COLSTON RESEARCH SOCIETY

COLSTON PAPERS

General Editor

R. L. GREGORY

This book is Volume XXXI of the Colston Papers. Previous volumes are:

Vol. I. 1948 *Cosmic Radiation*—Editor, F. C. Frank (out of print)
Vol. II. 1949 *Engineering Structures*—Editor, A. G. Pugsley (out of print)
Vol. III. 1950 *Colonial Administration*—Editor, C. M. MacInnes (out of print)
Vol. IV. 1951 *The Universities and the Theatre*—Editor, D. G. James (out of print)
Vol. V. 1952 *The Suprarenal Cortex*—Editor, J. M. Yoffrey (out of print)
Vol. VI. 1953 *Insecticides and Colonial Agricultural Development*—Editors, T. Wallace and J. T. Martin (out of print)
Vol. VII. 1954 *Recent Developments in Cell Physiology*—Editor, J. A. Kitching (out of print)
Vol. VIII. 1956 *The Neurohypophysis*—Editor, H. Heller (out of print)
Vol. IX. 1957 *Observation and Interpretation*—Editor, S. Körner (out of print)
Vol. X. 1958 *The Structures and Properties of Porous Materials*—Editors, D. H. Everett and F. S. Stone (out of print)
Vol. XI. 1959 *Hypersonic Flow*—Editors, A. R. Collar and J. Tinkler
Vol. XII. 1960 *Metaphor and Symbol*—Editors, L. C. Knights and Basil Cottle (out of print)
Vol. XIII. 1961 *Animal Health and Production*—Editors, C. S. Grunsell and A. I. Wright
Vol. XIV. 1962 *Music and Education*—Editor, Willis Grant (out of print)
Vol. XV. 1963 *Reality and Creative Vision in German Lyrical Poetry*—Editor, A. Closs
Vol. XVI. 1964 *Economic Analysis for National Economic Planning*—Editors, P. E. Hart, G. Mills and J. K. Whitaker (out of print)
Vol. XVII. 1965 *Submarine Geology and Geophysics*—Editors, W. F. Whittard and R. Bradshaw
Vol. XVIII. 1966 *The Fungus Spore*—Editor, M. F. Madelin
Vol. XIX. 1967 *The Liver*—Editor, A. E. Read
Vol. XX. 1968 *Towards a Policy for the Education of Teachers*—Editor, William Taylor (out of print)
Vol. XXI. 1969 *Communication and Energy in Changing Urban Environments*—Editor, D. Jones
Vol. XXII. 1970 *Regional Forecasting*—Editors, M. Chisholm, A. E. Frey and P. Haggett (out of print)
Vol. XXIII. 1971 *Marine Archaeology*—Editor, D. J. Blackman
Vol. XXIV. 1972 *Bone: Certain Aspects of Neoplasia*—Editors, C. H. G. Price and F. G. M. Ross
Vol. XXV. 1973 *Foreign Relations of African States*—Editor, K. Ingham
Vol. XXVI. 1974 *Structure of Fibrous Polymers*—Editors, E. D. T. Atkins and A. Keller
Vol. XXVII. 1975 *The Eruption and Occlusion of Teeth*—Editors, D. F. G. Poole and M. V. Stack
Vol. XXVIII. 1976 *Remote Sensing of the Terrestrial Environment*—Editors, R. F. Peel, L. F. Curtis and E. C. Barrett
Vol. XXIX. 1977 *Ions in Macromolecular and Biological Systems*—Editors, D. H. Everett and B. Vincent
Vol. XXX. 1978 *Tidal Power and Estuary Management*—Editors, R. T. Severn, D. L. Dineley and L. E. Hawker

Income Distribution: the Limits to Redistribution

Editors:
David Collard, Richard Lecomber and Martin Slater
(*Directors of the Symposium*)

Proceedings of the
Thirty-first Symposium of the Colston Research Society

held in the
University of Bristol March 1979

A HALSTED PRESS BOOK

JOHN WILEY & SONS
New York

Published in the U.S.A.
by Halsted Press,
a Division of John Wiley & Sons Inc.,
New York

British Library Cataloguing in Publication Data

Income distribution. – (Colston
papers; vol. 31).
1. Income distribution – Congresses
I. Collard, David
II. Lecomber, Richard III. Slater, Martin
IV. Series
339.2 HB601

ISBN 0 470-27099-3

Printed in Great Britain by
Henry Ling Ltd

a subsidiary of
John Wright & Sons Ltd
at the Dorset Press,
Dorchester.

FOREWORD

The Colston Papers, which are one of the results of the Colston Symposia, form in themselves a striking illustration of what a university does and of some of the ways in which it contributes to society. The prime purpose of the Symposia is to bring together groups of experts so that they may assist the university in the maintenance and extension of society's intellectual capital. But there are no disciplines among those forming part of the proper interest of a university which are without interest to a much wider audience, and rarely are there disciplines of little importance to society.

So it is with the present volume coming from the 1979 Symposium on the Limits to Redistribution. The subject could hardly be more topical: but then there never will be a time when it will be a dead issue. The way in which any society cares for each of its citizens, how far it can help them and how far it can trespass upon their freedom in doing so, are fundamental questions which lie behind the much more 'practical' questions discussed in this volume.

As always, it was a pleasure for Bristol University and for all of us to provide a home for a short while to acknowledged masters. Their intellectual distinction will be apparent from the pages which follow. What will not be so obvious is the friendliness and good humour which marked their discussions and which we as their hosts enjoyed so much.

A. W. Merrison

CONTENTS

SYMPOSIUM COMMITTEE

Professor D. A. Collard
Professor A. S. Deaton
J. R. C. Lecomber
M. D. E. Slater
Professor G. Whittington

SPEAKERS

Professor C. V. Brown	Department of Economics, University of Stirling
Professor J. Creedy	Department of Economics, University of Durham
F. Field	Child Poverty Action Group, London*
Professor L. Gevers	Faculté des Sciences Economique et Sociales, Universitaire Notre-Dame de la Paix, Namur
J. A. Kay	St John's College, Oxford
R. Layard	Centre for Labour Economics, London School of Economics and Political Science
A. McAuley	Department of Economics, University of Essex
Professor E. Maskin	Department of Economics, Massachusetts Institute of Technology
D. Piachaud	Centre for Labour Economics, London School of Economics and Political Science
C. A. Pissarides	Centre for Labour Economics, London School of Economics and Political Science
Professor C. T. Sandford	School of Humanities and Social Sciences, University of Bath
J. Seade	Department of Economics, University of Warwick
Professor E. Sheshinski	Department of Economics, Hebrew University of Jerusalem
Professor G. Szakolczai	Research Institute for Applied Computer Sciences, Budapest
A. Zabalza	Centre for Labour Economics, London School of Economics and Political Science

* The speaker is now MP for Birkenhead, and so is no longer with the CPAG.

DISCUSSANTS

J. A. Astin	Inland Revenue, Statistics Division, London
Professor D. A. Collard	School of Humanities and Social Sciences, University of Bath
F. A. Cowell	Department of Economics, London School of Economics and Political Science
Professor A. Deaton	Department of Economics, University of Bristol
Professor P. Hammond	Department of Economics, University of Essex†
A. G. Jackson	Department of Economics, University of Bristol
J. Le Grand	Department of Economics, London School of Economics and Political Science
Professor J. A. Mirrlees	Nuffield College, Oxford
J. Stern	Economic Advisers' Office, Department of Health and Social Security, London
D. Todd	H.M. Treasury, London
R. Van Slooten	Director, Central Economics Service, Northern Ireland Department of Finance, Stormont, Belfast
Professor G. Whittington	Department of Economics, University of Bristol

PARTICIPANTS

M. Barrow	School of Social Sciences, University of Sussex
Professor E. Bennathan	Department of Economics, University of Bristol
R. L. Berry	Department of Economics, University of Bristol
Professor B. Bobe	Directeur du Laboratoire d'Economie Publique Urbaine et Regionale, Université des Sciences et Techniques de Lille
J. R. Broome	Department of Economics, University of Bristol
M. J. Browning	Department of Economics, University of Bristol
Professor D. G. Champernowne	Trinity College, Cambridge
H. M. Clarke	Department of Economics, University of Bristol
Professor M. Cramer	University of Amsterdam (Visiting Professor, Department of Economics, University of Bristol)
I. R. Davidson	Department of Economics, University of Bristol
H. B. Davies	Department of Health and Social Security, London
J. S. Dodgson	Department of Economics and Commerce, University of Liverpool
F. Euvrard	Centre d'Étude de Revenus et de Coûts, Paris
N. Forward	Secretary, Royal Commission on the Distribution of Income and Wealth, London
M. Gregory	Department of Political Economy, University of Glasgow
P. G. Hare	Department of Economics, University of Stirling
D. Heald	Department of Social and Economic Research, University of Glasgow
R. Hemming	Department of Economics, Brunel University
S. Holterman	Department of Health and Social Security, London
J. R. King	Inland Revenue, London

† Professor Hammond is at present with the Department of Economics, Stanford University, California, USA.

PARTICIPANTS

S. Latham	Department of Economics and Commerce, University of Liverpool
J. R. C. Lecomber	Department of Economics, University of Bristol
A. Lewis	School of Humanities and Social Sciences, University of Bath
G. W. Lewis	Department of Economics, University of Bristol
I. C. Lincoln	School of Economics and Accounting, Leicester Polytechnic
F. McDonald	Department of Economics and Economic History, Manchester Polytechnic
Professor J. Muellbauer	Department of Economics, Birbeck College
E. Nabiel	Department of Economics, Lanchester Polytechnic
J. L. Nicholson	Policy Studies Institute, London
J. W. O'Hagan	Department of Economics, Trinity College, University of Dublin
M. O'Higgins	School of Humanities and Social Sciences, University of Bath
C. Pond	Civil Service College, London
P. Rice	School of Social Sciences, University of Sussex
M. J. Ricketts	School of Economics, University College at Buckingham
P. Ruggles	Policy Studies Institute, London
S. N. Sahay	Department of Economics, University of Bristol
M. Sawyer	Department of Economics and Related Studies, University of York
Professor W. J. Sheehan	University of Newcastle, Australia (Visiting Professor, Public Sector Economics Research Centre, University of Leicester)
M. D. E. Slater	Department of Economics, University of Bristol
G. A. Stephenson	Central Statistical Office, London
J. Vint	Department of Economics and Economic History, Manchester Polytechnic
P. T. Wanless	Department of Economics, University of Strathclyde
D. F. Winter	Department of Economics, University of Bristol
J. Yates	Visiting Fellow at the Universities of Leicester and Sheffield from Sydney, Australia

ACKNOWLEDGEMENT

The Editors are grateful to the Committee of the Colston Research Society for offering us the opportunity to organise the Symposium, to our colleagues at Bristol, particularly Esra Bennathan, Angus Deaton and Geoffrey Whittington, for their encouragement throughout, and to Jo Sowry for her efficient copy-editing.

LIMITS TO REDISTRIBUTION : AN OVERVIEW

D. A. Collard

School of Humanities and Social Sciences, University of Bath

Redistribution is a *process* whereby command over goods and services is transferred from one group of persons to another without the *quid pro quo* of exchange. The theme of this Symposium is the importance of the various limits encountered in the redistributive process. In this brief overview I list the principal limits, some, though not all, of which were discussed at various stages of the Symposium. I then discuss some of the main instruments of redistribution and their defects and conclude with suggestions for future research.

THE LIMITS TO REDISTRIBUTION

1. Legitimacy of the status quo

It is a commonplace of modern welfare economics that policy instruments should be designed so as to maximize social welfare. If the policy-maker would like a more equal distribution of income and wealth than currently exists, such preferences may be encapsulated in the social welfare function—for example, as an 'aversion to inequality'. Income is up-for-grabs; redistribution is firmly on the political agenda. Theorists of the Right have questioned this now conventional view. Nozick, for example, has argued that the individual is *entitled* to income which he has legitimately earned (or which his forbears had legitimately earned and voluntarily transferred to him). Compulsory redistribution has therefore no place on the agenda, a view which, if taken seriously, would constitute the most serious limit of all to redistribution. The only legitimate redistribution would then be voluntary. This view was not taken at this Symposium: an implicit assumption was that redistribution was, indeed, a proper concern of policy.

2. Consequent loss of output

One obvious limit to redistribution other than lump-sum redistribution is the possible loss of output as goods and services are redistributed from the more to the less productive, from the more enterprising to the less enterprising or from those with low rates of time preference to those with high rates of time preference. Thus a more egalitarian distribution of, say, education could result in inefficient investment in human capital, and, eventually, to a loss of output. There may, of course, be cases where no such 'trade-off' is called for. To the extent that education and health care raise the standard of literacy and lower the incidence of disease, discounted future output may even be higher as a result of redistribution-in-kind, not lower. In Western developed countries (though not in developing countries) one is probably well past this phase. Even so, the consensus of professional opinion is that the short-term effects of redistributive taxation are probably small, partly because of normal income effects and partly because of low substitution elasticities. Brown's paper is largely concerned with improving his earlier work to allow for kinks in the budget constraint. More ambitiously, Gevers attempts an estimate of the trade-off itself, using American data: he finds that some further redistribution was attainable at relatively little output loss. One is fairly safe in asserting that the short-term elasticity of output with respect to transfers is low but that we still remain largely ignorant of the longer term effects of tax on career choice and similar strategic decisions.

3. Consequent loss of utility

Most recent discussion concerns itself not with loss of output but with loss of *utility*. Thus the optimal income tax literature makes explicit use of the utility-maximizing assumption for the individual and *either* a utilitarian social welfare function or a more general welfare function, based nevertheless on individual utilities. Under redistribution the better-off suffer losses of utility. This is important in two ways. Firstly to the extent that the transfer imposes an excess burden it implies efficiency losses: losses associated with a distortion of the work-leisure choice and not necessarily with output reductions. Secondly the simple loss of utility may itself cause the better-off to resent (and even to oppose) transfers (but see 5 below). These utility effects can perhaps be ignored by the planner interested only in output and unafraid of political opposition. The planner taking a wider view of social welfare and operating in a democracy cannot ignore them.

Opponents of the 'conservative' nature of much of the optimal income tax literature could very well want to challenge the importance of its utility base. Suppose that a transfer from the better-off to the worse-off could be effected with no loss of output but with the better-off working sufficiently harder to maintain their own incomes *and* to make up any output loss by the worse-off. Would this be a good thing? Yes, if the planner had no interest in the leisure of the better-off. Probably not, if he had optimal tax theorists as advisors.

Economists in their concern for efficiency and output have been less aware of the second sort of utility effect (political opposition) that they might have been. But tax payers' revolts and the like now lie firmly in the domain of the new public economics.

4. Political power

In the economist's model, the 'policy-maker' maximizes social welfare, taking into account the trade-off between output and redistribution. Little attention is paid to whether the optimum is politically attainable. Given that income distribution is skewed, with the median less than the mean, simple majority voting would indicate some redistribution. One plausible assumption (see Gevers' paper) is that the preferences of the median voter are decisive with respect to pure public good provision and redistribution. Though convenient, the median voter approach implies a very naive theory of democracy. In a representative democracy, rather than one given to holding single issue referenda, the system might well operate *as though* the preferences of some other individual were decisive, e.g. the individual at the upper quartile of the income distribution. The relationship between actual tax structure and implied political decision rules seems a promising area for further research.

5. Self-interest

Closely associated with the two previous 'limits' is the self-interest of the electors. Unfortunately we know very little about the willingness of the electorate to support redistribution to the poor. So long as this can be achieved by redistribution from the rich to the poor, even quite selfish median voters may be expected to support it (particularly if they feel malevolent towards the rich!). But once the possibilities of such redistribution are exhausted, further redistribution has to be at the expense of voters from around the median income. It is often alleged that most redistribution takes place between middle income pressure groups because they are simply not interested in redistribution to the poor. The evidence of casual empiricism is that tax cuts are higher on their agenda than redistribution. Thus it is the self-interest of the bulk of the population, not merely of the rich, which acts as a potential limit to redistribution.

6. Government expenditure

One lesson of research into optimal income tax is that the optimal amount of redistribution will be less the greater the government's revenue requirement for financing its own expenditure on goods and services. Much of this expenditure will, of course, itself be redistributive and to that extent the two categories are not mutually exclusive. However, the analysis picks up, in a more sophisticated fashion, the intuitive notion that the marginal excess burden increases with total tax. If taken seriously this poses a major dilemma for socialist governments in social democracies if they wish to increase public expenditure on goods and services *and* redistribute income.

7. Imperfect revelation

Whatever is taken as the focus of redistribution (income, wealth, expenditure, ability, etc.) the individual will usually have some incentive to understate it. This is not only a question of self-interest on the one side but of morality and the strength of prevailing codes of conduct on the other. Some forms of tax evasion are widely considered to be 'fair game', others are not. Similarly tax avoidance, the relabelling of economic activities in such ways as to minimize tax, is widely viewed not merely as legal but as morally permissible. These are the obvious forms of imperfect revelation but it is now well-known (see the discussion of Maskin's paper) that it is difficult to devise decision rules which encourage individuals to reveal their correct endowments (of, say, ability) in a large economy. Advocates of expenditure taxes argue, amongst other things, that revelation is less imperfect under their systems (see Kay's paper). This major problem surely explains why the tax authorities have selected otherwise 'unsuitable' taxes such as the window tax, rates and revenue tariffs?

Readers will be able to think of other 'limits' to redistribution. Enough have been mentioned to indicate that here is material for several symposia.

METHODS OF REDISTRIBUTION

Several of the many methods of redistribution were discussed at the Symposium.

1. Lump-sum redistribution

A lump-sum tax has no efficiency effects and is generally believed by welfare economists to be 'impossible'. This is broadly correct but the emphasis in recent discussions has been on devising mechanisms for the correct revelation of endowments or abilities. The discussion of Maskin's paper at this Symposium stressed the very limited progress that has been made: no persuasive mechanism is in sight.

2. Price manipulation

A limited use of subsidies for redistributive purposes has been made in Western economies. The great difficulty with them is that, unless combined with something like a means test, receipts raised for the purpose go to all relevant users, including the better-off. At the Symposium relatively little was said about price manipulation in the Western context, the presumption being that it was an inefficient redistributive mechanism.

However, two papers one by Szakolczai and the other by McAuley, discuss the redistributive use of prices in Eastern Europe. This policy seems to have the expected high efficiency costs and has been rather ineffective in its redistributive goals—perhaps it has been more successful in promoting 'merit' goods such as cultural activities. Reforms are increasingly directed to moving prices back towards 'equilibrium' levels.

3. Redistribution in kind

Though there was no formal paper on redistribution in kind it was frequently cited as powerfully redistributive when financed by a progressive tax system. This is because benefits are very approximately equal *per capita*, the convention being to divide total expenditure by the number of people in the relevant group of beneficiaries (e.g. educational expenditure divided by the number of children of school age).

But there are several reasons for believing that the redistributive effect is overstated when calculated in this way.

(i) Some unallocated benefits (e.g. defence, the law, etc.) could in principle be held as conferring benefits proportional to, say, property.

(ii) Some benefits already allocated should perhaps be re-allocated to indicate that some groups benefit disproportionately from government expenditure: for example, the middle-classes are alleged to have better access to health service facilities or to the more desirable state schools.

Both of these indicate that benefits could very well be slightly regressive rather than proportional. Whether the whole system is then redistributive depends on whether the tax structure is more progressive than the benefits structure is regressive.

The third reason for believing that *per capita* allocation overstates redistribution is a quite different one.

(iii) Paternalism is a legitimate reason for wishing to redistribute in kind. But the measured benefit to the individual is then the *planner's valuation* of merit goods, not the individual's own money valuation. The per capita method implies that the average individual would, upon reflection, value (say) health care at its average cost of production. If he would, in fact, value it at less than this the per capita figure is an over-valuation of benefit. The element of paternalism creates a constant temptation to the beneficiary to frustrate the intentions of policy-makers. To the extent that he succeeds in this he actually *increases* the value of the benefit to himself.

All these considerations suggest that allocation of benefits in kind is by no means a simple matter: that the beneficiaries should be properly identified and their own valuations of the goods and services provided at least taken into account. Neither should it be forgotten that the aim of provision in kind is not merely redistributive: often it is not even *primarily* redistributive.

4. Redistribution in cash

Combined with exemption levels for taxation, benefits in cash are very effective in redistributing income. They have little of the paternalistic flavour of benefits-in-kind and may be valued unambiguously at their face value. They may be universal or selective. It is useful to distinguish between three classes of cash benefit:

(*a*) *Universal cash transfers.* These are the 'cleanest' form of redistribution and are paid to every household with given characteristics. Child benefit (formerly family allowances) are a clear case. Because of their obvious redistributive nature, cash payments have frequently been advocated as the basis of social dividend type schemes. One attraction of such 'dividends' is their non-selective nature: the recipient qualifies by virtue of some physically identifiable need, e.g. to feed and clothe children (see Field's paper). Under the simplest social dividend schemes, *everyone* would receive a basic cash payment, having met the minimal criterion of being alive. Practical variants have had to be watered down in various ways (see (*c*) below).

(*b*) *Social security benefits.* These are in principle insurance-based and may or may not be redistributive. At one extreme the individual voluntarily pays a stream of premiums during his working life which are actuarially balanced by benefits received during unemployment, sickness or old age: in such cases there is redistribution between periods for the individual but no redistribution between individuals. There are then no 'efficiency' effects. At the other extreme, both contributions and benefits could be progressive so that the poor gain at the expense of the rich and the insurance element is purely nominal. Of the papers on social security at this Symposium that by Creedy most clearly addressed itself to redistribution between persons. The redistributive effect of a state pension scheme depends on the relative terms of the state and private schemes and on freedom to contract out. Redistribution cannot be taken for granted in social security schemes: it all depends on their structure and on the exit rules.

(*c*) *Means-tested benefits.* Intended as a residual category, to wither away as the welfare state progressed, the means-tested cash benefit has shown extraordinary resilience. With allowances to cover children and insurance benefits to cover hard times they should gradually have disappeared. But they have not done so. It is difficult to see how they could except in the case of a full social dividend scheme with basic benefits set at or above current social security levels: an 'expensive' solution. Short of this there will always be special circumstances and crises for individual families, to be sorted out on a discretionary basis within a safety-net scheme. If redistribution to those in need were the only consideration, supplementary benefit would be a very attractive instrument but it does, of course, have the well-known disadvantages of means-tests, discretion, client-status and so on. It would be the cheapest way of ensuring that transfer took place only to those in real need and resistance by median income groups would be encountered at only an advanced stage in the transfer process. But further down the scale the well-known disincentive effects of the poverty trap could set limits to this particular instrument of redistribution.

5. Wages policy

Wages policies do have redistributive effects, but redistribution (see Layard's paper) has not, historically, been their main purpose in the West. Frequently the main motive has been macro-economic anti-inflation policy, of a short-term nature, so that little attention was paid to redistribution. The need to help the low paid is often mentioned but at least equal weight is given to the maintenance of 'differentials'. Both sets of considerations, macro-policy and redistribution, are likely to operate against efficient allocation of resources. This is not to say that the market and the market alone should determine wages: in the public sector particularly there is a need for a more-or-less permanent review body to consider rates of pay. But here again, efficiency considerations suggest supply and demand, rather than conscious redistribution, as the starting point. Unlike cash benefits or benefits-in-kind, wages policy does *not* seem to be a strong candidate as the prime instrument of redistribution (but see Szakolczai's paper for a contrary view).

6. Income tax

A progressive income tax, combined with cash or in-kind benefits, is the obvious, and indeed the most immediately attractive instrument of redistribution. The progressivity of the tax schedule (marginal rate being greater than the average rate) is ensured by exemption levels at the bottom even without an increasing marginal rate. No judgement may be made about its redistributive effect, however, without knowing the benefit structure—a steeply progressive tax system could finance provision of semi-public goods enjoyed only by the rich. But a progressive tax system gives redistribution a head start.

Criticisms of the UK system of income tax are almost too numerous to mention. Those concerned with its limitations as a *redistributive* device are primarily:

(i) Personal allowances have not automatically kept pace with inflation (though the Rooker-Wise amendments have helped in recent years). This, of course, makes the system less progressive.

(ii) There is a very small lower-band range, so the taxpayer finds himself paying at the standard rate very quickly as income rises.

(iii) The standard rate band is very long. With high personal allowances and a lower initial rate this would not be a serious matter but it does reduce the degree of progressivity.

(iv) The apparently progressive schedule at the highest rates is illusory since little income is taxed at these rates. This is due both to evasion and avoidance (discussed at the Symposium in papers by Sandford and Kay). Note that since the Symposium the highest UK rate has been reduced to sixty per cent.

(v) Overlap between the tax and social security systems can lead to very high marginal rates for those on low incomes. This is an inexcusable muddle and is a top priority for reform.

(vi) The tax base has been eroded, effectively redistributing in favour of owner-occupiers, those with heavy life-insurance and so on.

(vii) The more favourable treatment of expenses under Schedule D than under PAYE effectively redistributes income from the regular wage-earner to the self-employed.

7. An expenditure base

The UK value-added tax is slightly progressive and taxes on drink and tobacco are regressive. Since the Meade Report (1978) replacement of the income tax by an expenditure tax has been increasingly advocated. The argument has *not* primarily been a redistributive one though the tax could in principle be made progressive if combined with a social dividend. It would have an important bearing on two of the points about income tax just made. On point (iv) (about avoidance and evasion) an expenditure tax could be devised (see Kay's paper) so as to give less opportunity for this. On point (vi) (about erosion of the base) *all* income would be taxed at the point of expenditure so that, again, the base would be effectively widened. One would not, of course, wish to make a case for expenditure taxation on these two considerations alone, especially if the defects could be corrected in some other way. On the face of it the redistributive implications of an expenditure tax are slightly unattractive. One would have to be very careful to increase supplementary benefits, pensions and so on so that non-income-tax-payers did not suffer from the effects of, say, an expenditure tax effected by VAT. Alternatively the expenditure tax could be explicitly progressive in which case much of its simplicity would be lost.

8. Taxes on wealth

These were not discussed at the Symposium. Taxes on the transfer of wealth at death (or by gifts) are likely to have fewer and less important efficiency effects than simple taxes on wealth.

9. Anti-discrimination legislation

There is some risk of adverse employment effects for the group on whose behalf legislation is enacted. In principle this should not happen if there had been no rational basis for discrimination and Layard suggested that displacement was minimal in the case of UK labour-market sex-discrimination legislation. There was little further discussion of this theme.

10. Broader instruments

Some very important instruments of redistribution were not discussed at all at the Symposium as the programme was already a crowded one. The demarcation line is hard to draw because almost all policies have some redistributive implications, e.g. policy on inflation. But regional policy, youth employment policy, urban renewal policy, agricultural policy and trade protection policy all have clear redistributive intent and would be obvious candidates for discussion at a more extended conference.

COMMENTS ON RESEARCH NEEDS

Much of the work presented at this Symposium is part of a thriving and active 'research programme'. For example, good work on optimal income tax (e.g. Seade in this Symposium) continues to be produced as does empirical work on the efficiency effects of taxation (e.g. Brown in this Symposium). Social security, which was rather neglected until recently, is now attracting attention from theorists and econometricians (e.g. Sheshinski and Weiss, Zabalza et al. and Creedy in this Symposium). Research work develops a momentum of its own and goes ahead regardless of recommendations made at Symposia such as this. Nevertheless on a personal view there are a few areas in which it would be especially interesting to have further research work carried out.

The Trade-off

For many years economists have talked about the trade-off between output and redistribution. This is pre-eminently a question for positive economics: once the trade-off is known the policy-maker may impose his own value judgments. But the present state of play is that the economist is not even able to state the size of the trade-off. The policy-maker might legitimately ask of the profession: 'Suppose I want to reduce the Gini coefficient by x percentage points, using policy instrument r. How much output loss will there be?' Essentially this calls for an extension of recent work on putting redistributive policy into 'small' general equilibrium systems.

Political economy

Gevers' paper on trade-offs was based on a simple 'economic' theory of politics—single issue majority rule. More work needs doing on the relationship between policies, voter preferences and political decision rules. To some extent this is a matter of developing more sophisticated models. But is is also a matter of having more evidence of voters' preferences and attitudes—particularly their preferences about and attitudes towards redistribution.

Tax avoidance and evasion

It would be valuable to have further studies (like Kay's) on the susceptibility of different taxes to these problems. It would also be useful to explore the determinants of avoidance and evasion (e.g. how far can they be analysed purely selfishly?—prospective gains versus probability of getting caught and expected punishment—are moral standards important, and if so how far are these related to views on the fairness of the tax system?).

Relative income effects

These are ignored in most works. Layard suggested their importance, not only from a normative standpoint (though this is important enough) but in influencing behaviour.

Comparative studies

The papers by Szakolczai and McAuley and the stimulating discussions to which they gave rise indicate that there would be much interest in some across-country comparisons of redistributive instruments actually used and their effectiveness. One does tend to concentrate rather on taxation and on Western European and American institutions and problems.

ON FIRST-BEST TAXATION

E. Maskin

Department of Economics, Massachusetts Institute of Technology

1. INTRODUCTION

The theoretical literature on the redistribution of income (or endowments) through taxation to achieve ethical goals has grown considerably in the past decade. Most of this work on optimal taxation attempts only second-best optimization. That is, authors generally begin with the supposition that the details about preferences and abilities necessary for making differential lump-sum transfers are lacking, so that only distortionary or poll taxes are available. In many cases, therefore, they abandon the possibility of attaining a full optimum.

Only rarely do authors state explicitly why this information should not be available.* Indeed, income tax returns could, in principle, be made sufficiently detailed to provide it. Probably the most important barrier to lump-sum transfers, as Hammond [1979] has persuasively argued, is that if consumers understand how the information they report about themselves is to be used, they will ordinarily have an incentive to report falsely.

This paper studies the possibility of first-best taxation when the tax authority is *ex ante* not completely informed about consumers' characteristics and so has to rely on consumers' reports. Following much of the literature on optimal taxation, I assume that tastes are publicly known, but that endowments (for example, labour skills) are private information. A tax schedule is first-best relative to a (Paretian) social welfare function (SWF) if it leads to the SWF being maximized subject only to feasibility constraints; i.e., if it leads to a full social optimum.

First-best taxes exist for some social welfare functions even when the government is not well-informed about consumers' characteristics, but precisely which social welfare functions can be fully optimized depends on the government's ability to observe consumers' actions. When consumers work, for example, the government may be able to observe their output or number of labour hours or both. If consumers vary in skill and skill itself is unobservable, one quantity may not be deducible from the other. When only one of the quantitities is observable, the consumer may, therefore, be able to *misrepresent* the size of his endowment. If the government is able to observe only output, for example, the consumer might claim to consume less (or more) leisure than, in fact, is the case, by pretending to be less (or more) skilled than he in fact is. Such misrepresentation could be worthwhile if taxes are a function of leisure (or labour).

In many circumstances, understatement of endowments is considerably easier than exaggeration. Suppose, for example, that the government can monitor hours worked perfectly but that it can observe only the output that consumers choose to show it.

* See, however, Dasgupta and Hammond (1978), and Mirrlees (1977).

Despite this imperfect monitoring, exaggeration of endowment is ruled out; a consumer cannot exhibit more output than he has produced. It is difficult to see, however, how to prohibit understatement so easily. Because of the greater plausibility of understatement than of exaggeration, I shall confine myself to that case. One type of understatement is *endowment concealment:* understatement of the truth by the consumer, where the unstated (concealed) portion is retained for his own consumption. A prominent practitioner of endowment concealment is the able worker who claims to be inept while continuing to work skilfully. Being able, he can complete tasks in less time than someone less skilled. If the tax scheme, however, is to compensate the less able for their longer work hours, he might well benefit from announcing to the world that he is a less skilled worker than he is, while continuing to enjoy the greater leisure of an able worker.

If, in this labour-production example, the government can observe both hours worked and output, a form of misrepresentation is still available to the consumer; namely, he can misrepresent the *quality* of his labour, by not only *claiming* to be, but by *behaving* as though he were less skilled than he actually is. By behaving in all ways as an inferior worker, the consumer is, in effect, *destroying* part of his endowment. Nonetheless, such destruction may be *advantageous* under many tax systems.

Concealment corresponds to what we commonly call *tax evasion* and is ordinarily ruled out by assumption in the tax literature. Indeed, the tax authority can prevent it by monitoring consumption. *Endowment destruction*, on the other hand, is more easily disguised. Destruction is probably the greatest theoretical barrier to a tax on skill.

Understandably, the class of social welfare functions that can be fully optimized is smaller when the consumer can only destroy his endowment than when he can conceal it. The optimizable class also typically depends on whether the economy is large or small. (A large economy is one where each consumer contributes negligibly to the aggregate endowment. I consider small economies in order to make the results applicable to such problems as division of goods among a small group of agents.) Roughly speaking, when concealment of endowments is permitted, only a competitive social welfare function (a social welfare function for which competitive allocations are the only first-best allocations) can be fully optimized in a large, private-goods economy, even when the distribution of endowments is known. In a small economy, not even this social welfare function is optimizable. On the other hand, in both large and small economies, a fairly extensive class, including the Rawlsian maximin social welfare function, can be optimized when individuals can only destroy their endowments. These results and others are presented in section 4 of this paper.

The implicit assumption in the preceding discussion, as well as in virtually all the optimum tax literature, is that a consumer's utility-maximizing behaviour, given the tax schedule he faces, is independent of the behaviour of others; he has a *dominant strategy*. This will certainly be the case if the consumer's taxes are dependent only on his own choices. Although tax schedules that make one consumer's payments dependent on the actions of another may seem rather complicated, there can be large gains to be made in using them (and thus dropping the requirement of dominant strategies), in terms of expanding the class of implementable social welfare functions. In section 5, therefore, I consider tax schemes where consumers, in effect, play a noncooperative game. I begin the formal part of the paper in section 2 with notation and terminology. Section 3 considers distribution of a single good while section 4 extends the analysis to two or more goods. Section 6 summarizes the main results in tabular form.

2. TERMINOLOGY AND NOTATION

I shall consider an economy with l private goods. Since I shall be concerned with distributional issues, I shall assume pure exchange, although virtually everything I say carries over to economies with production. When the economy is finite, let n be the number of consumers. In this case, an allocation is an n-dimensional vector, $(x^1, \ldots, x^n)$, with $x^i \in R^l_{++}$† for each i, where x^i is consumer i's consumption bundle. Allocation $\boldsymbol{x}=(x^1, \ldots, x^n)$ is aggregately feasible for initial endowments $\boldsymbol{\omega}=(\omega^1, \ldots, \omega^n)$ if $\Sigma_i x \leqslant \Sigma_i \omega^i$. Let U_∞ be the class of utility functions from R^l_{++} to R that are differentiable, monotonically increasing and concave and whose indifference curves do not intersect the axes. A social welfare function (SWF) is a mapping F: $R^n \times R^{nl}_{++} \to R$, with the interpretation that the allocation $(x^1, \ldots, x^n)$ is socially preferable to $(\bar{x}^1, \ldots, \bar{x}^n)$ for utility profile $(u^1, \ldots, u^n)$ and endowment profile $(\omega^1, \ldots, \omega^n)$ if and only if $F(u^1(x^1), \ldots, u^n(x^n); \omega^1, \ldots, \omega^n) > F(u^1(\bar{x}^1), \ldots, u^n(\bar{x}^n); \omega^1, \ldots \omega^n)$. Call F Paretian if, for all v, $v' \in R^n$, $v > v'$ implies $F(v) > F(v')$.

In the case of a continuum of consumers, suppose that i, indexing consumers, ranges in the interval [0,1]. An allocation is a (Borel-measurable) mapping $x[\cdot]$: $[0,1] \to R^l_+$ where $x[\mathrm{i}]$ is consumer i's consumption bundle. The profile of initial endowments is given by the (Borel-measurable) mapping $\omega[\cdot]$: $[0,1] \to R^l_{++}$. Let Ω be the class of all such endowment profiles $\omega[\cdot]$. Feasibility entails that $\int x[\mathrm{i}]d\mathrm{i} = \int \omega[\mathrm{i}]d\mathrm{i}$. The profile of utility functions is given by a mapping $u[\mathrm{i}]$: $[0,1] \to U$, where $u[\mathrm{i}]$ is consumer i's utility function. Let $\mathscr{U}$ be the class of all utility profiles $u[\cdot]$. For a continuum of consumers, a social welfare functional is a mapping F: $I \times \Omega \to R$, where I is the space of (Borel-measurable) mappings from [0,1] to R, and Ω is the space of (Borel-measurable) mappings from [0,1] to R^l_{++}.

A tax scheme is a rule that associates a vector of taxes to each vector of messages provided by consumers. This paper considers messages which provide, among other things, some information, possibly untruthful, about the consumers' endowments. I shall suppose that consumer i's message space, S^i, is of the form $S^i = R^l_{++} \times M^i$, with typical element $s = (\omega^i, m^i)$. The ω^i component of the message is to be interpreted as consumer i's professed endowment, whereas m^i represents any additional information the consumer provides. As I mentioned in the introduction, I am particularly concerned with concealment and destruction of endowments. I therefore assume for each consumer i that if his true endowment is $\hat{\omega}^i$, then he may play those strategies with ω^i components satisfying $\omega^i \leqslant \hat{\omega}^i$. Formally, in the case of finitely many consumers, a tax scheme is a mapping T: $S^1 \times \ldots \times S^n \to R^{nl}$, such that if $\boldsymbol{s} = (s^1, \ldots s^n)$ is the vector of messages provided and $T(\boldsymbol{s}) = (T^1(\boldsymbol{s}), \ldots, T^n(\boldsymbol{s}))$, then $T^i(\boldsymbol{s})$ is consumer i's net transfer of commodities. For aggregate feasibility, I assume that $\Sigma_i T^i(\boldsymbol{s}) < 0$ for all $\boldsymbol{s}$. If consumer i can conceal his true endowment, $\hat{\omega}^i$, then his consumption bundle after taxes is $\hat{\omega}^i + T^i(\boldsymbol{s})$. If he is restricted to destruction only, and if $\boldsymbol{s} = ((\omega^1, m^1), \ldots, (\omega^i, m^i) \ldots, (\omega^n, m^n))$, then his final consumption is $\omega^i + T^i(\boldsymbol{s})$.

One can think of T as a game played by the consumers and, after adopting a suitable solution concept, one can speak of the equilibrium outcomes of T. Of course, nothing so far guarantees that outcomes be individually feasible, that consumers' final consumptions be non-negative. To avoid individual infeasibility I shall restrict attention to tax schemes with the property that, for each consumer i, for any $\boldsymbol{s}^{-i}$ (all components of the $\boldsymbol{s}$-vector except the ith) and any $s^i = (\omega^i, m^i)$, $\omega^i + T^i(s^i, \boldsymbol{s}^{-i}) \geqslant 0$. This assumption implies that, under either endowment concealment or destruction, all outcomes are feasible. It further implies that, under endowment concealment,

† R^l_{++} denotes the strictly positive orthant, whereas R^l_+ is the non-negative orthant.

consumer i must, in equilibrium, obtain at least the utility of his initial endowment, since if he takes $s^i=(0, m^i)$, he will, in fact, retain his endowment ('0' here is the zero vector).

For a given solution concept, let $E_T(\boldsymbol{u},\omega)$ be the set of equilibrium consumption allocation for tax scheme T when consumers are described by utility and endowment profiles $\boldsymbol{u}$ and $\boldsymbol{\omega}$. An outcome is a vector of final holdings. Let $G_F(\boldsymbol{u},\omega)=\{x|\ F(u^1(x^1), \ldots, u^n(x^n);\ \omega)$ is maximized on the feasible set$\}$. I shall say that T is acceptable for the social welfare functional F (with respect to the given solution concept) for profile $\boldsymbol{u}$ if, for all profiles ω, $E_T(\boldsymbol{u},\omega) \subseteq F(\boldsymbol{u},\omega)$ and $E_T(\boldsymbol{u},\omega)\neq\phi$. That is, if T is imposed, an equilibrium allocation exists, and all equilibria are optimal with respect to F for any choice of endowments $\boldsymbol{\omega}$. The definition captures the idea that endowments are unknown to the game designer and that he must accept what the consumers tell him.

For any $\boldsymbol{u}$, F is implementable for $\boldsymbol{u}$ if for all ω and $\forall a \in G_F(\boldsymbol{u},\omega)$, there exists a tax scheme T, acceptable for F for $\boldsymbol{u}$, such that $a \in E_T(\boldsymbol{u},\omega)$. This definition conveys the idea that a social welfare function cannot properly be considered implementable unless all its optima are attainable through some tax scheme. A non-attainable optimum might just as well be looked on as not an optimum at all.

For some applications, I shall require the notion of differential implementability. For any $\boldsymbol{u}$, F is differentially implementable if, for each ω and $a \in G_F(\boldsymbol{u},\omega)$, an acceptable tax scheme T (as above) exists, with the additional provisos that $S^i=R^l_+$ for all i and that T is differentiable with respect to each consumer's strategy.

I am concerned in this paper with two non-cooperative solution concepts, those of dominant and Nash strategies. The optimal tax literature has, virtually without exception, restricted itself to dominant strategies. A consumer i with utility function u^i and endowment $\hat{\omega}^i$ has a dominant strategy $\bar{s}^i=(\overline{\omega}^i, \bar{m}^i)$ in tax scheme T if for all $s^i=(\omega^i,m^i)$ and all $\boldsymbol{s}^{-i}$, $u^i(\hat{\omega}^i+T^i(\bar{s}^i,\boldsymbol{s}^{-i})\geqslant u^i(\hat{\omega}^i+T(s^i,\boldsymbol{s}^{-i}))$ in the case of endowment concealment and $u^i(\overline{\omega}^i+T^i(\bar{s}^i,\boldsymbol{s}^{-i})\geqslant u^i(\omega^i+T^i(s,\boldsymbol{s}^{-i}))$ for endowment destruction. That is, a strategy is dominant if the consumer is willing to use it regardless of the behaviour of others.

3. DOMINANT STRATEGIES: THE ONE-GOOD CASE

To begin the analysis, I shall consider the case $l=1$. This special case is of particular interest because many distributional questions involve the division of a single good, e.g. the distribution of income. There are several results. The first, entirely trivial, theorem, which applies to endowment concealment, states that, for given $\boldsymbol{u}$, the only social welfare functional that is implementable in dominant strategies for $\boldsymbol{u}$ is the 'no-transfer' SWF, i.e., the F such that $G_F(\boldsymbol{u},\omega)=\{\omega\}$. It holds for either small or large economies.

Theorem 3.1: For given $\boldsymbol{u}$, $F: R^n\times R^n_{++}\rightarrow R$ is implementable for u in dominant strategies when consumers can conceal their endowments if and only if $\forall\ \omega\ G_F(\boldsymbol{u},\omega)=\{\omega\}$ The same result holds for a continuum of consumers.

Proof of Theorem 3.1. For given $\boldsymbol{u}$, suppose that tax scheme T is acceptable for F for $\boldsymbol{u}$ (with respect to dominant strategies). By assumption on T, each consumer must in equilibrium get at least the utility of his initial endowment. Thus, in a one-good world he must, in fact, get his initial endowment. Thus, for any ω, $E_T(\boldsymbol{u},\omega)=\{\omega\}$, and so $G_F(\boldsymbol{u},\omega)=\{\omega\}$. The proof is the same for a continuum of consumers.

The second class of results characterizes the implementable SWF's for endowment destruction. Suppose first that the social welfare function F depends only on utilities (i.e. it is not a function of endowments). Then, theorem 3.2 asserts, essentially, that, if F is Paretian, it is implementable if and only if all utilities are 'normal goods' with respect to F. That is, if we think of F as a function representing preferences for different consumers' utilities, then, as 'income' rises, demand for each consumers' utility should also rise, if implementability is to be ensured.

Theorem 3.2[‡]: Suppose that $F : R^n \times R^n_{++} \rightarrow R$ is a continuous, twice piecewise differentiable function that is concave in its first n arguments. Suppose further that at any optimum all consumers have positive holdings. Consider the problem:

$$\max_{v^1, \ldots, v^n} F(v^1, \ldots, v^n; \omega^1, \ldots, \omega^n) \text{ subject to } \sum_i p_i v^i \leqslant y. \tag{3.2.1}$$

If consumers are confined to endowment destruction, then F is implementable for all $\boldsymbol{u}$ if and only if, for each vector of positive prices $(p_1, \ldots, p_l)$ and for all i, the optimal v^i in the solution to (3.2.1) increases in y. The same result holds for a continuum of consumers.

Proof: See Appendix.

The intuition behind Theorem 3.2 is quite clear: an individual will be induced not to destroy his endowment if, by announcing a higher endowment, he obtains higher utility. If utility is a normal good, then raising income in the artificial maximization problem (3.2.1) will raise utility. If one draws an analogy between aggregate endowment and income (and the proof of theorem does this formally) the theorem follows.

The conditions on F under which all utilities are normal are messy to express; they consist of n ratios of determinants involving the first and second derivatives of F. Because of their messiness, I think it useful to state a simple special case of Theorem 3.2 which, nonetheless, probably covers most social welfare functions of interest; e.g. utilitarianism and the maximin criterion. Suppose that, in addition to being Paretian, a SWF F satisfies an equity property, a condition that prohibits discrimination against the well-endowed, and one additional condition on its second partial derivatives. Then it is implementable.

Theorem 3.3: Suppose that $F : R^n \times R^n_{++} \rightarrow R$ is a continuous, twice piecewise differentiable social welfare function that is concave in its first n arguments. Suppose further that, for all $i \neq j$

$$\partial^2 F/\partial v^i \partial v^j \geqslant 0, \quad \partial^2 F/\partial v^i \partial \omega^i \geqslant 0, \quad \text{and} \quad \partial^2 F/\partial v^i \partial \omega^j = 0, \tag{3.2.2}$$

if these derivatives are defined. Then, if consumers are confined to endowment destruction, F is implementable in dominant strategies for all $\boldsymbol{u}$. The same result holds for a continuum of consumers.

Proof: The proof is simply a verification that, under the stated hypotheses, utilities are normal goods. The detailed argument is omitted.

The interpretation of the differential inequalities in the statement of Theorem 3.3 is quite straightforward. The condition $\partial^2 F/\partial v^i \partial v^j \geqslant 0$ is an equity condition. It states that one individual's improvement in welfare should not diminish another's weight in the social welfare function. The condition is satisfied by virtually all commonly discussed social welfare functions, including utilitarianism $(F(v^1, \ldots, v^n) = \Sigma v^i)$ and the Rawlsian maximin criterion $(F(v^1, \ldots, v^n) = \min v^i)$. It is sometimes argued that

‡ I am indebted to Kevin Roberts for a conversation during which a similar proposition emerged.

the maximin criterion is equitable or egalitarian, while utilitarianism is not. In terms of the behaviour of $\partial F/\partial v^i$ as v^j increases, this argument boils down to the observations that $\partial F/\partial v^i$ jumps from zero to one as v^j moves from below v^i to above v^i (in a two-person economy) for maximin social welfare, whereas $\partial^2 F/\partial v^i \partial v^j$ is identically zero under the utilitarian concept.

The condition $\partial^2 F/\partial v^i \partial \omega^i \geqslant 0$ prevents an individual's being penalized (in terms of his welfare weighting) solely because his endowment increases. I should emphasize that this condition is in no way anti-redistributive. In particular, the maximin criterion, which, assuming all utility functions are the same, prescribes equal consumption for all, satisfies it, since maximin makes *no* connection between one's endowment and one's welfare weighting. Indeed, any social welfare function (e.g. utilitarianism) in which weightings depend only on the distribution of utilities, rather than on the distribution of endowments, satisfies the condition $\partial^2 F/\partial v^i \partial \omega^i \geqslant 0$ automatically.

Corollary 3.4: The utilitarian ($F = \Sigma V_i$) and maximum ($F = \min V_i$) social welfare functions are implementable in dominant strategies if consumers are confined to endowment destruction.

I should emphasize that the sequences of quantifiers in Theorems 3.1 and 3.2 differ. The former theorem asserts that for any given profile of utility functions, F must take a particular form to be implementable. The latter (as well as Theorem 3.3) states that if F takes a certain form, then it is implementable for any $\boldsymbol{u}$.

4. DOMINANT STRATEGIES: TWO OR MORE GOODS

With two or more goods, the possibility of implementation for endowment concealment depends on whether the economy is large or small. I first characterize those SWF's that are implementable with a continuum of consumers under endowment concealment. The main result is that in a large economy a Paretian SWF is implementable if and only if it is competitive; i.e., optimal allocations are competitive allocations.

Theorem 4.1: Suppose that $F: I \times \Omega \to R$ is a Paretian social welfare function such that, for given $u[\cdot] \in \mathscr{U}_\infty$, for any given $\overline{\omega}[\cdot] \in \Omega$ and any $a \in G_F(u[\cdot], \overline{\omega}[\cdot])$, there exists a selection $V[\cdot]: \Omega \to \Omega$ with $V[\cdot](\omega[\cdot]) \in G_F(u[\cdot], \omega[\cdot])$ and $V[\cdot](\overline{\omega}[\cdot]) = a$ such that, for any consumer i, $V[\mathrm{i}]$ is differentiable with respect to $\omega[\mathrm{i}]$. For any such $V[\cdot]$, suppose that, if $\omega[\cdot], \omega'[\cdot] \in \Omega$ implies $\omega[\mathrm{k}] = \omega'[\mathrm{k}]$ for all $\mathrm{k} \neq \mathrm{i}$, then $V[\mathrm{j}](\omega[\cdot]) = V[\mathrm{j}](\omega'[\cdot])$ for all i and $\mathrm{j} \neq \mathrm{i}$. Then F is differentially implementable in dominant strategies if and only if F is the competitive SWF for $u[\cdot]$; i.e. $\forall\, \omega[\cdot] \in \Omega$ and $a \in G_F(u[\cdot], \omega[\cdot])$ if and only if a is a competitive equilibrium for $u[\cdot]$ and $\omega[\cdot]$.

Proof: See Appendix.

The hypotheses require, in effect, that, for any $a \in G_F(u[\cdot], \overline{\omega}[\cdot])$, we may choose a differentiable selection from $G_F(u[\cdot], \omega[\cdot])$ that includes a and that is differentiable with respect to each consumer's endowment. They imply, moreover, that any such selection must satisfy the property that changing a single consumer's endowment does not affect any other consumer's allocation.

Notice that Theorem 4.1 holds equally well if the tax authority knows the statistical distribution of endowments, provided that the distribution assigns positive density to any endowment which an individual might possibly profess to have. (If this last property were violated, then misrepresentation of endowments could be detected by observing that an individual's claim does not correspond to any endowment in the distribution). It therefore imposes a strong limitation on the possibility of first-best taxation. Indeed, if the economy is already competitive, no first-best taxes are possible.

The result is related to Theorem 5 in Hammond [1979]. The principal difference is that Hammond studies misrepresentation of *characteristics*, comprising both preferences and endowments, whereas I am concerned with the misrepresentation of endowments only. The distinction is significant because Hammond allows an individual to claim to have *any* characteristic, while I permit only *understatement* of endowment. One might have believed, *a priori*, that prohibition on overstatement would have allowed the implementation of SWF's other than the purely competitive one. (In the case of *Nash* implementation, the constraint on overstatement enormously increases the set of implementable SWF's); hence, the main motivation for Theorem 4.1. In my framework, Hammond's own theorem is about implementation possibilities when negative as well as positive concealment is allowed.

There are a number of other theorems, all of which establish competitive equilibrium as the unique optimum of certain SWF's or, often equivalently, as the unique equilibrium outcome of a certain game. The classical result along these lines is Edgeworth's observation, first formalized by Debreu and Scarf [1962], that, in a large economy, all core allocations are competitive. Recently, Mas-Colell [1978] has shown that, with a large number of players, the Nash equilibria of a trading game satisfying convexity, anonymity, non-degeneracy and neutrality properties must be competitive. Hurwicz [1979] has shown that, in the case where preferences are sufficiently rich, the only Paretian efficient and individually rational SWF's that are Nash implementable include the competitive allocations as optima.

Using Theorem 4.1, I can show that for small economies (strictly ones with only finitely many consumers) no Paretian social welfare function is implementable in dominant strategies when consumers can conceal their endowments. This is a result first proved by Postlewaite [1979]. Intuitively, the reason is that any implementable SWF for a finite economy has its infinite economy counterpart. But, as Theorem 4.1 shows, in an infinite economy, any implementable Paretian SWF in an infinite economy must be competitive. The same must be true in a finite economy. But it is then a simple matter to show that the competitive SWF is not implementable.

Theorem 4.2: If $F\colon R^n \times R^{nl}_{++} \rightarrow R$ is a Paretian social welfare function, then it is not differentially implementable in dominant strategies for any $\boldsymbol{u} \in U^n_\infty$ when consumers can conceal their endowments. Postlewaite, [1979].
Proof: See Appendix.

When consumers can misrepresent endowments only by destroying them, the possibilities for implementation improve. For given utility profile $\boldsymbol{u}$, the range of implementable SWF's is, in general, quite considerable. Nonetheless, the SWF's that are implementable for *all* profiles $\boldsymbol{u}$ are limited to the class of SWF's with 'L-shaped' social indifference curves.

Theorem 4.3: Suppose $F\colon R^n \times R^{nl}_{++} \rightarrow R$ is a Paretian, continuous, piecewise differentiable SWF. F is differentially implementable for all $\boldsymbol{u} \in U^n_\infty$ under endowment destruction, if and only if there exists an SWF, F^*, of the form:

$$F^*(\boldsymbol{u},\omega) = \max_t \{t \mid a^i(t,\omega) \leqslant u^i \text{ for all i}\}, \tag{4.3.1}$$

where, for all i, a^i is monotonically increasing in t and ω^i,

$\lim_{t\to\infty} a^i = \infty$ and $\lim_{t\to -\infty} a^i = -\infty$, such that $\forall \boldsymbol{u}\ \forall \omega\ G_F(\boldsymbol{u},\omega) = G_{F^*}(\boldsymbol{u},\omega)$.

Proof: See Appendix.

Condition (4.3.1) amounts to saying that F has 'L-shaped' social indifference contours. Various authors, including Dasgupta and Hammond [1978], Postlewaite [1979], Mirrlees [1977], have remarked that when $a_i(t,\omega) = a_i t$ (where a_i is a positive constant), F^* is implementable.

5. NASH STRATEGIES

The preceding sections demonstrate that, with dominant strategies, possibilities for first-best taxation are (at least with more than one good) quite limited. In this section, I weaken the requirement of dominant strategies by adopting Nash equilibrium as the solution concept. By making a consumer's tax depend not only on his own strategy but on those of others, I show that the class of implementable social welfare functions is very wide. Indeed, individual rationality—the property that ensures that each consumer obtains at least the utility of his initial endowment—is a necessary and sufficient condition for implementability when consumers can conceal their endowments. Still weaker conditions suffice for implementation when consumers are confined to destruction.

Definition: A social welfare function F is *individually rational* if $\forall i\ \forall \boldsymbol{u}\ \forall \omega\ \forall \boldsymbol{x} \in G_F(\boldsymbol{u},\omega)$, $u^i(x^i) \geqslant u^i(\omega^i)$

Theorem 5.1: Let $F\colon R^n_{++} \times R^{nl}_{++} \to R$ be a social welfare function. For $\boldsymbol{u}$, F is implementable for $\boldsymbol{u}$ in Nash strategies if and only if F is individually rational.

Proof: It is clear that an implementable F must be individually rational because a consumer could always conceal (and, hence, consume) his whole endowment. To see that individual rationality implies implementability, *see* the constructive proof in Hurwicz, Maskin and Postlewaite [1979].

Definition: A SWF, F, is *non-confiscatory* if $\forall i\ \forall \omega\ \forall \boldsymbol{u}\ \forall \boldsymbol{x} \in G_F(\boldsymbol{u},\omega)$, $x^i > 0$.

Theorem 5.2: A non-confiscatory SWF is implementable in Nash strategies for all $\boldsymbol{u}$, if consumers are confined to endowment destruction.

Proof: See Hurwicz, Maskin and Postlewaite [1979].

6. SUMMARY

It may be useful to summarize the main results of this paper in two tables.

Table 1. Paretian SWF's implementable in dominant strategies.

	Concealment	Destruction
Finite number of consumers:		
Economies with only one good	No transfer SWF	'Normal' SWF's
Economies with 2 or more goods	None	SWF's with 'L-shaped' indifference curves
Continuum:		
Economies with only one good	No transfer SWF	'Normal' SWF's
Economies with 2 or more goods	Competitive SWF	SWF's with 'L-shaped' indifference curves

Table 2. SWF's implementable in Nash strategies.

Concealment	Individually Rational SWF's
Destruction	Non-confiscatory SWF's

APPENDIX

In this appendix, I provide the proofs of those results (excluding Theorem 5.1 and 5.2) that were not proved in the main text.

Proof of Theorem 3.2: Suppose that F: $R^n \times R^n_{++} \to R$ satisfies the hypotheses of the theorem. Consider any $\bar{\boldsymbol{u}},\bar{\omega}$ and $\boldsymbol{x} \in G_F(\bar{\boldsymbol{u}},\bar{\omega})$. For the time being assume that F is twice differentiable, instead of just twice piecewise differentiable. Then, because optima are interior, we can choose $\bar{x}^*$: $R^n_+ \to R^n$ such that $\bar{x}^*(\cdot)$ is differentiable for all $\omega,\bar{x}^*(\omega) \in G_F(\bar{\boldsymbol{u}},\omega)$ and $\bar{x}^*(\bar{\omega})=\bar{x}$. That there exists a tax scheme T, acceptable for F for $\boldsymbol{u}$, such that $\bar{x} \in E_T(\boldsymbol{u},\omega)$, is equivalent to the property

$$\forall\omega \ \frac{\partial x^{i*}}{\partial \omega^i}\ (\omega)>0. \tag{A.1}$$

(because, if equation (A.1) holds, an individual cannot gain by understating his endowment and, therefore, telling the truth is a dominant strategy).

Consider problem (3.2.1) theorem 3.2. For given $\mathring{\omega}$, and any i let

$$p_i = \frac{\partial F}{\partial v_i}\ (\bar{u}_1(x^{1*}(\mathring{\omega}), \ldots, \bar{u}_n(x^{n*}(\mathring{\omega})); \omega) \tag{A.2}$$

and

$$y = \max\left\{\Sigma p_i v_i \mid \forall i \quad v_i = \bar{u}_i(x^i), \quad \sum_i x^i = \sum_i \omega^i\right\}. \tag{A.3}$$

Thinking of y as a function of $\boldsymbol{\omega}$, we can infer that $\partial y/\partial\omega^i > 0$. Let $V_l^{1*}(y), \ldots, V_l^{n*}(y)$ be a (differentiable) solution to (3.2.1) with p_i and y as defined in (A.2) and (A.3). Then, for all i,

$$\frac{\partial \bar{u}^i}{\partial x}\frac{\partial x^{i*}}{\partial \omega^i} = \frac{\partial V^i}{\partial y}\frac{\partial y}{\partial \omega^i}.$$

Since $\partial\bar{u}^i/\partial x$ is positive, we conclude that $\partial x^{i*}/\partial\omega^i$ is positive if and only if $\partial v^i/\partial y$ is positive. That is, F is implementable only if all utilities are normal goods. If F is only piecewise differentiable, the same argument can be applied to each point in a sequence of closer and closer differentiable approximations to complete the proof.

Proof of Theorem 4.1: Suppose, first, that F is differentially implementable for $u[\cdot]$. Then $\forall\, \omega[\cdot]\ \forall\, a \in G_F(u[\cdot], \omega[\cdot])$ there exists an acceptable tax scheme $T[\cdot]$ where $S^i = R^l$; where $a \in E_T(u[\cdot], \omega[\cdot])$ and where T[i] is differentiable with respect to consumer i's strategy. Without loss of generality (*see* Dasgupta, Hammond and Maskin [1979]), we may assume, that professing the truth is a dominant strategy. Because F is Paretian, we may invoke the second fundamental welfare theorem to conclude that there exist $p(\omega[\cdot]) \in R^l_+$ and $Y[\cdot]\,(\omega[\cdot]) \in I$ with

$\int_{j\in[0,J]} Y[j]\,(\omega[\cdot])dj=0$, such that $t^i = T[i]\,(\omega[\cdot])$ solves $\max_{t^i} u^i\,(\omega^i + t^i)$ such that

$p(\omega[\cdot]\cdot t^i \leqslant Y[i]\,(\omega[\cdot])$. That is, the equilibrium outcome is a competitive allocation with transfer payments (the Y[i]'s are the transfers).

Choose $\omega[\cdot] \in \Omega$. For any i and any $\omega^i \in R^l_+$, define $W_{\omega^i}[\cdot] \in \Omega$ so that

$$W_\omega[j] = \begin{cases} \overline{\omega}[j], & j \neq i \\ \omega^i, & j = i \end{cases}$$

Because $T[\cdot]$ $(\omega[\cdot])$ is a selection from $G_F(u[\cdot], \omega[\cdot])$, the hypotheses imply that $\forall j \neq i$ so $T[j]$ $(\overline{\omega}[\cdot]) = T[j]$ $(W_{\omega^i}[\cdot])$. Therefore $p(\overline{\omega}[\cdot]) = p(W_{\omega^i}[\cdot])$. Thus, for all $i, \omega^i = \overline{\omega}^i$ maximizes $u[i](\omega^i + T[i](W_{\omega^i}[\cdot]))$ subject to $\omega^i < \overline{\omega}^i$. From the Kuhn-Tucker theorem, there exist, for each consumer i, γ_k (k=1, ..., l) such that

$$\sum_{j=1}^{l} \frac{\partial u[i]}{\partial x_j} \frac{\partial T_j[i]}{\partial \omega_k[i]} = \gamma_k$$

at the maximum. Also, at the maximum, $p(\omega[\cdot]) \cdot T[i](W_\omega{}^i[\cdot]) = Y[i](W_{\omega^i}[\cdot])$, so that $\Sigma_j p_j(\partial T_j[i]/\partial \omega_k[i]) = \partial Y[i]/\partial \omega_k[i]$. Therefore, since p is proportional to $(\partial u[i]/\partial x_1, \ldots, \partial u[i]/\partial x_l)$ at the maximum (equilibrium is interior because $u[\cdot] \in \mathscr{U}_\infty$), $\partial Y[i]/\partial \omega_k[i] \geqslant 0$ for each k. That is, the income transfer that consumer i receives must be a non-decreasing function of the endowment he professes. Now suppose that, for some i, $Y[i](\overline{\omega}[\cdot]) < 0$. Then choose $\mathring{\omega}^i \leqslant \overline{\omega}[i]$ such that $((\partial u[i]/\partial x_1)(\mathring{\omega}^i), \ldots, (\partial u[i]/\partial x_l)(\mathring{\omega}^i))$ is proportional to $p(\mathring{\omega}[\cdot])$. (Such a choice is possible because $u[i] \in \mathscr{U}_\infty$).

Now if $Y[i](W_{\mathring{\omega}}{}^i[\cdot]) < 0$, then

$$\max \{u[i](\mathring{\omega}^i + t^i) | p(\overline{\omega}[\cdot]) \cdot t^i \leqslant Y[i] (W_{\mathring{\omega}}{}^i[\cdot])\} < u[i] (\mathring{\omega}^i).$$

But, if consumer i's endowment is $\mathring{\omega}^i$, he can guarantee himself the utility $u[i](\mathring{\omega}^i)$ by concealing his endowment. Thus $Y[i](W_{\mathring{\omega}}{}^i[\cdot]) \geqslant 0$.

But this, in combination with $Y[i](\overline{\omega}[\cdot])$, contradicts the fact that $Y[i]$ must be increasing in ω^i. Thus, for all i, $Y[i](\overline{\omega}[\cdot]) \geqslant 0$.

Since $\int Y[i](\overline{\omega}[\cdot])di = 0$ (transfers sum to zero), we conclude that $Y[i](\overline{\omega}[\cdot]) = 0$ for (almost) all i. Thus, the equilibrium outcome is a competitive equilibrium. We have shown, therefore, that any implementable SWF must be competitive. To see the converse, choose $\overline{\omega}[\cdot]$ $a \in G_F(u[\cdot], \omega[\cdot])$ and a selection $V(\omega[\cdot])$ from $G_F(u[\cdot], \omega[\cdot]$ such that $a \in V[\cdot](\omega[\cdot])$ as above. Define $T[\cdot](\omega[\cdot]) = V[\cdot](\omega[\cdot])$. It is straightforward to verify that T is acceptable for F.

Proof of Theorem 4.2: Suppose that F: $R^n \times R^{nl}_{++} \to R$ satisfies the hypotheses of the theorem but is implementable for some $\bar{\boldsymbol{u}} \in U^n_\infty$. Choose $u[\cdot] \in \mathscr{U}_\infty$ such that, $\forall i \in [0,1]$, $\bar{u}[i] = \bar{u}[S(in)]$, where $S(x)$ is the smallest integer greater than or equal to x. Consider F^*: $I \times \Omega \to R$ such that $\forall$ $\omega[\cdot]$, G_{F^*} $(\bar{u}[\cdot], \omega[\cdot])$ is defined as follows:

(i) If there exists $\overline{\omega}$ such that, for each k $\in \{1, \ldots, n\}$, $\omega[i/n] = \overline{\omega}^k$ for almost all i with $(k-1) \leqslant i \leqslant k$, then $x[\cdot] \in G_{F^*}$ $(\bar{U}[\cdot], \omega[\cdot])$ if and only if (a) there exists $\bar{\mathbf{k}} \in G_F(\bar{\boldsymbol{u}}, \overline{\boldsymbol{\omega}})$ such that $\forall i$ $x[i/n] = \bar{x}^i$ if $\omega[i/n] = \overline{\omega}^{s(i)}$ and (b) if $\omega[i/n] \neq \omega^{s(i)}$ for some i, then there exists $\bar{\bar{x}} \in G_F(\bar{\boldsymbol{u}}, (\omega^{s(i)}, \boldsymbol{\omega}^{-s(i)}))$ such that $x[i/n] = \bar{\bar{x}}^{-s(i)}$.

(ii) If no such $\overline{\omega}$ exists, then $x[\cdot] \in G_{F^*}(\bar{u}[\cdot], \omega[\cdot])$ if and only if $x[\cdot]$ is a competitive equilibrium with respect to $\bar{u}[\cdot]$ and $\omega[\cdot]$.

Intuitively, F^* is a replication of F if the continuum economy itself is a replication of an n-person economy, (i.e., if (i) applies) and the competitive SWF otherwise, (i.e., if (ii) applies). It is easy to see that F^* is differentially implementable: if (i) applies then consumers tell the truth for the same reason they do when F is the SWF; if (ii) applies, then consumers tell the truth, because, from theorem 4.1, the competitive SWF is implementable. But, from theorem 4.1 again, F^* itself must be the competitive SWF, since it is implementable. Because F^* is just a replication of F, we conclude that

F must be the competitive SWF. Therefore it remains only to show that the competitive SWF is not implementable for any choice of $\boldsymbol{u} \in U_\infty^n$. To do this, let us assume, for simplicity, that $n=2$ and $l=2$ (the argument is essentially the same for larger n and l). Choose $\bar{\boldsymbol{u}} \in u_\infty^2$. If the competitive social welfare function is differentially implementable for $\boldsymbol{u}$, then there exists an acceptable game form $T: R_{++}^l \times R_{++}^l \to R^l \times R^l$, differentiable in each argument, such that, for all $\omega=(\omega^1, \omega^2)$, $(\omega^1+T^1(\omega^1, \omega^2)$, $\omega^2+T^2(\omega^1, \omega^2))$ is a competitive equilibrium allocation for $\bar{\boldsymbol{u}}$ and ω. Let $p(\omega)$ be the prices associated with the equilibrium allocation $(\omega^1+T^1(\omega^1, \omega^2), \omega^2+T^2(\omega^1, \omega^2))$. By the assumptions on $\bar{\boldsymbol{u}}$ and T, p is differentiable with respect to ω^1 and ω^2. Now if consumer 1 is to be induced not to conceal any of his endowment, then for all $\boldsymbol{\omega}$ we must have

$$\frac{\partial u^1}{\partial x_1}\left(\omega^1 + T^1(\omega)\frac{\partial T_1^1}{\partial \omega_k^1}(\boldsymbol{\omega}) + \frac{\partial u^1}{\partial x_2}(\omega^1 + T^1(\boldsymbol{\omega}))\right)\frac{\partial T_2^1}{\partial \omega_k^1}(\boldsymbol{\omega}) \geqslant 0 \text{ for k} = 1,2. \quad \text{(A.4)}$$

Furthermore, from Walras' Law

$$p_1\frac{\partial T_1^1}{\partial \omega_k^1} + p_2\frac{\partial T_2^1}{\partial \omega_k^1} + T_1\frac{\partial p_1}{\partial \omega_k^1} + T_2\frac{\partial p_2}{\partial \omega_k^1} = 0, \text{ for k}=1,2. \quad \text{(A.5)}$$

Hence, from (A.4) and (A.5)

$$T_1^1\frac{\partial p_1}{\partial \omega_k^1} + T_2^1\frac{\partial p_2}{\partial \omega_k^1} \leqslant 0. \quad \text{(A.6)}$$

At every point in consumer l's consumption space, at least one of the two goods is (locally) normal for him.

Without loss of generality, suppose that good 1 is normal in a neighbourhood of radius ε of $\overline{\omega}^1$. Choose $\overline{\omega}^2$ for consumer 2 so that (A.4) $\omega^{-1}+T^1(\boldsymbol{\omega}^{-1})$ is within ε of ω^{-1}, (A.5) $\overline{\boldsymbol{\omega}}+T(\overline{\boldsymbol{\omega}})$ lies on the convex portions of the two consumers offer curves and (A.6) $T_2^1(\overline{\boldsymbol{\omega}})<0$. (Since the offer curves must be convex in a neighbourhood of the endowment, conditions (A.4) and (A.5) can be met simply by choosing $\overline{\omega}^2$ so that the resulting equilibrium does not lie too far from the initial endowments.)

Let $x^1(p_1,p_2,\omega^1)$ be consumer l's utility-maximizing consumption bundle, given prices (p_1,p_2) and endowment ω^1. Then

$$\frac{\partial}{\partial \omega_2}(\omega_2^1 - x_2^1) = \frac{p_1}{p_2}\frac{\partial x_1^1}{\partial \omega_2} > 0,$$

since good 1 is normal. That is, an increase in the endowment of good 2 induces consumer 1 to sell more of it; his offer curve falls. Because consumer 2's offer curve is convex in a neighborhood of $\overline{\boldsymbol{\omega}}+T(\overline{\boldsymbol{\omega}})$, the fall in the offer curve means that p_2 falls relative to p_1; i.e., if prices are normalized to lie in the unit simplex $\partial p_2/\partial \omega_2^1<0$ and $\partial p_1/\partial \omega_2^n>0$. Because $T_2^1(\overline{\boldsymbol{\omega}})<0$, and $T_1^1(\overline{\boldsymbol{\omega}})>0$, we have, therefore,

$$T_1^1\frac{\partial p_1}{\partial \omega_k^1} + T_2^1\frac{\partial p_2}{\partial \omega_k^1} > 0, \quad \text{(A.7)}$$

which contradicts equation (A.6). Thus F is not implementable after all.

Proof of theorem 4.3: Suppose that an F^* as hypothesized in equation (4.3.1) exists. For given endowments $\boldsymbol{\omega}$, F can be maximized by maximizing the following Lagrangian:

$$\max\ t+\sum_i \lambda^i(u^i(x^i)-a^i(t,\omega))+\sum_j \gamma_j(\sum_i x^i_j-\sum_i \omega^i_j). \tag{A.8}$$

The first order conditions for an (interior) maximum are

$$1=\sum_i \lambda^i \frac{\partial a^i}{\partial t}=0. \tag{A.9a}$$

$$\lambda^i \frac{\partial u^i}{\partial x^i_k}+\gamma_j=0 \quad \text{for all i, j} \tag{A.9b}$$

$$u^i=a^i \quad \text{for all i} \tag{A.9c}$$

$$\sum_i x^i=\sum_i \omega^i \tag{A.9d}$$

Let $\{x^{i*}\}$ and $\{t^*\}$ be a solution to the problem. Thinking of x^{i*} and t^* as functions of ω and making use of (A.9c) we obtain

$$\sum_k \frac{\partial u^i}{\partial x^i_k}\frac{\partial x^{i*}_k}{\partial \omega^i_j}=\frac{\partial a^i}{\partial t}\frac{\partial t^*}{\partial \omega^i_j}+\frac{\partial a^i}{\partial \omega^i_j} \quad \text{for all i, j.} \tag{A.10}$$

From (A.9b), if $\gamma_j>0$ for some j, then $\lambda^i<0$ for all i. But this contradicts (A.9a), since $\partial a^i/\partial t \geqslant 0$. Therefore, $\gamma_j \leqslant 0$ for all j. Now $\partial t^*/\partial \omega^i_j=-\gamma_j$. Therefore, from $\partial a^i/\partial \omega^i_j \geqslant 0$ and (A.10), we conclude that

$$\sum_k \frac{\partial u^i}{\partial x^i_k}\frac{\partial x^{i*}_k}{\partial \omega^i_j} \geqslant 0 \quad \text{for all i and j,}$$

implying that consumers will never understate their endowments. F is implementable.

Next suppose that F^* as hypothesized does not exist. Then not all F's indifference curves are 'L-shaped'. In particular, there exists a vector $\bar{v} \in R^n$ and integers i and j such that $(\partial F/\partial v_i)(\bar{v}) \neq 0 \neq (\partial F/\partial v_j)(\bar{v})$. For simplicity suppose $n=l=2$. In that case, if one of F's indifference curves is not L-shaped, there exists $\bar{v}$ such that $(\partial F/\partial v_1)(\bar{v}) \neq 0 \neq (\partial F/\partial v_2)(\bar{v})$.

Choose $\boldsymbol{u} \in U^2_\infty$ and $\boldsymbol{x} \in R^4_{++}$ such that

$$(u^1(\bar{x}^1),\ u^2(\bar{x}^2))=\bar{v} \qquad \text{and} \tag{A.11}$$

$$\frac{\partial F}{\partial v_1}\frac{\partial u^1}{\partial x_1}=\frac{\partial F}{\partial v_2}\frac{\partial u^2}{\partial x_1} \quad \text{and} \quad \frac{\partial F}{\partial v_1}\frac{\partial u^1}{\partial x_2}=\frac{\partial F}{\partial v_2}\frac{\partial u^2}{\partial x_2} \quad \text{at } \boldsymbol{x}=\bar{\boldsymbol{x}}. \tag{A.12}$$

Thus, $\bar{\boldsymbol{x}} \in G_F(\boldsymbol{u},\boldsymbol{x})$. Differentiating (A.12) with respect to ω_1 and supposing that $\partial u^1/\partial x_1$ and $\partial u^1/\partial x_2$ are nearly zero, we obtain

$$\frac{\partial x^{1'}_1}{\partial \omega_1}=\frac{\begin{vmatrix} \dfrac{\partial F}{\partial v_2}\left(\dfrac{\partial^2 u^2}{\partial x_1^2}+\dfrac{\partial^2 u^2}{\partial x_1 \partial x_2}\right) & \dfrac{\partial F}{\partial v_1}\dfrac{\partial^2 u^1}{\partial x_1 \partial x_2}+\dfrac{\partial F}{\partial v_2}\dfrac{\partial^2 u^2}{\partial x_1 \partial x_2} \\ \dfrac{\partial F}{\partial v_2}\left(\dfrac{\partial^2 u^2}{\partial x_1 \partial x_2}+\dfrac{\partial^2 u^2}{\partial x_2^2}\right) & \dfrac{\partial F}{\partial v_1}\dfrac{\partial^2 u^1}{\partial x_2^2}+\dfrac{\partial F}{\partial v_2}\dfrac{\partial^2 u^2}{\partial x_2^2} \end{vmatrix}}{D} \tag{A.13a}$$

and

$$\frac{\partial x_2^1}{\partial \omega_1} = \frac{\begin{vmatrix} \dfrac{\partial F}{\partial v_1}\dfrac{\partial^2 u^1}{\partial x_1^2} + \dfrac{\partial F}{\partial v_2}\dfrac{\partial^2 u^2}{\partial x_1^2} & \dfrac{\partial F}{\partial v_2}\left(\dfrac{\partial^2 u^2}{\partial x_1^2} + \dfrac{\partial^2 u^2}{\partial x_1 \partial x_2}\right) \\ \dfrac{\partial F}{\partial v_1}\dfrac{\partial^2 u^1}{\partial x_1 \partial x_2} + \dfrac{\partial F}{\partial v_2}\dfrac{\partial^2 u^2}{\partial x_1 \partial x_2} & \dfrac{\partial F}{\partial v_2}\left(\dfrac{\partial^2 u^2}{\partial x_1 \partial x_2} + \dfrac{\partial^2 u^2}{\partial x_2^2}\right) \end{vmatrix}}{\mathrm{D}} \qquad (A.13b)$$

where

$$\mathrm{D} = \begin{vmatrix} \dfrac{\partial F}{\partial v_1}\dfrac{\partial^2 u^1}{\partial x_1^2} + \dfrac{\partial F}{\partial v_2}\dfrac{\partial^2 u^2}{\partial x_1^2} & \dfrac{\partial F}{\partial v_1}\dfrac{\partial^2 u^1}{\partial x_1 \partial x_2} + \dfrac{\partial F}{\partial v_2}\dfrac{\partial^2 u^2}{\partial x_1 \partial x_2} \\ \dfrac{\partial F}{\partial v_1}\dfrac{\partial^2 u^1}{\partial x_1 \partial x_2} + \dfrac{\partial F}{\partial v_2}\dfrac{\partial^2 u^2}{\partial x_1 \partial x_2} & \dfrac{\partial F}{\partial v_1}\dfrac{\partial^2 u^1}{\partial x_2^2} + \dfrac{\partial F}{\partial v_2}\dfrac{\partial^2 u^2}{\partial x_2^2} \end{vmatrix}. \qquad (A.13c)$$

Suppose that u^1 and u^2, in addition to satisfying (A.11) and (A.12), satisfy

$$\begin{pmatrix} \dfrac{\partial F}{\partial v_1}\dfrac{\partial^2 u^1}{\partial x_1^2} & \dfrac{\partial F}{\partial v_1}\dfrac{\partial^2 u^1}{\partial x_1 \partial x_2} \\ \dfrac{\partial F}{\partial v_1}\dfrac{\partial^2 u^1}{\partial x_1 \partial x_2} & \dfrac{\partial F}{\partial v_1}\dfrac{\partial^2 u}{\partial x_1^2} \end{pmatrix} = \begin{pmatrix} -1 & 4 \\ 4 & -17 \end{pmatrix}$$

and

$$\begin{pmatrix} \dfrac{\partial F}{\partial v_2}\dfrac{\partial^2 u^2}{\partial x_1^2} & \dfrac{\partial F}{\partial v_2}\dfrac{\partial^2 u^2}{\partial x_1 \partial x_2} \\ \dfrac{\partial F}{\partial v_2}\dfrac{\partial^2 u^2}{\partial x_1 \partial x_2} & \dfrac{\partial F}{\partial v_2^2}\dfrac{\partial^2 u^2}{\partial x_2^2} \end{pmatrix} = \begin{pmatrix} -2 & 3 \\ 3 & -5 \end{pmatrix} \qquad (A.14)$$

Then, from (A.13*a*) and (A.13*b*),

$$\frac{\partial x^1}{\partial \omega_1} = \frac{-8}{17} \text{ and } \frac{\partial x^2}{\partial \omega_1} = \frac{-1}{17}.$$

Thus

$$\frac{\partial u^1}{\partial \omega_1}(x(^2\omega)) = \frac{\partial u^1}{\partial x_1}\frac{\partial x^1}{\partial \omega_1} + \frac{\partial u^1}{\partial x_2}\frac{\partial x^2}{\partial \omega_1} < 0.$$

Therefore, individual 1 has the incentive to understate his endowment, so that F is not implementable after all.

ACKNOWLEDGEMENTS

I am grateful to Peter Hammond for a long and very useful written discussion of my paper. I wish to thank him, James Mirrlees and Kevin Roberts for helpful conversations. The paper owes much to the work of Peter Hammond, Leo Hurwicz, James

Mirrlees, and Andrew Postlewaite. Indeed, theorem 4·2 of the theorems in the section on Nash equilibrium is derived from some on-going joint work by Hurwicz, Postlewaite, and me. I would like to thank the NSF for financial support.

REFERENCES

Dasgupta P. and Hammond P. J. (1978) *Fully Progressive Taxation*, Univ. Essex.

Debreu G. and Scarf H. (1963) A Limit Theorem on the Core of an Economy. *Int. Econom. Rev.*

Hammond P. J. (1979) Straightforward Individual Incentive Compatibility in Large Economies. *Rev. Economic Studies.*

Hurwicz L. (1972) On Informationally Decentralized Systems. In McGuire C. and Radner R. (ed.) *Decision and Organization*, Amsterdam, North-Holland.

Hurwicz L. (1979) On Allocations Attainable through Nash Equilibria. In Laffont J.-J. (ed.) *Aggregation and Revelation of Preferences*, Amsterdam, North-Holland.

Hurwicz L., Maskin E. and Postlewaite A. (1979) *Feasible Implementation of Social Choice Correspondences by Nash Equilibria.* Massachusetts Inst. Technology.

Mas-Colell A. (1978) *An Axiomatic Approach to the Efficiency of Non-cooperative Equilibrium in Economics with a Continuum of Traders.* IMSSS Technical Report No. 274.

Mirrlees J. (1977) *The Theory of Optimal Taxation.* Univ. Oxford.

Postlewaite A. (1979) Manipulation via Endowments. *Rev. Economic Studies.*

DISCUSSION

by **P. Hammond,** *University of Essex, and Stanford University*

Introduction: The Theoretical Limits to Redistribution

In my view it is entirely appropriate that the first paper of this symposium should be an examination of the theoretical limits to redistribution. And Eric Maskin's paper, which is part of his work on the intriguing subject of 'incentive compatibility', goes about exploring these limits in entirely the right sort of way, as I see it. It helps to bridge an important gap in the approaches which economists have become accustomed to using, as I shall now try to explain.

On the one hand, competent second-year economics undergraduates learn about lump-sum taxes and subsidies as means of redistributing income. Lump-sum taxes are often rather carelessly defined; they are taxes where the amount collected from any one agent is fixed in nominal terms—in particular, they are independent of the agent's market transactions. Thus, there is no divergence between prices before tax and prices after tax. Loosely speaking, there are no 'distortions' in the economy. In particular, by comparison with the income taxes which are often thought of as the right instruments for redistributing income, there is no disincentive to work, because the implicit marginal rate of tax is zero if the tax is a lump-sum tax. So, with lump-sum taxes there are no limits at all to redistribution.

The trouble with lump-sum taxes, as we all know, and as Samuelson ([1947], 247–8) and Graaff ([1957], 77–79) at least have been careful to point out, is that one wants to base these taxes on individual characteristics such as ability which are hard to observe directly. And if one does base a tax on ability, say, or the quality of labour actually provided, this creates disincentives regarding the *quality* rather than the quantity of labour. Individuals become reluctant to acquire skills or to reveal them by taking skilled jobs. (For an analysis of an optimal ability tax, in Mirrlees' 1971 model of income taxation, see Dasgupta and Hammond [1978]).

So one has lump-sum taxes on one side of the gap. They represent an impracticable ideal, perhaps, but at least their theoretical implications are well understood. Competent third-year economics undergraduates, at least if they specialize in public finance, then make a considerable leap to consider the effects and effectiveness of commodity taxes, income taxes, property taxes, etc. which are based very closely on market transactions. Distortions are introduced and quantities become affected. Again, the theory is fairly well developed, especially since the work of Diamond and Mirrlees [1971] on optimal commodity taxation.

The question which should be asked, however, before we resort to income taxes, commodity taxes, etc. is whether these really represent the best we can do. If we rule out lump-sum taxes because even they create undesirable incentive effects, need we go over all the way to the other, more customary, taxes of public finance which also create undesirable incentive effects? In some cases, and with some major qualifications, it seems that we must (as I have shown elsewhere in Hammond [1979]), but Maskin shows that in other cases a considerable degree of compromise may be possible. In the present context, although generally it may not be possible to have full redistribution of income, it may still be possible to have much more redistribution than recent public finance literature suggests.

By now it should be fairly clear that to bridge the gap between lump-sum taxes and public finance we need to consider rather carefully the problem of how to devise a mechanism for redistributing real income in the economy, or, more generally, for allocating resources. We should be careful to understand exactly what kind of information the mechanism relies on, and what incentives individuals have for providing that information. These are precisely the issues to which the work on incentive compatibility, including Maskin's paper, addresses itself.

In fact, the title, 'On First-Best Taxation', is itself quite thought-provoking. Usually, 'first-best' welfare economics assumes that lump-sum taxation is used to bring about an ideal income distribution; 'first-best taxation', therefore, should be optimal lump-sum taxation. But, as I have already argued, the lump-sum taxes one would like to have may rely on information about skills and other individual characteristics which individuals will choose to suppress, so many schemes of lump-sum taxation are simply not feasible. Taking into account the information which individuals choose not to suppress, Maskin's tax schemes really are 'first-best'.

For the most part, Maskin considers a general exchange economy of l private goods and n consumers. In the present paper, it is assumed that all consumers' preferences are known although elsewhere, in his work with Hurwicz and Postlewaite, Maskin considers what happens when they are not. It is endowments which are unknown. Production and public goods can also be included. The problem is to devise a scheme of taxation—a 'mechanism'—which yields good outcomes even when individuals choose to conceal or even to destroy some of their endowments. It is, I think, rightly assumed that individuals cannot overstate their endowments, because such overstatement can usually be detected.

Broadly speaking, there are two classes of mechanism which can be distinguished, both of which are considered. The first and simplest kind is a 'direct' mechanism in which each individual simply reports an endowment (not necessarily his true endowment) and nothing else. The second kind is an 'indirect' mechanism which, in the present paper, relies on each individual sending not only a report of his endowment but also an extra message in addition—very often a report of other agents' endowments. Where the mechanism is direct, dominant strategies are of especial interest, as considered in sections 3 and 4 of the paper. With indirect mechanisms, one looks instead for Nash strategies; section 5 summarizes the relevant results from Maskin's work with Hurwicz and Postlewaite.

The Simplest Case: Redistribution in a One-Good Economy

In a one-good economy, all that can be done is to redistribute the individuals' initial endowments of the single good, which will be called 'cake'. A transfer scheme, or mechanism, redistributes cake in response to individuals' messages. In section 3 of the paper, these messages are direct reports of endowments.

Now, in section 2, Maskin requires each individual to be able to achieve a non-negative consumption level whatever he reports. So, if he is allowed to conceal his endowment, the individual can always ensure that none of it is taken away from him by reporting a zero endowment. Thus an equilibrium outcome of the mechanism can never be worse for the individual than if he had just kept his original endowment—in other words, the outcome is 'individually rational'.

In a one-good economy of course, individual rationality means that, since nobody can finish up with less of the one good than he started off with, so nobody can finish up with more, and thus we stay where we started, with the initial endowment. This is rather uninteresting, (*see* Theorem 3.1).

Where endowments cannot simply be concealed, however, but have to be destroyed, then equilibrium outcomes need not be individually rational, and so interesting possibilities arise even in a one-good economy. Then formally, under endowment destruction, with $T^i(\omega)$ denoting the direct transfer mechanism, and $x^i(\omega)$ denoting i's resulting consumption, we have:

$$x^i(\omega)=T^i(\omega)+\omega^i \quad (\text{if } \omega^i \leqq \overline{\omega}^i).$$

Provided that $dT^i/d\omega^i>-1$, which ensures that $dx^i/d\omega^i>0$, then obviously i's dominant strategy is to announce $\overline{\omega}^i$.

This possibility is of some considerable interest. It includes, for instance, the perfect redistribution rule (under inequality aversion):

$$T^i(\omega)=\frac{1}{n}\sum_{j=1}^{n}\omega^j-\omega^i$$

under which, when every individual tells the truth,

$$x^i(\omega)=\frac{1}{n}\sum_{j=1}^{n}\omega^i$$

because, of course, $dT^i/d\omega^i=(1/n)-1$. In fact, any 'income' redistribution rule which maximizes a sum of (strictly concave) utility functions:

$$W=\sum_{i=1}^{n}u^i(x^i) \text{ subject to } \sum_{i=1}^{n}x^i=\sum_{i=1}^{n}\omega^i$$

can be truthfully implemented in this way, provided that $du^i/dx^i>0$ and $d^2u^i/d(x^i)^2<0$ for every i and every $x^i \geqq 0$. In this one-good economy then, when unreported endowments are destroyed, there are no effective limits to redistribution for a large class of social welfare functions, including utilitarianism and maximin. Maskin's Theorems 3.2 and 3.3 give far more general social welfare functions which are implementable in this way.

So much for direct mechanisms in the one-good economy. Let me now turn to indirect mechanisms, as in Maskin's section 5 on Nash equilibrium. When endowments can be concealed, Theorem 5.1 is not so interesting in a single good economy because, as I have already remarked, only the trivial mechanism of transferring nothing at all is individually rational in such an economy. Where endowments cannot be concealed, however, Theorem 5.2 is striking. It is based on constructing a very specific mechanism where each consumer announces an entire profile of endowments, but has to destroy his own endowment if he understates it. The mechanism is remarkably powerful, even in a one-good economy. It can implement any transfer rule under which, if the total endowment is positive, each agent always get some of it. The mechanism works by allocating all the total endowment to a single consumer unless all consumers announce identical endowment profiles. It encourages each consumer to claim that he has a large endowment himself. Other agents are encouraged not to understate one another's endowments, but to be the lowest overstaters. If just one agent overstates another's endowment, however, that overstater get nothing. By these extreme reallocations out of equilibrium, each consumer, as I say, is induced to state the true profile of endowments. There is no need to assume individual rationality or even (surprisingly enough) the monotonicity property which is usually needed for Nash implementation (Dasgupta, Hammond and Maskin [1979], Theorem 7.1.3).

Before moving on to a general many-good economy, let me remark on one special case which can be reduced to a one-good economy, even though it has many goods. This is an economy where equilibrium price ratios are fixed and known, either because the economy is a small open one with all goods traded, or because the nonsubstitution theorem applies (i.e. there are constant returns to scale, no joint production, and a single non-produced factor). Some combination of these two cases will also suffice, of course. Then the efficiency prices which support any Pareto-efficient allocation are effectively exogenous, and so all that matters is the value of each consumer's endowment at these prices. Of course, this is really just a version of Hicks' composite commodity theorem.

Redistribution with Many Goods: Direct Mechanisms

When there are many goods, the economy faces the problem of achieving an efficient allocation, as well as of trying to redistribute income. Leaving consumers with their initial endowments is most unlikely to be Pareto-efficient. But then, once one tries to move to towards the Pareto frontier, consumers will typically be able to gain by concealing their true endowments, as Maskin's Theorem 4.2 shows. Notice that any Pareto-efficient allocation is a competitive equilibrium with suitable lump-sum transfers, provided preferences are convex and the allocation is an interior one. So, in the pure exchange economy of Theorem 4.2, one can think of a price and transfer mechanism for producing efficient allocations. Now, if prices are held fixed, lump-sum transfers are likely to cause difficulties, as they did in the one-good economy (unless unreported endowments are destroyed). But if lump-sum transfers are ruled out, and prices are varied, we are using a competitive or Walrasian mechanism without lump-sum transfers. Then consumers expect to benefit by claiming to have smaller endowments of goods they are selling, which tends to raise those prices relative to the prices of the goods they are buying. That is true, at least, in a gross substitutes economy. And it provides a very loose and heuristic argument for the impossibility of achieving Pareto efficiency—by dominant strategies, at least—and goes a little way towards explaining Theorem 4.2.

When unreported endowments are destroyed, however, the situation does change somewhat. Note, however, that the competitive mechanism may well be vulnerable to destruction of endowments. We all know that a coffee-producing country may want to dump some of its coffee at sea, in a glut year, in order to drive up the price sufficiently to increase its total revenue. And a classroom example may serve to reinforce the point rather dramatically.

Suppose we have an economy with two goods—left gloves and right gloves—and two agents—one with an endowment of left gloves and one with an endowment of right gloves. Both agents want equal numbers of left gloves and right gloves; excess gloves of either kind, however, are worthless. In such an economy, unless the total endowments of left and right gloves happen to be exactly equal, one kind of glove must have a zero price. For suppose there are more right gloves than left gloves, and that all gloves have a positive price. Then the total demands for left gloves and right gloves must be equal, so both markets cannot clear simultaneously. Thus right gloves become a free good, and the agent who started with an endowment of right gloves never gets any left gloves, while the lucky agent who started off with left gloves gets the right gloves needed to match. This is the competitive equilibrium, which is highly inequitable. Suppose, however, that the original owner of the right gloves destroys some of his endowment, so that it is now left gloves which predominate. Then the equilibrium switches around; left gloves have a zero price, and their original owner gets no pairs of gloves, while the original owner of right gloves now gets all the pairs it is possible to put together. Obviously, then, each agent wants to destroy some of his endowment. This is true even if initially the number of left and right gloves are equal.

Theorem 4.3, however, shows that there are mechanisms, other than the competitive mechanism, in which agents will not want to destroy their endowments. Postlewaite [1979] has already presented an example of such a mechanism. Maskin presents a general class. In fact, the allocation mechanism, in a pure exchange economy, must be the one which maximizes a function of the form:

$$\min_{i} \varphi^i(u^i(x^i); \omega)$$

i.e. each consumer's utility gain from trade, measured in some interpersonally comparable utility units. It is required that φ^i be increasing in u^i but, when any component of ω^i increases, then φ^i does not rise relative to φ^j (all $j \neq i$). Then an optimal allocation has the property that each consumer does gain from having a larger endowment. So no consumer wants to understate his endowment. By making sure that consumers are actually expected to provide more if their endowments are larger, it is also possible, as in a one-good economy, to arrange that no consumer wants to overstate his endowment either.

Redistribution with Many Goods: Profile Mechanisms

When there are many goods, and when agents can keep their endowments whether they declare them or not, there is little one can achieve in small economies with direct mechanisms as Maskin's Theorem 4.2, discussed previously, clearly demonstrates. It is in these circumstances that the ingenious Maskin mechanisms exhibited elsewhere in the proofs of Theorems 5.1 and 5.2 come into their own.

In constructing these mechanism, Maskin has followed an idea due originally, I understand, to Karl Vind. Each agent, instead of reporting just his own characteristic, as he would with a direct mechanism, reports an entire profile of characteristics. In fact, perhaps we should call these 'profile' mechanisms.

The profile mechanism exhibited in the proof of Theorem 5.2 works, it should be recalled, when agents cannot conceal their own endowments. Also, it is expressly designed to deal with a many-good economy; when I described its operation in a one-good economy, that was merely for simplification. The extension to many goods is actually rather straightforward.

When agents are free to conceal their own endowments then, as has been argued above, for a social choice rule to be implementable at all by a profile mechanism, it must be individually rational. Theorem 5.1 claims that any individually rational social welfare function is implementable in Nash strategies.

The proofs of Theorems 5.1 and 5.2 both rest on the construction of particular profile mechanisms. Some of the features of this kind of profile mechanism are not entirely satisfactory. In the mechanism used to prove Theorem 5.1, all agents are expected to report not only an entire common profile of endowments, but also a common allocation which is optimal given those endowments. Now, if it is the true profile of endowments which is to be reported then it is reasonably simple for the agents to coordinate their reported profiles. But there may be alternative Nash equilibria in which the true profile is not reported, and some agents may be better off in an alternative Nash equilibrium. More seriously, the agents need to agree, in effect, on an allocation, and for this there is no obvious allocation to fall back on (as they can fall back on the true profile) unless it happens that the optimum is unique. In fact, we know that there must be cases where the optimum is *not* unique, because typically a social choice rule which always selects a unique optimum cannot be implemented (see Dasgupta, Hammond and Maskin [1979], Theorem 7.2.3). Where the optimum is not unique, of course, different agents will try to get different allocations put forward for the common proposal, and it is not at all clear how a Nash equilibrium could ever be arrived at.

Labour Endowments and Redistribution of Income

Sections 3 and 4 of Maskin's paper show how direct mechanisms could implement a certain class of allocation rules in an economy provided that consumers could not over-report their endowments and provided that under-reported endowments were destroyed. I agree with Maskin that these assumptions can make good sense when it is skills which are not known. A worker reveals his skill by exercising it in the job he does; with suitable monitoring of job performance, the worker who does not reveal his skill destroys it, in effect, because of course his pay relates to the skills he does reveal. On the other hand, with monitoring, a worker cannot pretend to have skills he actually lacks, and in that sense he cannot over-report his skills.

This can be demonstrated somewhat more formally. Let x denote a consumption vector, l denote hours worked, and q a vector of skills the worker uses in his job. Each worker, i, we assume, has a known utility function $u^i(x^i, l^i, q^i)$ (with q^i as an argument because workers are not indifferent to the type of job they do). In addition, worker i has a true vector of skill $\bar{q}^i$ and can supply any skill vector $\bar{q}^i$ satisfying the vector inequality $q^i \leqq \bar{q}^i$.

In this economy, a direct mechanism specifies each worker's consumption vector $x^i(\overline{\boldsymbol{q}})$, as well as hours worked $l^i(\overline{\boldsymbol{q}})$ and skills required $q^i(\overline{\boldsymbol{q}})$, as functions of the profile of skill announcements $\overline{\boldsymbol{q}}$. Feasibility depends upon how skill reacts with labour supply in the production set; in general, we can say that:

$$\sum_i x^i(q) \in X(\boldsymbol{l},\boldsymbol{q})$$

where $X(\boldsymbol{l},\boldsymbol{q})$ is the set of aggregate outputs of consumption goods which are possible given the profile of hours worked $\boldsymbol{l}$ and skills used $\boldsymbol{q}$. Implementability rests on the mechanism $\boldsymbol{x}(\bar{\boldsymbol{q}}),\boldsymbol{l}(\bar{\boldsymbol{q}}),\boldsymbol{q}(\bar{\boldsymbol{q}})$ rewarding skill—in the sense that:

$$q^i \geqq q^i \text{ implies } u^i(x^i(q^i,\bar{\boldsymbol{q}}^{-i}),l^i(q^i,\bar{\boldsymbol{q}}^{-i});\, \bar{q}^i) \geqslant u^i(x^i(\bar{\boldsymbol{q}}),l^i(\bar{\boldsymbol{q}});\, \bar{q}^i)$$

and also on skills being fully exploited—in the sense that $q^i(\bar{\boldsymbol{q}}) = \bar{q}^i$ (all i, $\bar{\boldsymbol{q}}$).§ The first condition ensures that no agent wants to underreport his skill, while the second ensures that exaggerated reports will be caught, because the worker will be asked to provide skills he does not have if he does exaggerate. On the assumption that more skill is productive and that doing a more skilled job provides no less utility (if x and l are unaffected) then any allocation which does not use all the skills of the workers in the economy is Pareto dominated by another which does. So 'good' allocation rules will then use all available skills. The problem then is simply to choose the best rule which does reward skill. Very often, it seems, the maximin rule will be the best rule of this kind (cf. Dasgupta and Hammond [1978]).

Conclusions

Maskin's paper is a useful and provocative exploration of the theoretical limits to the redistribution of incomes arising from the need to maintain incentives. His indirect profile mechanisms are powerful ways of implementing what are technically called 'individually rational' allocation rules. However, the requirement for each agent to report an entire profile of endowments in such mechanisms limits their plausibility somewhat. On the other hand, the superficially more appealing direct mechanisms do not work at all well in small economies except in special cases where unreported endowments are destroyed and over-reported endowments are not allowed (or else get corrected). Yet the case many of us have in mind in this connection, where it is labour skills which are unequally distributed and income which we wish to redistribute, is a special case of this kind. Then it is possible to use taxes on skill to get much closer to equality of utility, if not of income, than has previously been recognized.

All the analysis is based on the assumption that consumers' tastes are known. In particular, this implies that we know who is lazy and who is industrious. With tastes unknown, implementation becomes much less easy. This is an interesting topic for future research. The general conclusion survives, however: the theoretical limits to redistribution may be much less severe than is commonly thought, and in particular, income taxation is a very poor substitute for skill taxation when hours of work are flexible.

REFERENCES

Dasgupta P. S. and Hammond P.J. (1978) Fully Progressive Taxation, University of Essex Economics Discussion Paper No. 115. *J. Pub. Econ.* (forthcoming).

Dasgupta P. S., Hammond P. J. and Maskin E. S. (1979) The Implementation of Social Choice Rules: Some General Results on Incentive Compatibility. *Rev. Economic Studies* **46,** 185–216.

Diamond P. A. and Mirrlees J. A. (1971) Optimal Taxation and Public Production. *Am. Econom. Rev.* **61,** 8–27 and 261–78.

Graaff J. de V. (1957) *Theoretical Welfare Economics*. Cambridge Univ.

Hammond P. J. (1979) Straightforward Individual Incentive Compatibility in Large Economies. *Rev. Economic Studies* **46,** 263–82

Postlewaite A. (1979) Manipulation Via Endowments. *Rev. Economic Studies* **46,** 255–62.

Samuelson P. A. (1947) *Foundations of Economic Analysis*. Harvard Univ.

§ The expression $\bar{\boldsymbol{q}}^{-i}$ here signifies the profile $\bar{\boldsymbol{q}}$ without the component $\bar{q}^i$.

SUMMARY OF THE GENERAL DISCUSSION

Collard asked whether it might be possible for people to avoid disclosing their true endowment to the tax authorities while still managing to gain the advantages of revealing their full skills to their employer. One might argue to the tax authorities that one's good job was due to luck, over-valuation, etc., and that one's basic skill was not responsible for one's high position. Hammond agreed that it was an important assumption that skills could be observed, albeit indirectly, and that the tax authorities had access to the same information as employers in this respect.

Cowell wondered whether the assumption that unrevealed endowments would be lost was really a good one, particularly in the case of labour endowments. For instance, one way of avoiding the screening of endowments would be for people to become self-employed, in which case it would become much harder for the tax authorities to determine the quantity and quality of their labour inputs. Maskin agreed that this possibility was an important constraint on the nature of the optimal tax system. In his model, consumers always had the option of consuming their endowment instead of entering into trade, and this might be interpreted as self-employment. In order to encourage consumers to enter the market, the tax system must leave them with greater benefits than the non-market option.

Mirrlees said that Maskin's results were very interesting, but he would have liked to hear more about some of the questions raised, particularly the difficulties associated with Nash equilibria. There would be in principle many Nash equilibria and there would be a problem of ranking and choosing the best one, through the SWF. At the end of section 4 Maskin lists a number of cases where his mechanisms work, but exactly how restricted must the form of the SWF be to assure implementability? Maskin replied that the extent to which the SWF must be restricted depended on the potential possibilities about endowments and tastes in the economy. If we only made the general assumptions that preferences were convex, monotonic and continuous, then a dictatorial SWF would be required. But if we could assume Cobb–Douglas utility functions, uniqueness would be assured anyway. He felt that the more serious objection to Nash equilibria was the problem of how such equilibria might arise. There was no adequate theory of the dynamics by which a Nash equilibrium might be reached from an initial disequilibrium. One of the attractions of the dominance concept was that reaching equilibrium with dominant strategies was far more plausible.

Hammond asked whether a consistent allocation might be arrived at even where the individual agents were not telling the truth. Maskin replied that in Nash equilibrium it would never be optimal to lie, although one individual might perceive that he could be better off outside a particular Nash equilibrium by lying. Cowell wondered whether the results of the paper might suggest that the government should be happy with a situation in which individuals were generally understating their tax liabilities if such a situation seemed to work. Maskin agreed. The aim was not to make people to tell the truth, but to get the best possible allocation of resources.

Collard sought to draw out the implications of the paper for the theme of the conference. A practical method of first-best taxation was really the philosophers' stone of redistributionists; a mechanism for making truthful declaration a dominant strategy would undoubtedly be ideal, but seemed to be quite impossible. It was more possible to engineer a game with Nash equilibria, but this concept had difficulties. More work might provide some more answers, but meanwhile one must soldier on with second-best solutions.

LeGrand wondered whether the paper could be summed up as 'the optimal amount of tax evasion'. Maskin disagreed. He felt that his optimum described a position in which evasion did not occur. LeGrand said that was true of the dominant solution but not of the non-dominant case. Kay said that when the aim was to tax an unobservable attribute, there was a difference between the policy of finding some other attribute that is observable and taxing that, and the policy of taxing the unobservable and taking the consequences of misreporting and evasion.

Hammond felt that the real lesson of the paper was that we might be able to get closer to lump-sum taxation than we had previously thought.

EFFICIENCY AND INCOME EQUALITY: SOME AMERICAN TRADEOFFS

L. Gevers and J. Rouyer

Facultés Universitaires Notre-Dame de la Paix
Faculté des Sciences Economiques et Sociales,
Rempart de la Vierge, 8, B-5000 Namur, Belgium

INTRODUCTION

What would have been the state of the US economy in 1961 and 1970 if government had pursued more leftist or more rightist policies? We shall attempt to provide a partial answer to this question: but will have to make major simplifications. Crucial aspects we have chosen to single out are in line with the neoclassical tradition.

We assume that households are interested only in three goods: of the two produced goods one is private and the other is collective in nature, while the third good is a nonproduced private factor of production. The entire tax system is amalgamated into a linear income tax, which is the only source of government finance.

Government is considered as a veil: its decisions are the very ones which would be selected directly by the method of majority voting. Voters are exclusively interested in their consumption plans, they are impervious to envy and pity. They display intermediate preferences in the sense of Grandmont (1978) and the median income-earning household turns out to be decisive.

The paper is organized as follows: first, we set out our theoretical model, and from it we derive two equations which we proceed to estimate econometrically. With the help of these estimates, it is possible to reconstruct the median voter's preference ordering. We then provide a description of the preference ordering of all consumers in 1961 and 1970 at the cost of an additional assumption, which we regard as fairly innocuous. This enables us to describe a sample of policies which various income groups consider best from their standpoint. As the marginal income tax rate varies, so do distortions throughout the economy. So also do the attendant efficiency losses. On the other hand, fiscal policies have a direct effect on the distribution of income. We measure these two-sided effects carefully, and obtain as a final product a clear picture of the tradeoffs between total income gains and changes in income equality. The paper ends with appendices containing technical arguments.

The present work was stimulated at an early stage by Aaron and McGuire (1970). It has been developed by building on Gevers and Proost (1978), and by drawing upon recent work by Reynolds and Smolensky (1977), and Hausman and Wise (1976).

We are not entirely happy with the theoretical framework. In particular, a theory which views government decisions as equilibrium outcomes of a direct voting process, may seem very constraining. In this respect, a fruitful research avenue may have been opened by Kramer (1977). More generally, we are well aware that our assumptions are overly simplistic and that our conclusions are tentative. We shall not discuss these matters further. Instead, we refer the interested reader to Musgrave's (1978) detailed discussion.

We are thankful to H. Glejser, G. H. Kramer, J. Mirrlees and S. Proost for their suggestions and also to M. Pietquin for computing assistance. We retain responsibility for remaining errors. A french version of the present paper is available upon request.

THE MODEL

We shall consider an economy consisting of an odd number of consumers, a private productive sector, and a public sector. Consumers are identified with help of index i, which runs from 1 to n.

There are only three goods. Of the two produced goods, one is a private consumption good and the other is a collective good in the sense of Musgrave-Samuelson. The third good is a private factor of production.

As we intend to concentrate on the debate over income taxation and public expenditure, we shall treat the productive section summarily. By our choice of units, we assume that one unit of productive factor can produce one unit of private goods or $1/p$ units of collective goods. Constant returns to scale are assumed. Output is delivered on order and sold at cost.

Each consumer, i, is directly interested in his consumption plan, a triple $(x_i,y_i,Z_i) \in E^3$, where x_i stands for private consumption, y_i denotes the amount of productive factor delivered to firms, while Z_i denotes collective good consumption.

Let Z stand for the total amount of collective good which is made available. In view of the above assumptions, the basic material scarcity constraints which our economy faces may be spelled out as follows:

$$Z_i \leqslant Z, \ \forall i, \tag{1}$$

and

$$p\,Z + \sum_i x_i \leqslant \sum_i y_i. \tag{2}$$

When selecting a plan (x_i,y_i,Z_i) consumer i is limited both by inequality (1) and by a private financial constraint. This constraint is expressed as follows:

$$x_i \leqslant a + by_i, \tag{3}$$

where a is a lump sum subsidy and b is equal to one minus the marginal income tax rate, which is assumed constant.

A consumption plan which satisfies (1) and (3) is not necessarily feasible physically. We shall assume that it must also be an element of a consumption set X_i, a closed and convex subset of E^3. In particular, we require x_i,y_i and Z_i to be nonnegative, and we set a maximum $Y_i > 0$ to the quantity of input which can be delivered by i to the productive sector. Thus $y_i \leqslant Y_i$ for every i and, Y_i may be interpreted as the earning capacity of i.

The public sector is responsible for the choice of a triple (a,b,Z), which we call a *public plan*. For some public plans, each agent i has the opportunity to choose a consumption plan which satisfies (1) and (3), and which lies within X_i. The set of all public plans which fulfil this condition will be denoted by S.

Every consumer i is assumed to have a continuous preference ordering over X_i, which displays strict monotonicity with respect to x_i and Z_i. Given any (a^s,b^s,Z^s) in S, there exists at least a most preferred consumption plan (x_i^s,y_i^s,Z_i^s) in X_i which satisfies (1) and (3). In this case, we shall say that (x_i^s,y_i^s,Z_i^s) is a *response to*

(a^s,b^s,Z^s). When the response is unique, one can speak of a response function R_i from a subset of E^3 to a subset of X_i. As the basis of our econometric work, we shall assume that R_i takes up a fairly specific form, inspired by the work of Hausman and Wise (1976).

Assumption 1

Let c and k be nonnegative parameters. Let $S \subset \left\{(a,b,Z) \in E^3_+, b^c \leqslant a^k\right\}$. For every i, R_i is defined on S as follows:

$$x_i = a + b^{c+1} a^{-k} Y_i,$$
$$y_i = b^c a^{-k} Y_i,$$
$$Z_i = Z.$$

We rule out the possibility that c and/or k be negative to guarantee that the compensated own price derivative of the labour supply be nonnegative. Indeed, we want, for every $Y_i > 0$,

$$\frac{\partial y_i}{\partial b} - y_i \frac{\partial y_i}{\partial a} = \frac{c}{b} y_i - y_i \left(\frac{-k}{a} y_i \right)$$
$$= \frac{y_i}{b} (c + k\, b^{c+1} a^{-k-1} Y_i) \geqslant 0.$$

The expression in parentheses is always negative if both c and k are negative. If c and k are of opposite sign this will be negative for some values of Y_i. Thus, we require both $c \geqslant 0$ and $k \geqslant 0$.

For each i, we define an induced preference relation on S as follows; consumer i is said to weakly prefer $(a^\circ,b^\circ,Z^\circ)$ to (a',b',Z') if, and only if, he weakly prefers any response of his to the former public plan to any consumption plan which is consistent with the latter.

Proposition 1

For each i, a utility function having as image on S

$$u_i = U(Y_i \frac{b^{1+c}}{1+c} + \frac{a^{1+k}}{1+k}, Z; Y_i) \tag{4}$$

where U has positive derivatives U_1 and U_2, is a representation of an induced preference relation which is consistent with assumption 1.

Proof: by Roy's relation,

$$y_i = \frac{\partial u_i / \partial b}{\partial u_i / \partial a}$$
$$= \frac{U_1\, Y_i\, b^c}{U_1\, a^k} = Y_i\, b^c\, a^{-k}.$$

The value of x_i may then be derived easily in view of (3). Moreover as, $U_2 > 0$, $Z_i = Z$.

Now that we have specified individual preferences on S we must concern ourselves with collective choice. We shall assume that a public plan is selected by the method of majority voting and that people vote sincerely. We define next an appropriate equilibrium concept and stress the decisive role of the median voter.

The set of *feasible public plans* consists of all triples $(a,b,Z) \in S$ which satisfy the public sector's budgetary constraint:

$$p\,Z + n\,a \leqslant (1-b)\sum_{i} y_i. \tag{5}$$

Letting $z = \dfrac{Z}{n}$ and $\bar{y} = \dfrac{1}{n}\sum\limits_{i} y_i$, we divide (5) through by n to get

$$p\,z + a \leqslant (1-b)\bar{y}. \tag{6}$$

A feasible plan will be called an *equilibrium plan* if there does not exist any other feasible plan which is strictly preferred to it by a majority of voters.

Let m be the index value associated with the voter whose earning capacity Y_m is a median of the distribution (Y_i). Let a *median plan* be a feasible plan which is most preferred by voter m.

Suppose it turns out that a plan is weakly preferred to another by a majority of voters if, and only if, it is also weakly preferred by voter m; then we say that the latter is *decisive*. Under these circumstances, a median plan is an equilibrium plan and vice versa.

Let us first assume that Z is fixed *a priori*, so that voters are concerned only with a and b. We thus examine the state of individual preferences within a given plan.

Proposition 2

Suppose assumption 1 holds. Then, for every (a°,b°,Z), $(a',b',Z) \in S$, the former is weakly preferred by a majority of voters to the latter if, and only if, it is preferred by voter m.

The proof is omitted, as it follows the same pattern as the proof of proposition 4 below.

If assumption 1 holds, we can use past observed values of a and b to estimate c and k. For this purpose we characterize next the plan which is most preferred by voter i, under a balanced budget constraint.

Proposition 3

For each i, for every preassigned value of Z, the public plan lying in the interior of S which maximizes u_i under constraint (6), satisfies

$$\frac{y_i}{\bar{y}} = 1 - \frac{c(1-b)y_i}{by_i} - \frac{k(1-b)y_i}{a}, \tag{7}$$

and the second order condition

$$c\,\frac{\bar{y}}{pz} \geqslant k\left(\frac{by_i}{a}\right)^2. \tag{8}$$

The proof, which is less instructive than lengthy, is relegated to appendix A.

Looking at (7), we require $a \geqslant 0$, and $z \geqslant 0$, which implies $b \leqslant 1$, so that it is necessary to have $y_i \leqslant \bar{y}$ to get an interior solution. In particular, $b = 1$ implies $y_i = \bar{y}$. This case is uninteresting as it implies $a = z = 0$. Moreover, if $1+c < c/b$, i.e. if $b < c/(1+c)$, (7) has no meaningful solution. Thus, every i having $y_i \geqslant 0$ wants to have $b \geqslant c/(1+c)$.

Once we drop the assumption that Z is fixed, we are no longer sure that voter m is decisive, and an equilibrium plan may fail to exist. Assumption 1 is not strong enough for this purpose. A proof may be found in Gevers and Proost (1978, proposition 7). See also Parks (1978).

Our next task is to provide a more specific form of utility function than (4); this will enable us to derive a demand equation for public goods the coefficients of which we shall proceed to estimate econometrically in the following section.

Assumption 2

Let q,r,s and $\beta > 0$ be given parameters. Every i's induced preference relation on S is represented by a utility function having as image

$$u_i = (Y_i \frac{b^{1+c}}{1+c} + \frac{a^{1+k}}{1+k} - qY_i - r)\,(Z - ns)^{\beta}. \tag{9}$$

The set S is so defined that each factor in (9) is nonnegative. Moreover S satisfies the same condition as in assumption 1.

The first thing we would like to check is that under assumption 2, an equilibrium plan does exist.

Proposition 4

If assumption 2 holds, the median voter is decisive.

Proof: In effect, we shall prove a more general proposition. Voter m is indeed decisive if we replace (9) with the more general formulation:

$$u_i = K(a,b,Z)\, h(Y_i) + H(a,b,Z)$$

where K and H are numerical functions defined on S, and h is a continuous, strictly increasing numerical function defined on the real line.

To prove our point, pick any two plans $(a^\circ,b^\circ,Z^\circ)$, (a',b',Z') in S. Let K°,H°, K',H' stand for the corresponding values taken up respectively by K and H. Voter i weakly prefers the former plan if, and only if, $K^\circ h(Y_i) + H^\circ \geqslant K'h(Y_i) + H'$. Now either $K^\circ = K'$, or $K^\circ > K'$, or $K^\circ < K'$. If $K^\circ = K'$, all agents weakly prefer plan zero. If $K^\circ > K'$, our inequality becomes

$$h(Y_i) \geqslant \frac{H' - H^\circ}{K^\circ - K'}$$

after rearrangement. As h is strictly increasing, and continuous, there is a critical value Y^* such that all i having $Y^* \leqslant Y_i (Y_i \leqslant Y^*)$ weakly prefer plan zero (plan one). Therefore, if $Y^* \leqslant Y_m$, plan zero is weakly preferred by a majority, and conversely. If $K^\circ < K'$, an analogous argument applies.

Assumption 2 would be more transparent if we were able to express the utility function in direct form. Unfortunately, this can be done only if $k = 0$.

Proposition 5

Suppose each voter's preference relation on X_i may be represented by a utility function of the form

$$u_i = (v_i - qY_i - r)(Z_i - ns)^\beta, \tag{10}$$

where
$$v_i = x_i - \frac{c}{c+1} y_i^{\frac{c+1}{c}} Y_i^{-\frac{1}{c}}, \tag{11}$$

$$v_i \geqslant qY_i + r, \text{ and } Z_i \geqslant ns.$$

Then assumption 2 holds for $k = 0$.

Proof: Substituting from (3) in (11) and differentiating, we get

$$y_i = b^c Y_i, \tag{12}$$

$$x_i = a + b^{c+1} Y_i,$$

so that
$$v_i = a + b^{c+1} Y_i - \frac{c}{c+1} b^{c+1} Y_i$$

$$= a + \frac{b^{c+1}}{c+1} Y_i. \tag{13}$$

There remains to substitute in (10), and to compare with (9).

Thus, in (10), private goods are weakly separable from collective goods. There are two subsistence levels: ns is the minimal amount of collective good and $qY_i + r$ is the minimal amount of v_i. An interpretation of v_i can easily be offered: consider any plan $(x_i^\circ, y_i^\circ, Z_i^\circ)$ and the corresponding amount v_i°, defined by (11); we observe that voter i is indifferent between $(v_i^\circ, 0, Z_i^\circ)$ and $(x_i^\circ, y_i^\circ Z_i^\circ)$. In other words, v_i° is the amount of rentier income which is equivalent to the initial plan, from the point of view of consumer i.

To conclude this section, we turn to the demand for collective goods. This appears to be very unwieldy if $k > 0$. We shall therefore assume that $k = 0$.

Proposition 6

If assumption 2 holds, and $k = 0$, the public plan which lies in the interior of S and maximizes u_i under constraints (1) and (6), satisfies (7) and

$$pz - ps = \frac{\beta}{1+\beta} \left(\frac{\bar{y}}{c+1} - qY_i - r - ps \right). \tag{14}$$

A proof may be found in Gevers and Proost (1978, proposition 8). Equation (14) lends itself easily to econometric treatment.

ECONOMETRIC ESTIMATES

In this section, we attempt to fit our theoretical model to US data, over the period 1950–1976. We do this in three stages: (i) we look at the distributions of tax burdens and benefits by income groups put together by Reynolds and Smolensky (1977), interpreting these data as resulting from a linear tax system; the parameters of the three linear tax functions fitted respectively for the years 1950, 1961 and 1970 are an essential ingredient of the estimation carried out at the next stage; (ii) is devoted to estimating the elasticities of the factor supply with respect to factor reward (c) and nonlabour income (k), using (7); (iii) we rely on (14), which describes the median voter's demand for collective goods, to estimate other parameters.

(i) To begin stage one, consider the US public sector as financing its expenditures for collective goods exclusively by means of a linear income tax. In this context, voter i's income y_i should be interpreted as his contribution to NNP.

As we implicitly assumed away intertemporal allocation problems in our theoretical model, it seems appropriate to define x_i as that part of the contribution to NNP which is not taxed: it is a quantity of private goods which can be used by i for private consumption or private investment. Thus, $(y_i - x_i)$ stands for the net tax levied on i. In some cases this can be negative.

Reynolds and Smolensky (1977) provide, for the three years 1950, 1961 and 1970, a breakdown of the estimated taxes, both direct and indirect, which were supported by each of a number of income groups; analogous estimates are presented for the specific goods which benefit each group, taking into account a narrow definition of collective goods. (Relevant definitions and a sample sheet of computations are provided in appendix B.) For each income group, we decided to use the algebraic sum of all these amounts as a measurement of $(y_i - x_i)$. For the three years 1950, 1961 and 1970 we carried out a weighted least-square adjustment of the tax function

$$(y_{jt} - x_{jt}) = (1 - b_t)y_{jt} - a_t$$

where subscript j identifies each income group. Our results are recorded in table 1.

Table 1. Estimated linear tax functions

t	a_t (1972 \$)	$a_t/\bar{y}_t$	b_t	Number of observations (income groups)	R^2	$y_{mt}/\bar{y}_t$
1950	1 547	0·127	0·755	7	0·982	0·808
1961	2 353	0·167	0·681	9	0·965	0·801
1970	2 806	0·183	0·664	11	0·975	0·782

The fit is reasonably good, but a closer look at the residuals suggests that there might be a more appropriate two-parameter tax function.

We conclude this preliminary work by observing that the ratio of median to average contribution to NNP, can also be estimated from the same source. When computing the median we assumed that the distribution of income within the median class was the same as across classes. A loglinear adjustment proved necessary to move from the income groups used by Reynolds and Smolensky to the NNP contribution concept.

(ii) Having availed ourselves of the necessary data, we proceed with an estimation of the factor supply elasticities. In view of proposition 2, we know that, for given z, the median voter is responsible for the choice of a and b, under assumption 1.

There are two elasticities to estimate from three observations (using (7)); moreover, both elasticities must be nonnegative.

Our constrained least squares estimate i turns out to be zero, the constraint being binding. Looking at residuals, a time trend does however show up as far as c is concerned. Letting $k = 0$, (7) may be rearranged to yield

$$c = \frac{b}{(1-b)}\left(1-\frac{y_{\mathrm{m}}}{\bar{y}}\right). \tag{15}$$

For $t = 1950$, $c_t = 0{\cdot}59$, for $t = 1961$, $c_t = 0{\cdot}425$ and for $t = 1970$, $c_t = 0{\cdot}431$. We decided to retain $k_t = 0$ for all t and to use the above c_t values in our analysis of the demand for collective goods.

(iii) We shall now attempt to estimate parameter β which was introduced under assumption 2 and which is used in our specification of the median voter's demand for collective goods.

Three other parameters are used in (14) *viz* q,r, and s. We believe that their value varies over time. Let us try to explain how they do so. We pointed out that our theoretical model neglects intertemporal choices at the individual level. The same is also valid at the collective level: there is no such thing as a public debt and we shall treat government deficits or surpluses as a part of the random noise affecting (14).

We do however believe that preferences vary over time in a systematic fashion. Assume that subsistence levels, $(qY_{\mathrm{i}}+r)$ and ns, are influenced by past consumption. More specifically, let

$$q_t Y_{\mathrm{i}t}+r_t = \lambda v_{\mathrm{i},t-1} \tag{16}$$

where λ is a constant parameter, which we proceed to estimate.

For this purpose we need to compute $v_{\mathrm{i},t-1}$, at least for the decisive individual. Gevers and Proost (1978) show that, if assumption 1 holds and $k = 0$,

$$v_{\mathrm{m}} = \frac{\bar{y}}{1+c} - pz \tag{17}$$

so that, when c is known, v_{m} is a difference between observable variables.

Next, we justify (16), not only for the median voter, but for every i, in order to make sure that the estimated model satisfies assumption 2. We do this by introducing a new assumption, *viz* that for every period t, there exist two numbers g_t and h_t such that, for each t,

$$Y_{\mathrm{i},t-1} = h_t + g_t Y_{\mathrm{i},t}. \tag{18}$$

Then substituting in (16) successively from (13) and (18), we get

$$q_t Y_{\mathrm{i}t}+r_t = \lambda\left(a_{t-1}+b_{t-1}^{c+1}\frac{Y_{\mathrm{i},t+1}}{c+1}\right) \tag{19}$$

$$= \lambda a_{t-1} + \frac{\lambda}{c+1}\, b_{t-1}^{c+1} h_t + \frac{\lambda}{c+1}\, b_{t-1}^{c+1} g_t Y_{\mathrm{i}t}.$$

The values of q_t and r_t may be readily computed from the right hand side. Due to lack of data, however, we cannot estimate q_t, r_t, h_t or g_t. Therefore, we limit ourselves to estimating λ.

Turning next to each individual's subsistence level with respect to public goods, $n_t s_t$, it seems worthwhile to recognize that years of unusually high military involvement may have a special effect. For this reason, we shall define a dummy variable W_t equal to unity in such years and zero otherwise; letting μ and γ be parameters, we write for all t,

$$n_t s_t = \mu Z_{t-1} + \gamma W_t. \tag{20}$$

To see the combined effect of these new assumptions pertaining to subsistence levels, we substitute from (16), (17) and (20) into (14), to get, after rearrangement

$$p_t z_t = \frac{\beta}{1+\beta}\left(\frac{\bar{y}_t}{c_t+1} - \lambda v_{m,t-1}\right) + \frac{1}{1+\beta} p_t s_t, \tag{21}$$

$$p_t z_t = \frac{\beta}{1+\beta}\left(\frac{\bar{y}_t}{c_t+1} - \lambda \frac{\bar{y}_{t-1}}{c_t+1} + \lambda p_{t-1} z_{t-1}\right) + \frac{\mu}{1+\beta}\frac{p_t Z_{t-1}}{n_t} + \frac{\gamma}{1+\beta}\frac{p_t W_t}{n_t}.$$

We fitted equation (21) to US time-series data for the period 1952–1976 to obtain estimates of β, λ, μ and ω. To this effect, we reformulated (21) as

$$(1+\beta)\, p_t z_t - \lambda\beta p_{t-1}\, z_{t-1} - \frac{\beta}{c_t+1}(\bar{y}_t - \lambda\bar{y}_{t-1}) = \mu\frac{p_t Z_{t-1}}{n_t} + \gamma\frac{p_t W_t}{n_t}. \tag{22}$$

Observe that the left-hand side depends only on λ, β and known time-varying values of z, $\bar{y}$ and c. For a grid of values of λ and β, we applied ordinary least squares to (22) using first differences; this procedure resulted in much improved estimates from the point of view of multicollinearity and autocorrelation. The set of estimates which minimizes the sum of square deviations between observed and predicted values of z is recorded in table 2.

Table 2. Regression results, equation (21)

	Standard error
$\beta = 0{\cdot}13$	
$\lambda = 0{\cdot}72$	
$\mu = 0{\cdot}892$	0·012
$\gamma = 4{\cdot}093728$	3·053

For 24 observations, $R^2 = 0{\cdot}72$

REDISTRIBUTION FRONTIERS

Next consider alternative states of the economy which might have emerged in 1961 and 1970 if various income groups had been decisive. As a preliminary step, we first narrow down assumption (18), which describes the evolution of individual earning capacity Y_i over time. This enables us to describe fully the taxpayers' preference structure in 1961 and 1970. Secondly, we define precisely the income concept and the summary measures of income inequality we shall use. Finally, we associate, for every public plan under study, two measures of inequality with a measure of efficiency. The shape of the two redistribution frontiers, which are defined in this manner, hardly changes from 1961 to 1970.

Our data and the estimates listed in the last section give us a complete picture of the median voter's preference structure. We made clear, under (18), that our data shed an incomplete light on the subsistence level of the individuals who are not decisive. As we would like to know what the latter would do if they were wielding power, we shall supplement our data and estimates with an assumption which is more specific than (17). For $t = 1961$ and 1970, we assume that the distribution of individual earning capacity $(Y_{i,t})$ is the same as $(Y_{i,t-1})$ up to a rescaling: for some positive number g_t,

$$Y_{i,t-1} = g_t Y_{i,t}. \tag{23}$$

In view of (7), it follows readily that

$$b_{t-1} = b_t \tag{24}$$

for t = 1961 and t = 1970. Moreover, as $\bar{y}_t = \bar{Y}_t b_t^c$, it follows that

$$g_t = \frac{\bar{Y}_{t-1}}{\bar{Y}_t} = \frac{\bar{y}_{t-1}}{\bar{y}_t}\ . \tag{25}$$

Substituting from (6), (12), (22), (23) and (24) in (18), we get

$$q_t Y_{it} + r_t = \lambda[(1+b_t)\,\bar{y}_{t-1} - p_{t-1} z_{t-1}] + \frac{\lambda}{c+1}\ b_t^{c+1} - \frac{\bar{y}_{t-1}}{y_t}\ Y_{it}\ .$$

In conclusion, we now have all the information we need to evaluate q_t and r_t for the years 1961 and 1970, and the preferences of every voter i are fully determined. From 1961 to 1970, average earning capacity has gone up by 23 per cent. Indeed, in 1972 \$, $\bar{Y}_{1961}$ = 14 311, while $\bar{Y}_{1970}$ = 17 652. Simultaneously, the subsistence level with respect to collective goods has gone up by 19 per cent. Finally, the increase in average subsistence level with respect to private goods amounts to 11 per cent.

In the following table, we record firstly the indifference curves for a sample of voters and, secondly the public plan they most prefer, taking into account (7) where k = 0, (14) and (6).

We have deliberately excluded from the above sample policies which lie at the boundary of S. Boundary solutions are reached in 1961 for b = 0·489 and b = 0·751. The corresponding figures for 1970 are b = 0·507 and b = 0·724. When the lower bound is reached, the highest income group is confined to its subsistence level with respect to private goods ($\lambda v_{i,t-1}$), and the corresponding public plan is best from the point of view of the lowest income group, and vice versa.

Table 3. Sample of preference structures

	1961					1970				
	Parameters									
$\frac{Y_i}{\bar{Y}}$	0·608	0·679	0·740	0·791	0·835	0·602	0·675	0·736	0·788	0·832
β			0·130					0·130		
c_t			0·425					0·431		
$p_t s_t$			1 981					2 365		
$v_{,t-1}$	3 686	3 977	4 220	4 428	4 606	4 774	5 148	5 462	5 729	5 958
	Most preferred plan									
b_t	0·52	0·57	0·62	0·67	0·72	0·52	0·57	0·62	0·67	0·72
a_t	2 992	2 634	2 221	1 758	1 250	3 780	3 345	2 841	2 275	1 652
$p_t z_t$	2 210	2 221	2 216	2 224	2 234	2 615	2 616	2 621	2 629	2 640

Note: Revised estimates are given in the Postscript (table A3)

The most striking feature of table 3 are the rapid decrease of a_t and the slow increase of z_t as we move from left to right and b_t increases. Turning to (14), we observe that

$$\mathrm{d}pz = \frac{\beta}{1+\beta}\left(\frac{\mathrm{d}\bar{y}}{c+1} - q\mathrm{d}\,Y_\mathrm{i}\right),$$

where $\frac{\beta}{1+\beta}$ is small and the other term is a difference between two terms which remains moderate over the relevant range. This explains the stability of z.

Next, we explore the efficiency and inequality aspects of the array of public plans depicted in table 3. To start with, we make precise the income concept we shall be using. Suppose two public plans have in common the quantity of collective goods which is provided. Then, as we pointed out in the section on econometric estimates, v_i may be considered as a natural income concept: it amounts to the rentier income which leaves consumer i indifferent with whatever pair $(x_\mathrm{i}, y_\mathrm{i})$ he actually chooses.

When any two public plans $(a^\circ, b^\circ, Z^\circ)$ and (a,b,Z) are to be compared, the same idea can be pushed one step further, in line with the general notion of consumer surplus. Let us take the former plan as a reference. Suppose consumer i derives from his response to the reference plan a utility level

$$u_\mathrm{i}^\circ = (v_\mathrm{i}^\circ + q\,Y_\mathrm{i} - r)\,(Z^\circ - ns)^\beta.$$

Similarly, for the other plan,

$$u_\mathrm{i} = (v_\mathrm{i} - q\,Y_\mathrm{i} - r)\,(Z - ns)^\beta.$$

In order to obtain an unambiguous income comparison, we shall compare v_i°, not with v_i, but with w_i which is implicitly defined by

$$u_\mathrm{i} = (w_\mathrm{i} - q\,Y_\mathrm{i} - r)\,(Z^\circ - ns)^\beta.$$

Thus, w_i and Z° are indifferent with the response to (a,b,Z), and the quantity of collective good is now the same as in the reference plan, which makes things comparable. Combining the last two equations, we get

$$w_\mathrm{i} = (v_\mathrm{i} - q\,Y_\mathrm{i} - r)\left(\frac{z-s}{z^\circ - s}\right)^\beta + q\,Y_\mathrm{i} + r. \tag{26}$$

Keeping our reference plan constant, we have in effect defined a new utility function which has a straightforward physical interpretation. We shall call w_i consumer i's real income. The reference plans we shall use are those predicted by our model when we assume that the public plan is selected by the individual who wishes to have $b = 0{\cdot}67$. This particular value was chosen because it lies approximately halfway between the b values observed in 1961 and 1970, which amount respectively to 0·681 and 0·664.

Our next task is to study the effects of the sample of plans described in table 3 on efficiency. Samuelson's classical conditions for an efficient allocation in an economy with public goods require, among other things, that the marginal rate of substitution between private goods be the same in production and in consumption. When $b<1$, this condition is not met. There is a distortion, the cost of which we want to assess. A natural yardstick seems to be the mean real income ratio w/v°. This can be decomposed as a weighted sum using (25):

$$\frac{\bar{w}}{\bar{v}^\circ} = \frac{1}{\bar{v}^\circ}\;(\bar{v} - q\bar{Y} - r)\left(\frac{z-s}{z^\circ - s}\right)^\beta + \frac{q\bar{Y} + r}{\bar{v}^\circ} \tag{27}$$

$$= \frac{\bar{v}}{\bar{v}^\circ}\left(\frac{z-s}{z^\circ-s}\right)^\beta + \frac{q\bar{Y}+r}{\bar{v}^\circ}\left[1-\left(\frac{z-s}{z^\circ-s}\right)^\beta\right]$$

Special interest attaches to $\frac{\bar{v}}{\bar{v}^\circ}$, as this term measures the combined effect of change in a and b, assuming that z takes up its reference value z°.

Using (13) and (6), we can write,

$$\frac{\bar{v}}{\bar{v}^\circ} = \frac{a+\frac{\bar{Y}}{c+1}b^{c+1}}{a^\circ+\frac{\bar{Y}}{c+1}(b^\circ)^{c+1}} \tag{28}$$

$$= \frac{\frac{\bar{Y}}{c+1}b^{c+1}+(1-b)\,b^c\bar{Y}-pz}{\frac{\bar{Y}}{c+1}(b^\circ)^{c+1}+(1-b^\circ)\,(b^\circ)^c\bar{Y}-pz^\circ}$$

$$= \frac{b^c-\frac{c}{c+1}b^{c+1}-\frac{pz}{\bar{Y}}}{(b^\circ)^c-\frac{c}{c+1}(b^\circ)^{c+1}-\frac{pz^\circ}{\bar{Y}}}$$

Table 4. Efficiency analysis

Year	1961					1970				
b	0·52	0·57	0·62	0·67	0·72	0·52	0·57	0·62	0·67	0·72
$\bar{v}/\bar{v}^\circ$	0·93447	0·96068	0·98234	1·00	1·01408	0·93374	0·96023	0·98213	1·00	1·01426
$\bar{w}/\bar{v}^\circ$	0·93266	0·95887	0·98116	1·00	1·01568	0·93238	0·95871	0·98109	1·00	1·01576

This expression will prove useful for the interpretation of table 4. We observe that the $\bar{v}/\bar{v}^\circ$ line hardly changes from 1961 to 1970. In view of (27), there are three reasons for this observation: firstly c_t changes little between 1961 and 1970; secondly, $z^\circ/\bar{Y}$ also changes little between these dates (from 0·156 to 0·152), and, thirdly z_t remains very close to z_t° in both years. The last reason, together with our first observation, provides an explanation for the stable behaviour of $\bar{w}/\bar{v}^\circ$, which is another salient feature of table 4.

If b changes from 0·72 to 0·62, i.e. if the marginal tax rate changes from 0·28 to 0·38, real national income per head, as measured by $\bar{w}$, is reduced by 3·7% in 1961; in 1970, the figure amounts to 3·5%. If the marginal tax rate is raised from 0·33 to 0·43, i.e. if b changes from 0·67 to 0·57, real national income per head is reduced by 4·11% in 1961, and by 4·13% in 1970.

So much for the inefficiencies induced by taxation. We turn next to the analysis of income inequality. Let us look at the ratio of the difference in real income to the same difference in the reference situation for consumers i and j:

$$\frac{\Delta w}{\Delta v^\circ} = \frac{w_i-w_j}{v_i^\circ-v_j^\circ}$$

Substituting from (25) and (13), we get

$$\frac{\Delta w}{\Delta v^\circ} = \frac{\Delta v^\circ}{\Delta v^\circ}\Bigg[(a+ \frac{b^{c+1}}{c+1} \;Y_i - qY_i - r) \left(\frac{z-s}{z^\circ - s}\right)^\beta + qY_i + r$$

$$- (a+ \frac{b^{c+1}}{c+1} \;Y_j - qY_j - r) \left(\frac{z-s}{z^\circ - s}\right)^\beta - qY_j - r\Bigg] \tag{29}$$

$$= \frac{c+1}{(b^\circ)^{c+1}(Y_i - Y_j)} \left[(\frac{b^{c+1}}{c+1} - q)\left(\frac{z-s}{z^\circ - s}\right)^\beta + q \right] (Y_i - Y_j)$$

$$= \frac{c+1}{(b^\circ)^{c+1}} \left[(\frac{b^{c+1}}{c+1} - q)\left(\frac{z-s}{z^\circ - s}\right)^\beta + q \right]$$

$$= \frac{b^{c+1}}{(b^\circ)^{c+1}} \left(\frac{z+s}{z^\circ - s}\right)^\beta + \frac{q(c+1)}{(b^\circ)^{c+1}} \left[1 - \left(\frac{z-s}{z^\circ - s}\right)^\beta \right].$$

Observe that $\Delta w/\Delta v^\circ$ does not depend on the particular pair (i,j) we started with. It can thus be taken as a measure of real income inequality.

Like (27), equation (29) can be expressed as a weighted sum with help of (27), and it is then easy to trace the effect of each policy parameter in $\Delta w/\Delta v^\circ$. The effect of a vanishes identically. If $z = z^\circ$, the effect of a change in b is described by

$$\frac{\Delta v}{\Delta v^\circ} = \left(\frac{b}{b^\circ}\right)^{c+1},$$

while the discrepancy between $\Delta v/\Delta v^\circ$ and $\Delta w/\Delta v^\circ$ is accounted for by the fact that $z \neq z^\circ$ and by interaction effects.

Finally, if G and G° denote the values of the Gini concentration coefficient corresponding to (a,b,Z) and $(a^\circ,b^\circ,Z^\circ)$, then by definition,

$$\frac{G}{G^\circ} = \frac{\Delta w/w}{\Delta v^\circ/v^\circ}.$$

Table 5 summarizes our empirical results pertaining to real income inequality.

Table 5. Inequality analysis

Year	1961					1970				
b	0·52	0·57	0·62	0·67	0·72	0·52	0·57	0·62	0·67	0·72
$\frac{\Delta v}{\Delta v^\circ}$	0·69686	0·79426	0·89537	1·0	1·0801	0·69581	0·79349	0·89495	1·0	1·10848
$\frac{\Delta w}{\Delta v^\circ}$	0·69700	0·79368	0·89458	1·0	1·11008	0·69611	0·79313	0·89429	1·0	1·11048
$\frac{G}{G^\circ}$	0·74733	0·82773	0·91176	1·0	1·09294	0·74660	0·82728	0·91152	1·0	1·09326

The similarity between the two panels is striking. The residual effect of z being different from z°, measured by

$$\frac{\Delta w}{\Delta v^{\circ}} - \frac{\Delta v}{\Delta v^{\circ}},$$

is of varying sign, and its absolute value is negligible, except for $b = 0{\cdot}72$. Here, the effect of an increase in z is regressive, in the sense that real income disparity is increased by 3%.

A 10% increase in b increases $\Delta w/\Delta v^{\circ}$ by approximately 21% and the Gini coefficient by about 18%, as can be expected from the definition of G/G° and from our earlier observations about the elasticity of $\bar{w}/\bar{v}^{\circ}$ with respect to b.

To sum up our analysis we associate with every value of our efficiency measure w/v° the corresponding values of both inequality indices, defining in this way two alternative redistribution frontiers. Each 1961 frontier is so close to its 1970 counterpart that they would be indistinguishable on a normal sized chart.

To assess the elasticity of each inequality index with respect to the efficiency index, we carried out four OLS loglinear adjustments. Our results are recorded in table 6. In each case, there are five observations.

Table 6. Loglinear approximations of redistribution frontiers

Dependent variable	Intercept (1961 = 1970)	Elasticity 1961	Elasticity 1970	R^2 (1961 = 1970)
$\Delta w/\Delta v^{\circ}$	1·005	5·424	5·419	0·995
G/G°	1·005	4·424	4·419	0·993

To conclude, we emphasize the remarkable stability of the redistribution frontiers, despite the changes in earning capacities and subsistence levels. The explanation must be sought in the above paragraphs. Indeed, each frontier is, by definition, the graph of a composite function, the elements of which are themselves quite stable over time, as we have shown in tables 4 and 5.

APPENDIX A: PROOF OF PROPOSITION 3

In view of proposition 1, our problem reduces to maximizing $Y_i \dfrac{b^{1+c}}{1+c} + \dfrac{a^{1+k}}{1+k}$ with respect to a and b, under the constraint

$$pz = (1-b)\, b^c\, a^{-k}\, \bar{Y} - a, \tag{30}$$

which can be obtained by combining (6) with assumption 1.

Having formed the Lagrangian expression

$$L = Y_i \frac{b^{1+c}}{1+c} + \frac{a^{1+k}}{1+k} + \lambda \left[pz - (1-b)\, b^c\, a^{-k}\, \bar{Y} + a \right],$$

we differentiate it:

$$\frac{\delta L}{\delta a} = a^k + \lambda \left[k(1-b)\, b^c\, a^{-k}\, \bar{Y}(1/a) + 1 \right]$$

$$\frac{\delta L}{\delta b} = Y_i\, b^c - \lambda \left[c(b^c/b)a^{-k}\, \bar{Y} - (c+1)\, b^c\, a^{-k}\, \bar{Y} \right].$$

We let these derivatives vanish and we get rid of λ, obtaining an expression which says that the marginal rate of substitution between a and b must equal the corresponding rate of transformation along the graph of (30)

$$-Y_i\, b^c\, a^{-k} = \frac{c(b^c/b)a^{-k}\, \bar{Y} - (c+1)\, b^c\, a^{-k}\, \bar{Y}}{k(1-b)\, b^c(a^{-k}/a)\, \bar{Y} + 1}\ . \tag{31}$$

Dividing through by $b^c\, a^{-k}\, \bar{Y}$, and substituting from assumption 1

$$-\frac{y_i}{\bar{y}} = \frac{(c/b)-(c+1)}{(k/a)\,(1-b)\,\bar{y}+1}\ .$$

Rearranging, we get

$$(k/a)\,(1-b)\,y_i + (y_i/\bar{y}) = c+1-c/b, \tag{32}$$

from which (7) is easily obtained.

It remains to establish the validity of (8). For a maximum lying in the interior of S, we require the marginal rate of substitution not to decrease faster than the marginal rate of transformation along (30).

To evaluate the change in the marginal rate of substitution, we differentiate the left hand side of (31) which is, by assumption 1, equal to $+y_i$

$$-\left.\frac{dy_i}{db}\right|_{u_i} = -c(y_i/b) + k(y_i/a)\,(-y_i)\ . \tag{33}$$

To evaluate the change in the marginal rate of transformation, we rewrite the latter as N/D,

$$\left. D\frac{d(N/D)}{db}\right|_Z \begin{aligned} &= c(c-1)\,(\bar{y}/b^2) - c(c+1)\,(\bar{y}/b) - y_i \left[(c+1)\,k(\bar{y}/a) - c\,k(\bar{y}/ab) \right] \\ &\quad + y_i \left[c\,k(\bar{y}/ab) - (c+1)\,k(\bar{y}/a) + k(1+k)\,(1-b)\,(\bar{y}\,y_i/a^2) \right]. \end{aligned} \tag{34}$$

As $D>0$, we require this expression not to exceed

$$-D\left.\frac{dy_i}{db}\right|_{u_i} = -\left[k(1-b)\,(\bar{y}/a)+1 \right] \left[c(y_i/b) + k(y_i^2/a) \right]. \tag{35}$$

Hence

$$\begin{aligned} &-c(y_i/b) - k(y_i^2/a) - c\,k(1-b)\,(\bar{y}/a)\,(y_i/b) - k^2(1-b)\,\bar{y}(y_i/a)^2 \\ &\quad \geqslant c(c-1)\,(\bar{y}/b^2) - c(c+1)\,(\bar{y}/b) - 2(c+1)\,k(\bar{y}/a)y_i + 2\,c\,k(\bar{y}/a)\,(y_i/b) \\ &\quad + k(1+k)\,(1-b)\,\bar{y}(y_i/a)^2\ . \end{aligned}$$

By (32), $\quad k(1-b)\,(y_i/a)\,\bar{y} = \bar{y} + c\,\bar{y} - (c/b)\bar{y} - y_i\ .$

Substituting and rearranging:

$$\begin{aligned} &-c(y_i/b) - k(y_i^2/a) - c(\bar{y}/b) - c^2(\bar{y}/b) + (c/b)^2\bar{y} + c(y_i/b) \\ &\quad \geqslant c(c-1)\,(\bar{y}/b^2) - c(c+1)\,(\bar{y}/b) - 2(c+1)\,k(\bar{y}/a)y_i + 2\,c\,k(\bar{y}/a)\,(y_i/b) \end{aligned}$$

$$+(k+2k^2)(1-b)\bar{y}(y_i/a)^2,$$

$$-k(y_i^2/a)\geqslant -c(\bar{y}/b^2)-2[(c+1)-(c/b)]k(y_i/a)\bar{y}+(k+2k^2)(1-b)\bar{y}(y_i/a)^2.$$

Rearranging, substituting from (31) and using (6)

$$0\geqslant k(y_i^2/a)-c(\bar{y}/b^2)-2[(k/a)(1-b)y_i+(y_i/\bar{y})]k(y_i/a)\bar{y}+(k+2k^2)(1-b)y(y_i/y)$$

$$0\geqslant k(y_i^2/a)-c(\bar{y}/b^2)-2[k(y_i^2/a)+k(1-b)\bar{y}(y_i/a)^2$$

$$c(\bar{y}/b^2)\geqslant k(1-b)\bar{y}(y_i/a)^2-k\,a(y_i/a)^2 = k(y_i/a)^2 z\,.$$

After a final rearrangement, we obtain (8).

APPENDIX B: DATA BASE

Data used in stage (i)

See table A1 opposite.

Data used in stage (iii)

Time-series cover the period 1952–1976 (annual data)

Net national product (1972 \$ 10^9)
550·3 571·2 560·9 599·8 611·7 621·8 618·6 658·0 672·5 689·2 731·2 760·6 801·6 850·0 901·1 923·5 963·4 985·9 977·8 1055·9 1065·7 1122·5 1096·9 1079·9 1148·7
Source: Survey of Current Business

Expenditures on collective goods, undeflated \$ 10^9
62·941 68·896 65·857 62·934 60·247 65·947 68·714 71·917 73·259 78·768 84·483 88·021 90·172 94·380 109·080 123·239 135·239 141·867 145·984 152·222 166·231 181·038 196·831 224·174 241·045
Figures obtained by subtracting from total public expenditures the following items: education, agriculture, net interest, public assistance, and other welfare, veterans benefits. This concept seems to match closely the concept used by Reynolds and Smolensky (1977).
Source: Survey of Current Business

Public expenditures deflator
47·4 48·5 48·9 49·7 52·1 54·4 56·1 57·2 58·0 59·2 61·1 62·6 64·0 66·0 69·2 72·6 76·7 81·0 87·5 93·7 100·0 106·9 118·3 128·9 136·7
Source: Survey of Current Business

NNP deflator
57·7 58·6 59·4 60·7 62·4 64·5 65·4 66·9 68·1 68·8 70·2 71·3 72·5 74·2 76·7 79·0 82·5 91·2 95·9 100·0 106·0 116·3 126·5 133·0

Number of families + unrelated individuals (10^6)
49·879 50·589 50·902 51·842 52·740 53·225 54·161 55·132 56·203 56·702 57·863 58·309 58·817 60·104 60·749 61·540 63·168 64·579 66·064 67·669 69·894 71·484 73·640 74·812 76·754
Source: Statistical Abstract

Dummy variable W_t
1 1 1 0 0 0 0 0 0 0 0 0 0 0 0 1 1 1 1 1 1 0 0 0 0 0

Estimated c_t
0·59 0·59 0·59 0·59 0·59 0·425 0·425 0·425 0·425 0·425 0·425 0·425 0·425 0·425 0·425 0·431 0·431 0·431 0·431 0·431 0·431 0·431 0·431 0·431

Table A1. Income distribution USA 1970, (in '70 $)

Income class	under 2 000	2 000–2 999	3 000–3 999	4 000–4 999	5 000–5 999	6 000–6 999	7 000–7 999	8 000–9 999	10 000 14 999	15 000–24 999	25 000–and over	All groups
Number of families (×1 000)	7 458	4 356	4 092	3 828	3 960	3 960	4 026	7 986	14 586	9 372	2 442	66 064
Factor income before taxes, per family (y_j)	981	2 590	3 828	5 481	6 929	8 370	10 003	11 928	16 294	25 429	64 927	13 419
Total taxes per family	576	1 189	1 712	2 269	2 683	3 026	3 437	4 054	5 089	7 435	25 755	4 553
Benefit from specific goods, per family	1 917	3 178	3 111	3 128	2 568	2 270	2 184	2 192	2 348	2 581	4 702	2 546
Net taxes, per family ($y_j - x_j$)	−1 341	−1 989	−1 399	−859	115	756	1 253	1 862	2 741	4 854	21 053	2 007
Balance (x_j)	2 322	4 579	5 227	6 340	6 814	7 614	8 750	10 006	13 553	20 575	43 874	11 412

Source: Reynolds and Smolensky (1977), Appendixes B, C, D, E.

Notes: The number of families is adjusted to match the time-series data given in appendix B. Consequently item 2 is also adjusted.
Total taxes include federal, state and local taxes.
Specific goods: all federal, state and local expenditures excluding national defence, international affairs and 'other general expenditures'.

REFERENCES

Aaron H. and McGuire M. (1970) Public goods and income distribution. *Econometrica* **38,** 907–921.
Burtless G. and Hausman J. A. (1978) The effect of taxation on labor supply: evaluating the Gary negative income tax experiment. *J. Political Economy* **86,** 1109–1131.
Gevers L. and Proost S. (1978) Some effects of taxation and collective goods in postwar America. *J. Publ. Economics* **9,** 115–137.
Grandmont J. M. (1978) Intermediate preferences and the majority rule. *Econometrica* **46,** 317–330.
Hausman J. A. and Wise D. A. (1976) Evaluating of results from truncated samples: The New Jersey Income Maintenance Experiment. *Ann. Econom. Soc. Measurement* **5,** 421–445.
Kramer G. H. (1977) A dynamical model of political equilbrium. *J. Economic Theory* **16,** 310–334.
Musgrave R. A. (1978) *Notes on Fiscal Sociology.* Discussion Paper 642, Harvard Institute of Econ. Research.
Parks R. P. (1978) *Comments on Some Effects on Taxation and Collective Goods in Postwar America,* CORE Discussion Paper, Université Catholique de Louvain, (forthcoming, *J. Pub. Econ.*)
Reynolds M. and Smolensky E. (1977) *Public Expenditures, Taxes, and the Distribution of Income.* New York, Academic.

POSTSCRIPT

Following the conference, some improvements were made to the estimation of the preference structures (tables 2 and 3). Equation (21) was re-expressed using (17) and (20) as:

$$p_t z_t = \frac{\beta}{1+\beta}\left(\frac{\bar{y}_t}{1+c_t} - \lambda\,\frac{\bar{y}_{t-1}}{1+c_{t-1}} + \lambda p_{t-1} z_{t-1}\right) + \frac{1}{1+\beta}\,\frac{p_t}{n_t}\left(uZ_{t-1} + \gamma W_t\right) \quad . \tag{21A}$$

Using a grid of λ values, this was estimated in first difference form; this procedure gave much improved estimates from the point of view of multi-collinearity and auto-correlation. Residual least squares were minimised for $\lambda = 0$ with the results shown in table A2.

Table A2. Regression results, equation 21A

Parameter	Estimate and Standard Error	Structural Parameters	Estimate
λ	0		
$\frac{\beta}{1+\beta}$	0·042 (0·046)	β	0·043
$\frac{\mu}{1+\beta}$	0·862 (0·130)	μ	0·899
$\frac{\gamma}{1+\beta}$	0·961 (3·080)	γ	1·003

$\lambda = 0$ allows a considerable simplification of (16) *viz.* $q_t = r_t = 0$. It follows that the subsistence level for collective goods has risen by 34% between 1961 and 1970. table 3 is accordingly revised as follows:

Table A3. Sample of preference structures—revised estimates

	1961					1970				
			Parameters							
$\frac{Y_i}{\bar{Y}}$	0·608	0·679	0·740	0·791	0·835	0·602	0·675	0·736	0·788	0·832
β			0·043					0·043		
c_t			0·425					0·431		
$p_t s_t$			1 722					2 300		
			Most preferred plan							
b_t	0·52	0·57	0·62	0·67	0·72	0·52	0·57	0·62	0·67	0·72
a_t	3 237	2 867	2 450	1 982	1 473	3 804	3 354	2 841	2 270	1 644
$p_t z_t$	1 964	1 977	1 990	2 000	2 011	2 589	2 604	2 619	2 633	2 646

These revisions resulted in revisions to tables 4 and 6. These were mostly rather small and for reasons of space are not given here. They are however obtainable from the authors and will appear in *Cahiers du Semonaire d'Econométrie.*

Our estimate of c is correct if k is set equal to zero. As Mirrlees suggests, lifting this constraint leads to a positive estimate of k. Nevertheless, we decided to retain the constraint. Indeed, without it we would have had insufficient data to estimate the demand for collective goods.

DISCUSSION

by **J. A. Mirrlees,** *Nuffield College, Oxford University*

The paper has two parts. First the authors use American data to estimate a utility function for the typical American consumer. This utility function expresses his preferences in regard to private consumption, public consumption, and labour. It depends on one parameter, Y, that varies within the population, and on other parameters that are the same for everyone, and are estimated. In the latter part of the paper, the authors use this utility function to work out estimates of the extent to which greater income equality requires a sacrifice of efficiency, and *vice versa.*

I find it easiest to understand this exercise by starting at its end and working back to the beginning. The end is the trade-off between efficiency and equality. These two concepts are here quantified by using the estimated utility function. Any utility function would do, for by using the utility function, each individual's real income in any situation can be calculated as the private consumption that would, along with a reference level of public consumption and zero labour, yield precisely the utility that the situation in question makes available. The population average level of real income thus measured is a reasonable measure of efficiency (if the utility function is correct), while the rate at which real income varies in the population (in this paper, the derivative of real income with respect to Y, which happens, in the special case considered, to be constant) is a reasonable measure of inequality. That granted, one might think that the right way of representing the trade-off between efficiency and equality is to find the possibility frontier for the two variables so defined. That is not what Gevers and Rouyer do. They work out how efficiency and equality would vary as individuals with different Y are allowed to be dictators; i.e., as the level of public consumption, and the linear tax system, are chosen so as to maximize the utility of different individuals within the population. (But see the addendum below.)

The efficiency–equality possibility frontier may not be very different from the frontier derived in the paper. But I do not understand why the trade-off was calculated as the authors have done. It is one thing to advance the political theory that the median voter's preferences determine the equilibrium policies of the State. It is quite another to display the possibilities available to the State under the constraining assumption that the only feasible policies are those that would be selfishly chosen by at least one person. None of the individuals, let it be noted, happens to care about either efficiency or equality as here measured. If calculations of the alternative possible efficiency–equality configurations are useful—and I am by no means convinced that they are—it must be because intelligent voters, advisors, educators, and ministers of the State, take efficiency and equality (as defined) to be important ends. If they are the only important ends, there is no reason to be constrained, other than by the weak necessities of majority voting. If, more plausibly, there are other important ends (such as individual utility) to be considered, it is not of much use to present the tradeoffs between equality and efficiency without looking at the way in which the other ends also vary.

Even if we accept the restrictive constraint implicit in the Gevers/Rouyer treatment, we may question the linear production possibilities implicit in the assumption that the marginal product of labour and the marginal cost of producing public goods do not vary from one equilibrium to another. For small changes, it is unlikely that the neglect of curvature in the production frontier matters, but it is not clear that the changes contemplated in the paper are always small.

Quantitatively, the last point is not likely to be important. What matters most is the method of estimating the utility function. The interesting feature of the function used, which has a considerable effect on the final estimates, particularly of inequality, is the dependence on private and public consumption in the previous period. But I was most particularly struck by the way in which estimates of preferences, both between consumption and leisure and between private and public consumption, are based on observations of public policy: on the one hand the redistributive system of taxes, on the other the level of public expenditures. To justify this, a particular theory of behaviour of the State is necessary. Gevers and Rouyer assume that policy is the outcome of majority voting, so that, with the particular utility function used, the preferences of the median voter determine public policy. Time series then allow the parameters of the utility function to be estimated.

I have three comments on this ingenious procedure. In the first place, it is troubling that only three time periods can be used for the estimation of consumption/leisure preferences. It may be remarkable that nevertheless the most convenient value, $k=0$, is found; but I must report that the particular way I used least squares in attempting to replicate the estimate gave a quite different value of k. Since it is extremely implausible that labour supply should be independent of lump-sum income, I was relieved by my own failure to find that k should vanish. The more orthodox estimates of consumption/leisure preferences, from labour supply behaviour, likewise yield positive k. My second point is that the market behaviour of consumers must in any case be a much more reliable guide to preferences among private goods than such a political theory as this. Thirdly, I am by no means persuaded that a median-voter theory provides an adequate description of the determination of public expenditure for a country where 'logrolling' is apparently an important feature of the system.

The central point is that we need to try to estimate preferences for public goods. It is an important problem, and a fascinating one. A thoroughgoing attempt to carry out and use such an estimation is much to be welcomed.

Addendum

In discussions during the Symposium, after these comments were presented, Louis Gevers and I realized that the true efficiency–equality frontier and the one calculated in the paper are, for the particular model used, and within a certain range, the same. Consequently my criticisms must be read as either methodological, or, for the model under review, largely wrong. The 'real-income' measure of utility v_i in the paper is linear in Y_i (earning capacity), and can be written

$$v_i = A + BY_i$$

where A and B are determined by public policy. Efficiency is measured (essentially) by the average of the v_i:

$$\bar{v} = A + B\bar{Y}$$

and inequality is measured by B. Thus any weighted average of efficiency and equality can be written.

$$\lambda\,(A + B\bar{Y}) - \mu B$$

with positive λ and μ; and this can in turn be written

$$\lambda[A + B(\bar{Y} - \frac{\mu}{\lambda})].$$

A man with earning capacity $Y_i = \bar{Y} - (\mu/\lambda)$ would maximize exactly this (if he could dictate the outcome), and therefore put the economy on the true efficiency–equality frontier. It is interesting (and understandable) that dictatorship by a man with income greater than *mean* income takes the economy inside the efficiency–equality frontier, with efficiency sacrificed in order to create inequality.

SUMMARY OF THE GENERAL DISCUSSION

The most important point to come out of the discussion, following Mirrlees, was whether Gevers' 'trade-off' was the same as an equity–efficiency frontier. (In Gevers' model one is constrained by the levels of public good chosen by the median individual). This led to an extended discussion on voting and redistribution and to Mirrlees' addendum above. Deaton suggested interpreting the results in terms of dictatorships by different decile groups. Winter remarked that the selfish rich man would vote for a zero marginal tax rate; Collard suggested that altriuism might be important but stressed the difficulty of distinguishing between selfish and non-selfish voting outcomes. Mirrlees believed that the median-voter model could more plausibly be interpreted in terms of 'representative' rather than 'simple' or 'direct' democracy. Another modifying factor, in view of the slowness of legislative change, was that it would be short-sighted for voters to confine their attention to the interests of their current income groups; their future position might well change and they should therefore give consideration to the interests of other groups to which they might subsequently belong; thus individuals might behave *as if* a microcosm of society. O'Higgins believed that voters were allowed effective choice only over very marginal questions.

In response to Nicholson, Gevers estimated that a reduction of 5·4 per cent in income 'spread' would 'cost' about 1 per cent of national income; this seemed rather a small cost. Champernowne agreed that the size of the trade-off was important and central to the Symposium but was uncertain as to what precisely was being estimated and questioned the robustness of the assumptions—on this latter point Gevers had nothing to add.

Several contributors expressed anxiety about the method of estimation being used. In response to Mirrlees, Gevers agreed that price changes between public and private goods had not been properly taken into account. He defended his 'rickety' method of estimating labour supply on the grounds that he was really interested in 'factor supply' not just labour supply. Following a mention of 'log-rolling', Deaton doubted its importance in a one public good model: he also questioned whether, if public goods entered separably into utility functions, consumption data could pick up these preferences. Could we employ the same consumption $\rightarrow$ welfare methodology as in standard consumption theory? This led to a brief discussion of preference revelation, Layard stressing willingness to pay, Hammond commenting that the problem also arose for private goods in 'small economies' and Stern and Seade mentioning local public goods.

There was widespread interest both in this and other discussions in the possibility of inferring preferences for public goods and/or income redistribution from actual decisions under various assumed majority voting systems.

OPTIMAL NON-LINEAR POLICIES FOR NON-UTILITARIAN MOTIVES

J. Seade

Department of Economics, University of Warwick

INTRODUCTION

This paper studies optimization by a principal, e.g. a government or a firm, whose choice among social alternatives is constrained to those it can decentralize, as in the non-linear taxation literature, but whose ranking of these alternative equilibria is not constrained to be of any special form, such as utilitarian or profit-maximizing. Accordingly, we shall define welfare directly on the various quantities arising in the economy, on the consumption vectors of consumers in full detail, without necessarily processing this information in any particular way.

The exercise is of interest, we think, partly for purely 'theoretical' (or 'mathematical') reasons, namely to provide a framework of analysis for the incentives problem as such and to explore features of solutions arising from its general structure rather than from any specific maximands. In this sense, these are notes on the problem of 'optimization subject to optimization', where the maximands at the two levels are not necessarily related in any given way. To this view of the exercise, some might answer that only a few special cases really matter at all, such as utilitarian taxation or pricing by governments or benevolent firms, or non-linear pricing by profit maximizers. But even then there is a case for gaining perspective on these models, to aid our understanding of each special problem or indeed of their relationship, by placing them in a suitable wider context that contains them.

Alongside the above remarks on formalism or interpretation, we offer the following more practical motivations for the exercise. We start with the usual utilitarian objective in mind, and introduce various reasons why this may be too restrictive in applications.

Egalitarianism

It has been argued strongly, for example by Sen (1973), that utilitarianism is not the natural vehicle to capture a concern with equality, despite the principal's freedom to 'concavify' utility functions before adding them. For one thing, the *distribution* of utilities may matter, e.g. some notion of distance between top and bottom utilities, which might even result in negative welfare weights at the top, under certain allocations. This would call for a general individualistic approach (welfare defined on utilities), not necessarily Paretian (i.e. increasing in its arguments), let alone utilitarian. Furthermore, there is no special reason why 'egalitarianism' should have to be defined on utilities at all; maybe a particular 'egalitarian' government is concerned about the distribution of income itself, or of cross-section consumption at a point in time rather than in a life-cycle sense. This would require welfare to be defined on consumption vectors directly.

Paternalism

A second type of reason for relaxing the utilitarian, or even individualistic, framework is given by paternalistic considerations: that consumers' preferences are socially 'wrong' in some respect or that, equivalently, they act on the basis of the wrong information. For example, it is an old view to regard utility time-discounts as 'impatience' or *myopia* (see, e.g. Pigou, 1929, part 1, ch. II), which the government should not abide by when comparing social states. Similarly (see e.g. Diamond 1977), various forms of social security schemes we observe in practice can be seen as important instances of paternalistic behaviour by the government, since they impose floors on individual consumption of certain goods and services as well as on total consumption per period (the ability to borrow against future security payments being usually very limited). Otherwise, if redistribution and insurance were the only purposes of such schemes, a simpler poll transfer ought often to have been observed in its place.

Other objectives

One would often wish to move further away from the usual utilitarian set-up than suggested above. For example, the utilitarian non-linear-tax model we have discussed elsewhere applies directly to the problem of utilitarian pricing by public firms, whenever charges can be made non-linear in quantities.† But, more often than not, public utilities are required to include some profit variable in their maximands alongside their consumers' welfare proper (Goldman et al., 1977, allow for this). The non-negativity condition on profits, imposed in the usual utilitarian model, is only an extreme form of this interdependence.

Similarly, governments often wish to maximize national income, tax revenue or employment, or to bring balance of payments considerations to bear on the decision to tax certain goods more than others. Clearly, all these variables should ideally not be given any weight in themselves but taken into account via their indirect effect on welfare. But governments do behave in this Dutch-school-like 'flexible targets' manner, presumably because the short-run and gross economic indicators are all too important for them—just as managers of private firms may well care for non-profit variables. Whatever the objective function, the incentives problem remains essentially the same.

The outline of the paper is as follows. First we present the model and discuss various aspects of it: individual behaviour and participation, the welfare function and the interpretation of the model for some special cases. Then we derive and discuss the necessary conditions for an optimum, including the solution for optima with corners, which has not been considered in detail or generality in the literature. In the next section we discuss specific features of optima: end-points taxation which takes a readily intuitable form for the general case; some further implications of the end-points result for special cases, in particular revenue or profit maximization; relations between tax rates; and some remarks on the signs of distortions in the optimum—i.e. on tax rates. A brief stock-taking is offered in the final section.

† The interpretation of the taxation model for the utilitarian pricing of consumption goods whose retrading can be prevented was noted in Seade (1977, p. 229). An implication was, as also noted there, that no distortion should be imposed at the top and perhaps the bottom (if all consumers are buyers) of optimal pricing schedules. Recent papers from the pricing literature have studied essentially the same model, under a special assumption on preferences (equation 3) which arises naturally in that context, and obtained again the no-distortion result, among others (*see* Goldman et al 1977; Roberts, 1978 and Willig, 1978). Goldman et al allow for a somewhat more general maximand (giving weight to profits, alongside utilities); Goldman et al and Roberts derive other features of the model they consider, some of which we refer to below.

THE MODEL

Preferences, skills and income

Consider an economy whose consumers' utility functions are

$$u = u(a,b,h) \tag{1}$$

where a is a numeraire commodity, b a vector of other goods, which for expediency we shall mostly refer to as a scalar, and h a parameter that captures individual ability, income, tastes or whatever central differences amongst consumers a given model is to concentrate on. We assume h to follow a well-behaved (in particular, bounded) density function $f(h)$, and denote the *support* of the latter (the smallest interval that contains all h's actually observed in the population) by $[\underline{h}, \bar{h}]$,‡ although we shall later feel free to give a different interpretation to these 'extreme' values of h.

We impose the convention that, unlike preferences, consumers' opportunity sets are all identical. Essentially this amounts to defining a and b as they occur in production (efficiency-hours of work rather than time worked, for example), and measuring them as *net trades* with the market. Thus, if endowments do differ with h, these differences simply affect the utility which different consumers derive from a given pair of *trades* (a,b), if final consumption is what matters. This is already allowed for in equation (1).§

It may be useful to relate equation (1) to special structures that have been studied in the literature. To study labour supplies and the generation of income, it is natural to focus on the way in which the wage rate varies across consumers, so that we get h=wage, with a and b representing, by our previous convention, consumption and gross income. This gives equation (1) the form

$$u = U(a,b/h), \tag{2}$$

which is Mirrlees' (1971) well-known income-tax model. Alternatively, still concentrating on income differences across consumers, one could disregard labour-supply decisions and set h=income, directly, so as to focus attention on the expenditure side of behaviour. Then, writing x for consumption of the numeraire, b for the commodity subject to tacation or discriminatory pricing and $a = a(b)$ for the total expenditure on the latter, individual budget constraints reduce to $x + a = h$. Thus, if preferences are otherwise identical among consumers, a unique underlying $U(x,b)$ becomes

$$u = U(h - a,b), \tag{3}$$

again a special form of equation (1). This is the utility-structure used by Goldman et al. (1977) as well as (implicitly) by Roberts (1978) and Willig (1978).

We assume u to be strictly concave, twice differentiable and, for convenience, increasing in a and b. We also need to make sure that h is an unequivocal ordinal index for consumers' economic behaviour. For this, writing s for the marginal rate of substitution of a for b,

$$s(a,b,h) = u_b/u_a, \tag{4}$$

‡ The support need not be a single (i.e. connected) interval, as stated for simplicity in the text; it could be the union of a finite number of such intervals, i.e. f can be zero in the interior of its domain. This would not affect the analysis, except that an additional utility–continuity condition across neighbouring branches of the support would (normally) be required.

§ If labour is truly heterogeneous, for example (not reducible to homogeneous 'efficiency units'), the model becomes one with a continuum of commodities rather than *two* as we have assumed. Finally, we assume away differences in consumption sets across consumers, of an essential kind or induced by the redefinition and measurement of (a,b) as described.

we assume

$$s_h \equiv \partial s/\partial h > 0. \tag{5}$$

That is, indifference curves always turn in the same direction, at each point in (a,b)-space, as h increases. Thus, a and b are weakly monotonic in h whatever the budget line consumers face. (In fact equation (5) implies more, that a is non-increasing and b non-decreasing in h, but this is purely by our convention on the actual signs of s_h and of u_a,u_b. Single-signedness is what matters.) It is easy to check what equation (5) amounts to in the examples considered above: equation (2) satisfies it if (but not only if) consumption, a, is non-inferior (Seade, 1980), while equation (3) does if the taxed good, b, is normal.

Social Welfare

Following the motivation given in the introduction, we make welfare dependent directly on each individual's consumption of a and b. With a continuum of consumers, these 'lists' of quantities, one for each h, become entire functions of h. For lack of standard notation, I shall denote by $a|$ the whole arc of the a-allocation:

$$a| \equiv a|_{\underline{h}}^{\overline{h}} \equiv \{a(h) \text{ for } \underline{h} \leqslant h \leqslant \overline{h}\} \tag{6}$$

(c.f. the usual under-bar for vectors), and similarly write $b|$ for the arc of $b(h)$ and u for that of utilities across values of h. Welfare, W, may then be written||:

$$W = W(a|, b|). \tag{7}$$

Particular examples of interest are easily written down to put equation (7) to work on applications such as those suggested in the introduction. But, as soon as one does that, one loses sight of the common structure of alternative examples, and sacrifices generality. No doubt an important obstacle to a general analysis is the lack of a notation for functionals which is easy to write and grasp.¶ By way of contrast, we notice that, for a problem closely related to the present exercise, but where the representation of consumers by a continuum is unnecessary, Diamond and Mirrlees (1971) do use the discrete counterpart to equation (7) for as long as the analysis permits, treating the individualistic form as a special case worthy of further study. Nevertheless, it will prove convenient not to insist on 'too' much generality, and to adopt a form of equation (7) which is both general enough for our purposes, and easier to handle. Thus, we impose additive separability of welfare across consumers,

$$W = \int_{\underline{h}}^{\overline{h}} \hat{u}\ (a,b,h)\ f(h)\ \mathrm{d}h, \tag{8}$$

where the function $\hat{u}\ (a,b,h)$ has a natural interpretation: it is the *social* (or principal's) *utility* from h's consumption. This still allows W to depend in any linear form on utilities (individual or paternalistic), on the variance of utilities or of specific goods such as income, on aggregates such as profits or revenue, or variables depending on aggregates (linearly) such as various 'macro' objectives.

|| I avoid calling equation (7) *Bergsonian* because this term is very often (though incorrectly) applied to the *individualistic* welfare function—apart from the fact that Bergson's definition was in a finite-dimensional context.

¶ A functional analyst would of course simply write equation (7) as $W(a,b)$, where the arcs a and b are mere points in a suitable space, but this is no less abstract than equation (7) and can be inconvenient if notation is to allow for particular realizations of the functions a and b too.

One can notionally relax additive separability, replacing the derivatives of the functional equation (8) at any given point, $\hat{u}_a,\hat{u}_b$, by the corresponding derivatives of the functional equation (7) with respect to local arc-changes,** $W_a(h)$, $W_b(h)$. One would then just modify accordingly all the equations we shall obtain below, and perhaps draw a qualitative feel as to how non-separability of W would affect the optima (an example is given on p. 63). But the actual computation of solutions would be complicated enormously, as the usual set of differential equations one obtains for the description of the optimum would be replaced by an integro-differential or a difference-differential system with forward *and* backward 'memory' (derivatives $\mathrm{d}a/\mathrm{d}h$ and $\mathrm{d}b/\mathrm{d}h$ depending, at each point, on the state of the system at other points in both directions), which do not appear to have been studied at all in the mathematical literature.

Constraints

(i) The principal's problem is to make an optimal selection, relative to its objective equation (8), of two allocation-functions $a(h)$, $b(h)$, which should arise through decentralization and meet some 'isoperimetrical' constraint on the value of resources available to the planner, which can variously be interpreted, for example, as a production constraint, government's revenue requirement, or minimum permissible profits for a public firm.†† Linearizing, this constraint can be written as:

$$\int_{\underline{h}}^{\bar{h}} \{a(h)+pb(h)\}\, f(h)\, \mathrm{d}h \leqslant A, \tag{9}$$

where p is the relative shadow price of b at the optimal equilibrium.

(ii) Let us turn now to the decentralization condition on the allocations. All the government can do, we assume, is to offer consumers a *budget set*, a set of points in (a,b)-space from which to choose their consumption. If the (north-east) frontier of this set is smooth, interior individual maximization for people taking part in the scheme imposes

$$u_a a' + u_b b' = 0, \tag{10}$$

where $a' \equiv \mathrm{d}a(h)/\mathrm{d}h$, etc; this is derived and discussed in Seade (1977). The ratio a'/b' is the trade-off between the two goods as faced by the consumer at the margin, so that equation (10) is an *envelope condition* for the economy: tangency of preferences with the budget constraint for each consumer. On the other hand, this tangency may come 'from the wrong side', i.e. give a minimum. It is a simple exercise in the use of indifference-curve diagrams to check, given equation (10) and assumption (5) on

** The *variational derivative* of W w.r.t. a at h^1 is defined as

$$W_a(h^1) = \lim\, [\delta W / \int_{h^0}^{h^2} \delta a\, f\, \mathrm{d}h]$$

as $|\delta a| \to 0$, $h^2 > h^1 > h^0$, $(h^2 - h^0) \to 0$. This derivative is unique when it exists: Gelfand and Fomin (1963, pp. 12, 27–29).

†† The first interpretation of equation (9) is obvious. For the second, write $t(h)$ for the amount of tax an h-man ends up paying in a given equilibrium and y for his gross transfer income. The individual budget constraint is then $a+pb+t=y$ which, imposing $\int t \geqslant R$ (revenue), yields equation (9) with $A \equiv \int y - R$. For equation (9) as profits $\geqslant -A$, think of pb as production cost and $-a$ as the price-function for consumers, their required outlay on buying quantity b.

preferences ($s_h > 0$), that maximization occurs iff $b' \geqslant 0$ for all h. This is rigorously proved by Mirrlees (1976, appendix). We must, therefore, ensure that‡‡

$$b' \geqslant 0. \tag{11}$$

Notice that equations (10) and (11) also hold for most h's consuming on a corner *of the budget set*: there, a' and b' are simply zero over an h-range. It is only corners *of the allocation functions* ($a(h)$, $b(h)$), which are not unrelated to the former, that pose difficulties for these equations. Corners of the former kind are important and will be studied for optima, while those of the latter are not, in that they will only arise at a few values of h—at any rate if the variational analysis is to be applicable at all. But it is clear by continuity of $u(\cdot)$ that if 'nearly' all consumers are maximizing utility then *all* consumers are, so that imposing equation (10) (for points of differentiability) suffices as far as necessary conditions for (interior) maximization by all h is concerned. Equivalently, a condition that applies directly also at non-differentiabilities of $a(h)$, $b(h)$ is used by Mirrlees (1976), namely that $\mathrm{d}u/\mathrm{d}h = \partial u/\partial h$.

(iii) The above conditions, equations (10) and (11), are necessary and sufficient for an individual optimum from amongst the set of possibilities offered by the government. This applies only by consumers actually maximizing on that set, which in certain contexts (the usual closed-economy optimal-tax set-up) can be taken to be *all* consumers in the population. More generally, however, consumers have the option of leaving the market altogether, becoming tax-exiles for example. A *participation constraint* is required: that each consumer who does stay in derives not less utility than a certain minimum $\bar{u}$, presumably that associated with his best alternative (net of costs involved), which would normally differ across consumers:

$$u(a(h), b(h), h) \geq \bar{u}(h). \tag{12}$$

It would be incorrect to impose equation (12) for all h in the population, however, for it must only hold for values of h 'captured' by the scheme. A full treatment of the problem must incorporate a choice of the captured ranges of h as one of the controls, and only apply equation (12) in these ranges. One can clearly not say, for the general case, what the partition of the population into participants and leavers will be like in the optimal equilibrium, as this will depend, among other things, on the nature of the exogenous schedule $\bar{u}(h)$ in equation (12). Separate analysis of this aspect of the problem is required, and this will be presented elsewhere. But it is clear that the interior necessary conditions, for the case where the marginal values of h between participation regimes are chosen optimally, must be the same as those one would obtain by treating those optimal marginal h's as fixed—only the relevant end-point conditions will be sensitive to this added dimension of choice. We can therefore think of the interval $[\underline{h}, \bar{h}]$ as denoting a given participation arc rather than the whole, exogenously given population; if these consumers are to be induced to stay in in the optimum, clearly equation (12) must hold for each of them. We want to study the nature of the tax or price schedules these (and other!) consumers will face in the optimum.

One last point one should mention in this connection is that it is no longer clear whether the domain of welfare should be the set of consumers who stay in, or the

‡‡ We have not placed an *upper* limit on b', i.e. on the 'speed' at which demands vary across different people. The limit case $b'(h_d) = \infty$ amounts essentially to a discontinuity or multi-valuedness at $b(h)$ at h_d, i.e. the tax function running along h_d's relevant indifference curve over an arc. Goldman et al (1977) give an example of this possibility and Mirrlees (1971) gives conditions under which discontinuities are ruled out for the income-tax case (Theorem 2-v). We assume away discontinuities of allocations. Were they to arise, our analysis would apply all the same to each continuous arc, with the point of discontinuity h_d playing the role of $\bar{h}$ and $\underline{h}$ for two successive continuous arcs—only transversality conditions would be affected at these points: equilibrium utility must be continuous in h through the point h_d (see note ¶¶, below).

whole population; it can be either. But by additive separability, this does not upset the optimization within each participation range—it only affects the choice of the extent of participation.

THE OPTIMUM: CHARACTERIZATION

Necessary conditions

So as to facilitate reference of multipliers to associated constraints, let us write in full the Lagrangean for the problem:

$$\max_{a,b} \int_{\underline{h}}^{\bar{h}} F\,\mathrm{d}h, \quad \text{where}$$

$$F \equiv \{[\hat{u} - \lambda(a+pb)]f + \mu(u_a a' + u_b b') + vb' + \pi(u - \bar{u})\}, \tag{13}$$

where the arguments of all functions have been omitted. Non-negativity constraints on (a,b) are here neglected, but can be brought in in given cases as the need arises.

First order conditions for equation (13) are constraints (9), (10), (11) and (12), the first one and last two of these having complementary slack with $\lambda \geq 0$, $v \geq 0$, $\pi \geq 0$, respectively, plus the following:

$$(\hat{u}_a - \lambda)\, f + (\pi - \mu')\, u_a = \mu\, u_{ah}, \tag{14}$$

$$(\hat{u}_b - \lambda p) f + (\pi - \mu')\, u_b = \mu\, u_{bh} + v', \tag{15}$$

with transversality conditions $\mu\, u_a = \mu\, u_b + v = 0$ (see Seade, 1977, pp. 224–5) at either end-point whose value of h is *fixed*, i.e. one which is not a frontier between participation regimes, as discussed at the end of the previous section. Hence for such fixed-h end-points§§,

$$\mu(\underline{h}) = \mu(\bar{h}) = v(\underline{h}) = v(\bar{h}) = 0. \tag{16}$$

On the other hand, at arc end-points interior to the population the relevant part of equation (16) does not hold, but a continuity condition on end-point utilities replaces it in closing the system, as we shall see below.

To put conditions (14)–(15) in a more useful form, it is most convenient to treat values of h where consumption is changing separately from those where it is not. It is clear from assumption (5) on preferences ($s_h > 0$) that, for demands actually observed in the population, consumption is constant at $(\bar{a},\bar{b})$ over an h-range if and only if $(\bar{a},\bar{b})$ lies on a corner of the opportunity set (tax function) consumers face. That is, discussing constancy of $a(h)$, $b(h)$ is tantamount to discussing possible corners of the optimal tax function.

Taxes on smooth arcs

Over an h-range where consumption is changing, the value of v is and remains zero, so that v' in equation (15) vanishes. It will be easier to interpret the first-order conditions if we define

$$\hat{s} \equiv \hat{u}_b / \hat{u}_a. \tag{17}$$

§§ Notice that, with a fixed, 'captive' population, as in Seade (1977), one always gets $\mu(\underline{h}) = \mu(\bar{h}) = 0$, despite the fact that this may or may not translate into zero distortions at the endpoints (cf equation (18), below), depending on whether bunching occurs there. This point is often overlooked in interpreting equation (16) directly in terms of taxes.

This is the *social* (or principal's) *marginal rate of substitution*, or constant-welfare trade-off, on an h-man's consumption of $a(h)$, $b(h)$, derived from the social evaluation of his consumption, $\hat{u}(\cdot, \cdot; h)$. Eliminating terms in $(\pi-\mu')$ from equations (14) and (15) and re-arranging, one obtains

$$\lambda(s-p)=\hat{u}_a(s-\hat{s})+u_a s_{\underline{h}}\, \mu/f, \tag{18}$$

where s is h's *private* marginal rate of substitution of a for b, defined in equation (4). The left-hand side of equation (18) is the distortion on the (relative) price of b an h-man should face in the optimum: the excess of marginal price he pays $(=s)$ over producers' price p.

It is of interest to note that, for a given value of $\mu(h)$, the last term in equation (18) is exactly the usual one describing the optimal utilitarian distortion—indeed this is obvious from equation (18) itself, as $s=\hat{s}$ under utilitarianism (or individualism, more generally). To this component of the tax, the term $\hat{u}_a(s-\hat{s})$ is now added, which has a natural interpretation: it measures the social value of the divergence between private and social preferences. More precisely, it is the compensating change in the quantity of numeraire the individual reckons he needs for constant utility as b changes, over society's computed compensation, $\hat{s}$, both valued at the social value of numeraire in h's hands, $\hat{u}_a(\cdot,\cdot;h)$. Thus, the first term in equation (18) arises directly from differences between social and private preferences, and might be called the 'paternalistic' motive for taxation. It might also be viewed as the 'first-best' component of the tax, as it describes the line on which the first-best set of allocations would fall, were it achievable. In contrast, the second term in equation (18) is the 'individualistic', or 'second-best' motive for the tax, which arises purely from the incentives nature of the problem, from the need to resort to decentralization of equilibrium allocations.

The above remarks are only suggestive of interpretation, and not meant to be operational, for the actual value of $\mu(h)$ will depend critically on the choice of the function $\acute{u}(\cdot,\cdot;h)$, as well as on the remaining data for the problem. We obtain $\mu(h)$ by direct integration of equation (14):

$$\mu(h)=\mu(\underline{h})\exp\left(-\int_{\underline{h}}^{h}\frac{u_{ah}}{u_a}\,\mathrm{d}h'\right)+\int_{\underline{h}}^{h}\left\{\frac{\hat{u}_a-\lambda}{u_a}f+\pi\right\}\exp\left(-\int_{h'}^{h}\frac{u_{ah}}{u_a}\,\mathrm{d}j\right)f\,\mathrm{d}h'. \tag{19}$$

If $\underline{h}$ is fixed (no exclusion at the bottom), $\mu(\underline{h})=0$. If $\bar{h}$ is fixed, $\mu(\bar{h})=0$.

The characterization of the optimum (leaving apart possible constancy-ranges of consumption), is now complete. At each point, either $\pi=0$ or utility is given by equation (12). Using this, equations (10), (18) and (19) can be transformed into a system of three differential equations in $a(h)$, $b(h)$ and $\mu(h)$, or in $\pi(h)$, $b(h)$ and $\mu(h)$. The particular solution of interest will be the one that satisfies condition (9) on total demands plus, at the bottom, $\mu(\underline{h})=0$ if $\underline{h}$ is fixed, or else $u(a(\underline{h}), b(\underline{h}), \underline{h})=\bar{u}(\underline{h})$[||||]; similarly for h.

Corners

We now turn to intervals of h where consumption remains constant at a corner. To simplify things, let us assume away the participation constraint, which would seem unlikely to start biting within a corner, but which could easily be accounted for if necessary.

|||| That is, equality in equation (12) must always hold at the boundary points, between regimes where equation (12) is met and those where it is violated. This follows from *continuity* of equilibrium allocations *of utility*, itself imposed by continuity of $u(\cdot,\cdot; h)$ on h.

Over an interval of constancy of the allocation functions, say for $j \in [h_0,h_1]$, the term v' in equation (15) does not generally vanish. However, at both end-points of that interval the associated constraint, (11), is 'just' biting, $v(h_0)=v(h_1)=0$, and everywhere inbetween v is non-negative. Moreover, it is easy to show that v (as well as μ) is continuous throughout the schedule¶¶. It follows, integrating equations (14) and (15), that

$$\int_{h_0}^{j} \{(\hat{u}_a-\lambda)\, f-\mu'\, u_a-\mu\, u_{ah}\}\, \mathrm{d}h \equiv 0, \tag{20}$$

and

$$v(j)= \int_{h_0}^{j} \{(\hat{u}_b-\lambda p)\, f-\mu' u_b-\mu u_{bh}\}\, \mathrm{d}h \geq 0, \tag{21}$$

both $\forall\, j \in [h_0,\, h_1]$, and that

$$\int_{h_0}^{h_1} \{(\hat{u}_b-\lambda p)\, f-\mu' u_b-\mu u_{bh}\}\, \mathrm{d}h=0. \tag{22}$$

All one needs to know about a range of constancy is how long it should be, i.e. the value of h_1 if we think of the solution as being worked out from the bottom. Equation (22) can be used to find h_1 (with equation (21) providing a continuous check as the integration is performed), for all the other information which equation (22) requires is known to us on reaching the point h_0***. In particular, notice that equation (14), and hence the solution for $\mu(h)$, and equation (19), are independent of v and hold at corners too. This characterization, however, is indirect and not at all operational, involving rather complicated expressions for μ and μ'. To simplify things, notice that, when $a(h)$ and $b(h)$ are constant, say at $(\bar{a},\bar{b})$, $\mathrm{d}u_a/\mathrm{d}h=u_{ah}$. We can therefore integrate by parts the middle terms of these equations:

$$\int_{h_0}^{j} \mu' u_a \mathrm{d}h=\mu u_a \Big|_{h_0}^{j} - \int_{h_0}^{j} \mu u_{ah}\, \mathrm{d}h, \tag{23}$$

similarly for u_b in equations (21)–(22). The last terms of equations (20) and (23) cancel each other, as do those in the corresponding equations for u_b. Hence, equations (20)–(21) become

$$\int_{h_0}^{j} (\hat{u}_a-\lambda)\, f\, \mathrm{d}h=u_a^j\mu^j-u_a^0\mu^0,$$

$$\int_{h_0}^{j} (\hat{u}_b-\lambda p)\, f\, \mathrm{d}h \geq u_b^j\, \mu^j-\, u_b^0\mu^0,$$

(with equalities at $j=h_1$), where u_a^0 denotes $u_a\,(\bar{a},\bar{b},h_0)$, $\mu^j=\mu(j)$, and so on. Eliminating μ^j from here, we finally obtain

$$\int_{h_0}^{j} \{(\hat{u}_b-\lambda p)\; -s^j(\hat{u}_a-\lambda)\}\, f\mathrm{d}h \geq u_a^0\mu^0\, (s^j-s^0), \tag{24}$$

$\forall\, j \in [h_0,\, h_1]$, and

¶¶ Multipliers are continuous inside smooth arcs of the allocation-functions $a(h)$, $b(h)$; at corners of these (where a constancy range starts and ends), standard variational analysis requires continuity of $F_{a'}$ and $F_{b'}$ (*see* Geldfand and Fomin, 1963, sec. 1.6) i.e., in this case, of $\mu\, u_a$ and $\mu\, u_b+v$, which imply the result. This continuity property of the multipliers is essential for the present argument and at other points below.

*** The only previous solution for corners I am aware of is in (Mirrlees, 1971, Theorem 2-iv); he uses essentially forms of equations (21) and (22) for the income-tax case, with μ and μ' from equation (19).

$$\int_{h_0}^{h_1} \{(\hat{u}_b - \lambda p) - s^1 (\hat{u}_a - \lambda)\} f \, \mathrm{d}h = u_a^0 \mu^0 (s^1 - s^0). \tag{25}$$

Equation (25) determines, in a rather direct form, the solution-value for h_1, or equivalently the 'exit' right-slope of the tax function at the corner, s^1. We need not worry about multiplicities of solutions, which in all probability will be a feature of equation (25): the relevant solution is the *smallest* $h_1 \geq h_0$ that solves it; this is because at that point v in equation (21) has fallen from having a strictly positive value to being zero, and moving beyond that point will generically render v negative, which involves a violation of equation (24). (This is not inconsistent with a possible degenerate case of two corners merging into a single one at h_1—the value of v 'bouncing back' into the positive after reaching zero at the point h_1. The computation would simply re-start there.)

Equation (25) has a simple enough structure that invites interpretation, but we have not been able to find an intuitive explanation for it. Both equations (25) and (24), can be further simplified, in search of an explanation, if we consider the utilitarian case and treat h_1 as being 'close enough' to h_0, so that $s^j - s^0 \approx s_h^0(j - h_0)$. Then, equation (24) requires that, within a corner,

$$\int_{h_0}^{j} \{\lambda(s^j - s^0) - u_a (s^j - s)\} f \mathrm{d}h \geq 0, \tag{26}$$

with equality being the signal for the next smooth regime to start.

FEATURES OF OPTIMA

Optimal tax schedules can have very diverse properties, depending critically on the principal's objective and the way h is assumed to enter individual preferences (given by the structure of the problem at hand), and even on the specific functions being used. This is true for the familiar utilitarian taxation (or pricing) problem, and consequently all the more so in the present more general model. Only a few properties of taxes are known to hold fairly generally under utilitarianism: the non-negativity of optimal *income* tax rates (Mirrlees, 1971); the no-distortion (e.g. zero marginal tax) requirement at end-points where bunching does not occur (Seade, 1977); Atkinson–Stiglitz's (1976) condition on the undesirability of differential taxation across commodities entering utility separately from h; these are three such features that come to mind.††† Our purpose in this section is to see what becomes of these results when more general optimal schedules are considered. We omit various details of proofs or of precise conditions under which results hold, whenever these follow closely their counterparts in the above-mentioned articles.

Tax treatment at the end-points

Let us ignore for the moment the participation constraint. The values $\underline{h}$ and $\bar{h}$ are then fixed and correspond with the actual extreme values of h in the population (but see fn. §), rather than with policy-determined extreme points of a given taxation interval, where it borders with possible h-ranges on either side, where people choose to withdraw from the scheme.

††† Another general property of optimal taxes is Mirrlees' (1976) very general but obscure Pareto-efficiency condition, on a relation that must hold between optimal non-linear taxes on different commodities.

With fixed $\underline{h}$ or $\bar{h}$, the transversality condition (16) applies, so that $\mu(\underline{h})=0$, or $\mu(\bar{h})=0$ respectively. It follows, under weak regularity conditions on the way preferences vary with h (boundedness of u_{ih}), that $s_h\mu/f$ also vanishes at the points $\underline{h}$ and $\bar{h}$, regardless of whether or not density f is zero at this point (Seade, 1977, p. 228). One must be cautious, however, as to what is implied for tax rates: the bottom value of the parameter for the population, $\underline{h}$, can be identified with the bottom *of the tax schedule* only if there is no bunching of consumers with $h>\underline{h}$ at the consumption point observed for $\underline{h}$. Otherwise, if a non-zero range of consumers $[\underline{h}, h^*]$ all maximize utility at the same point on the tax schedule, e.g. choosing not to work at all, then it is still true that $\mu(\underline{h})=0$, but the bottom tax rate now relates, via equation (18), to the lowest h with an interior solution, namely h^*; and $\mu(h^*)$ will not normally be zero. If there is no bunching, however, the bottom of the h- distribution and of the (interior) tax schedule can be identified with each other, and the optimal tax rate for that point is indeed given by equation (18) with its last term set equal to zero. That is, without exclusion or bunching,

$$\lambda(s-p)=\hat{u}_a(s-\hat{s}), \quad \text{at } h=\underline{h},\bar{h}. \tag{27}$$

A corollary to this is the result (Seade, 1977) that, whatever the structure of the specific problem at hand may be, optimal tax or price schedules for utilitarian objectives display no distortion at the end-points in the absence of bunching.‡‡‡ (The same is true for *each* tax schedule, if b, and accordingly s and p, are interpreted as vectors.) The following generalization is immediate from equation (27): bunching or exclusion apart, distortions at end-points are zero for any optimal Paretian, or more generally individualistic, tax or price schedule, regardless of the complexity of interactions across utilities which render the full problem virtually insoluble quantitatively, as indicated on p. 57 above.

Before turning to the interpretation of the more general form of the end-points condition (27), it is of interest to discuss briefly the crucial role of the no-bunching and no-exclusion assumptions in securing this result. For ease of exposition, let us refer to the utilitarian closed-economy case. The no-distortion requirement follows intuitively from the fact that, without bunching, a marginal tax at an end-point has *all* the population on one side of it, so that the motive for distorting prices, essentially to raise revenue from some to pump it back directly or indirectly to others, is not met. The end-point distortion's yield is, under those circumstances, a pure deadweight waste. But if there is bunching, say at $\underline{h}$, there will be a certain fraction of the population not paying any tax on the bottom rate, so that some distortion will (normally) remain desirable on distributional grounds. Similar remarks apply when there is 'exclusion'—if, say, $\underline{h}$ is only the lowest h-value among those who choose to stay in in the optimum. In that case, a change in the marginal tax at the bottom changes the position of the bottom point itself, the value of $\underline{h}$, affecting revenue, distribution and welfare in other forms than those suggested by the simple argument above.

Let us now seek an interpretation for the end-points optimality condition (27). A possible tack would be simply to adapt the 'efficiency *vs* equality' argument used for the utilitarian version of equation (27): that is, for the general case, that at the end-points the second-best motive for the tax disappears, and all the weight should be given to the 'efficiency' element, correcting only for differences between individual and social preferences, as in equation (27), and not for the government's inability to allocate consumption directly. This view of equation (27) has the advantage that it relates the present problems of interpretation directly to that which arises naturally

‡‡‡ Versions of this result for the utilitarian problem were noted in footnote †, p. 54.

for the utilitarian case. But by the same token, the explanation does not add much to our understanding of the simple result for utilitarianism. Let us, instead, rearrange this expression and write it as:

$$s = \frac{\hat{u}_b - \lambda p}{\hat{u}_a - \lambda} \equiv \hat{\sigma} \quad \text{at} \quad h = \underline{h}, \bar{h}\ . \tag{28}$$

This condition has an interesting interpretation which, in particular, puts the utilitarian result in a different light, as an instance of a more general principle. Notice that $\hat{u}_b$ represents the social gain from giving an extra unit of b to an h-man, while λp is the cost of doing that, namely the unit production cost of b. Hence $\hat{u}_b - \lambda p$ is the *social profit* of the given man's consumption of b at the margin. Similarly, $\hat{u}_a - \lambda$ is the social marginal profit from adding to his consumption of a. The right-hand side of equation (28), which we have denoted by $\hat{\sigma}$, thus emerges as (minus) the slope of the *social 'net' indifference curve* between consumption of a and b by an h-man. Hence, in contrast with the straightforward *gross* counterpart to this measure defined on (social) utilities alone ($\hat{s} \equiv \hat{u}_b/\hat{u}_a$), $\hat{\sigma}$ computes social-utility trade-offs taking due account of the cost-side of consumption. Therefore equation (28) is a condition for *generalized Pareto efficiency* (in a non-Paretian world) at the end-points, i.e. tangency of individual and social net indifference curves. The reason for this is of course not that preferences embodied in s matter *per se*, but that without it it is possible to increase $\hat{u}$ at (and near) the end-points at no extra resource cost, as exemplified in figure 1.

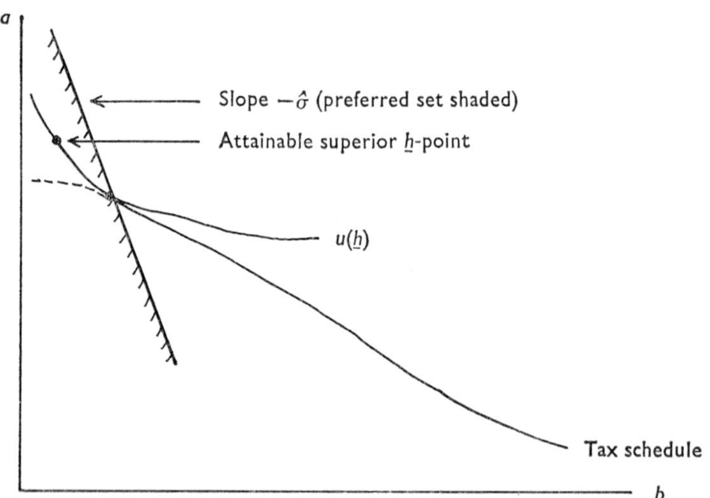

Figure 1. Inefficiency at end-point.

Implications of the end-points condition: examples

With a utilitarian welfare function, equation (28) reduces to $s = p$ at the end-points, as mentioned above. One can, however, still write this condition as $u_b/u_a = (u_b - \lambda p)/(u_a - \lambda)$, and interpret it in terms of private *vs* social net preferences as above.

It would be useful to explore the type of implications which equation (28) may have for taxes in non-utilitarian contexts. Consider first Mirrlees' (1971) income tax model, retaining its given structure on consumers' preferences and behaviour, but let welfare be non-utilitarian. For example, very high incomes may be unwanted *per se*, out of direct regard for the distribution of income that emerges. If so, the constant-utility consumption-cost of extra income for the top-man is higher in $\hat{u}$ than in u, i.e. $\hat{s}>s$. From equation (27), this implies $p>s$ at the top, where in this case p is the real wage rate paid by producers. Therefore, the marginal tax rate at the top turns out to be positive in the optimum, despite all purely Paretian considerations to the contrary. Preferences that give rise to this may be what many of us have in mind when feeling a certain discomfort with the end-point no-distortion prescription as applied to the top of the income scale. A similar, perhaps less plausible, argument could be made for the bottom of the income tax on the very same lines, namely an interest in narrowing the spread of incomes. There, $\hat{s}<s$ would reflect a greater social than private preference for the working poor to earn more by working harder. Personally, I would probably not subscribe to this particular mixture of puritanism and paternalism but it sounds familiar. If adopted, one would have $s>p$ at the bottom (a higher net than gross marginal wage), which means a *negative* marginal income tax, again upsetting a rather general property of utilitarian income taxes: the non-negativity of marginal tax rates—to which we return below.

A second non-utilitarian example of interest—both intrinsic interest and as an illustration of the issues involved—is that of a *revenue-maximizing* government or firm. For small movements around an optimum, and a correspondingly fixed value of aggregate transfer income, maximizing revenue is equivalent to minimizing private consumption (of leisure and goods), so that the welfare function (9) reduces to

$$W = - \int_{\underline{h}}^{\bar{h}} (a+pb) f \mathrm{d}h. \tag{29}$$

That is, $\hat{u}(a,b,h) = -(a+pb)$ here. The same notation applies to the profit-maximizing firm (see footnote ††). The special, striking feature of this example is that, in the optimum, the constraint (10) on total demands will *not* be tight: one is maximizing W subject to a *floor* on W. Hence the multiplier dual to equation (10) vanishes: $\lambda=0$. Also, from equation (29), $\hat{u}_a = -1$, $\hat{u}_b = -p$. Substituting these values into equation (28), we get the same no-distortion condition as under utilitarianism, $s=p$; thus *optimal tax schedules for revenue (or profit) maximization have a zero distortion at either end-point where bunching and exclusion do not arise.*

This result, as stated, holds with the same generality as that of its utilitarian counterpart, i.e. regardless of the specific structure of preferences imposed by the problem at hand. But a crucial difference with the utilitarian result arises through violations of the no-bunching, no-exclusion provisos made in the statement of the result. Under utilitarianism, these conditions may or may not be met, depending on the alternatives to participation consumers of different kinds have, $\bar{u}(h)$ in equation (12), as well as on the specific form of their preferences, density and so on. It is therefore natural, short of performing a taxonomy of possibilities or specific discussion of special cases, simply to rule out by assumption both bunching and non-participation in the statement of the end-points result. For the revenue maximizer the situation is rather different: *no optimum can exist before and unless the participation constraint bites.* Intuitively, the government's exploitation of consumers can only be stopped by its own wish (the choice of W), electoral or other form of defeat (not considered), or (the threat of) migration. To prove the result, put $\lambda=0$ and $\hat{u}_a=-1$ in equation (19), giving:

$$\mu(h) = \mu(\underline{h}) \exp(\cdot) + \int_{\underline{h}}^{h} (\pi - \frac{f}{u_a}) \exp(\cdot) \,\mathrm{d}h. \tag{30}$$

Now suppose that all consumers participate in the scheme. This implies that $\pi(h)=0\ \forall\ h$, and that $\underline{h}$ and $\bar{h}$ are fixed as given in the population, so that equation (16) applies at both ends, $\mu(\underline{h})=\mu(\bar{h})=0$. But differentiating equation (30), with $\mu(\underline{h})=\pi=0$, one gets $\mu'<0\ \forall\ h$, which implies a contradiction. Thus it is a general property of optimal taxes for revenue-maximization that some consumers are induced to opt out of the system—including the possibility of an endogenous mortality rate for a slave economy. Depending on which ranges of h first choose to leave, which can clearly not be ascertained without assumptions on the fine structure of the problem, the no-distortion result may hold at $\underline{h}$, $\bar{h}$, none or both.

Other properties of optimal taxes

While omitting routine details, let us see what the counterparts are, for the present formulation, of other well-known features of utilitarian taxes.

Commodity taxes

A result by Atkinson and Stiglitz (1976) for utilitarianism states that no distortion should be imposed within a vector of commodities x^1 which enter utility in a form that is weakly separable from h: $u=U(\varphi(x^1), x^2,h)$, where the vector (x^1,x^2) is the same as (a,b), but split in some different way, with b here interpreted as a vector. Now under more general social preferences, this rule is modified in much the same way as the utilitarian no-distortion condition for the end-points. That is, given separability of x^1, only an 'efficient' distortion amongst the components of x^1 should be imposed, given precisely by equation (28) again, where the rates of substitution and relative prices s, $\hat{s}$, p, apply to pairs of commodities within the vector x^1.

An immediate implication is that a counterpart to Atkinson–Stiglitz's result applies to *revenue or profit maximization* too: percentage mark-ups over marginal costs should be the same for all commodities in each consumer's basket, assuming that those commodities enter utilities in a separable form from consumer's 'income' h. This follows from equation (28), noting again that, under profit maximization, $\lambda=0$, u_a-1, $u_b=-p$. Price-discrimination takes the same simple, easily implementable form discovered by Atkinson and Stiglitz for utilitarian taxation. Equal costs to producers (of two different baskets) implies equal prices to consumers; only total expenditure matters.

Rates of taxation

Mirrlees (1971) shows that, for the income tax case (u as in (2)), $du_a/dh<0$ implies that the optimal marginal income tax is positive at all levels of income where it is defined. His argument, and this result, extend directly to the general utilitarian problem: u_a decreasing in h implies a positive marginal tax of a relative to b throughout the schedule. That is, rather naturally, taxation will be used to transfer the numeraire in that direction where it is more 'useful' in consumption.

The problem, alas, is that the final schedule of u_a's is an endogenous component of the whole optimization exercise. One would expect single-signedness of du_a/dh in a wide range of cases, but exceptions can easily arise; the condition is not a valid 'primitive' assumption (one on the data) and needs to be checked in particular cases. For the income-tax problem, for example, it can be shown to hold if leisure and consumption are non-inferior (Seade, 1980).

With non-utilitarian preferences the above result still holds, now stated in terms of single-signedness of $d\hat{u}_a/dh$ but more importantly, now applying only to the 'second-best' element of the tax in equation (18). The total sign of the distortion will depend on the interaction between this effect and the 'efficiency' element of the tax, the first term in equation (18), $\hat{u}_a(s-\hat{s})$. For example, referring again to the income-tax problem, one could think of a government interested in redistribution (in an ex-post sense), i.e. with $d\hat{u}_a/dh<0$, but whose views on leisure are more puritanical than consumers', so that it would like to see people, generally, work harder. The first of these motives for taxation, on the limit to redistribution due to decentralization, will call for a positive marginal tax throughout, tailing-off towards zero near the end points of the schedule; the second motive will be of the opposite sign: a marginal subsidy as an incentive to effort. The latter would probably not dominate throughout the schedule in most cases of interest, but any such effect would render marginal rates negative in some ranges of income, approaching the (negative) end-point values given by equation (28).

CONCLUDING REMARKS

The purpose of this paper was to provide a formulation of the optimization-cum-incentives problem which would, on the one hand, unify the two main special cases which have already been studied, utilitarianism and profit-maximization, bringing out their common structure and results; while at the same time putting the problem in a more general form. This generality is meant not only to cater for further examples beyond those mentioned above, for example those suggested in the introduction but, more importantly, to put special cases in perspective, hopefully enhancing our understanding both of the working of the general incentives problem, and of specific results.

As far as results are concerned, we were expecting fewer to hold for the general case, and those that did to be less amenable to intuition than under utilitarianism, but this turned out not to be the case. In particular, the optimal taxation (or pricing) of the 'richest' and 'poorest' members of the community takes a simple and intuitable form even when the principal's objective is not spelled out. Moreover, the same 'efficiency' condition that must hold at the end-points describes the way in which taxes on commodities which are separable from the individual parameter h in utility functions should be related, generalizing the well-known no-excise-taxes result of Atkinson and Stiglitz (1976). When applied to the profit maximization case, this condition reduces to exactly the same form found by these authors for utilitarianism, which simplifies the kind of price-discrimination a monopolist selling many goods should or would use.

Unlike the above, most other results we discussed held only for special cases, such as the general requirement for revenue or profit maximizers to exclude part of the population, or the conditions under which the distortions on relative prices can be signed. Considerable generalizations are possible in many of these cases.

Finally, results apart, it was also of interest to note the simplicity of the conditions describing the optimum in the general case: the decomposition of taxes into a 'first-best' or 'paternalistic' motive and a 'decentralization' motive, and the simple treatment which can be given to corners of optima, which had not been treated in any detail in the contexts of previous analyses.

ACKNOWLEDGEMENTS

A preliminary version of this paper was read at the 1978 Winter Symposium of the Econometric Society (Sindelfingen, Germany; January) and at seminars in Hull, Nuffield College and Warwick (SSRC Economic Theory Study Group). I am grateful to the members of these seminars, and in particular to James Mirrlees and David Starrett for useful remarks.

REFERENCES

Atkinson A. B. and Stiglitz J. E. (1976) The design of tax structure: direct *vs* indirect taxation. *J. Pub. Econ.*, **6**, 55–75.

Diamond P. A. (1977) A framework for social security analysis *J. Pub. Econ.* **8**, 275–298.

Diamond P. A. and Mirrlees J. A. (1971) Optimal taxation and public production *Am. Econ. Rev.* **61,** 8–27 and 261–278.

Gelfand I. M. and Fomin S. V. (1963) *Calculus of Variations.* Englewood Cliffs, N. J., Prentice-Hall.

Goldman M. B., Leland H. E. and Sibley D. S. (1977). Optimal nonuniform prices. Bell Labs. Economics Discussion Paper No. 100.

Mirrlees J. A. (1971) An exploration in the theory of optimum income taxation. *Rev. Econ. Studies* **38,** 175–208.

Mirrlees J. A. (1976) Optimal tax theory: a synthesis *J. Pub. Econ.* **6,** 327–358.

Pigou A. C. (1929) *The economics of welfare.* London, Macmillan.

Roberts K. W. S. (1978) Welfare considerations of nonlinear pricing, Massachusetts Institute of Technology (mimeograph).

Seade, J. K. (1977) On the shape of optimal tax schedules. *J. Pub. Econ.* **7**, 203–235.

Seade J. K. (1980) On the sign of the optimum marginal income tax Univ. Warwick. Economics Discussion Paper No. 166.

Sen A. K. (1973) *On economic inequality.* Oxford, Oxford Univ.

Willig R. D. (1978) Pareto-superior nonlinear outlay schedules, *Bell J. Econ.* **9**, 56–69.

DISCUSSION

by **D. Todd,** *H.M. Treasury, London.*

As a public servant, one is conscious that a relatively small number of able academics are working in a difficult area on an important topic—important in the practical sense that many people over the political spectrum feel that the burden of income tax is too high. A number of other industrialized countries feel this also. The question is whether anything valuable is emerging from this work which might provide some insights for public policy. There is much to discuss in Seade's paper because, as far as I can see, the principles on which it is based can be applied to a wide range of issues in the public sector. I will therefore confine my remarks to one aspect of his work, namely income taxation.

The first point to note is that optimal income tax models are really about tax design rather than tax reform. Hence we are concerned largely with the construction analytically of income tax schedules. The problem posed is a very old one in economics. Fundamentally, it draws attention to the distinction between income and substitution effects of a relative price change. One tries to choose an income tax schedule so as to maximize a Social Welfare function subject to a given central government revenue constraint. Further, this choice must be made in such a way as to minimize distortions or disincentives. Thus the income effect emerges in the attempt to satisfy the revenue constraint and the substitution effect measures the degree to which any distortions are created. By making specific assumptions about the form of a social welfare function, the distribution of labour skills and the elasticity of labour supply, it becomes possible to compute a variety of alternative tax schedules.

Typically, from the numerical calculations in the literature, one finds relatively low marginal rates of income tax but these marginal rise rates tend to rise initially and then either stabilize or decline through the higher income levels. In general, results from this work are relatively few and are a very long way removed from what we observe in practice.

Seade's approach to the problem is significant in that he departs from the more conventional and widely-used utilitarian form of social welfare function (SWF). In his model, government is allowed explicitly (and realistically) to have preferences of its own. Hence his function is not simply an aggregation of individual's preferences under the assumption of separability. The moment one follows this approach it becomes clear that a very wide variety of possibilities emerge. Depending on the weights and arguments appearing in the SWF, virtually any degree of progressivity is possible in the optimal tax schedule. It is easy to see intuitively that the few general results for the utilitarian case need not hold any more, simply because governments may demand or require more or less equality. However it may be possible to obtain results similar to those of Seade whilst remaining with the more conventional framework. Atkinson, for example, has demonstrated that by applying simple transformations to utililitarian welfare functions it becomes possible to derive tax schedules more closely approximating those which we actually observe.

Again, suppose one assumes, realistically, that the existing distribution of skills is skew. The concentration or mass of this function can now be characterized by the mode. One can now hypothesize further and say that the mass of individuals around the mode have a collective desire to be more 'like' a relatively wealthy person in the tail than the latter has of being further removed from them in terms of earnings. In other words there are externalities in preference formation which would in these circumstances lead to a mode-dominated welfare function. Whilst the model would have to be specified precisely and this may be difficult, I am sure that this would yield results not unlike those of Seade but, whilst remaining within the utilitarian framework. Further, it seems to me that a formulation along the above lines would be broadly in accordance with our experience of incomes policies over the past few years. On entirely pragmatic grounds therefore, a maxi-mode specification may well have something to commend it.

Lastly, I have two points of detail. The first concerns the role of the participation constraint. Again in practical terms this could be of importance. The welfare of a non-working married woman could be affected by changes in the tax function. If she is thinking of entering the labour market but is then discouraged by a tax policy change, then confining welfare to include active participants only, will misrepresent the cost or benefit to society. This point is recognized more easily with indirect taxation, e.g. tobacco and alcohol duties. Secondly, the 'bunching' problem, or kinks in the schedule considered by Seade, seems to say something in principle about where jumps or discontinuities in the tax function ought to be. The schedules observed in practice on the face of it bear no relation to this, which suggests that administration and political constraints are required in a full analysis.

SUMMARY OF THE GENERAL DISCUSSION

There was considerable discussion of why the existing tax structure was so different from the allegedly 'ideal' structures which emerged from optimal tax theory. Seade felt that the 'common-sense' objection to the theoretical conclusion of zero marginal tax rates for the richest arose simply because the whole assumption of utilitarianism was in fact itself objectionable.

Todd speculated whether the difference between 'theory' and practice might actually be due to a genuine preference for the present system, and wondered whether one could identify the assumptions which would justify the present system. He felt that a utilitarian SWF dominated by the mode of the income distribution might be sufficient.

Champernowne doubted whether such an exercise was worthwhile. The present tax-structure had not resulted from a set of consistent decisions, but had grown up in a very haphazard fashion, and if there were any guiding principle, it was surely administrative convenience.

Lecomber, however, felt that the idea of a 'maxi-mode' decision rule was quite attractive; it was at least as reasonable as the more popular maximin criterion. Collard commented that some work had in fact been done on this.

Nicholson said that in his opinion the present system was not that far removed from the ideal. There was great confusion between marginal and average rates of tax. In practice, the system was not all that progressive if you took into account national insurance contributions. Because of evasion and avoidance, effective marginal tax rates at high incomes might be very low indeed. In his view, the real defect of the present system was its complexity.

There were several questions on various technical points of the analysis. LeGrand noted that the social welfare function in equation (8) appeared to allow the possibility of externalities. Did this mean that externalities made no difference to the results? Seade agreed that this was so but only if the externality part of utility was additively separable, an assumption that seemed unnatural in that interpretation.

Cowell felt that it was important that the upper limit of the ability distribution should be bounded and observable. The tax structure was clearly sensitive to the exact point at which the marginal rate should go to zero, and one therefore had to be able to fix this precisely.

Hare questioned the assumption on p. 55 that the consumers' opportunity sets were all identical. He wondered whether this was really as innocuous as Seade thought. However, Seade said that this was only a question of the definition of units provided underlying homogeneous units for each of the two goods existed.

Champernowne queried whether the results would still hold if the distribution of income were Paretian. Seade replied that the tail of the Pareto distribution did not decline as fast as the Log–Normal Distribution did. Whereas with the latter distribution the results would always hold, the Pareto distribution would only work with certain utility functions.

Deaton felt that the results of the paper were unfortunately rather negative. One of the benefits that had come out of optimal tax theory in the past was that at least certain tax structures and practices had been shown to be inconsistent. But Seade's framework was so general that almost anything could go.

UNCERTAINTY AND OPTIMAL SOCIAL SECURITY SYSTEMS

E. Sheshinski and Y. Weiss

Department of Economics, Hebrew University of Jerusalem and Tel Aviv University

INTRODUCTION

The effects of social security have been discussed within the framework of an overlapping-generations model by Barro (1974).† His analysis can be summarized quite simply. If social security is *fully funded*, i.e. contributions to the system are invested at the market rate of interest, it is a perfect substitute for private savings. Consequently, a forced increase in social security will reduce private savings by an equal amount. Consumption, bequests and aggregate savings will be unaffected. If social security is financed on a *pay-as-you-go* basis, i.e. taxes on the currently working population are used to finance benefits to the retired population, it is a perfect substitute for private bequests. Hence, a forced increase in social security will reduce bequests by an equal amount. Consumption, private savings and aggregate savings will be unaffected. In such models the optimal level of social security is clearly undetermined.

In this paper we analyze social security in a somewhat more realistic context. The duration of life is assumed uncertain and the annuity aspect of social security benefits is incorporated explicitly. We use a simplified two-period version of Yaari's model (1965) to determine the demand for annuities. Optimal social security is defined as the amount of annuities demanded by a representative individual. Our working hypothesis is that all such insurance is provided publicly. Although in principle the private market could also satisfy this demand, in practice the public supply appears to be dominant.‡

The demand for social security depends upon the mode of financing. Under a fully funded system, demand is determined by each generation so as to maximize its lifetime utility, taking into account the welfare of future generations. A pay-as-you-go system involves transfers from the younger generation to the old. Demand is therefore defined from the point of view of the old, taking into account the social security taxes paid by the young.

Under an actuarially fair, fully-funded social security system, perfect insurance against life uncertainty is feasible. The representative individual will prefer that option which enables him to equate the marginal utility of bequests across states of nature. Consequently, at the optimum, private savings are reserved for bequests while social security benefits are used solely for consumption. The same pattern appears in an optimal pay-as-you-go system.

A steady state is defined as a path along which all the choice variables, in per-capita

† See also Feldstein (1974) and the exchange between Barro (1976), Buchanan (1976) and Feldstein (1976). Samuelson's (1975) analysis is different since, following Diamond's (1965) discussion of the effects of national debt, he disregards bequest motives and hence voluntary intergenerational transfers.

‡ In the US, pension funds provide less than 50 per cent of the total benefits to retirees.

terms, remain fixed. There is a unique steady-state path associated with each mode of financing the social security system. It is shown that for any values of the exogeneous variables, these steady-state paths are equivalent in the following sense:

(i) Consumption, aggregate savings and individual utility are the same in both systems;

(ii) The sum of private savings and social security contributions under a fully-funded system is equal to private savings under a pay-as-you-go system; and

(iii) The product of the population growth rate and the level of social security taxes under a pay-as-you-go system is equal to the product of the rate of return and the level of social security taxes under a fully-funded system. As an immediate implication, when the rate of return exceeds the population growth rate, then the optimal level of social security under a pay-as-you-go system exceeds that under a fully-funded system. These conclusions are made consistent through adjustments in the optimal level of bequests.

We analyze the effects of two demographic changes which were the subject of recent discussion: an increase in life expectancy and a decrease in the birth rate. Under certain conditions, an increase in life expectancy is shown to increase the optimal level of social security, to decrease private savings and to increase aggregate savings. These results are expected since, with a given income, an increase in life expectancy calls for a decrease in the flow of lifetime consumption but to an increase in total consumption during the retirement period, which is financed by social security benefits. The implications of a decrease in the birth rate are unambiguous: bequests, private and aggregate savings decrease, while the optimal level of social security increases. The reason for these results is that a reduction in the birth rate and, correspondingly, in the size of optimal bequests, increases consumption during retirement and hence social security benefits. The above results apply to the long run, comparing steady states, and to the short run, with given initial endowments.

Finally, we consider the short-run effects of an imposed change in the level of social security. Starting at the optimum, an increase in the level of a fully-funded social security system is shown to be only partially compensated by a decrease in private savings, thereby increasing aggregate savings. Full compensation occurs only in the absence of uncertainty, which is the case discussed by Barro (1974). Under additional assumptions concerning risk-aversion, the same conclusions apply when the initial level of social security exceeds the optimal level. An imposed increase in the level of a social security system based on pay-as-you-go will increase aggregate savings and bequests. However, under uncertainty, the increase in bequests does not fully compensate for the increased taxes on the younger generation.

A non-optimal level of social security leads to a random distribution of bequests, generated by lifetime uncertainty. Consequently, steady states, or the long-run effects of a change in social security, should be discussed in terms of stable distributions. We have not included such an analysis in this paper.

The only type of uncertainty here considered relates to the duration of life. The inclusion of other uncertain elements, such as health and future wage income, may change some of the conclusions that we have reached. It will be important in these extensions to specify which decisions by the individual are made *ex ante* and which *ex post*.

OPTIMAL SOCIAL SECURITY SYSTEMS

We shall analyze a model in which all annuities are supplied by the public sector through a social security system and focus on the determination of its optimal level.

Two methods of financing will be considered: a fully-funded system and a system based on a pay-as-you-go principle.

Our point of departure from previous literature is the emphasis on life uncertainty, which implies that social security is not a perfect substitute for private savings. We extend the standard model of overlapping generations (Samuelson, 1958; Diamond, 1965) to include uncertain lifetime. Life of a representative individual is divided into two periods: a working period of fixed duration and a retirement period whose length is random. Wages in each period are assumed fixed. Utility depends upon own consumption in each period, the length of life and the expected utility of the next generation. Each generation may affect the welfare of the next one through the transfer of bequests.

Two types of assets are available: an annuity which yields a given return for the duration of retirement and regular savings. Due to the uncertain lifetime, the rate of return on annuities is random. We assume that the rate of return on savings is certain.

Let c_0^i and c_1^i be the consumption flows in the first and second periods, respectively, of generation i. Let B^i be the level of per-capita bequests left by generation i to generation $i+1$. The fraction of the potential retirement period which is actually realized is denoted by θ, where $0 \leqslant \theta \leqslant 1$. The distribution of θ is assumed to be the same for all generations.

The budget constraint for a representative member of generation i is

$$c_0^i = w + B^{i-1} - a^i - s^i \tag{1}$$

$$GB^i = Rs^i + (R'a^i - c_1^i)\theta$$

where w is first-period earnings, a^i the investment in annuities and s^i the amount of savings, R the return on savings, R' the benefit–investment ratio on annuities and G the number of children. It is assumed that w, R, R' and G are fixed. Note also that there is no reinvestment of funds during the second period.

The determination of R' depends on the method of financing the social security system. In an *actuarially fair*, fully-funded system, expected benefits are equal to the return on the investment in the system. That is,

$$R' = R/\bar{\theta} \tag{2}$$

where $\bar{\theta}$ is the expected length of the retirement period in the population.

With a pay-as-you-go system, expected benefits to retirees are equal to social security taxes collected from the working population, i.e.,

$$R' = G/\bar{\theta}. \tag{3}$$

Equations (2) and (3) assume that risk pooling is feasible. The social security system can therefore offer a non-random benefit rate to each individual.

We shall first analyze a funded system.

Funded Social Security

Since a funded system does not involve intergenerational transfers, its optimality can be analyzed from the point of view of a single generation.

For a given optimal policy of the next generation, each generation's indirect utility depends on its initial endowment. We can therefore write the expected utility of generation i as a function of its consumption and the level of bequests. We assume the following additive form:

$$V^i = u(c_0^i) + \underset{\theta}{E}\,[v(c_1^i,\theta) + Gh(B^i)] \tag{4}$$

where $u(c_0^i)$ is first-period utility, $v(c_1^i,\theta)$ second-period utility and $h(B^i)$ is the evaluation of the next generation's representative individual indirect utility. Each of these functions is assumed to be invariant over time and to satisfy, for any θ, the usual monotonicity and strict concavity assumptions. Note that both c_1, the fixed flow of consumption, and θ, its duration, affect second period's utility.

All the variables, except B^i, are chosen by the individual *ex ante*, i.e., prior to the realization of θ. To ensure an interior solution, we assume that

$$u'(0) = v_1(0,\theta) = h'(0) = \infty, \qquad \text{for any } \theta, \tag{5}$$

where $v_1 = \partial v/\partial c_1$. The maximization of (4) subject to (1) yields the following first-order conditions (FOC):

$$\partial V/\partial s = -u'(c_0^i) + RE[h'(B^i)] = 0 \tag{6}$$

$$\frac{\partial V^i}{\partial a} = -u'(c_0^i) + \frac{R}{\bar\theta}\,E[\theta h'(B^i)] = 0. \tag{7}$$

$$\partial V^i/\partial c_1 = E[v_1(c_1^i,\theta) - \theta h'(B^i)] = 0. \tag{8}$$

The objective function can be shown to be globally strictly concave in the variables s, a and c_1, and thus the solution to (6)–(8) is unique.§ We shall denote the solution for each i by (s^{*i}, a^{*i}, $c_1{}^{*i}$), which are functions of B^{i-1}. By (1) we obtain the corresponding c_0^{*i} and B^{*i}.

Due to assumption (5), only interior solutions need to be considered. It follows directly from these conditions that $c_0^* > 0$, $c_1^* > 0$ and $B^* > 0$ for all θ. Furthermore, a^* and s^* must be strictly positive. First, $B^* > 0$ implies, by (1), that either a^* *or* s^* is positive. Second, suppose that $s^* = 0$ and $\partial V/\partial s \leqslant 0$. It then follows from (6)–(7) that $\mathrm{Cov}[h'(B),\theta] \geqslant 0$. However, by (1), $Ra^* - c_1^* > 0$ and hence B is increasing in θ. Due to risk aversion, $h''(B) < 0$; the above covariance must therefore be negative, which is a contradiction. A similar argument shows that $a^* > 0$.

The condition

$$\mathrm{Cov}[\theta,h'(B)] = E[\theta h'(B)] - \bar\theta E[h'(B)] = 0 \tag{9}$$

§ The Hessian Matrix of our problem

$$\begin{bmatrix} u'' + \frac{R^2}{G}E[h''] & u'' + \frac{R^2}{\bar\theta G}E[\theta h''] & -\frac{R}{G}E[\theta h''] \\ u'' + \frac{R^2}{\bar\theta G}E[\theta h''] & u'' + \frac{R^2}{\bar\theta^2 G}E[\theta^2 h''] & -\frac{R}{\bar\theta G}E[\theta^2 h''] \\ -\frac{R}{G}E[\theta h''] & -\frac{R}{\bar\theta G}E[\theta^2 h''] & E[v_{11}] + \frac{1}{G}E[\theta^2 h''] \end{bmatrix}$$

is negative-definite. The diagonal elements are negative by strict concavity. The principal minor of order 2 is equal to

$$(R^2/\bar\theta^2 G^2)\{Gu''E[(\theta-\bar\theta)^2 h''] + R^2(E[\theta^2 h'']E[h''] - E[\theta h'']^2)\} > 0.$$

The second term in the above expression is positive by Schwartz's inequality. The determinant can be reduced to

$$\frac{R^2}{G^2}\left[\left(u'' + \frac{R^2}{\bar\theta^2}E[v_{11}]\right)\left(E[\theta^2 h'']E[h''] - E[\theta h'']^2\right) + \frac{Gu''E[v_{11}]}{\bar\theta^2}E[(\theta-\bar\theta)^2 h'']\right] < 0.$$

which follows from (6) and (7) implies, since B is monotone in θ and $h''<0$, that B^* is *constant* for all θ. This, of course, is a well-known result. Annuities enable the individual to transfer consumption across states of nature and it is optimal to equate the marginal utility of bequests, $h'(B)$, in all states. Further, it follows from (1) that

$$C_1{}^{*i}=Ra^{*i}/\bar{\theta} \quad \text{and} \quad GB^{*i}=Rs^{*i}. \tag{10}$$

That is, annuities are used exclusively for consumption during retirement while all savings are reserved for bequests. Clearly, in the absence of a bequest motive, $h'(B)\equiv 0$, and the individual's portfolio would contain only annuities.

Substituting (10) into (4), the objective function becomes

$$V^i=u(c_0^i)+E\left[v\left(\frac{R}{\bar{\theta}}\,a^i,\theta\right)\right]+Gh\left(\frac{Rs^i}{G}\right), \tag{11}$$

which is to be maximized subject to the constraint $c_0^i+a^i+s^i=w+B^{i-1}$. The problem is thus reduced to a problem of choice under certainty. This does not imply, of course, that uncertainty is redundant in our model. On the contrary, in the absence of life uncertainty the optimal level of social security is indeterminate, being a perfect substitute with private savings. However, the achievement of complete insurance at the optimum facilitates the comparative static analysis.

Two types of comparative static analyses are of interest. One, a short-run analysis for generation i, which holds initial endowments, i.e., $w+B^{i-1}$, constant. Second, a long-run steady-state analysis along a path satisfying $B^{i-1}=B^i$, which implies that all the choice variables remain fixed. In both cases we restrict ourselves to partial equilibrium, holding w and R constant.

We shall discuss here the steady-state effects of two demographic changes which have been the subject of recent discussion: an increase in life expectancy and a decrease in the birth rate.

Recalling that $h(B^i)=F(V^{*i+1}(B^i))$, where V^{*i+1} is the optimal level of utility for generation i+1 and F is a monotone increasing function, we can rewrite condition (6) in recursive form

$$-u'(c_0^i)+RF'(V^{*i+1})u'(c_0^{i+1})=0. \tag{12}$$

Hence, in a steady-state, $c_0^i=c_0^{i+1}$, we have $F'=h'/u'=1/R$. A sufficient condition for a unique steady state is that, when marginal utilities of consumption are equalized across generations, the following 'selfishness' condition is satisfied:

$$u''-Rh''>0. \tag{13}$$

In subsequent discussion we shall assume that condition (13) holds.

Using equation (11), the FOC (6)–(8) and rewriting $\theta=\bar{\theta}+\varepsilon$, where ε is a random variable independent of $\bar{\theta}$ with zero mean,|| we obtain

$$\frac{da^*}{d\bar{\theta}}=\frac{1}{\Delta}\,h'\left(u''-\frac{R}{G}(u''-Rh'')\right)\left(-\frac{E[v_{11}]c_1}{E[v_1]}+\frac{E[v_{12}]\bar{\theta}}{E[v_1]}-1\right) \tag{14}$$

$$\frac{ds^*}{d\bar{\theta}}=\frac{1}{\Delta}\,h'u''\left(\frac{E[v_{11}]c_1}{E[v_1]}-\frac{E[v_{12}]\bar{\theta}}{E[v_1]}+1\right) \tag{15}$$

where $\quad \Delta=-\dfrac{R\bar{\theta}}{G}\,h''u''-\left(u''\left(1-\dfrac{R}{G}\right)+\dfrac{R^2h''}{G}\right)\dfrac{R}{\bar{\theta}}\,E[v_{11}]<0.$

|| Since θ is restricted to [0,1], the described shift is not strictly spread preserving.

Similar to standard models of savings under uncertainty, the effect of a spread-preserving shift depends upon whether the relative change in expected marginal utility of future consumption,

$$-\frac{E[v_{11}]c_1}{E[v_1]}+\frac{E[v_{12}]\bar{\theta}}{E[v_1]},$$

is larger or smaller than one. An increase in $\bar{\theta}$ affects expected marginal utility directly and indirectly through the decrease in the flow of social security benefits during retirement. It is reasonable to assume that $v_{12}>0$ and thus the sum of the above two expressions will be positive. It is only with stronger conditions, however, that one obtains the 'intuitive' outcome $da^*d\bar{\theta}>0$ and $ds^*/d\bar{\theta}<0$.¶ The effect on aggregate savings, i.e., a^*+s^*, also depends on the same condition. The source of the ambiguity concerning the optimal level of social security is quite clear. For given labour inputs and income, an increase in life expectancy calls for a reduction in the flow of second-period consumption, c_1. However, expected total consumption, $\bar{\theta}c_1$, which is provided by social security taxes, may increase or decrease.

The implications of a decrease in the birth rate are unambiguous. A reduction in G leads to a decrease in the size of bequests and hence in private savings. Per-capita bequests will, however, increase and so will second-period consumption and thus the optimal level of social security. While a^* and s^* change in opposite directions, their sum, i.e., aggregate savings, will decrease. Specificially,

$$\frac{ds^*}{dG}=-\frac{Rs^*}{\Delta G^2}\left(\bar{\theta}u''h''-\frac{R}{\bar{\theta}}E[v_{11}]\,(u''-Rh'')\right)>0 \tag{16}$$

$$\frac{dc_1^*}{dG}=\frac{R}{\bar{\theta}}\frac{da^*}{dG}=\frac{R^2s}{\Delta G^2}h''u''<0 \tag{17}$$

$$\frac{dB^*}{dG}=\frac{R^2s^*}{\Delta G^2\bar{\theta}}u''E[v_{11}]<0 \tag{18}$$

$$\frac{d(a^*+s^*)}{dG}=\frac{R^2s^*}{\Delta G\bar{\theta}}E[v_{11}]\,(u''-Rh'')>0. \tag{19}$$

The short-run effects of changes in $\bar{\theta}$ and in G are qualitatively identical to the long-run effects presented above. The usual relation between the short-run and long-run effects holds in this case: the long-run elasticities, across steady states, exceed (in absolute values) the short-run elasticities.

Pay-As-You-Go System

A pay-as-you-go system involves transfers across generations. An optimal social security must weigh the welfare of the retired recipients against that of working population. We assume that the social planner's point of view is identical in this respect with that of the older generation at each point of time. At a point in time when the population consists of generations i and i+1, the problem solved by a member of the older generation i is

¶ A special case of some interest is $v(c_1,\theta)=\hat{v}(c_1)\theta$. Then $-(E[v_{11}]c_1/E[\hat{v}_1])=(v''(c_1)c_1/v'(c_1))$, which is the standard definition of relative risk aversion, and $(E[v_{12}]\bar{\theta}/E[v_1])=1$. Hence, $da^*/d\bar{\theta}>0$, $ds^*/d\bar{\theta}<0$, and $(d(a^*+s^*)/d\bar{\theta})>0$.

$$\max_{a^i, c_1^i} E[v(c_1^i, \theta) + Gh(B^i - a^i)] \tag{20}$$

subject to

$$GB^i = Rs^i + \left(\frac{Ga^i}{\bar{\theta}} - c_1^i\right)\theta \tag{21}$$

where s^i is predetermined. The FOC are given by

$$E[h'(B^i - a^i)(\theta - \bar{\theta})] = 0 \tag{22}$$

and

$$E[v_1(c_1, \theta) - \theta h'(B^i - a^i)] = 0. \tag{23}$$

We shall denote the solution to (22) and (23) by $(\hat{a}^i, \hat{c}_1^i)$ which depends on s^i. The nature of the optimal solution is similar to the one obtained in the case of the funded system; namely, social security benefits are used solely for consumption. Bequests are adjusted to the level of private savings and are thus non-random:

$$G\hat{a}^i = \hat{c}_1^i \bar{\theta}, \qquad \hat{B}^i = Rs^i/G. \tag{24}$$

The long-run, steady-state effects can be analyzed with the additional restriction that $\hat{a}^i$ is time invariant, which implies that all the other choice variables are also constant. Accordingly, in addition to conditions (22) and (23), we also have condition (25) which determines the optimal level of savings

$$-u'(c_0) + RE[h'(B - a)] = 0, \quad \text{where } c_0 = w + (Rs/G) - a - \hat{s}. \tag{25}$$

The endogeneous steady-state level of s is denoted by $\hat{s}$.

There is a simple correspondence between the steady-state solutions of the two methods of financing the social security system:

$$\hat{a} = Ra^*/G \quad \text{and} \quad \hat{s} = s^* + a^*. \tag{26}$$

Using relation (26), it can be verified that the system of equations (6)–(8) and (23)–(25) are equivalent.

When $R = G$ the two systems yield identical optimal levels of social security and the same aggregate savings. When $R > (<) G$, the optimal social security tax will be larger (smaller) under a pay-as-you-go system than under a funded system. However, bequests adjust so that the net transfer between generations remains unchanged. Consequently, the steady-state levels of consumption, aggregate savings and utility are identical under the two systems.

This result has a direct bearing on the Feldstein–Barro controversy [Feldstein (1974, 1976) and Barro (1974, 1976)] with regard to the effect of social security on aggregate savings. Our discussion indicates that when social security is optimally chosen, the method of financing has no long-run effects. The concept of an optimal level of social security played no role in the above controversy since lifetime uncertainty was disregarded. The discussion focused on imposed changes in the level of social security. We shall turn to this question in the next section.

Short-run analysis for the pay-as-you-go system can be applied to the older generation, for which private savings are given. Thus, condition (25) need not hold. The results for the optimal level of social security are qualitatively the same as in the long run.

DEPARTURES FROM THE OPTIMAL LEVEL OF SOCIAL SECURITY

There are marked differences in the effects of an imposed social security system under conditions of certainty and uncertainty. Under certainty, the maximum level of utility is independent of the level of a. If social security is funded then a is a perfect substitute for s and if financed on a pay-as-you-go basis then a is a perfect substitute for B. Hence any change in a will be exactly compensated by either s or B. None of the other variables will be affected. Under uncertainty, there is no perfect substitute for a which, by assumption, is the only form of insurance available. Consequently, the maximum level of utility depends on a as well as initial resources. As a simplifying assumption, however, we shall continue to assume that the utility of bequests depends on B in the case of a funded, and on $B-a$ in the case of a pay-as-you-go system. This is equivalent to the assumption that each generation is concerned with the expected wealth, rather than the expected utility, of the next generation.** In other words, each generation disregards the risk aversion of subsequent generations.

When a is imposed at an arbitrary level, the definition of a steady state is considerably more complicated than when a is optimally chosen. When complete insurance is not feasible, bequests become random. A steady state can then be defined as a stable distribution of B. We shall not attempt to characterize this distribution. Instead, the analysis will be confined to impact effects for a given generation, starting from the optimum a^*. As in the previous section, we shall discuss in turn a funded system and a pay-as-you-go system.

The maximization problem which we discuss is identical to the one in the previous section except that a is predetermined.

Differentiating totally the FOC (6) and (8) with respect to a, we obtain

$$\frac{\mathrm{d}s^*}{\mathrm{d}a}=\frac{G}{\Delta'}\left\{-Gu''(c_0)E[v_{11}(c_1,\theta)+\theta^2h''(B)]-\frac{R^2}{\bar{\theta}}E[v_{11}(c_1,\theta)]E[\theta h''(B)]\right\}<0 \tag{27}$$

$$\frac{\mathrm{d}c_0^*}{\mathrm{d}a}=-\left(\frac{\mathrm{d}s^*}{\mathrm{d}a}+1\right)=-\frac{R^2}{\Delta'}\left\{\frac{GE[v_{11}(c_1,\theta)]}{\bar{\theta}}(\bar{\theta}E[h''(B)]-E[\bar{\theta}h''(B)])\right.$$
$$\left.+(E[h''(B)]E[\theta^2h''(B)]-E[\theta h''(B)]^2)\right\} \tag{28}$$

where

$$\Delta'=Gu''(c_0)(GE[v_{11}(c_1,\theta)+E[\theta^2h''(B)])+R^2GE[v_{11}(c_1,\theta)]E[h''(B)]$$
$$+R^2(E[h''(B)]E[\theta^2h''(B)]-E[\theta h''(B)]^2)>0. \tag{29}$$

The last term on the RHS of (28) and (29) is positive by Schwartz's inequality. It follows that $1+\mathrm{d}s^*/\mathrm{d}a>0$ if Cov $[h''(B),\theta]\geqslant 0$. We have already seen that at (a^*, s^*, c_1^*) B is non-random and thus $\mathrm{Cov}[h''(B),\theta]=0$, satisfying the above condition.

** Expected wealth is defined as the expected present discounted value of consumption, including expected bequests. By (27),

$$c_0^i+\frac{c_1^i}{R}+\frac{GE[B^i]}{R}=w+B^{i-1}.$$

In the case of a pay-as-you-go system, the definition includes *net* bequests, i.e. bequests minus the taxes paid by the next generation. By (1) and (3)

$$c_0^i+\frac{c_1^i}{R}+\frac{GE[B^i-a]}{R}=w+B^{i-1}-a.$$

Hence, if the level of social security happens to be equal to the optimal annuity holding level for the individual, then $1+\mathrm{d}s/\mathrm{d}a>0$. This result means that a forced increase in the level of social security will reduce private savings but increase total savings.

Under the additional assumption of non-increasing absolute risk aversion in the utility of bequests, which implies $h'''(B)\geqslant 0$, we can extend the previous result to levels of social security which exceed the optimum level, a^*. This can be shown as follows.

By concavity, $\partial V/\partial a \lesseqgtr 0$ as $a \lesseqgtr a^*$, when (6) and (8) are satisfied. Hence, by (6) and (7), $\mathrm{Cov}(h'(B),\theta)\lesseqgtr 0$ as $a\lesseqgtr a^*$. Consider the case $a\geqslant a^*$. Since $h'(B)$ is strictly monotone in θ it must be decreasing in θ in order to satisfy $\mathrm{Cov}(h'(B),\theta)\leqslant 0$. Therefore, B is increasing in θ and if $h'''(B)\geqslant 0$ then $\mathrm{Cov}(h''(B),\theta)\geqslant 0$. Hence, by (28), $1+\mathrm{d}s^*/\mathrm{d}a>0$ for $a\geqslant a^*$.††

The above result may be interpreted as follows. Consider an experiment in which a is increased and s decreases by an equal amount. Under certainty such a shift in asset composition does not change the consumption and bequest possibilities and thus this would be the optimal adjustment. However, under uncertainty such a change affects the probability distribution of bequests. If $a>a^*$ and thus $(Ra/\bar{\theta})-c_1^*>0$, then for a given level of c_1, the variance of bequests increases while the mean remains unchanged. The assumption that $h'''>0$ implies, in this case, that the expected marginal utility of bequests increases. This result is retained when c_1 adjusts so as to satisfy (8).‡‡

Another question of interest is the effect of social security on expected bequests. Using the FOC (6) and (8) we find that

$$\frac{\mathrm{d}E(B)}{\mathrm{d}a} = R\left(\frac{\mathrm{d}s^*}{\mathrm{d}a}+1\right) - \frac{\mathrm{d}c_1^*}{\mathrm{d}a}$$

$$= -\frac{1}{\Delta'}\left\{\frac{R^2GE[v_{11}]}{\bar{\theta}}\left(E[\theta h''(B)]-\bar{\theta}E[h''(B)]\right)\right.$$

$$\left. + \frac{Gu''(c_0^1)}{R}\left(E[\theta^2 h''(B)]-\bar{\theta}E[\theta h''(B)]\right)\right\}. \tag{30}$$

In general, the sign of (30) is indeterminate. However, at a^*, B— and hence $h''(B)$— is independent of θ, which implies that (30) is negative, $\mathrm{d}E(B)/\mathrm{d}a<0$. Notice that under certainty $\mathrm{d}E(B)/\mathrm{d}a=0$ for all a, which is in accordance with the observation made previously that the sum $s+a$ remains constant for changes in a.

Consider now the short-run impact of an increase in social security payments to generation i financed by an increased tax on generation (i+1). The only choice variable for generation i is c_1^i, since savings are predetermined. Differentiating (23) with respect to a yields

$$\frac{\mathrm{d}\hat{c}_1}{\mathrm{d}a} = \frac{1}{\bar{\theta}}\,\frac{E[\theta(\theta-\bar{\theta})h'']}{E[v_{11}]+(i/G)E[\theta^2 h'']}\,. \tag{31}$$

Evaluated at $\hat{a}$, $\mathrm{d}\hat{c}_1/\mathrm{d}a>0$, since h'' is constant. It follows that $1>\mathrm{d}E[B]/\mathrm{d}a>0$. In contrast to the case of certainty, the increase in bequests does not fully compensate for the increased taxes on the younger generation.

†† Notice that if $h'''(B)=0$, i.e. utility of bequests is quadratic, then $1+\mathrm{d}s^*/\mathrm{d}a>0$ for *all a*.

‡‡ When c_1 increases, the variance would still increase since $\mathrm{d}c_1/\mathrm{d}a<R/\bar{\theta}$, i.e. part of social security benefits is left for bequests. However, the mean bequest decreases, due to the reduction in savings. These two effects combine to increase the expected marginal utility of bequests. When $\mathrm{d}c_1/\mathrm{d}a<0$, both the mean and the variance of B increase. Our result indicates that the latter effect is dominant.

Consider now the effects of the increase in social security taxes on the working population. Starting at the steady-state values $(\hat{a},\hat{s})$, we differentiate equations (23)–(25) with respect to a. The change in first-period consumption is given by

$$\frac{d\hat{c}_0}{da} = -\left(\frac{d\hat{s}}{da}+1\right) = -\frac{Rh''}{\Delta' G}\left\{\left(1+\frac{R}{G}\right)h''V_\theta + RE[v_{11}]\right\} < 0 \tag{32}$$

where

$$\Delta' = \left(u'' + \frac{R^2h''}{G}\right)E[v_{11}] + \frac{u''h''E[\theta^2]}{G} + \frac{R^2h''^2}{G^2}V_\theta > 0$$

and $V_\theta = E[\theta^2] - \bar{\theta}^2$ is the variance of θ. Notice that c_0 would decrease even in the absence of uncertainty. This is because initially endowments are held fixed. In the long run, endowments will vary with bequests and, in the case of certainty, c_0 will remain invariant.

Aggregate consumption in any period is the sum of the older generation's total consumption, $\bar{\theta}c_1$, and the younger generation's total consumption, Gc_0. Thus, the change in aggregate consumption is, by (31) and (32),

$$\bar{\theta}\frac{dc_1}{da} + G\frac{dc_0}{da} = \left\{\Delta'\left(E[v_{11}] + \frac{h''E[\theta^2]}{G}\right)\right\}^{-1}\left\{h''V_\theta\left((u''-Rh'')\left(E[v_{11}] + \frac{h''E[\theta^2]}{G}\right) - \frac{R^2h''^2\bar{\theta}^2}{G^2}\right) - R^2E[v_{11}]h''\left(E[v_{11}] + \frac{h''E[\theta^2]}{G}\right)\right\} < 0. \tag{33}$$

As in a fully-funded system, the initial impact of an increase in social security is to increase aggregate savings.

ACKNOWLEDGEMENT

This research was partially supported by National Science Foundation Grant SOC-00587.

REFERENCES

Barro R. J. (1974) Are Government Bonds Net Wealth. *J. Political Economy* **82,** 1095–1117.

Barro R. J. (1976) Reply to Buchanan and Feldstein. *J. Political Economy* **84** 343–350.

Buchanan J. M. (1976) Barro on the Ricardian Equivalence Theorem. *J. Political Economy* **84,** 337–342.

Diamond P. A. (1965) National Debt in a Neoclassical Growth Model. *Am. Econom. Rev.* **60,** 1126–1150.

Feldstein M. S. (1974). Social Security, Induced Retirement and Aggregate Capital Accumulation. *J. Political Economy* **82,** 905–926.

Feldstein M. S. (1976) Perceived Wealth in Bond and Social Security: A Comment. *J. Political Economy* **84,** 331–336.

Samuelson P. A. (1958) An Exact Consumption Loan Model of Interest with or without the Social Contrivance of Money. *J. Political Economy* **66,** 467–482.

Samuelson P. A. (1975) Optimum Social Security in a Life-Cycle Growth Model. *Int. Econom. Rev.* **16,** 538–544.

Yaari M. E. (1965) Uncertain Lifetime, Life Insurance, and the Theory of the Consumer. *Rev. Economic Studies* **32,** 137–150.

DISCUSSION

by **A. G. Jackson,** *Department of Economics, University of Bristol*

Eytan Sheshinski and Yoram Weiss use the Samuelsonian overlapping-generations model to analyze different methods of social security funding. Their model contains all the usual ingredients. In the first period of the two-period lives everyone works and is paid the same amount of perishable good, which can be either consumed or exchanged for some claim on future consumption such as savings or annuities. During the second period of life labour productivity is nil, enforcing retirement and the redemption of financial claims for survival. The advance that Sheshinski and Weiss make is to have the age of death uncertain. However the distribution of age at death is known and fixed so that complete insurance is possible within the older generation.

Each individual has the same utility function with, as arguments, first and second period consumptions and the utility of one's descendants. Thus there is a bequest motive and Sheshinski and Weiss go further to make bequests indispensable in equation (5), which is the equivalent of the Inada condition in growth models. Although I do not doubt that some individuals have the financial capacity and desire to make bequests I think the usual statistics lead us to overestimate the importance of bequests for two reasons. Uncertainty and miscalculation of the length of life imply that savings are not drawn down to nothing under risk aversion, even if the parent does not want to leave anything to his children. Secondly, durability and quality are closely related characteristics of a good. A house that literally falls to pieces on the owner's death will be too ramshackle and unsafe to be usable or give utility for some time before its collapse. Passing on a house, a work of art or any durable good to one's children does not necessarily reflect familial altruism at all, but the nature of commodity technology; things that work well both give pleasure and last a long time.

Sheshinski and Weiss contrast two types of social security provision: fully-funded and pay-as-you-go. The former is equivalent to a life-contingent annuity and the latter requires some governmental intervention to enforce the intergenerational transfers.

The amazing result is that the two systems are equivalent in their real effects. 'Amazing' because both the financial instruments and the objective functions differ. Usually, different choice objects and maximands imply different solutions. A better way of understanding this result is to note that risk aversion implies that risk minimization maximizes utility, *ceteris paribus*. In this system risk can be removed completely. If savings are left untouched during the second period the bequest is certain, and the annuity pay-off is also a steady certain stream. Under a fully-funded scheme a certain result is possible and if the pay-as-you-go scheme were suddenly imposed then individuals would indulge in some home-made leverage, equation (26), to unwind the financial instruments. For this result to hold, the bequest motive is needed: if the tax burden on the young is too high then savings by the older generation are increased to give the desired net intergenerational transfer. But the objective functions are different also: in a fully-funded system people maximize their lifetime utility, but in a pay-as-you-go system the government maximizes the older generation's welfare. From the additive utility function (4), one's lifetime utility is the sum total of utility when young and old. So the two different objectives are nested. In equation (25), which seems to embody the need that the system is decentralizable, the missing first-order condition is re-inserted into the problem (cf. equation (6)). To put the crux more simply you cannot maximize lifetime utility without maximizing second-period utility conditional on the first period's utility.

The comparative statics results all seem reasonable and plausible, but the utility function is quite specific in its form and I hazard a guess that untypical comparative statics results can be fairly easily generated.

Some limitations to and extensions of the paper come readily to mind. Strictly the paper is about retirement uncertainty, because everyone lives through the work period. If people can die young, then this uncertainty within the working generation could be washed out with life insurance.

At first sight, the Sheshinski–Weiss paper seems like a further nail in the coffin of liberal macroeconomics, since if government bonds are not net wealth how can macro policy work? The more interesting macroeconomic question concerns behaviour off a steady-state equilibrium path, be it in disequilibrium or some cyclical equilibrium that is not *optima optimorum* because of information deficiencies. In a sense the comparative statics for a system with non-optimal social security apply to a disequilibrium which by construction is not optimal. In this case fiscal policy is non-neutral and in the right direction!

To return to the theme of this conference, Sheshinski and Weiss have presented a most elegant example in which private selfish decision-making provides the limit to intergenerational redistribution.

SUMMARY OF THE GENERAL DISCUSSION

Hammond raised the issue of whether a social security system could ever really be described as 'optimal'. The consensus of recent discussion seemed to be that the market could take care of uncertainty, and that therefore a social security system could only be *at best* as efficient as a market system. However, in practice we had neither perfect capital markets nor perfect initial distribution, while the problem of moral hazard arose both for public and private provision.

Gevers considered what might happen if there were two types of people in society, one with a low rate of time discount and the other with a high rate. Without intervention, capital would eventually be almost entirely held by the class with the low discount rate, and the characteristics of the steady state would be dominated by their preferences.

Zabalza expressed a view that bequests were in practice more a residual phenomenon than a planned one. Sheshinski agreed—in his model, although agents might plan a *desired* level of bequests, θ was still a random variable, and therefore an individual's *actual* bequest was also random.

Seade made the point that, when considering an infinite time-horizon, maintaining a fully-funded system was clearly less efficient than switching to a pay-as-you-go system, because once-and-for-all gains could be made by so doing. One had here an example of the infinite consumption–loan problem.

Cowell suggested that many intergenerational transfers did not actually occur through inheritance, but were made when both parties were still alive. Stern also felt that transfers from children to parents were not unimportant, although these were more usually made in kind than in cash.

SOCIAL SECURITY, LIFE-CYCLE SAVING AND RETIREMENT

A. Zabalza, C. A. Pissarides and D. Piachaud

Centre for Labour Economics, London School of Economics

INTRODUCTION

The social security system in Britain, as in most other countries, has transferred income along two dimensions. First, there has been a transfer from younger workers (men under 65 and women under 60) to older, mostly retired, individuals. The greater the reliance of the system on a pay-as-you-go method of financing, the greater normally is the extent of this transfer. Second, there has been a transfer from more highly-paid to less highly-paid persons, since contributions are earnings-related, whereas at least until recently benefits were largely independent of pre-retirement income and depended only to some limited extent on post-retirement income and wealth.† Up to the late 1970s the main objective of the system appeared to be the guarantee of a *minimum* income irrespective of income and wealth holding. In 1977, the year of this study, benefits were fixed at a level below the mean net earnings of workers approaching retirement age, so that if individuals did not wish to suffer a significant drop in their consumption after retirement they had to supplement their social security wealth with other savings of their own.

The extent of income transfer built into the social security system, and the degree to which the policy objectives of the system are achieved, clearly depend on the responses of individuals. Our main objective in this paper is to consider some of these responses, concentrating, in particular, on the labour supply response of people nearing retirement (what may be called the disincentive effect of social security). We also look into the portfolio substitutions induced.

We are not aware of any British work in this area. On the other hand, American work‡ has concentrated on the estimation of participation equations with social security entitlement as one of their independent variables. The estimated effect was assumed to be the sole effect of social security on retirement. In fact, there are two effects of social security that must be taken into account in attempting to estimate the labour supply response. First, social security alters the relative price of work and leisure; this has been the primary focus of the American work referred to above. Second, social security alters the composition of individual portfolios; in particular, if housing and consumer durables are excluded, social security is likely to be the most important asset in most people's portfolios, and so its existence is likely to have significant effects on saving patterns in other assets; since these other assets also influence the labour supply decision near retirement, social security influences the latter indirectly, via asset substitution.

† See below, section on the samples and definition of variable p. 87. New and substantial changes introduced in the late 1970s will eventually lead to a greater dependence of benefits on pre-retirement income.

‡ e.g. Boskin (1977) and Quinn (1977). For a recent survey see Clark et al. (1978).

As with the first (direct) effect, we are not aware of British work on asset substitutions induced by social security. Some relevant work in the US by Feldstein and his collaborators (Feldstein, 1974, 1976) has found that the introduction of social security in the US has led to substantial (possibly dollar for dollar) substitution between private savings and (forced) savings in social security. If Feldstein's claim is correct, then clearly the effect of social security on retirement is the difference between the positive effect estimated directly from participation equations and the negative effect that results from the crowding-out of other assets in the portfolio. Thus, conceivably, portfolio substitutions may work to offset completely the direct effect of social security on retirement.

Unfortunately our sample is not rich enough to enable us to estimate fully the portfolio substitutions induced by social security. For this reason our analysis of portfolio substitution will have to be very tentative; it is designed mainly to suggest the extent to which our direct estimates may have to be qualified. We are able to offer more rigorous estimates of these direct effects, which is the main purpose for which the data employed here were collected.

We first develop a simple model of retirement decisions. Next, we describe briefly the data and define the variables used in the subsequent analysis. We then present empirical estimates of participation equations with potential earnings, assets (including social security) and personal characteristics as independent variables. We find that, in general, pensions (both state and private) and other savings encourage earlier retirement, whereas potential earning capacity encourages continued participation. The estimated effects of asset holdings (retirement pensions and other savings) on the probability of participation are not significantly different from each other, so clearly the net effect of social security on participation depends on the extent of asset substitution following the introduction of social security. We are unable to find any evidence in favour of substitution of social security for private savings, although much more detailed information on people's wealth holding is needed before we can be more definite about the extent of asset substitution.

Finally we present our conclusions. Overall we find that the evidence favours the view that, in Britain, social security has acted as an important disincentive for continuing work after reaching the statutory retirement age.

RETIREMENT DECISIONS

We begin by considering the effects of social security on the individual's decision within a static model, where the individual is free to choose any point on a given budget line. Dynamic problems which introduce endogeneities into the budget constraint, and market-imperfection problems which restrict the individual's choice along the given budget lines, are considered later.

Within the static model, the social security system can be characterized simply as an income-guarantee and an earnings rule. The system guarantees a minimum income for most individuals above a certain age (65 for men and 60 for women) equal to the state retirement pension (*RP*). The receipt of this pension is not conditional on full retirement but, for men aged 65–70 and women aged 60–65, earnings exceeding a certain minimum are subject to a tax which is set against pension entitlement. At the time that our data were collected, earnings up to £35 per week were exempt, the next £4 were taxed at 50% and any further earnings taxed at 100% until the full pension entitlement was exhausted. The earnings rule did not apply to unearned income. Unearned income for the age groups that we are considering consists mainly of an occupational pension (*OP*) and income from assets (*AI*).

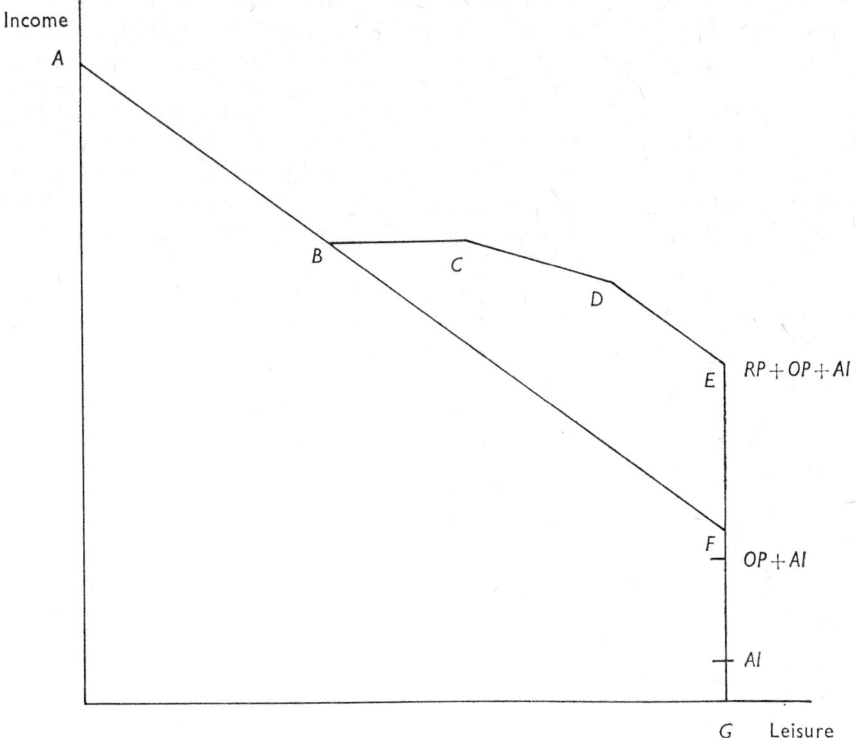

Figure 1. The effect of the earnings rule on the budget constraint.

The effect of the earnings rule on the individual's budget constraint is shown in figure 1. Ignoring income taxes and social security contributions, the introduction of a state pension subject to an earnings rule changes the budget constraint from *ABFG* to *ABCDEFG*. If the individual maximizes a utility function representable by income–leisure indifference curves that are convex to the origin then the chosen point may lie on one of the three branches (*AB*, *CD* or *DE*) or at any of the four corners (*A*, *C*, *D* or *E*), but it will not lie along *BC* where there is an implicit tax rate of 100%.

Individuals in the age ranges subject to the earnings rule have the option of deferring their pension for a higher pension when they do retire. At the time of our sample the increase in the pension achieved by deferring for a year was 6·5% of the pension. The effect of current deferments is to shift the branch *AB* of the budget constraint up, parallel to itself, by an amount equal to the present value of the increments for that week's deferment that will be gained from whenever the pension is claimed until death; on average this amounts to 25% of the retirement pension. By contrast, the effect of past deferments that have already been credited to the individual is to shift up the 'bulge' *BCDE*. Thus unlike the earnings rule, which acts as a disincentive to work after the statutory retirement age, the possibility of deferment acts both as an incentive to work because it raises net earnings and as a disincentive because deferment raises potential retirement income.

A person will retire (work zero hours) if his utility at point *E* is greater than his utility at any other point on the budget constraint. For a given utility function, whether this is the case or not will depend on his net income at zero hours, on his net marginal wage if he decides to work, and on a variety of other personal characteristics affecting the marginal utility of leisure. In this paper we attempt a quantification of the effects of social security and other variables on the decision to retire by estimating conventional participation (retirement) equations. This approach admits only two states for each individual: zero hours of work, or point E, and the point that the individual is most likely to choose if he elects to participate. For each individual in our sample we calculated net weekly income if he were to participate and the same if he were to retire. Both of these calculations involve estimating potential earnings and retirement incomes, and then netting them according to the rates of income tax and earnings rule in force at the time of the sample. The methods used are described below.

It is well-known that conventional participation equations cannot cope with adjustments in hours of work. We avoided estimating hours equations at this stage because the several corners introduced into budget constraints by the earnings rule and income taxes render unsatisfactory any estimation method other than a full maximum-likelihood method with fully specified budget constraints and utility functions.§ As expected, given the institutional constraints on hours, most studies of labour supply of groups with a significant proportion of non-participants (e.g. married women), find that the main supply response to changes in economic variables comes from the choice of whether or not to participate, rather than from adjustments in hours worked.|| Thus little is lost by restricting our analysis to the participation decision, while the awkward problems posed by non-linear budget constraints and endogenous marginal wages are largely avoided.

A linear specification of the participation equation would be

$$P=\alpha_0+\alpha_1 Y+\alpha_2 X+\text{ other variables }+\varepsilon \tag{1}$$

where P is the probability of participation, Y is net weekly earnings, X is net income at zero hours of work, ε is an error term and α_1 and α_2 are estimated parameters. In order to avoid endogeneity problems introduced by variations in hours we standardized Y for hours, by assuming that if individuals decide to participate they will all work the same number of hours, H.

The variable Y was then defined as H multiplied by a gross wage rate (observed or predicted for each individual), net of income taxes and the earnings rule. Y is the only variable influenced by the earnings rule; the other element of the social security system, RP, is included in X. For generality we do not restrict the coefficient α_2 to be the same for all sources of unearned income; its various components are included separately in the regression.

It is interesting to notice that taxes (including the earnings rule) that influence the budget constraint at points other than point E, will have an influence on participation only if the individual is not able to choose his desired hours of work. In a neoclassical framework, where the individual may select any point on the budget constraint, the only information that is needed to decide whether the person will participate or not is the height of point E and the slope of the budget constraint at that point. If point E lies on a higher indifference curve than points along DE, it must lie on a higher indifference curve than any other point on the budget constraint. Since we believe that workers are constrained in their choice of hours, we restricted work possibilities to

§ We hope to report estimates obtained from maximum-likelihood estimation in a future paper. Since the methods at present available are still somewhat tentative, we believe that estimates obtained from conventional participation equations are of considerable interest in their own right.

|| For a study based on UK data, see Layard, Frederking and Zabalza (forthcoming).

'full-time' (40 hours per week for men and 35 hours for women); in this context the earnings rule and other taxes may discourage participation.¶

In addition, some individuals may be restricted in their choice of occupation by mandatory retirement from their main lifetime job, (or, in general, by involuntary loss of that job). Fortunately, we have information on the reasons for giving up the main lifetime job, so we are able to test whether involuntary loss of job has any effect on retirement behaviour.

Finally, the model summarized in figure 1 should be qualified for the portfolio adjustments that the individual is likely to make when he anticipates the state pension early in his lifetime. Thus, whereas figure 1 is applicable to an elderly individual who is unexpectedly offered a windfall state pension, if the pension is anticipated the accumulation of private savings and private pension rights is likely to be affected adversely. The implication is that the introduction of the state pension does not simply add the 'bulge' to the budget constraint shown in figure 1, but it also shifts the whole constraint down, (at least for those intending to benefit from the state scheme). However, since the shift is parallel to itself no econometric problems are introduced by this adjustment—this qualification should simply be borne in mind in the interpretation of the results. (We look at the portfolio substitutions induced by private and state pensions later in the paper.)

THE SAMPLE AND DEFINITION OF VARIABLES

The Retirement Survey was based on a sample of men aged 55–72 and women aged 50–72 interviewed by the Office of Population Census and Surveys in February and March 1977; it was commissioned jointly by the Departments of Employment and of Health and Social Security. This sample used various sampling fractions to ensure adequate representation of certain groups. Overall there were almost equal numbers of men and women, distributed fairly evenly over the two age ranges; 41·2% of men and 51·2% of women were above pensionable age (65 for men and 60 for women).

The work status of respondents exhibited some clear (and rather surprising) patterns that suggested some of the selection procedures used in our regression analysis. Among men under 60, 95% were working full-time (over 30 hours per week, with a mean of 40 hours), 1% were working part-time, and the remaining 4% were retired.** In the age group 60–64 the proportions changed to 79%, 3% and 18% respectively. But when social security and most other (occupational) pensions became available at age 65 the proportions changed dramatically to 9% full-time, 16% part-time and 75% retired within the 65–69 age group. Thus it is clear that there is a sharp break at age 65 in the behaviour of men, so that a common sample that includes both under-65s and over-65s is unlikely to provide very useful information about the effects of small changes in pensions, earnings, etc. In this paper we concentrate on the analysis of the male sample over 65 years of age, since our main interest is in the disincentive effects of social security which do not operate in the younger sample.

The behaviour of women is rather different. Equal proportions of working women under pensionable age work full-time and part-time, but as with men more women work part-time over pensionable age. There is also a clear break in the participation of women at age 60, with the proportion retired rising from 21% in the age group

¶ A more general specification would take into consideration three states, full-time work, part-time work, and retirement. We intend to look at this three-way choice in a future paper, using the maximum-likelihood estimation method.

** We have excluded a small proportion that described themselves as 'unemployed and looking for a job.'

55–59 to 62% in the age group 60–64. For the reasons already discussed we shall concentrate our analysis on the sample over pensionable age.

The remainder of this section describes the variables used in the regressions, and gives some more information about the two samples used.

Dependent variable

The equation estimates the probability that a person will not retire. We thus define our dependent variable as a 0/1 dummy with value 1 for those that participate and 0 for those who are retired. We defined retirement as zero hours of work. Overall, our samples consisted of 639 men and 525 women, with the dependent variable (proportion *not* retired) taking a mean value of 0·19 for men and 0·23 for women.

Independent variables

State retirement pension

As discussed above, we want to measure the potential level of this variable should the person decide to retire. If the individual is entitled to a retirement pension, the value of the benefit should enter irrespective of whether he is actually receiving it or not. Otherwise, if we measured RP by actual pension benefits we would be introducing a serious endogeneity bias, because full-time participants would tend to be associated with $RP=0$, retired people with $RP>0$. We therefore assigned the full pension benefit to all individuals in our sample (£15·30 for single persons and married women and £24·50 for married men). In addition, we increased the pension entitlement of retired men who had deferred claiming their pension and of working men aged 65–69 who are *not* claiming the pension, and are therefore deferring (about 75% of full-time workers);†† for every year of deferment we increased the pension by 6·5%, representing the return to deferment at the time of our sample.

There are a number of other smaller payments made by the Social Security system to families in need (e.g., some allowable expenses, rent and rate rebates, etc). The only information provided in the survey was which individuals had no unearned income other than a retirement pension and so were entitled to the receipt of some kind of supplementary benefit. We took this into account by introducing a 0/1 dummy, taking the value 1 if the person was in that category.

Occupational pension

To measure potential occupational pensions we followed similar criteria to those applied to the retirement pension. Those who were receiving a pension are assigned its actual value. For those not receiving one, but who declared that they *would* receive one in the future, we estimated their *potential* occupational pension and assumed they could receive it at age 65 (60 for women). This was done by means of an equation, run on actual receivers, in which the value of the occupational pension was determined by earnings in the main job, socio-economic group to which their main occupation belonged, current age, and number of past employers. Finally, to those not receiving an occupational pension, and who declared that they are not entitled to one, we assigned the value $OP=0$. About 50% of men and 15% of women were receiving (or due to receive) occupational pensions.‡‡

†† For women we did not make any adjustment, since we could not determine from the data whether, and for how long, they have been deferring.

‡‡ See appendix table A1 for the equation predicting occupational pensions, and appendix table A3 for the mean values and standard deviations of all the variables used in the regressions. It was necessary to estimate a *potential* pension for those not receiving it, because although the Survey asked about entitlement. it did not ask about the amount expected for those not receiving a pension at the time of the Survey. We had to predict pensions for only 2% of men over 65 entitled to one, and 9% of women over 60 with entitlement.

Asset income

This variable was defined as income from savings; it is not very reliable since it had to be calculated by applying a gross interest rate at the mid points of four very wide ranges of declared savings.§§ The chosen gross interest rate was 10% per annum. This, together with the under-reporting associated with this type of variable, makes the results on this variable somewhat tentative.

The above three variables were netted by using (where applicable) the standard tax rate on income, adjusted by the corresponding tax allowance. At the time of our sample, the tax allowance for those aged 65 and over was £29·90 per week for married people and £19·42 per week for single, and the standard tax rate was 35%.

House ownership

Where the individual owns his own home, it is common to add to the asset-income variable an owner-occupier's imputed rent. In most cases, given the absence of data on the valuation of houses, imputed rent is effectively a 0/1 dummy for house ownership. However, given the different nature of income from financial assets and imputed income from housing, it is likely that their effect on retirement is different. We therefore took into account the effects of house ownership by adding a 0/1 dummy for house ownership to the above unearned income variables.

Earnings

This variable cannot be observed for non-participants, nor is it possible to have a clear idea of the hours that a retired person would work should he decide to participate. This means that for non-participants it is impossible to obtain their potential net earnings precisely. We dealt with this problem by first calculating for each individual his gross wage rate should he decide to participate, and then multiplying this by 40 (35 for women) to find the gross weekly earnings from full-time work.|||| The gross figure was then netted according to the income tax allowances and tax rate given above, and also according to whether the person would find it worthwhile to defer his pension or be subject to the earnings rule.¶¶ We assumed that individuals would defer if their potential earnings plus the gains from deferment exceeded their potential earnings net of the earnings rule plus the state pension. In terms of figure 1 this implies that only people to the left of point C will defer, but some closer to C than B may not defer. The earnings rule in force at the time of our sample was described on p. 84.

Where gross wage rates were available we used the actual figures reported by the individual; if these were not available (because the individual did not currently have a job) we predicted them by means of a wage equation run on the participants of our sample.*** The wage equation is of the form.

$$\ln w = \beta_0 + \beta_1 S + u$$

where w is the gross wage rate, u an error term, and S is a vector of characteristics affecting productivity, including education, age, (age)^2, socioeconomic group of (last) occupation and health. (See appendix table A2.) The independent variable used in the participation equation was net weekly earnings obtained from this wage equation.

§§ The ranges were 0–300, 300–1500, 1500–2500 and over 2500, all in £. We used mid-points where possible, and £3500 for the last group. In addition some people declared zero savings.

|||| Boskin (1977) also used net earnings for reasons similar to ours, but Quinn (1977) used gross wage rates.

¶¶ Notice that the earnings rule operates on pre-tax earnings, so we first net earnings according to the rule and subsequently according to income tax.

*** Participants over pensionable age were over-sampled, so we have a sufficient number of observations for the wage predictions. In the participation equations, this over-sampling was corrected by using weights that brought the sample fractions to the average for the population.

If predicted earnings were found to be high enough to make deferment of the pension optimal, we added to net earnings an untaxed amount for the returns to deferment. For every week of deferment individuals receive an extra 0·125% of pension for ever after retirement. Thus the benefit from deferment will depend on the expected lifetime of deferrers, on the rate at which they discount future income and on the time that they are expected to retire. In calculating this return we used 77 years for the life expectancy, 10% for the discount rate, and 2·5 years for the average deferment period.

Health

The effects of health on retirement (in contrast to those of economic variables) are controversial. In general, studies based on survey tables compiled from questionnaires find that poor health is the most important factor leading to early retirement, but more objectively based regression analyses do not always confirm these conclusions. Thus, Steiner and Dorfman (1959) attributed early retirement to poor health, while Boskin (1977) found that health effects were altogether insignificant. Recently, Quinn (1977), using regression analysis, found that both health and economic factors are significant determinants of retirement, but that health has a larger quantitative effect (i.e. it explains a larger fraction of early retirements). We believe that these conflicting results may be largely due to the manner in which this variable has been defined. Those studies which have found health an insignificant contributor to retirement have used 'objective' measures of the individual's health, while those which have found significant effects have tended to use 'subjective' measures of this variable. We are able to confirm this claim since we have both objective and subjective measures of health at our disposal. In the equations below we report only estimates obtained with the subjective measure—'would you say in general your health is good, fair, or poor?'—which is entered as a 0/1 dummy, 0 for 'good 'or 'fair' and 1 for 'poor'. This health variable is the only one that gave significant estimates. The 'objective' alternative—number of weeks in bed during the past year—was always insignificant.

'*Working status of spouse*' *and* '*living with spouse*'

If the leisure of husband and wife are complementary goods, we would expect retired people to be associated with non-working spouses. However, since this variable may also proxy the earning capacity of the spouse, there is also a financial effect working in the opposite direction. Thus, we cannot be certain as to its net effect *a priori*. (The variables used in the regressions below were two 0/1 dummies, with 1 standing for 'married and living with spouse' in the first variable, and for 'spouse working' in the second.)

Age

It is to be expected that the older the person, the higher is his probability of retirement. In itself, however, this variable could just reflect the effect of health or of accumulated assets on retirement. On the other hand, when included in conjunction with health and economic variables, it is more likely to reflect institutional or social factors which make older people more likely to retire.

Involuntary loss of main job

Respondents were treated as having left their main job involuntarily if they gave as the reason for leaving one of the following: 'Was made redundant', 'Had to retire', 'Fired or sacked from job', 'Business was sold/went bankrupt', 'Temporary/casual/

part-time work ended'. The variable used in the regressions was a 0/1 dummy, taking value 1 in all the above cases and 0 otherwise.

From the theoretical discussion above, it is clear that the two economic variables that determine the participation decision are net earnings and net income at zero hours of work. However, aggregating all unearned incomes into a single income variable may not capture the different nature of the components of income at zero hours. It is clear that there are substantial differences, from a life-cycle perspective, between income from assets on the one hand, and income from state or occupational pensions on the other. It is therefore to be expected that their effect on retirement will also be different. Boskin (1977) finds that the effect of pensions is much greater than that of income from assets. As he points out, this is reasonable because pensions are guaranteed for life (and possibly indexed) and because, to the extent that bequests are planned, personal wealth can be transferred whereas pensions cannot. We will take account of these differences by entering the components of unearned income separately, and by testing statistically the differences in their estimated coefficients. Since the only significant variation in the state pension across individuals is related to marital status, the state pension cannot be entered separately, so it is always added to occupational pension to form a common total pension variable.

EMPIRICAL RESULTS FOR PARTICIPATION EQUATIONS

Table 1 presents the results of regressing the participation equation for men and women over the statutory retirement age (*see overleaf*).

Economic variables

Our set of data corroborates the hypothesis that state and occupational pensions affect the decision to retire. This variable takes the expected sign for both men and women and it is statistically significant for men. Income from savings also has the expected negative sign, but is not statistically significant at the 10% level. The other asset-ownership variable, house ownership, is also insignificant. However, the data suggest that a better specification of the participation equation would constrain the coefficients of pensions and income from savings to equality. This is done in columns (2) and (4), and in both cases the increase in the residual sum of squares resulting from the restriction is not significant. These results are in contrast to Boskin's (1977) findings, which show a coefficient on social security benefits seven times as large as the coefficient on income from savings. Our estimates would imply that if the individual responded to the state pension by reducing his private savings on a £-for-£ basis, then social security would not influence the retirement decision significantly. However, whether this substitution takes place or not for our set of data is an unsettled issue. (But see p. 93 for a more detailed analysis of this question.) In general the imposition of this restriction does not alter the other coefficient estimates. As expected, people entitled to supplementary benefit, be they men or women, are more likely to be retired than people of the same characteristics but without this entitlement.

Net earnings are also significant (although for women only at the 10% level) and with the expected positive sign. The higher are earnings, net of taxes and reductions under the earnings rule, the lower is the probability that a person will retire. Comparing the coefficients on unearned income and net earnings in columns (2) and (4), we find that while the effect of unearned income is greater for men than for women, that of net earnings is greater for the latter. In the case of men, the effect of net earnings on retirement is less than the effect of unearned income, while for women

Table 1. Participation equations
Dependent variable: probability of participation. Samples: men 65 and over, women 60 and over

Independent variables	Men		Women	
	(1)	(2)	(3)	(4)
Economic:				
state and occupational pensions (£ pw)	−0·0068		−0·0029	
	(0·0020)		(0·0035)	
income from savings (£ pw)	−0·012		−0·0058	
	(0·008)		(0·0091)	
total unearned income (£ pw)		−0·0071		−0·0032
		(0·0019)		(0·0033)
house ownership (0, 1)	0·017	0·013	−0·055	−0·057
	(0·033)	(0·032)	(0·039)	(0·037)
supplementary benefit (0, 1)	−0·11	−0·095	−0·13	−0·12
	(0·04)	(0·036)	(0·05)	(0·04)
net earnings (£ pw)	0·0014	0·0014	0·0038	0·0039
	(0·0007)	(0·0007)	(0·0023)	(0·0023)
involuntary loss of main job (0, 1)	−0·15	−0·14	−0·16	−0·16
	(0·03)	(0·03)	(0·04)	(0·04)
Personal:				
age (years)	−0·0072	−0·0070	−0·027	−0·027
	(0·0063)	(0·0063)	(0·005)	(0·005)
health (0,1)	−0·18	−0·18	−0·27	−0·27
	(0·05)	(0·05)	(0·07)	(0·07)
marital status (0, 1)	0·073	0·076	−0·076	−0·080
	(0·042)	(0·042)	(0·050)	(0·048)
spouse working (0, 1)	0·25	0·25	0·11	0·11
	(0·05)	(0·05)	(0·05)	(0·05)
Constant	1·02	1·00	1·94	1·92
	(0·44)	(0·44)	(0·36)	(0·35)
$\bar{R}^2$	0·11	0·11	0·15	0·15
N	639	639	525	525

Note: Figures in brackets are standard errors.

the two effects are very similar (but the effect of unearned income is not statistically significant). Our results imply that the indexation of pensions to average earnings during inflations, assuming earnings rise faster than prices, should bias the decision of elderly men in favour of retirement, but should have no significant effect on the retirement of women.

Finally, having lost the main lifetime job involuntarily is a strong inducement to retire from the labour force altogether. This may be due to loss of potential earnings capacity accumulated at the main job, or simply to the fact that the job choices open to these individuals are restricted.

Non-economic variables

Health and age have figured prominently as determinants of retirement in previous studies. In our case health is quite a significant determinant of retirement for both men and women (quantitatively more important for the latter), whereas age is significant for women but not for men. Our results are in agreement with Quinn's (1977) who also used a subjective measure of health, but not with Boskin's (1977) who used an objective measure (our objective variable also gave insignificant results as discussed above).

However, to measure the overall effect of these two variables, we should also take into account the indirect influence they may have on retirement through earnings, since they are included among the personal characteristics used to predict wage rates. As can be seen from the wage equation for men (*see* appendix table A2), both health and age are significant. Therefore it is quite correct to conclude that, at least for our sample, poor health and old age contribute significantly to the retirement of men. Similarly, despite the fact that these variables do not contribute significantly to the explanation of women's earnings, they both influence their participation decisions directly.

Marital status influences the participation decisions of both men and women. Men living with their wives are more likely to participate, perhaps indicating their higher financial responsibility. Among married men, those whose wives are working tend to participate more than those whose wives are at home, indicating that husband's and wife's leisure are complementary. On the other hand, married women who live with their husband are less likely to participate, but if their husband is working they tend to participate more, indicating, again, the complementarity of leisure.

LIFE-CYCLE SAVINGS

It is clear from the above that both social security and other life-cycle savings have significant effects on the decision to retire. Since social security contributions are compulsory, whereas most other forms of saving, in particular non-contractual saving, can be adjusted independently by individuals, variations in social security benefits may be offset in individuals' portfolios through variations in other savings. Thus, in calculating the *net* effect of social security on retirement, we must look into the portfolio substitutions induced by social security.

It cannot be overemphasized that our sample is inadequate for a satisfactory analysis of portfolio substitutions. We have just four ranges of 'other savings', which includes all wealth held other than social security, occupational pensions, and housing. We have information on occupational pensions actually received by retired people, but only on entitlement for people before retirement, so we are forced to predict the level of the latter by using the former sub-sample (*see* appendix table A1). Finally we have information on house ownership, but not on the value of the house, so we are forced to use a house-ownership dummy, for wealth in housing.

Despite these difficulties we attempted to obtain some information on portfolio substitutions, by carrying out two types of analysis. First, we computed post-retirement income for men aged 65–70 by source, and obtained the ratio of this to predicted net earnings at age 65. This type of analysis provides information on the relative significance of social security in people's portfolios and also on income maintenance after retirement. Second, we estimated regressions of the general form estimated by Feldstein and others (1974, 1978) for the United States, where voluntary savings (what Feldstein calls 'fungible' wealth) are regressed on earned income, pensions, including social security, and other individual characteristics.

The *simple* life-cycle model predicts that consumption after retirement should not be very different from consumption before retirement. Our computations with respect to post-retirement portfolios and income maintenance indicate that on average income from all pensions and savings is about 65% of net labour earnings at age 65, whereas *actual* income received after age 65 (i.e. including any labour earnings from continued work) raise this to 73%.††† On portfolio composition, we found that social security is a very important asset indeed, accounting on average for about 75% of post-

††† In appendix table A4 we report more fully income-maintenance ratios for our sample.

retirement income. Occupational pensions, which also have an element of compulsion, account for 20%, and the remaining 5% is accounted for by other savings, which is the only asset in portfolios that can be varied freely and independently by individuals. These findings are clearly unfavourable to the simple life-cycle view of savings (e.g. as put forward by Ando and Modigliani, 1963), being closer to Diamond's (1977) findings for the United States. However, rather than rejecting the life-cycle model altogether, what this indicates is that the proper model for the analysis of social security may not be the simple life-cycle model, but extended versions that include important real-world elements like uncertainties and capital-market imperfections, and, of course, explicit pensions and social security provisions.

Our regression results with respect to portfolio substitutions resulting from social security and other pensions are also unfavourable to the simple life-cycle view, as expressed for instance by Feldstein and Pellechio (1978). Following the latter we write the ratio of post-retirement to pre-retirement income as

$$\frac{AI+OP+RP}{Y} = \alpha_0+\alpha_1 \frac{OP+RP}{Y} + \alpha_2 Y+\alpha_3 Z \tag{2}$$

where AI is asset income, OP occupational pension, RP social security pension, Y earnings and Z a vector of personal characteristics. Feldstein and Pellechio take the ratio of *wealth* to income, but our approach is equivalent (and less prone to error and biasses introduced from using inappropriate rates of discount and survival probabilities) provided individuals consume, on average, the income from their savings without running down the stock.‡‡‡

Since $OP+RP$ may induce earlier retirement Feldstein and Pellechio introduce a term $(OP+RP)/Y$ in equation (2), where α_1 should be positive but less than one.§§§ Then they arrive at an estimated equation of the form

$$AI=\beta_0+\beta_1(OP+RP)+\beta_3 Y+\beta_4 Y^2+\beta_5 YZ+u \tag{3}$$

where β_0 should be close to zero and β_1 close to -1 if the simple life-cycle model is confirmed, and between 0 and -1 if the introduction of state and occupational pensions leads to earlier retirement or increased bequests. For the United States they find that the coefficient estimated for social security (i.e. our RP, excluding OP) is indeed negative, less than one in absolute value, but closer to unity than zero.

Our findings are probably less reliable than theirs, but they are so different that it is doubtful whether even better data based on our interviewees can confirm the American findings. In all the tests that we tried, β_1 is positive and significantly different from zero. In table 2 we report estimates for β_1 for men of two age groups, 55–64 and 65–69 years of age, with independent variables the constrained $OP+RP$ and the unconstrained OP and RP. The other independent variables include predicted net earnings, which is a proxy for 'permanent' income, the same variable squared, and the same variable interactive with each of the personal characteristic variables used in the participation equations. The full equations for the constrained case are reported in appendix table A5.

It is clear that the coefficient estimates obtained on the pension variables do not make sense within the simple life-cycle model used by Feldstein and his collaborators. If anything, our regressions show that, even when we control for income and personal characteristics, people with higher pensions are also likely to have higher savings.

‡‡‡ We tested for the latter by including age as one of the independent variables in the regressions reported below, but there was no evidence of decreasing stocks with age (or indeed any dependence of the stock of 'other savings' held on age).

§§§ If the introduction of pensions leads to increased bequests, as Barro (1974) claims, then α_1 should also pick up this effect and be significantly positive.

Table 2. Saving substitutions induced by pensions

	Coefficient estimates, β_1, with standard errors	
	Age 55–64	Age 65–69
OP+RP	0·013	0·019
	(0·002)	(0·006)
OP	0·013	0·019
	(0·002)	(0·006)
RP	0·164	0·018
	(0·064)	(0·105)

We do not, however, wish to interpret this as a 'recognition effect' along the lines of Cagan (1965) and Katona (1965). Rather, we would emphasize again, that conclusions about the effects of social security on life-cycle allocation should not be drawn from the simple model but from an extended version that takes into account social security and other imperfections.

CONCLUSIONS

The results presented in the section on empirical participation equations suggest that both economic variables and health and other non-economic variables have important effects on retirement. As expected, the larger is the level of potential income at retirement (i.e. state retirement and occupational pensions, and income from savings) the more likely is the person to retire; conversely, the larger is the level of net potential earnings from work, the more likely is the person to participate. Men appear to be more influenced by their unearned income, whereas women are influenced more by their potential earnings.

Our overall results indicate that in Britain the Social Security system has a significant influence on retirement decisions. On the one hand, by providing a pension it has encouraged people to retire earlier than they would otherwise; this is the effect measured by our 'unearned income' variable. On the other hand, the presence of the earnings rule has reduced potential net earnings from work, and so has acted as a disincentive for continuing work after the statutory retirement age.

Concerning the first effect of the Social Security system, our results show that the influence of state pensions on retirement is not significantly different from that of other types of unearned income. Thus, the net effect of social security on retirement depends on the degree of asset substitution. We attempted to estimate these substitutions, despite the paucity of our data in this respect; we found no evidence of asset substitutions, indicating that the existence of social security has a significant influence on retirement.

Concerning the disincentive effects of the earnings rule, we found that variations in the rule influence participation via their effect on net earnings. In this paper we concentrated on two states, full-time work and retirement, so we are not able to offer a precise quantitative measure of the disincentive effects of the earnings rule. Such a measure should also take into account the possibility of changing from full-time to part-time work when the rule affects the individual, given that part-time earnings will not normally be subject to the earnings rule. We intend to study this three-way choice in a future paper. However, in this paper we found that the effect of net earnings on retirement, although statistically significant, is quantitatively very small, so we would not expect a change in the earnings rule to have a very important effect on labour supply.

APPENDIX

*Table A*1. Occupational pension equations.
Dependent variable: amount of occupational pension (£ per week)
Sample: those receiving any occupational pension

	Men	Women
Constant	6·07	0·15
	(4·45)	(5·30)
Gross weekly earnings in main occupation	0·21	0·23
	(0·02)	(0·04)
Whether over pension age (dummy)	−4·7	2·0
	(1·5)	(2·1)
Number of different employers in life	−0·69	−0·81
	(0·38)	(0·46)
Socio-economic group (main job):		
professional and managerial	16·7	6·2
	(3·8)	(3·5)
other non-manual	12·1	4·2
	(3·7)	(3·1)
skilled	4·7	
	(3·7)	
semi-skilled manual	5·4	−4·2
	(3·9)	(3·4)
other	3·3	
	(23·6)	
$\bar{R}^2$	0·56	0·40
N	271	106

Note: Figures in brackets are standard errors.

*Table A*2. Wage equations.
Dependent variable: log gross hourly wage.
Samples: working men 65 and over and working women 60 and over

	Men	Women
Age	−1·69	0·039
	(0·72)	(0·256)
(Age)^2	0·012	−0·0006
	(0·005)	(0·0020)
Health	−0·16	−0·044
	(0·06)	(0·058)
Education completion age	0·10	0·12
	(0·03)	(0·02)
Time in job	0·065	0·054
	(0·016)	(0·015)
Socio-economic group (last job):		
professional and managerial	0·39	0·41
	(0·10)	(0·11)
other non-manual	0·045	0·061
	(0·071)	(0·060)
skilled manual	−0·029	−0·091
	(0·085)	(0·091)
semi-skilled manual	−0·12	−0·099
	(0·08)	(0·059)
other	0·053	−1·23
	(0·480)	(0·41)
Constant	58·71	−0·66
	(24·68)	(8·32)
$\bar{R}^2$	0·23	0·30
N	379	356

Note: Figures in brackets are standard errors.

Table A3. Means and standard deviations of variables in the participation equation

	Men	Women
Participation (0, 1) (dependent variable)	0·19 (0·39)	0·23 (0·42)
State and occupational pension (£ pw)	27·66 (8·82)	12·23 (7·96)
Income from savings (£ pw)	2·45 (2·52)	2·08 (2·48)
House ownership (0, 1)	0·45 (0·50)	0·46 (0·50)
Supplementary benefit (0, 1)	0·38 (0·48)	0·35 (0·48)
Net earnings (£ pw)	25·43 (22·35)	21·35 (9·22)
Involuntary loss of main job (0, 1)	0·38 (0·49)	0·19 (0·39)
Age	68·35 (2·40)	65·68 (3·77)
Health (0,1)	0·09 (0·28)	0·08 (0·26)
Marital status (0, 1)	0·79 (0·41)	0·54 (0·50)
Spouse working (0, 1)	0·10 (0·30)	0·23 (0·42)
N	639	525

Table A4. Income maintenance after retirement
Sample: men aged 65–69

Range	Cumulative frequency, %	
	(1)	(2)
0–0·3	0·5	5·9
0·3–0·4	5·3	9·9
0·4–0·5	20·7	20·2
0·5–0·6	40·1	35·5
0·6–0·7	62·4	53·7
0·7–0·8	81·7	68·6
0·8–0·9	90·8	78·1
0·9–1·0	95·7	85·3
1·0–1·1	97·4	89·7
1·1–1·2	98·3	92·7
1·2–1·3	99·1	95·4
1·3–1·4	99·6	97·7
1·4+	100·0	100·0
Mean	0·659	0·732
Standard deviation	0·192	0·453
N	414	421

Notes: Column (1): ratio of potential income at zero hours of work to net earnings at 65

Column (2): ratio of actual (reported) income after age 65 to net earnings at age 65

Table A5. Savings equations: men
Dependent variable: stock of savings held

Independent variables	Age 55–64	Age 65–69
State and private pensions	11·28	15·63
	(1·89)	(5·34)
Net earnings	−53·14	−90·55
	(36·37)	(76·69)
Net earnings squared	0·46	1·11
	(0·35)	(0·58)
Net earnings multiplied by:		
health	−0·59	−0·39
	(0·39)	(0·29)
spouse working	6·16	−0·77
	(2·23)	(3·79)
house ownership	10·05	15·31
	(2·32)	(2·76)
marital status	10·57	6·29
	(3·43)	(3·74)
age	0·68	0·30
	(0·40)	(0·87)
Constant	−143·08	1087·69
	(636·49)	(1337·47)
$\bar{R}^2$	0·29	0·30
N	776	408

Notes: Figures in brackets are standard errors.
The dependent variable used was the *stock* of savings, so to convert this to an income-from-savings variable all coefficients should be multiplied by the weekly rate of return on savings. The figure we used in our earlier work, and in reporting the coefficients in table 2, was 0·0012, indicating an annual rate of return of 6%. We have five points of the dependent variable, indicating mid-points of the ranges reported in our sample: 0, 150, 900, 2000 and 3500, all in £.
We also estimated the coefficients by specifying the variables as in equation (2), because (3) may suffer from heteroskedasticity. However, the results were very similar.

ACKNOWLEDGEMENTS

This work was carried out at the Centre for Labour Economics, London School of Economics. We are grateful to M. Barton and J. Gomulka for computational assistance, and to R. Layard, S. Nickell and M. Stewart for comments on a previous draft of this paper. We would also like to thank the Department of Health and Social Security for their financial support and comments, and the Office of Population Censuses and Surveys who collected the data. The analysis and conclusions are entirely the authors' responsibility.

REFERENCES

Ando A. and Modigliani F. (1963) 'The Life-Cycle Hypothesis of Saving: Aggregate Implications and Tests', *Am. Econom. Rev.* **53,** 55–84
Barro R. J. (1974) 'Are Government Bonds Net Wealth?'. *J. Political Economy* **82,** 1095–1117
Boskin M. J. (1977) 'Social Security and Retirement Decisions'. *Economic Inquiry* **15,** 1–25
Cagan P. (1965) *The Effect of Pension Plans on Aggregate Saving*, New York, NBER
Clark R., Kreps J. and Spengler J. (1978) Economics of Aging: A Survey. *J. Econom. Lit.* **16,** 919–962

Diamond P. A. (1977) A Framework of Social Security Analysis. *J. Pub. Econ.* **8,** 275–298

Feldstein M. S. (1974) Social Security, Induced Retirement and Aggregate Capital Accumulation. *J. Political Economy* **82,** 905–926

Feldstein M. S. (1976) Social Security and Saving: The Extended Life Cycle Theory. *American Economic Review Papers and Proceedings* **66,** 77–86

Feldstein M. S. and Pellechio A. (1978) *Social Security and Household Wealth Accumulation: New Microeconomic Evidence.* NBER Working Paper No. 206.

Katona G. (1965) *Private Pensions and Individual Savings,* Ann Arbor: Survey Research Center, Inst. Social Res., University of Michigan

Layard R., Frederking M. and Zabalza A. Married Women's Participation and Hours. *Economica* (to be published).

Quinn J. F. (1977) Microeconomic Determinants of Early Retirement: A Cross-Sectional View of White Married Men. *J. Hum. Res.* **12,** 329–346

Steiner P. O. and Dorfman R. (1957) *The Economic Status of the Aged,* Berkeley, University of California

DISCUSSION

by **D. A. Collard,** *School of Humanities and Social Sciences, University of Bath*

I like to believe that the interest recently shown in pensions reflects not a tired and ageing profession but an important and neglected subject with analytical issues of sufficient difficulty to attract high-powered research. That this is so was confirmed by the giving up of the whole of a recent issue of the *Journal of Public Economics* (**10,** 1978) to retirement and related issues.

The present paper by Zabalza et al. arises out of work being done at the Centre for Labour Economics at the LSE and concerns itself with the analysis of the disincentive effects of retirement pensions.

Participation

The linear participation equation has as its dependent variable the probability that a person will participate (0, 1). The independent variables are: the state retirement pension, occupational pension, asset income, house ownership (0, 1), earnings or potential earnings, health (0, 1), age and involuntary loss of main job (0, 1). The samples used for the regressions were 639 men and 525 women and the interviews were carried out by the Office of Population Censuses and Surveys.

The two principal findings are unsurprising. (i) State and occupational pension schemes negatively affect the decision to participate; (ii) potential net earnings affect the decision to participate. You are more likely to carry on working after 65 (60 for women) the greater the *gain* in income by not staying at home. But unless the specification is changed there are some slightly surprising insignificant variables—among them pretty well all the zero-work income variables for women, savings and house-ownership. Again the income variable is less significant for women.

Several features of this part of the paper call for comment. The first thing to strike one is the number of (0, 1) dummies, *including* the dependent variable. As a non-econometrician I can see that this could give rise to difficulties and it is a less sophisticated approach than that of, for example, Boskin and Hurd (1978) who use a logit equation. However, the sample size is large so perhaps it does not matter very much. I leave it to the econometricians.

My second point is the estimation of potential earnings. Earnings could not, of course, be found directly for non-participators. For them a wage equation (on participators) was used, based upon personal characteristics such as education, age, socio-economic group and health. The wage equation has several significant variables at the 95% level but explains very little of the total variation. Perhaps it would have been better to have used earnings prior to retirement as a predictor of potential post-retirement earnings? That the figure must have been available is clear from the savings analysis and I cannot think that endogeneity problems would be of great importance.

My third point is about housing. There is a positive but insignificant coefficient on the (0, 1) house ownership dummy which is seen simply as a financial asset. It would have been interesting to see whether the coefficient would go negative and significant if all house owners with residual mortgages were excluded.

Fourthly there is apparently some controversy as to whether 'health' is a significant explanatory variable. Zabalza et al. are probably correct in believing that this hangs on whether objective or subjective valuations are used; it is the latter which turn out to be important. Boskin's (1977) paper is cited for the insignificance of the health variable but it emerged as important in Boskin and Hurd (1978). Boskin and Hurd's probability of retirement figure is almost doubled by the presence of bad health. In this study health is significant for both men and women with the expected sign.

Fifthly there is evidence of a Darby-and-Joan effect. If one retired spouse stays at home the other is (*cet. par.*) more likely to do so.

On the whole, the evidence in this part of the paper is in accord with what one would predict from economic theory with the important variables having significant coefficients.

Saving

The other major investigation is into the savings equation. The rationale for doing this is that variations in social security benefit will have some effect on other forms of saving, possibly fully offsetting them. Thus social security could have an *indirect* effect on the participation decision, participation depending on total unearned income, including both state and occupational pensions and income from savings. It would be useful to know, therefore, whether an increase in social security would or would not increase total unearned retirement income. In the case of perfect offsetting it would not.

The authors run savings against: state and private pensions, net earnings (and net earnings squared) and a number of personal characteristics weighted by income. In this equation savings are a stock (table A5, appendix) but they are reduced to a flow for comparison with work by Feldstein and Pellechio (1978). The important coefficient here is β_1, that of asset income against occupational and retirement pensions. For complete substitution $\beta_1 = -1$. The coefficient found by Zabalza et al. is dramatically different from this: it was *positive* and significantly different from zero. Hence, *cet. par.*, an increase in the retirement pension leads to an increase in other forms of saving, an increase in the inducement to stay at home and a decrease in the participation rate.

The weak link in this chain of argument is the role of income from savings in the participation decision. It clearly requires savings to be significant here. It just so happens (see table 1) that the coefficient on savings is not significant even at the 10% level. However, the authors respecify their equation with equal coefficients on pension income and savings income. The case for this respecification is weak, however, as they acknowledge when comparing with Boskin's (1977) results. With respecification they are perfectly right to argue 'our estimates imply that if the individual responded to the state pension by reducing his private savings on a pound for pound basis, then social security would not influence the retirement decision significantly'. But without respecification, pensions would have *six times* the effect on retirement of savings even if there was complete portfolio substitution. I cannot see why the authors are so wedded to the indirect effect via perverse portfolio substitution rather than the direct effect as in the non-respecified equations.

Retirement and the Limits to Redistribution

There are good social reasons for wishing to have state retirement pensions which do indeed act as a disincentive to carry on working. It is difficult to see such disincentives among the elderly as a limit to redistributive policies. May I close with two speculations? (i) The more redistributive is the state pension the more likely it is (*cet. par.*) that the better-off will participate once retired; (ii) schemes for early retirement, from say 50 onwards are normally justified on efficiency grounds: the redistributive effects of the amounts offered in compensation will turn out to be very important in the next decade or so.

REFERENCES

Boskin and Hurd (1978) Effect of Social Security on Early Retirement. *J. Pub. Econ.* **10,** 361–377. *J. Pub. Econ.,* 1978.

SUMMARY OF THE GENERAL DISCUSSION

Replying to Collard, Zabalza explained that the zero-one dummy variable approach to participation had been adopted because the alternative method using hours worked was less tractable. Also, this simple method did pick up most of the relevant variation: Layard, Frederking and Zabalza had discovered that, with working women, 82% of labour supply response was due to the participation/non-participation decision; only 18% was due to hours adjustment. He was not too worried about the low $\bar{R}^2$ in the wage equation (Collard, pp. 99–100)—this was not unusual in cross-sectional work. The alternative of using past earnings as a proxy for earning power had been considered, but post-retirement earnings are not usually gained from the same sort of employment as pre-retirement earnings. The authors agreed that a more sophisticated econometric treatment was in principle desirable, but felt that the results would be unchanged.

It was suggested by Brown that one possible defence of the zero-one dummy approach could be that people do have to accept a fixed number of hours employment, and are not free to vary their hours worked.

In reply to a question from O'Hagan, to what extent retired people genuinely did have a free choice whether to work or not, the authors explained that whereas many retired people had obviously been compelled to give up their *original* job, this did not mean that they were unable to get *a* job. Everyone in the sample had considered that they could get some sort of a job if they wanted.

Replying to some other points from Collard's discussion, Pissarides said that they did not have adequate information on mortgages (Collard, p. 100). He defended the respecification of the participation equation (Collard, p. 100) as being better on statistical criteria. The effect on early retirement was anyway very small, income from savings being only 5% of total income. On intergenerational redistribution, at present 18% of those eligible retire early, the main reasons being ill-health and the option of taking occupational pensions early.

Piachaud defended the use of the 'subjective' measure of health. It was not a perfect indicator, but more 'objective' measures such as 'weeks in bed per year' were not really very good indicators of health in relation to working possibilities. Evidence from invalidity pensions seemed to corroborate the subjective answers. Le Grand agreed. In his view the ultimate behavioural factor was whether people *felt* well enough to work. Lecomber felt that one should be cautious about using subjective measures—the answers would probably depend on the form of the question. Brown commented that the analysis presupposed that the causation was from health to retirement, whereas in fact retirement might easily affect health.

Judge asked how important were employers' contributions in portfolio substitution. The authors replied that they had no information on how the various occupational schemes were funded, but really it was only the benefits that should affect retirement behaviour, not the contributions.

Gregory was concerned about the form of the equations reported in table 1. Were they reduced form equations or demand-for-participation equations? What was being assumed on the supply side? Pissarides replied that supply was assumed to be unconstrained. Layard added that a weaker assumption could be that any job rationing that did occur did not depend on the variables in these equations. Stern commented that if there were no supply-side restrictions it would indeed be important not to use previous earnings as a proxy for earning-power. He also asked whether the authors had considered treating full-time and part-time employment separately. Pissarides said that the authors had in fact tried this—but it had not made any difference to the results.

PENSION SCHEMES AND THE LIMITS TO REDISTRIBUTION: SOME POLICY ALTERNATIVES

J. Creedy

Department of Economics, University of Durham

INTRODUCTION

Redistribution and contracting out

This paper examines the limits to the redistribution of lifetime earnings which is possible using various kinds of government pension schemes. It is obvious that an actuarially sound pension scheme will not involve any systematic redistribution. But the recognition that the retired form a high proportion of the poor has led to pressure for government schemes which provide an adequate pension for all individuals, irrespective of their previous capacity to accumulate a fund which may provide an annuity in retirement. The scheme proposed by Beveridge (1942) is well known, and recommends the principle of flat rate contributions and benefits. However, recent years have seen the introduction of earnings-related schemes which, it has been claimed, still involve redistribution.

The first almost platitudinous point to make is that any scheme which results in redistribution will usually involve some individuals obtaining a rate of return on their contributions which is less than the market rate of return (where the scheme is funded and self-contained). If, therefore, individuals are allowed to contract out of the state scheme they must nevertheless be obliged to pay a proportion of their earnings into the pension fund, for some redistribution to be possible.† Thus, when discussing the development of state pensions, Atkinson (1977) has remarked that, 'it proved possible to devise contracting-out systems which left the redistributive and subsidy element of the state scheme more or less intact. This could only be done, of course, by limiting the option to *partial* contracting out'.‡ The suggestion that partial contracting out leaves redistribution 'more or less intact' is rather surprising. It is therefore of interest to examine not only the potential redistribution which is implied by a compulsory state scheme, but also the practical limitations to redistribution where some individuals are allowed to contract out of the scheme and obtain interest on their savings at the fixed market rate.

† This point has also been made by Diamond (1977): 'proposals to allow individuals to opt out of Social Security must decrease its redistributive purpose or continue taxation for redistributive purposes of those who do opt out'.

‡ He went on to say that, 'there has been no question of reverting to the arrangements which obtained before 1948 under which, in certain circumstances, a private pension could stand in place of the whole state pension'. (Atkinson, 1977.) Nevertheless it is shown below that this kind of scheme may have significant advantages over the current scheme.

A simple model

There are obviously many different ways in which redistribution takes place in pension schemes. The rules involving eligibility for benefits, transfer of pension rights, the measure of earnings on which the pension is based, and differential mortality are just a few of the factors which can have significant redistributive implications.§

In order to concentrate on the limits to possible redistribution in the two situations where contracting out is or is not allowed, this paper considers a very simple model which abstracts from most of the complicating factors. Thus lifetime is divided into two periods only: the working life and retirement. The pension scheme is assumed to be funded. No allowance is made for population or productivity growth, factors which usually allow a pay-as-you-go system to pay higher pensions than a fund. The ith individual ($i=1, \ldots, N$) earns y_i over the first period and pays contributions of $T(y_i)$ into a pension fund. The fund then accumulates at the interest rate of $100r\%$, and the N individuals receive a pension of $P(y_i)$ in the second period. It will be seen that even within this highly simplified framework the analysis of policy alternatives is not straightforward.

An immediate problem arises with the use of the simple model used here, since in practice the length of time over which contributions are paid is much longer than that over which the pension is received. It can, however, be shown that the consideration of a number of sub-periods affects simply the rate of interest used. Comparisons should therefore use quite high values of r, although it will be clear from the formulae that many of the results are independent of its level (such as the number contracting out). Although comparisons of absolute values are rather difficult, this does not affect the consideration of the nature of the policy trade-offs involved; that is, the extent to which one policy variable must be changed as a result of a change in some other policy variable, in order to finance the scheme. This aspect of the model is furthermore not crucial for the comparison of measures of relative inequality under different schemes.

The assumption that all individuals live until the same age is also unrealistic, and in practice differential mortality would reduce the extent of systematic redistribution. It may also seem unusual that one of the motives for insurance, the fact that the length of working life and the period of retirement are uncertain, has been ignored here. ‖ Nevertheless it is not crucial when examining the motives for contracting out, since both state and private schemes pay a pension up to death, irrespective of the length of life.¶

It should also be noted that this paper considers only the inequality of net income (after the deduction of contributions and payment of pensions) rather than, say, the inequality of 'utility' which results from the receipt of income.

Flat rate and proportional schemes

A system whereby each individual pays contributions of c during the first period and receives a pension of $c(1+r)$ during retirement in the second period is clearly the simplest case. Total net income over the two periods is $(y_i-c)+c(1+r)=y_i+cr$. The addition of a constant amount to each person's earnings reduces relative inequality, as shown in more detail below. The flat rate system therefore involves some equalizing

§ An analysis of different schemes using simulation methods is presented in Creedy (1978a).

‖ For further discussion of this aspect of pensions, see Diamond (1977).

¶ This does, however, raise the question of the extent to which different private pension schemes attempt to screen individuals. The issues concerning risk-rating and screening cannot be discussed here, however.

Table 1. Values of η_z. Flat rate pension with no contracting out.

$t=0{\cdot}05$		$t=0{\cdot}10$		$t=0{\cdot}20$	
$r=0{\cdot}2$	$r=0{\cdot}6$	$r=0{\cdot}2$	$r=0{\cdot}6$	$r=0{\cdot}2$	$r=0{\cdot}6$
0·443	0·430	0·416	0·400	0·336	0·307

redistribution, although in this special case there is no incentive for individuals to contract out of the scheme since the rate of return to contributions is the same for everyone.

It is obvious that a system which uses directly proportional contributions and pensions involves no redistribution. In this case $T(y_i)=ty_i$ and $P(y_i)=py_i$. If the arithmetic mean of y_i is $\bar{y}$, then total contributions of $Nt\bar{y}$ simply finance total pensions of $Np\bar{y}$. Thus $p=t(1+r)$ and total net income is $y_i(1+rt)$. This simple result will clearly not hold if some allowance is made for 'time preference' (with the rate differing between individuals), although this complication is ignored here for analytical convenience.

PROPORTIONAL CONTRIBUTIONS AND FLAT-RATE PENSIONS

Although it is obvious that the combination of proportional contributions with flat-rate benefits will lead to greater equality in the distribution of total net income than in that of earnings, it is nevertheless of interest to compare this important case with other schemes discussed below. Here the total accumulated contributions of $Nt\bar{y}(1+r)$ must finance total pensions of Nb where b is the flat-rate pension. Thus $b=t(1+r)\bar{y}$, and total net income over two periods is equal to $y_i(1—t)+t(1+r)\bar{y}$. The effect on relative inequality therefore occurs through the addition of the term $t(1+r)\bar{y}$.

If η_y is the coefficient of variation of y, it can be shown that the coefficient of variation of total net income is $\gamma\eta_y$, where $\gamma=(1-t)/(1+rt)$.** Values of η_z for some alternative combinations of r and t are shown in table 1.

This type of system therefore seems to offer an effective method of reducing inequality, provided that full participation in the scheme by all individuals is compulsory. The incentive to contract out of such a scheme is considered in the next section.

Individual rates of return

If the implicit rate of return on contributions for person i is denoted by r_i, then this is obtained by definition from

$$(1+r_i)=P(y_i)/(T(y_i). \tag{1}$$

Substituting for P and T from the previous section gives

$$(1+r_i)=(1+r)\bar{y}/y_i \tag{2}$$

and all individuals with earnings greater than the arithmetic mean obtain a rate of return which is less than the market rate of interest which is earned by the pension fund. These people would be tempted to contract out of the state scheme if possible. But if this is allowed then the amount available for redistribution in flat-rate pensions would fall, thereby introducing a further group of people who would have an

** In general it can be shown that if $z=\xi y+\psi$ then $\eta_z=\eta_y\{1/(1+\psi/\xi\bar{y})\}$.

incentive to leave the system. This position is obviously unstable, resulting in everyone but the poorest member of society leaving the state scheme.

A stable system of contracting out

A simple expedient, which bears some resemblance to more realistic schemes, is to allow individuals to contract out of the scheme but to force them to contribute a proportion, δt say, of their earnings into the state fund. No pension is paid to those who leave the system, however. As more people contract out of the scheme the total amount of ineligible contributions increases, and the number over whom the total fund must be shared decreases. Furthermore the effective rate of interest which individuals are able to obtain in the market is reduced to $(1-\delta)(1+r)$, since if total savings remain at ty_i a proportion $(1-\delta)$ only is 'invested' for retirement. Consequently there is some level of earnings, y^* say, below which there is no further incentive to contract out of the state scheme.

Suppose, then, that individuals with earnings above y^* contract out of the scheme. The total contributions to the fund are

$$Nt[\int^{y^*} y\mathrm{d}F(y)+\delta\int_{y^*} y\mathrm{d}F(y)]$$

$$= Nt\bar{y}\left[\frac{1}{\bar{y}}\int^{y^*} y\mathrm{d}F(y)+\delta\{1-\frac{1}{\bar{y}}\int^{y^*} y\mathrm{d}F(y)\}\right]$$

$$= Nt\bar{y}\,\{\delta+(1-\delta)\,F_1(y^*)\} \tag{3}$$

where $F(y)$ is the distribution function of y, and $F_1(y)$ is the first moment distribution of y, defined by $F_1(y)=(1/\bar{y})\int^y u\mathrm{d}F(u)$.

Total contributions are now spread over $NF(y^*)$ people, rather than N, so that the pension per person, b after interest is added to the fund, is given by:

$$b=(1+r)t\bar{y}\,\{\delta+(1-\delta)\,F_1(y^*)\}/F(y^*). \tag{4}$$

By equating the effective market rate of return for those contracting out with the rate of return offered to a person with earnings of y^* by the state scheme, the following is obtained:

$$(1-\delta)(y^*/\bar{y})=\{\delta+(1-\delta)F_1(y^*)\}/F(y^*).$$

A higher value of δ will clearly increase y^* and thereby reduce the number of individuals who contract out. The relationship between values of δ and y^* is most clearly seen from

$$F(y^*)(y^*/\bar{y})-F_1(y^*)=\delta/(1-\delta). \tag{5}$$

It should be noted that equation (5) does not contain terms in either the contributions rate t or the market rate of return r. For any functional form, F, for which a convenient first moment distribution exists it is therefore possible to calculate the value of δ which is associated with any value of y^*. The feasible redistribution arising from choices of δ and t can then be obtained. The policy alternatives indicated by equation (4) and (5) can be examined using the assumption that y is lognormally distributed as $\Lambda(y/\mu, \sigma^2)$. In this case there is a convenient relationship between the various moment distributions (see Aitchison and Brown, 1957). The jth moment distribution, denoted by Λ_j, is given by:

$$\Lambda_j(y\,|\,\mu, \sigma^2)=\Lambda(y\,|\,\mu+j\sigma^2, \sigma^2).$$

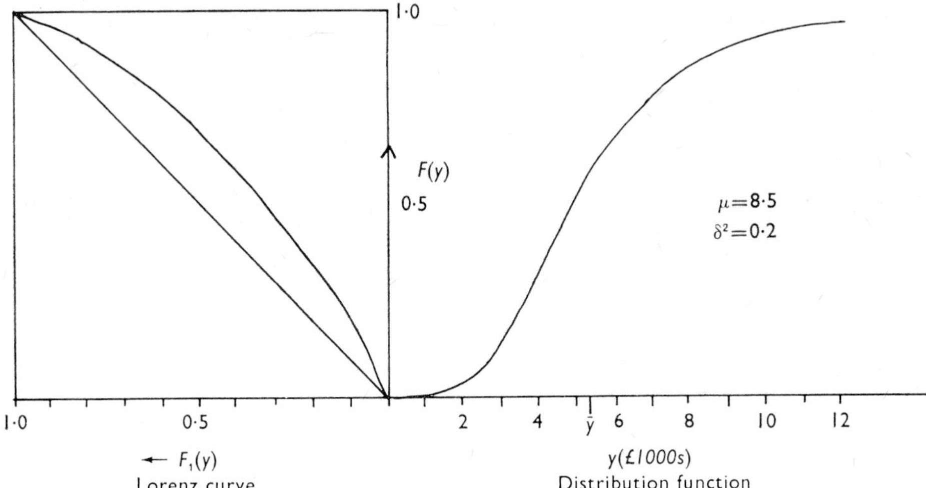

Figure 1. Distribution of earnings.

The required integrals (for $F(y^*)$ etc) can also be computed using the approximation discussed in Aitchison and Brown (1957), p. 71).

The values of 8·5 and 0·2 were used throughout the paper for μ and σ^2 respectively, since they correspond fairly closely to measures of the distribution of annual average life earnings.†† These values imply, under lognormality, that the coefficient of variation of y, η_y, is equal to 0·471 (since $\eta^2 = \exp[\sigma^2 - 1]$), and that the arithmetic mean of y, $\bar{y}$, is equal to £5431. The distribution function and Lorenz curve for this distribution are shown in figure 1. This may be used to make appropriate transformations between income, y, the proportion of individuals with income not greater than y, $F(y)$, and the proportion of total income earned by those individuals, $F_1(y)$.

It is first necessary to use equation (5) to show the value of δ required to achieve any given y^*. Figure 2 shows the variation in the proportion of individuals remaining in the state scheme as δ increases. Figure 1 may be used to obtain the corresponding values of y^* and $1 - F(y^*)$. The latter, along with δ, gives the amount of income which is contributed to the fund by those contracting out. Clearly, $F(y^*)$ approaches unity as δ increases. For example, in order to 'prevent' people with earnings up to £7000 contracting out (that is to keep 79% of the population within the state scheme) it is necessary to impose a proportional tax of $27t$% on the earnings of those who contract out. Note that, although δ is independent of t and r, the actual proportional tax rate will depend on these other variables.

The nature of the constrained policy choices may be considered as follows. It has been shown that with the flat-rate pension and no contracting out, $b/\bar{y} = (1+r)t$. The policy trade-off is therefore shown by the 45° line in figure 3. Where contracting out is allowed, the slope of the line decreases although it still passes through the origin (as shown by equation (4), the slope is $\delta + (1-\delta)F_1(y^*)/F(y^*)$). This implies that a higher contributions-rate is required to finance any given level of flat-rate pensions. Further details are shown in table 2. Clearly as δ increases and the number of people who contract out is reduced, a given increase in the flat-rate pension can be achieved

†† For further details see Creedy (1978a).

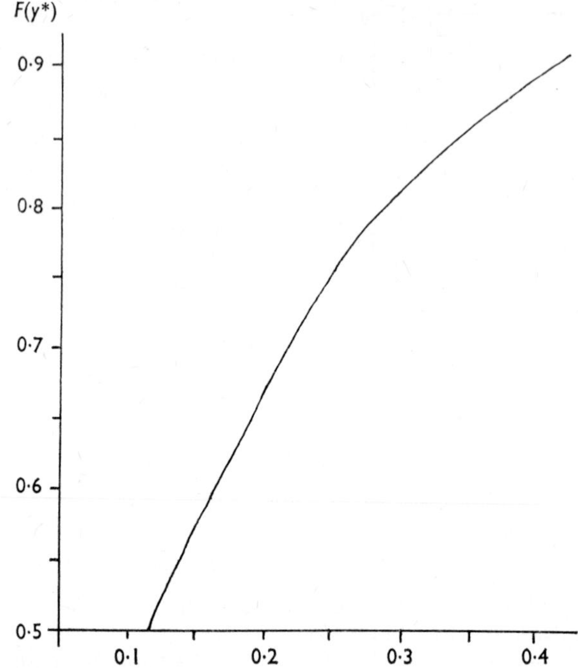

Figure 2. **Contracting out: flat rate pension.**

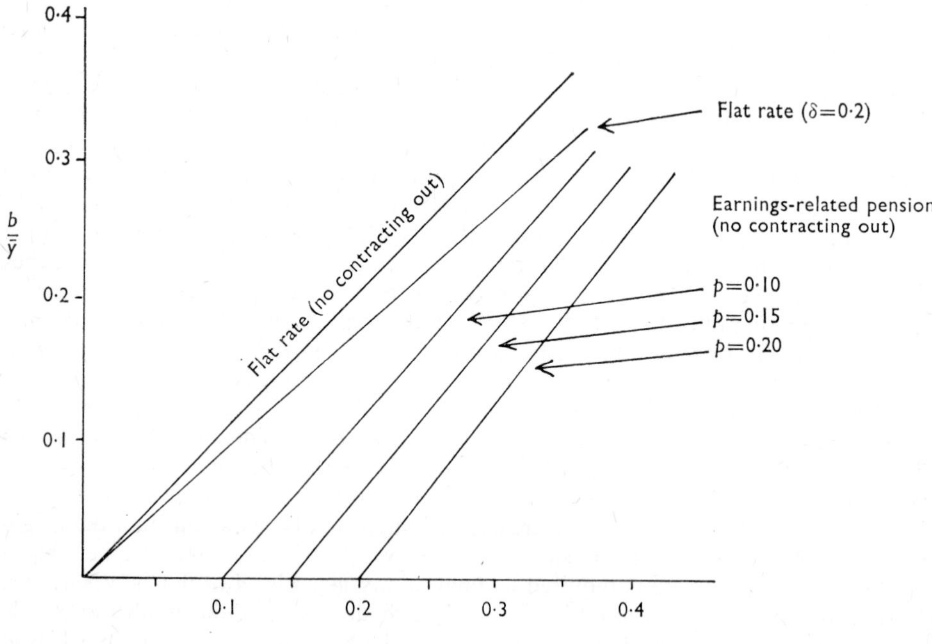

Figure 3. Trade-off between $b/\bar{y}$ and $(1+r)t$.

Table 2. Ratio of flat-rate pension to $(1+r)t$.

δ	$b/\{(1+r)t\}$	$b/\{(1+r)t\bar{y}\}$
0·12	4412	0·81
0·20	4826	0·89
0·27	5080	0·94
0·35	5228	0·96
0·41	5314	0·98

with a smaller increase in the proportional tax rate (as the gradient of the line OP increases).

The inequality of total net income

The effect on the inequality of total net income is not, however, as clear as in the first two cases considered above. There is a clear transfer from those who are contracted out to those remaining in the state scheme, although within this higher income group there is no change in relative inequality. In addition there is a certain amount of redistribution within the group whose earnings are below y^*. The inequality of total net income therefore depends on the two 'within-group' components and the 'between-group' component.

This paper considers the coefficient of variation of total net income, η_z, where z_i is the ith person's net income. The measure is used because it is most tractable in this situation, and can be easily decomposed. It should be noted that if the distribution of earnings is lognormal, this will not in general be the case for net income. The problem is to obtain η_z where the sample is divided into two groups according to the transformation between z_i and y_i. For those in the state system $z_i = y_i(1-t)+b$ (with b given by equation (4)), while for those contracted out, $z_i = y_i\{(1-t)+t(1-\delta)(1+r)\}$. Before examining these special cases, it is perhaps useful to consider the more general problem of obtaining the mean and variance of two sub-groups where $z_i = \xi y_i + \psi$, say. It can be shown that for those contracted into the system

$$E(z|y<y^*) = \xi\bar{y}F_1(y^*)/F(y^*) + \psi$$

and

$$V(z|y<y^*) = \frac{\xi^2\{V(y)+\bar{y}^2\}F_2(y^*)}{F(y^*)} - \frac{\xi^2\bar{y}^2F_1(y^*)^2}{F(y^*)^2}$$

where $F_2(y^*)$ is the second moment distribution defined by $F_2(y) = \int^y u^2 \mathrm{d}F(u)/\int u^2\mathrm{d}F(u)$. The corresponding mean and variance of the group above y^* are obtained as

$$E(z|y>y^*) = \frac{\xi\bar{y}\{\{1-F_1(y^*)\}+\psi}{\{1-F(y^*)\}}$$

$$V(z|y>y^*) = \frac{\xi^2\{V(y)+\bar{y}^2\}\{1-F_2(y^*)\}}{\{1-F(y^*)\}} - \frac{\xi^2\bar{y}^2\{1-F_1(y^*)\}^2}{\{1-F(y^*)\}^2}.$$

The appropriate substitutions for ξ and ψ can then easily be made, and the groups combined in the usual way to obtain the overall mean and variance.

Table 3. Values of η_z with contracting out.

δ	$t=0{\cdot}05$ $r=0{\cdot}2$	$t=0{\cdot}05$ $r=0{\cdot}6$	$t=0{\cdot}10$ $r=0{\cdot}2$	$t=0{\cdot}10$ $r=0{\cdot}6$	$t=0{\cdot}20$ $r=0{\cdot}2$	$t=0{\cdot}20$ $r=0{\cdot}6$
0·12	0·461	0·458	0·451	0·446	0·433	0·425
0·20	0·456	0·451	0·442	0·434	0·414	0·401
0·27	0·452	0·446	0·434	0·423	0·399	0·382
0·35	0·449	0·442	0·428	0·416	0·387	0·367
0·41	0·447	0·439	0·423	0·410	0·378	0·357

Note: $\eta_y=0{\cdot}471$.

Values of the coefficient of variation of total net income, η_z, are then shown in table 3 for alternative rates of δ, t and r. (Note that the values of b which can be financed under each set of alternatives can be obtained directly from table 2.) Thus for any given δ, the value of η_z decreases as t and r increase. These values may be compared with η_y of 0·471, but it is more instructive to compare them with the values which would result from a state scheme which did not allow contracting out (shown in table 1 above). Obviously, when $\delta=0$, the value of η_z is the same as that of η_y, and as δ increases then η_z approaches asymptotically its value under the flat-rate pension with no contracting out. Figure 4 shows the variation in η_z against δ for two proportional rates of contributions and two rates of interest. This diagram therefore clearly shows the extent to which contracting out reduces the ability of the pension scheme to redistribute lifetime income.

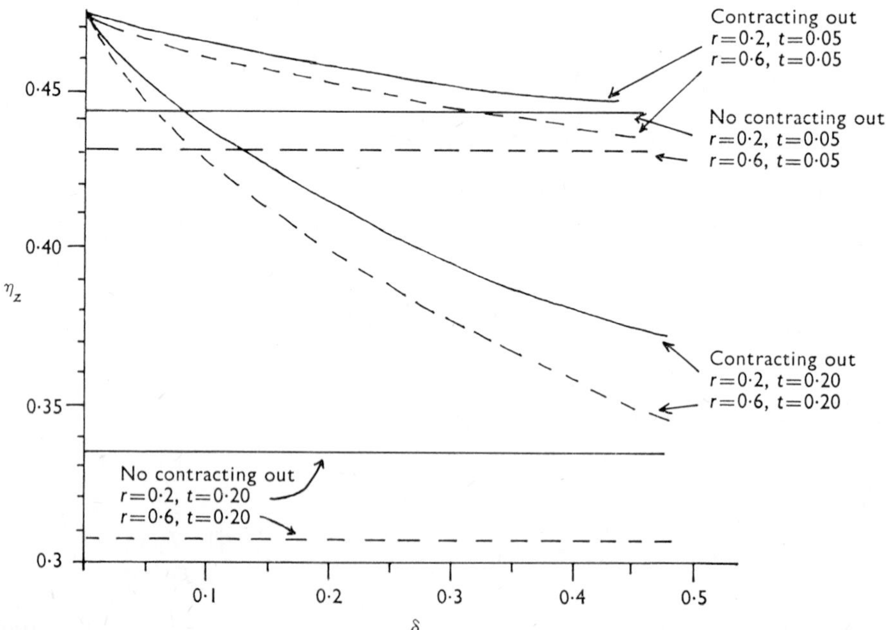

Figure 4. Inequality: flat-rate pension with contracting out.

PROPORTIONAL CONTRIBUTIONS WITH A TWO-TIER PENSION

A compromise between the above flat-rate pension and proportional contributions scheme is one where a basic flat-rate pension of b is paid to all individuals, and an additional proportional pension is obtained, based on the excess of earnings over the flat-rate pension. Thus the pension formula is given by:

$$\begin{aligned} P(y_i) &= b + p(y_i - b) \qquad & y > b \\ &= b & y \leqslant b\,. \end{aligned} \tag{6}$$

The amount needed to finance the unconditional flat-rate pension is therefore Nb, while the amount required for the earnings-related second tier of the pension is equal to

$$\begin{aligned} &Np\textstyle\int_b (y-b)\,\mathrm{d}F(y) \\ &= Np[\bar{y}\{1-F_1(b)\} - b\{1-F(b)\}]. \end{aligned} \tag{7}$$

Table 4. Values of $t(1+r)$ for two-tier pension.

b(£'s)	$b/\bar{y}$	$p=0{\cdot}05$	$p=0{\cdot}10$	$p=0{\cdot}15$	$p=0{\cdot}20$
800	0·15	0·19	0·23	0·28	0·32
1200	0·22	0·26	0·30	0·34	0·38
1600	0·30	0·33	0·37	0·40	0·44

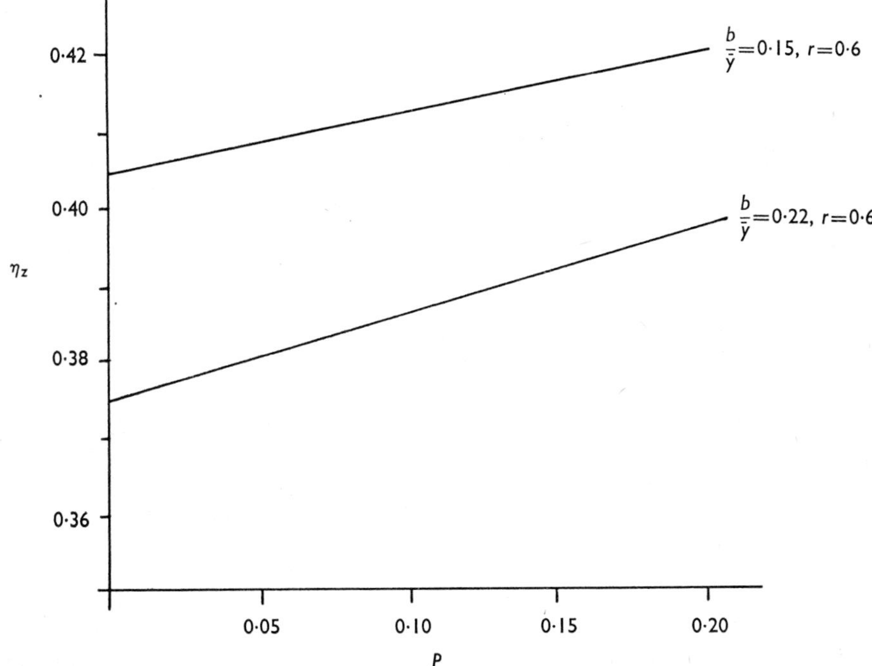

Figure 5. Inequality: two-tier pension (no contracting out).

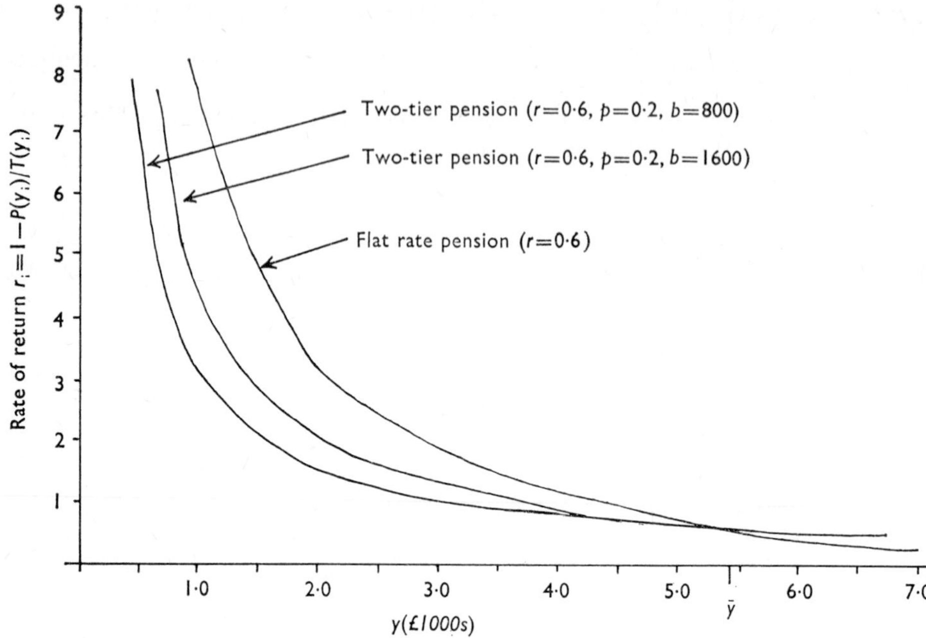

Figure 6. Individual rates of return (no contracting out).

It is clearly not possible to make independent choices of the three policy variables t, p and b. The relationship between them is given by:

$$t(1+r)\bar{y} = b + p[\bar{y}\{1 - F_1(b)\} - b\{1 - F(b)\}]\,. \tag{8}$$

This can be used to obtain any one of the three variables, given two others. Computationally it is most convenient to set b and p, and then determine t. Some idea of the constraints affecting policy choices is given in table 4, which shows values of $(1+r)t$ which are required to finance given levels of b and p.

The relationship is also shown in figure 3 for three values of the proportional pension rate, p. These lines are approximately linear, and are closer to linearity as $b/\bar{y}$ decreases. (Since, when b is small, $F(b) \approx 0$ and equation (8) gives $t(1+r) = p + b(1-p)/\bar{y}$.)

Figure 3 clearly shows the large difference between the contribution rate which is required to finance the two-tier scheme and that required for the flat-rate pension, even where contracting out is allowed in the flat-rate scheme.

Figure 5 shows the variation in η_z as the value of the earnings-related proportion, p, increases, for two alternative values of b and a value of r of 0·6. Figure 6 shows only cases where contracting out is not allowed. Note that this relationship is linear, a point which is not obvious from the derivation. (A similar result in a different context is given in Creedy (1978*b*).) The proportional contribution rate necessary to finance each scheme may be obtained from figure 3. The intercept of each line in figure 5 is of course the value of η_z for the appropriate flat-rate pension (with $p=0$).

Further details are given in table 5 for rates of interest of 0·2 and 0·6. Notice that for given values of b, higher rates of interest lead to higher η_z; whereas on the simple flat-rate scheme increases in r lower η_z. The explanation is simply that higher r (with

Table 5. Values of η_z for two-tier pension.

$b/\bar{y}$	$p=0{\cdot}1$		$p=0{\cdot}2$	
	$r=0{\cdot}2$	$r=0{\cdot}6$	$r=0{\cdot}2$	$r=0{\cdot}6$
0·15	0·410	0·413	0·418	0·421
0·22	0·381	0·386	0·392	0·398
0·30	0·353	0·361	0·367	0·375

Note: $\eta_y=0{\cdot}471$.

fixed b) enables the contributions rate to be reduced. In the former case, higher r would finance higher values of b.

The effect of η_z and on policy choices under a similar system which allows contracting out can now be examined. However, it is first of interest to consider the individual rates of return from the two-tier pension.

It was shown by equation (2) that under a scheme of flat-rate pensions with proportional contributions, the individuals with earnings above the arithmetic mean obtain a rate of return from the pension scheme which is less than the market rate of interest. This is illustrated in figure 6, for a rate of interest of 0·6. Very few individuals would actually obtain the high rates indicated for those with income less than £2000. The variation in individual rates of return under the two-tier pension scheme is also shown in figure 6, where those with $y>\bar{y}$ also have $r_i<r$. This last point is not obvious; it may most easily be seen by examination of equation (8) for small values of b, such that $F(b)$ may be neglected. In this case $t(1+r)\bar{y}=b(1-p)+p\bar{y}$ and the individual rate of return is given by:

$$(1+r_i)=(1+r)\left\{\frac{b(1-p)+py_i}{b(1-p)+p\bar{y}}\right\}\frac{y_i}{\bar{y}}\,.$$

A stable two-tier system of contracting out

The modification to allow for an earnings-related supplement to the flat-rate pension also complicates the problem of examining the effects of different rules for contracting out. The method adopted in the current UK pension scheme is to allow individuals to contract out of the second tier of the pension. Again contributions are reduced to $\delta t y_i$, rather than $t y_i$. The problem is to find that level of earnings, y^*, below which it is not profitable for individuals to contract out. The feasible limits to redistribution can then be considered.

Total contributions are given in equation (3). Since everyone receives the flat-rate component, the amount needed to finance this part of the scheme is Nb, as before. The total amount needed to finance the earnings-related section is then given by:

$$Np\int_b^{y^*}(y-b)\,\mathrm{d}F(y).$$

Following the simplification used above this can be shown to be:

$$Np[\bar{y}\{F_1(y^*)-F_1(b)\}-b\{F(y^*)-F(b)\}]. \tag{9}$$

which may be compared with equation (7). Total contributions must then be equated to total pensions, giving

$$(1+r)t\bar{y}\{\delta+(1-\delta)F_1(y^*)\}=b+pG(y^*,b) \tag{10}$$

where $G(y^*, b)$ is the term in square brackets in equation (9). Comparison of equation (10) with equation (4) shows the additional complication introduced by the need for two parameters of the pension scheme (b and p). Any set of values which satisfy equation (10) must also satisfy the condition that the rate of return from the pension for earnings of y^* is equal to the 'effective' market rate of return on the same savings. This means that the following condition must also hold:

$$(1+r)(1-\delta)=\{b+p(y^*-b)\}/ty^*. \tag{11}$$

The policy combinations available can then be examined by combining equations (10) and (11) to eliminate $(1+r)t$ so that:

$$\frac{b+p(y^*-b)}{(1-\delta)y^*}=\frac{b+pG(y^*, b)}{\bar{y}\{\delta+(1-\delta)F_1(y^*)\}}. \tag{12}$$

Equation (12) can then be rearranged to give:

$$\frac{\delta}{1-\delta}=\frac{\{b+pG(y^*, b)\}y^*}{\{b+p(y^*-b)\}\bar{y}}-F_1(y^*),$$

which corresponds to equation (5) in the analysis of the simple flat-rate scheme, and can be used to obtain δ, given y^*, b and p. After solving for these values, substitution into (11) easily gives $(1+r)t$.

When contracting out is allowed with a simple flat-rate pension, it was shown (pp. 106–9) that the proportion of people leaving the state scheme can be controlled within reasonable limits. Thus to increase the proportion of the population within the state scheme from 51% to 67% requires an increase in δ from 0·12 to 0·20. In the two-tier scheme, where equation (13) is complicated by the introduction of p and b, control is much more difficult. The values of δ required for given y^* are shown in table 6, for given p and b. The required value of δ is seen to be much more sensitive to changes in the value of p than in y^* (or b). This raises severe difficulties of policy control since the tax rate necessary to finance alternative schemes would be expected to be rather more sensitive to the number of people who contract out. These are shown in table 7.

Table 6. Values of δ for given y^*. Two-tier pension.

	$b/\bar{y}=0{\cdot}15$		$b/\bar{y}=0{\cdot}22$		$b/\bar{y}=0{\cdot}30$	
$y^*/\bar{y}$	$p=0{\cdot}1$	$p=0{\cdot}2$	$p=0{\cdot}1$	$p=0{\cdot}2$	$p=0{\cdot}1$	$p=0{\cdot}2$
0·92	0·27	0·21	0·30	0·25	0·32	0·28
1·66	0·28	0·19	0·32	0·23	0·35	0·27

Table 7. Values of $(1+r)t$ needed to finance given policies.

	$b/\bar{y}=0{\cdot}15$		$b/\bar{y}=0{\cdot}22$		$b/\bar{y}=0{\cdot}30$	
$y^*/\bar{y}$	$p=0{\cdot}1$	$p=0{\cdot}2$	$p=0{\cdot}1$	$p=0{\cdot}2$	$p=0{\cdot}1$	$p=0{\cdot}2$
0·92	0·33	0·42	0·45	0·52	0·57	0·63
1·29	0·27	0·36	0·36	0·44	0·45	0·52
1·66	0·25	0·33	0·32	0·40	0·40	0·47

The required values of $(1+r)t$ may be compared with those in table 4. For high y^* (for example $y^*/\bar{y}=1{\cdot}66$) the tax rates are only slightly higher than when contracting out is not allowed, but (not surprisingly) when y^* is much lower the rates must be increased significantly.

The inequality of total net income

The problem of obtaining the coefficient of variation of total net income is again complicated by the introduction of a further group. The three relevant groups are those receiving only the basic flat-rate pension, those whose earnings are between b and the contracting out level y^*, and those who have contracted out. Thus

$$\begin{aligned} z_i &= y_i(1-t)+b && \text{for } y<b \\ &= y_i(1-t)+b+p(y_i-b) \\ &= y_i(1-t+p)+b(1-p) && \Big\} \text{ for } b<y_i\leqslant y^* \\ &= y_i[(1-t)+t(1-\delta)(1+r)]+b && \text{for } y_i>y^*. \end{aligned}$$

The appropriate means and variances for the first and third group can be obtained from appropriate substitutions into the expressions given in the next section, while for the second group it can be shown that:

$$E(z|b<y<y^*) = \frac{\xi\bar{y}\{F_1(y^*)-F_1(b)\}}{\{F(y^*)-F(b)\}}+\psi.$$

The expression for $V(z|b<y<y^*)$ can then easily be obtained by comparison.

The coefficient of variation of total net income, η_z, under different policies, is shown in table 8. Unlike the other schemes reported above, the values of η_z are not sensitive to variations in the rate of interest (for given y^*, b and p). However, this may simply appear because of the nature of the comparisons. (δ, p and b are first set, then t is obtained from $(1+r)t$. An increase in r would, however, allow p or b to be changed rather than t, and these have more effect on η_z.) Table 8 clearly shows how the introduction of contracting out reduces the ability to reduce inequality. The values of η_z in table 8 are significantly higher than corresponding values in table 5. Indeed for low y^* and high p, the value of η_z actually exceeds η_y. (This is even more noticeable for $p=0{\cdot}25$.)

Thus the two-tier system combined with contracting out (of the second tier) offers very limited scope for redistribution, and can even increase the dispersion of total net income above that of earnings. Nevertheless, a comparison of this section with the results of the previous section indicates that the main limitation is caused not so much by contracting out as by the introduction of the earnings-related tier to the pension formula. Contracting out causes much greater policy problems where there is an earnings-related pension than when only a flat-rate scheme (with proportional contributions) is used.

Table 8. Values of η_z: Two-tier pension with contracting out.

	$b/\bar{y}=0{\cdot}15$		$b/\bar{y}=0{\cdot}22$		$b/\bar{y}=0{\cdot}30$	
$y^*/\bar{y}$	$p=0{\cdot}1$	$p=0{\cdot}2$	$p=0{\cdot}1$	$p=0{\cdot}2$	$p=0{\cdot}1$	$p=0{\cdot}2$
0·92	0·467	0·470	0·466	0·470	0·467	0·472
1·29	0·460	0·465	0·457	0·464	0·455	0·463
1·66	0·443	0·448	0·430	0·439	0·417	0·431

The new Government scheme introduced in April 1978, along with schemes operated in a number of other countries, has the additional complication that no contributions are paid or pension received on earnings above a certain upper limit. This is considered in the next section.

PROPORTIONAL CONTRIBUTIONS WITH TWO-TIER SYSTEM AND UPPER LIMIT

The pension scheme introduced in the United Kingdom in April 1978 is the same as that considered in the previous section, except that there is an upper limit to earnings, beyond which no contributions are paid or earnings-related pension received. With a limit of m, which applies to both contributions and pensions, the pension formulae are:

$$\begin{aligned} P(y_i)&=b && \text{for } y_i<b \\ P(y_i)&=b+p(y_i-b) && \text{for } b<y_i<m \\ P(y_i)&=b+p(m-b) && \text{for } y_i>m. \end{aligned}$$

In this case total contributions to the scheme, with no contracting-out arrangements, are equal to

$$Nt[\bar{y}F_1(m)+m\{1-F(m)\}].$$

These would accumulate at the market rate of interest, r, and would be required to finance flat-rate benefits (a total of Nb) plus the earnings-related second tier. The amount required for this latter part is given by:

$$N[p\bar{y}\{F_1(m)-F_1(b)\}-pb\{F(m)-F(b)\}+\{b(1-p)+pm\}\{1-F(m)\}]$$

Again the range of constrained policy choices available is obtained by equating accumulated contributions to total pensions. In the UK system a further degree of freedom in the policy options is lost by the desire to set m at approximately seven times the flat-rate pension. (i.e. $m=7b$). The effect of relaxing this constraint can therefore also be examined.

First, the values of $(1+r)t$ required to finance alternative policies are shown in table 9. These may be compared with values in table 4, where the differences are greatest for the lowest value of $b/\bar{y}$. Similarly, when the ratio of m to b is raised from 7 to 10, the values of 100 $(1+r)t$ are reduced by approximately 7% for $b/\bar{y}=0{\cdot}15$, but are only slightly lower for the $b/\bar{y}=0{\cdot}30$.

The inequality of total net income

In obtaining the coefficient of variation of total net income, the population is now divided into three groups, within each of which inequality declines. Total net income, z_i, is given by

$$z_i=y_i(1-t)+b \qquad \text{for } y_i<b$$

$$\left.\begin{aligned} z_i&=y_i(1-t)+b+p(y_i-b) \\ &=y_i(1-t+p)+b(1-p) \end{aligned}\right\} \text{for } b<y_i<m$$

$$\left.\begin{aligned} z_i&=y_i-tm+b+p(m-b) \\ &=y_i+\{b(1-p)+m(p-t)\} \end{aligned}\right\} \text{for } y_i>m$$

The values of η_z are shown in table 10; these are comparable to those given in table

Table 9. Values of $(1+r)t$: Two-tier system with upper limit $m=7b$.

$b/\bar{y}$	$p=0{\cdot}05$	$p=0{\cdot}10$	$p=0{\cdot}15$	$p=0{\cdot}20$
0·15	0·29	0·33	0·37	0·41
0·30	0·34	0·38	0·41	0·45

Table 10. Values of η_z. $(m=7b)$.

	$p=0{\cdot}1$		$p=0{\cdot}2$	
$b/\bar{y}$	$r=0{\cdot}2$	$r=0{\cdot}6$	$r=0{\cdot}2$	$r=0{\cdot}6$
0·15	0·448	0·434	0·448	0·431
0·22	0·401	0·397	0·408	0·403
0·30	0·363	0·367	0·375	0·378

Note: $\eta_y=0{\cdot}471$.

Table 11. Values of η_z. $(m=10b)$.

	$p=0{\cdot}1$		$p=0{\cdot}2$	
$b/\bar{y}$	$r=0{\cdot}2$	$r=0{\cdot}6$	$r=0{\cdot}2$	$r=0{\cdot}6$
0·15	0·425	0·420	0·429	0·422
0·22	0·387	0·390	0·397	0·399
0·30	0·355	0·362	0·369	0·376

5, for the two-tier system without an upper limit. The effect of increasing the ratio of m to b from 7 to 10 is shown in table 11, where it can be seen that the values of η_z are much closer to those in table 5. The additional constraints imposed on policy choices within the new government scheme by the desire to have the same upper limit for both contributions and pensions, and to have $m/b=7$, are therefore rather severe. The reasons for introducing these characteristics into the pension scheme have not been made clear in any of the White Papers, however.

CONCLUSIONS

The purpose of this paper has been to examine the extent to which alternative government pension schemes may be able to affect the inequality of net lifetime income; that is, income after deduction of contributions and payment of pensions. For reasons of tractability the measure of relative inequality used was the coefficient of variation. Special attention was given to the feasible range of policy alternatives where the pension scheme must be self financing, and the additional problems which arise where individuals are allowed to contract out of the government scheme. The basis of contracting-out arrangements is that the government must prevent all individuals from leaving the state system by reducing the effective rate of return which can be obtained in the market. This is done by collecting proportional contributions to the government pension fund from those contracting out, which nevertheless do not entitle individuals to full pension rights.

Of the various schemes examined it was shown that the system of proportional contributions and flat-rate pensions resulted in the greatest reduction in the inequality of lifetime income (further reductions could obviously be achieved by the use of a progressive system of contributions).‡‡ The redistributive ability of such a scheme was shown to be significantly constrained by allowing individuals to contract out.

The introduction of an earnings-related second tier to the government pension formula was shown to involve less redistribution than the flat-rate scheme combined with contracting out. However, when contracting out is allowed with the two-tier pension, the ability to redistribute lifetime income virtually disappears. Furthermore, it was shown that the choice of policy variables becomes extremely difficult with contracting out, because of the high sensitivity of the number of individuals who leave the system to their rate of contributions to the state scheme.

The results, therefore, strongly suggest that if it is desired to have a pension scheme with an earnings-related component, it would be very unwise to allow contracting out. If, however, the ability to contract-out of a state scheme is regarded as being of paramount importance, then it would be much better to have a simple flat-rate government pension.

The conclusions show that departure from the original Beveridge suggestion of an 'adequate' flat-rate pension leads to severe administrative difficulties, and considerably reduces the redistributive element of pension schemes. Finally, it is perhaps worth noting that the calculations reported above have been made on the assumption that the administrative costs of running pension schemes is zero. It is, however, obvious that the costs of running an earnings-related scheme (based on an average of earnings over many years) are significantly higher than those of running a flat-rate pension.§§

ACKNOWLEDGEMENTS

I am very grateful to Linda Roberts for computing assistance and to S. J. Prais for comments on an earlier draft. The paper was written at the National Institute of Economic and Social Research.

REFERENCES

Aitchison J. A. and Brown J. A. C. (1957) *The Lognormal Distribution.* Cambridge, Cambridge University, p. 12.

Atkinson J. A. (1977) The developing relationship between the state pension scheme and occupational pension schemes. *Social and Economic Administration,* **11,** 3, p. 216.

Beveridge W. (1942) *Social Insurance and Allied Services,* HMSO Cmd. 6404.

Creedy J. (1978a) *An analysis of Government Pension Schemes.* National Institute of Economic and Social Research Discussion Paper, No. 12.

Creedy J. (1978b) Negative Income taxation and income redistribution. *Oxford Bulletin of Economics and Statistics* **40,** 4.

Diamond P. A. (1977) A framework for Social Security analysis. *J. Pub. Econ.* **8.**

DISCUSSION

by **J. Stern,** *Economic Advisers' Office, Department of Health and Social Security*

In his paper John Creedy ingeniously models the effects on the distribution of lifetime income achieved by the Labour Government's new pension scheme known as *Better Pensions.* In his paper, he establishes a baseline position for comparisons—a pensions

‡‡ An analysis of various negative income taxation schemes shows that they can be much more effective in reducing inequality, but this should not be too surprising. See Creedy (1978b).

§§ These conclusions, furthermore, cast a shadow over the optimism expressed by Atkinson (1977, p. 225) when he states, 'We are attempting something which, to my knowledge, is paralleled nowhere in the Western World. I cannot pretend to predict precisely how the relationship between occupational schemes and the State scheme will work out over future years, but the arrangements now evolved seem to have attracted sufficient general support to serve as the basis for a period of ordered and fruitful development in this field'.

scheme with proportional contributions and flat-rate pensions and then shows the differences made by (i) partial contracting out; (ii) a pension with a flat-rate element and a proportional upper tier; (iii) a two-tier pension with partial contracting out from the upper tier only and (iv) a two-tier pension with partial contracting out from the upper tier but with pensions and contributions subject to an upper limit. It can be seen from this that he has built into his analysis all the main features of the Better Pensions, with great technical finesse. There are, of course, some features that he could not build in. To make the analysis tractable, he assumes a constant population, constant productivity growth and a funded pension scheme. These assumptions imply that, in the paper before us, he cannot analyze some of the interesting but less central elements of the pensions scheme, such as the 'best 20 year provision', or the earnings-dynamizing and inflation-proofing elements in the context of growing productivity and a pay-as-you-go scheme. The omission of these elements is not all loss, however, as it allows a clearer focus on the central features. The exception to that is that the potential instability of the two-tier scheme with partial contracting out, identified by Creedy, may be reduced by the omitted features. (There are also empirical factors that may reduce the potential instability. *See below*.)

The analytic conclusions of Creedy's paper can be (baldly) set out as follows:

(i) The pensions scheme that has most potential for redistributing lifetime income is a scheme with flat rate pensions and proportional contributions;

(ii) The incorporation of either partial contracting out or a proportional earnings-related upper tier of pension both reduce the ability of the pensions scheme to redistribute lifetime income—the latter more than the former;

(iii) The combination of a two-tier pension having a proportional (earnings-related) upper tier with partial contracting out from the upper tier implies that there is 'very limited scope for redistribution', with contracting out causing much greater problems than for a flat rate pension;

(iv) Curiously, if my reading of tables 6, 9 and 11 is correct, the imposition of an upper limit to earnings of 7 times the basic pension level for both contributions and pensions increases the degree of lifetime redistribution when partial contracting out is allowed compared with the position when there is no upper limit. However, a higher limit to earnings (of 10 times the pension level) shows more redistribution than the 7 times variant.

On the basis of the results set out above, Creedy's conclusions for pensions policy are that it is extremely unwise to allow contracting out in a pensions scheme with an earnings related element. If contracting out is required, then it is better to have a flat-rate government pension.

My comments on Creedy's paper fall into two groups. The former is related to the choice of policy criterion for judging pensions schemes and the rationale for the current scheme and the latter relates to the facts of state- and occupational-scheme coverage, which affect the degree of applicability of his results for the operations of the new pensions scheme.

As the more interesting issues arise under the first heading, I will deal with them first. Stated in a nutshell, my contention is that pensions policy has not been conceived in this country as an engine of redistribution but as a method of poverty relief for the old and that successive pensions reforms have primarily reflected changes in our views on poverty. Creedy's paper is relevant to the relative costs (in terms of contribution and/or tax rates) of achieving policy goals, but in my view it otherwise misrepresents the objectives of mainstream thinking on pensions in the UK. Creedy quotes from Sir Alec Atkinson's 1977 paper as showing that policy makers are designing pensions schemes so as to be redistributive in Creedy's sense. I am not entirely clear in what sense the Atkinson paper uses the term redistribution (I think he means redistribution from young to old) but I am quite sure he does not mean lifetime redistribution, where the higher earners are likely to receive a lower rate of return on their total savings from earnings for retirement purposes than lower earners, which is what Creedy means. The clearest statement of Atkinson's position is when he writes 'The late Minister of State (Social Security), the Rt. Hon. Brian O'Malley, used to say that he was in favour of occupational schemes flourishing because he was in favour of bigger pensions—and people would get a higher *total* pension income in retirement if occupational schemes flourished than if they didn't'. (Atkinson, page 218.) After dealing with the problems of cutting back existing occupational schemes, Atkinson concludes the paragraph as follows: 'If on those, or other grounds, it is accepted that the Government should do all they legitimately can to help occupational schemes flourish, a prima facie case has been made for allowing good occupational schemes to stand in place of part of the State scheme because in this way their contribution will be maximized. How is this best done? The search for the answer has occupied many ingenious minds both outside and inside Government over the past two decades.'

My view is that the main determinant of pension policy is the simple one of how to ensure that old people do not live in poverty, i.e. the provison for them of a standard of living that society believes as the minimum necessary for a reasonable life contingent on previous living standards. To the extent that Governments have had explicit problems on redistribution, they have been conceived and discussed as part of taxation policy to be implemented by the Inland Revenue, or implicitly through educational policies.

My own interpretation of attitudes to pensions policy runs as follows:

(i) The nineteenth-century surveys, e.g. by Booth, Rowntree and their twentieth-century successors showed that the single most important cause of poverty was old age. The remedy that was assigned was a pension paid for through a contributory system that came to fruition as National Insurance. This developed out of nineteenth-century friendly-society and union funds;

(ii) The programme outlined achieved universal coverage after 1945 with a flat-rate pension at a subsistence rate paid for by flat-rate contributions. However, with the increased cost of pensions not least due to their increasing roughly in line with real earnings, there was increasing criticism of the sharply regressive nature of flat-rate contributions. This in itself limited the growth of pensions, as well as encouraging the move to earnings-related contributions;

(iii) In the post-war period, the view has grown up that the goal of National Insurance is to assure a level of benefit related to previous earnings rather than to subsistence, which is generated through Supplementary Benefit. One way of describing this is to say that 'job rights' should be carried into benefits. Thus, an earnings-related pension is to give those who do not have one, the 'job right' benefit of an occupational pension. The Labour Party has been greatly involved for over 20 years in the design and introduction of earnings-related benefits (e.g. Earnings Related Supplement in 1965) and the Better Pensions reform has its origins, as I understand it, in proposals made by Professor Abel-Smith and others in the 1950s. But at that time contracting out from occupational pensions schemes would not have seemed the problem it is today, as most of the growth in the numbers covered by occupational pensions took place in the period 1957–63;

(iv) There are two major beliefs encouraging the growth of earnings-related pensions and other benefits. The first is the idea that the income one needs to maintain a similar standard of living when elderly, sick or unemployed is higher for those with higher incomes, e.g. because of pre-existing financial commitments. This belief is directly counter to the idea of using benefits to equalize lifetime incomes, but is partially consistent with equalizing redistribution across generations at a point in time. The other major belief is that people will not 'stand for' paying earnings-related contributions for a flat-rate benefit. Such a policy, it is claimed, violates the 'National Insurance principle'. The argument is justified on a variety of grounds. The strongest, it seems to me, is that social security gains in public esteem from being financed through a hypothecated tax set aside for that alone. But the major gain from having a hypothecated tax is that people can see themselves directly benefitting as well as all others in the society, in which case they may be more willing to pay for higher benefits for others. This allows some redistribution, but if that is pushed too far, then the identification of the benefits of others with the benefits to oneself is lost and the gains from hypothecation disappear. In that event, the level of basic benefit any Government can provide could well be held back. However, whatever the reasons, there can be little doubt that many people, certainly inside DHSS, rightly or wrongly believe that to have earnings-related contributions with only flat-rate benefits would imperil the National Insurance system. In these days of tax revolts (particularly against direct taxation and current marginal rates), it is an argument economists might like to consider more seriously.

Although Creedy's paper bypasses most of the debate about pensions in a National Insurance framework, his results are relevant in other areas, e.g. the consideration of income guarantees, negative income tax and similar systems where benefits and taxation are more fully integrated. The new pensions scheme will only remove from poverty those pensioners who retire from now on. They do not affect the currently retired and will not greatly augment the incomes of those who retire over the next decade or so. If one wanted to augment the incomes of these groups, then one way of doing so would be via a tax-assessed income guarantee. Creedy's results confirm one's expectation that that would be the least expensive way to relieve current pensioners from poverty (in terms of implied tax and contribution rates) whatever its other problems (e.g. administrative costs, introduction of a means test for pensioners, etc.). It is interesting to note the growing interest in the income guarantee route of reforming social security.

I would now like to deal briefly with a few empirical points that affect John Creedy's paper:

(i) For the contracting-out options, Creedy assumes that all those with earnings above a certain level (y^*) contract out and those below stay in. He then sets the partial contribution rate (δ) to obtain various proportions of the working population contracted in;

(ii) This technique has obvious power in an analytical model, but the real world situation is surprisingly different. The latest report of the Occupational Pensions Board shows 11·5 million occupational pensions members, of whom about 10–11 million are believed to have contracted out.

According to the Government Actuary's Department Survey 5·4 million occupational pensioners are in the public sector and I would have expected virtually all these to have contracted out of the new pension scheme. The public sector includes all the local authority and NHS manual workers, who are almost always classed as low paid, and other relatively low-paid groups such as busmen or coal-mining surface workers. In the private sector, with the legal requirement for contracted-out occupational pensions schemes to have a final salary-based pension, the 5 million so covered are heavily represented by large corporations, both financial and industrial, who tend to cover their workers irrespective of pay levels.

(iii) The actual structure of contracting out is thus rather different from Creedy's and is likely to modify his conclusions—particularly on the stability of pensions schemes.

I would like to congratulate John Creedy on writing a very stimulating paper which forced me to consider more carefully the objectives of pensions policy.

REFERENCE

Atkinson J. A. (1977) The developing relationship between the State pension scheme and occupational pensions schemes. *Social and Economic Administration.* **11,** 3, p. 216.

SUMMARY OF THE GENERAL DISCUSSION

Creedy explained that he had been forced to make various large assumptions to keep the analysis tractable. There was very little that was behavioural in the paper; what it really showed was the *upper* limit to redistribution via pensions schemes. He wondered about Stern's point on the 'National Insurance Principle' and the difficulty of having flat-rate benefits with graduated contributions. Was that really the case? Judge said he would be more persuaded of Stern's 'hypothecated tax' argument if there weren't an exchequer subsidy to National Insurance. In reply, Stern said that pay-as-you-go had become necessary in order to alleviate particular problems quickly, but that within the DHSS the 'National Insurance Principle' was still taken very seriously.

Cowell noted that Creedy's definition of lifetime income did not allow for time-discounting. This was potentially worrying, because the results might well be sensitive to intertemporal weighting. (As a result of Cowell's comment, Creedy subsequently produced an Addendum to his paper, which is available from the author on request.)

O'Hagan enquired what exactly was meant by 'actuarially sound'? Creedy explained that this was a requirement that the fund could always meet its expected obligations, in this case over the second period of the model. Champernowne wondered how a resource problem could arise in this case. Financing was only a veil.

Brown enquired whether there was any hard evidence on the differential effects of employers' and employees' contributions. Stern replied that he did not know of any.

Nicholson recalled that he had once compared three schemes of NI: the Beveridge scheme, the Crossman scheme and the Keith Joseph scheme. The most redistributive was the original Beveridge scheme, with flat-rate contributions and benefits. In his view, the reason was that benefits are always more redistributive than taxes, and that flat-rate benefits are the most redistributive of all. Thus flat-rate benefits which are only half financed by flat-rate contributions are very redistributive.

Clarke said that a constant population did not necessarily imply a constant age-structure. One problem in the UK had been the increasing proportion of pensioners, but this was now stabilizing. Also he noted that pensions produced a redistribution between sexes, because of sex-differential mortality. Pond noted that differential mortality across occupations produced a similar important redistribution.

Lecomber asked whether it was true that it was the richer people who contracted out? Stern agreed that many low-paid people, particularly in the public sector, were contracted out. A comparatively low percentage of private-sector employees were contracted out.

Creedy concluded by saying that he thought redistribution had to consider life-time incomes rather than a single-period 'snap-shot'. However, it did not seem from his analysis that pension schemes were a very suitable vehicle for redistribution.

WAGES POLICY AND THE REDISTRIBUTION OF INCOME. THE COLSTON RESEARCH SOCIETY ANNUAL LECTURE, 1979

R. Layard

Centre for Labour Economics, London School of Economics

SUMMARY

The question I want to discuss is: 'Should wages policy be one of the instruments of redistribution?' The answer of leader writers and politicians seems increasingly to be 'Yes'. My own answer is increasingly 'No', and I see a real danger that increasing concern with wages will divert attention from the vital task of building a more equal and coherent fiscal system.

My doubts about wages policy come under three heads, and it may help if I summarize them rather dogmatically straight away so that you can see where I am going. First, there is the doubtful relevance of wages policy to the problem of family poverty. It is not true that the workers in the poorest families are mostly low-paid, nor that low-paid workers are mainly in the poorest families. This is because families differ not only in wages but also in their needs and in the number of earners they include. So wages policy, even if feasible, could have only a limited impact on inequality. And through its employment effects it could hurt some of those that it is designed to help.

Second, there is the problem of enforceability. Recent incomes policies have had much less effect on wage inequality than is generally thought, because they have been systematically evaded. To make even an agreed wages policy stick seems impossible in a reasonably free society.

Third, there is the difficulty of securing agreement. It is a pipe-dream to suppose that by prolonged discussion a consensus could be reached on what is a just wage structure. One must distinguish here between horizontal and vertical equity. There *is* a reasonably objective test of horizontal equity between two occupations requiring similar basic abilities: relativities are correct if there is no more pressure of people wanting to enter the one occupation than the other. This should be the main test used by the new Standing Commission on Pay Comparability. But there is *no* objective test of vertical equity, which could determine what wage differential was fair as between occupations requiring different basic abilities. No series of colloquia or of national commissions will ever achieve a stable consensus on this point. Indeed many people are personally schizophrenic on this issue. I remember vividly hearing the then Chairman of the TUC explain on the radio that the two main objectives for the next pay round should be to raise the relative position of the low-paid and to restore differentials. However, I personally would reject the idea that vertical equity could attach to wages as such rather than to family income in relation to needs. The latter kind of equity can only be achieved via the fiscal system.† Meanwhile, efficiency arguments indicate that wages should be settled in the market place.

However, though we should avoid a wages policy with distributional objectives, we do need a wages policy that is designed to fight inflation. Inflation reduces welfare (as judged by opinion polls) even when real wages are on average increasing, as in the early and late 1970s. This is partly because of uncertainty, but partly because of the way in which inflation leads to continual reordering of the wages league table. Such reordering makes the losers lose more contentment than the gainers gain. It should therefore be a major objective of policy to stabilize the wage structure. It would be good if relative wages could be got to something near their equilibrium levels. But it is almost as important to keep them fairly stable. Month-by-month indexation would be an excellent way to do this and is probably the best available policy for the next pay round.

THE RELATION BETWEEN LOW PAY AND POVERTY

Let me begin again at the beginning. There are two main variants of an equalizing wages policy: a national minimum or a comprehensive policy for all levels. Consider first a national minimum wage. The question is: How much would this do to reduce poverty? This depends of course on the strength of the relation between low pay and poverty. Table 1 presents the basic evidence. The table relates to workers, full-time

Table 1. Distribution of 1000 typical employees by income relative to supplementary benefits (SB) and by individual hourly earnings (1975).

	Income as percentage of SB			
	140 or less	140–200	Over 200	All
Hourly earnings (pence)				
Under 62·5	20	34	39	93
62·5 to 87·5	28	64	95	187
87·5 and over	58	194	468	720
All	106	292	602	1000

Notes : 1. Excludes people under 21 or over pensionable age.
2. Income relative to SB measures the net annual income of the household to which the employee belongs relative to the household's long-term Supplementary Benefit (SB) entitlement. Housing costs are deducted from income and also excluded from SB.
Source: General Household Survey tapes, as used in Layard, Piachaud and Stewart, (1978).

and part-time, but excludes people under 21 since they could have a lower minimum wage than adults. The table includes both men and women, since they would have to be subject to the same minimum. It then shows the pay and welfare levels of the workers concerned. Pay is measured by hourly earnings, since this is how a minimum wage would have to be specified. The welfare of the worker is measured by the income 'per head' of his or her household; and this in turn is measured by the household's annual net income relative to what it would receive if it were on long-term Supplementary Benefit. I am not using SB here as an absolute poverty standard, but simply

† In the fiscal system I include public expenditure on education and training, affecting the productivity of workers.

as a method of adjusting income for family size. So the table examines how far adult workers on low hourly wages are in poor households and vice versa.

The results are rather striking. In 1975 nearly 10% of workers earned under 62·5 pence an hour. And just over 10% were in families with income per head below 140% of the SB level. But the overlap between the two groups was very low. *Only one in five of those in the poorest families* (bottom 10%) *were among the lowest-paid* (bottom 10%).‡ So a policy to raise only the lowest pay would leave most poverty unaffected. This may be why the TUC in 1974 proposed a higher minimum pay target equal to two-thirds of average male earnings.§ In 1975 two-thirds of average male earnings was slightly over 87·5p, but what is striking is that a minimum wage of that level would still leave unaffected over half of the workers in the poorest families.

The reason is that most of those on low hourly wages are married women, and married women workers are not usually in the poorest families. The poorest families are mostly ones in which there are a number of children and only one earner. If that earner is a man he is unlikely to be low-paid, even though the family is poor. For example, of the men workers in the poorest families (bottom 10%) only a third earned below 87·5p. The other two-thirds would have been left unaffected if an 87·5p minimum had been established. The main group of poor families that might gain from a minimum wage would be those headed by a single-parent mother. But at the same time an 87·5p minimum would have raised wages of rather over half of all women workers and of about 10% of men, despite the fact that in each group the minority of the workers affected are 'poor'.

Of course such a measure would have some mild equalizing effect, and one would always welcome any equalization, provided it did not have excessive efficiency costs. However, wage hikes of this kind would almost inevitably have employment effects, which would be both inefficient and inequitable.‖ In the US there is a good deal of evidence that increases in minimum wages have reduced employment and increased unemployment, at any rate for youths. But in Britain we have what might look like a counter-example. Between 1973 and 1976 the wages of women rose by 15% relative to men without any obvious employment effects—in fact the employment of women rose relative to men. However the interpretation of that episode is not yet clear. One explanation is that pay rose due to the Equal Pay Act and that there were no employment effects. Another explanation points to two disconcerting facts. First, women's employment rose as much due to a shift of total employment towards female-intensive industries, as to an increased proportion of women within each industry. Second, both for manual and non-manual workers, the relative wage increase was the same in the public and the private sectors, whereas equal pay was already meant to prevail in the public sector. This would suggest that women's wages rose partly due to the demand shifts towards female-intensive industries. Until more is known about this episode I would prefer to rely on the cumulated evidence of studies of labour demand in America and Britain. These have almost invariably shown that the pattern of labour demand responds substantially to changes in relative wages. I am therefore pretty confident that, if a minimum wage target were imposed there would be more unemployment, especially of women, without any adequate offsetting equity gain.

But have I underestimated the equity gain that would result from a wages policy, especially if it were a comprehensive policy and not just a minimum wage? The most

‡ The correlation between the two variables is 0·27. *See also* Layard and Zabalza (1979).

§ The TUC has since then adopted a flexible attitude to low pay and has never favoured a national statutory minimum.

‖ Given that low wages are already above market-clearing levels, there is no obvious reason why the efficiency cost of a *small* rise in the wage would be less than the equity gain (net of the equity effects of unemployment).

obvious criticism is that I have focussed unduly on those sources of inequality (especially family size) which are essentially transitory. There is, after all, a good case for looking at equity questions in terms of lifetime income per head rather than annual income per head. How would this change our conclusions? For simplicity let us assume that each family has over its lifetime the same number of children and that only the husband works, receiving the same wage in each year. Then the distribution of lifetime income per head is more equal than the distribution of annual income per head, since it is not affected by the number of children at home in a particular year. And a policy of wage equalization would eliminate a higher fraction of the inequality of lifetime income per head than of annual income per head, since there are no non-wage sources of lifetime income inequality.

What follows? In my view nothing. If social welfare is an additive function of individual incomes (of the kind assumed by Tony Atkinson) and if incomes are approximately log-normally distributed, then changes in inequality can be measured by changes in the variance of the log of income.¶ And in our example the changes in the log of the income variable are the same in the lifetime and the annual context. So moving to the lifetime case does not strengthen the argument for wages policy. And in fact our example is artificial. For individual wages vary a great deal from year to year. An equalizing wages policy would compress not only the distribution of permanent income but also of transitory income. But the second type of compression would have no effect on the distribution of lifetime income. So wages policy would have less effect on lifetime than annual income inequality. Thus moving to the lifetime framework does not increase our impression of the equity gains to be set against the efficiency costs of equalization via wages policy. I therefore conclude that a wages policy, even if it could be made to stick, would be much less equalizing than is generally supposed. And the equity gains would be likely to be offset by the efficiency losses.

THE ENFORCEABILITY OF WAGES POLICY

However our whole discussion so far is relevant only in so far as wages policy actually can alter the long-term wage distribution. What evidence would we like to have on this? Let us consider first a comprehensive policy covering pay in all occupations, with the prescribed wage structure more equalizing than the pattern that would have prevailed under the free market. If the policy is not counter-inflationary, the average prescribed wage will be the same as the free market average would have been. It follows that, if the wages policy has been imposed, there will then be market pressure upwards on wages above the average and market pressure downwards on wages below the average. Could such a policy stick? We should need to know whether it is possible to enforce both wage maxima and wage minima. On the other hand if the policy is also counter-inflationary it might be that all market rates would be above the prescribed levels, and only maxima need be enforced. By contrast, if we were concerned not with a comprehensive pay policy but only with a minimum wage, all we would need to know is the enforceability of wage minima.

So what is the evidence? On wage maxima, the main evidence comes from the experience of the incomes policies of 1972–1977. As is well known, these policies were all breached, though the wage increases which occurred may of course have been

¶ The argument is spelt out more fully in Layard (1979). With a log-normal distribution

$$\ln E = -\tfrac{1}{2}\varepsilon \operatorname{Var}(\ln Y)$$

where E is Atkinson's equality measure, ε his coefficient of inequality aversion ($\varepsilon > 0$) and Y income.

Table 2. Percentage change in average weekly earnings: prescribed and actual.

	Policy	Prescribed	Actual
November 1972–April 1973	Freeze	0	1·8
April 1973–November 1973	£1+4% (£5 max.)	6·7	10·3
November 1973–August 1974	£2.25 or 7% (£7 max.)+'threshold'	13·0	14·9
August 1974–August 1975	No limit	No limit	25·9
August 1975–August 1976	£6	10·4	14·3
August 1976–August 1977	5% (£2.50 min, £4 max.)	4·5	7·3

Note: 1. *Actual* earnings. There is no monthly series which distinguishes between men and women. The table therefore relates to both sexes.

The data are from the *Department of Employment Gazette*, May 1978, pp. 633–5 and relate to full-time and part-time workers.

For the period April–April they can be compared with the results for full-time workers from the New Earnings Survey and the results are similar. For the period October–October they can be compared with the results for full-time manual workers from the 'October survey' and are again similar.

2. The *prescribed* series does not allow for the exceptions to incomes policy allowed where women's pay was increased relative to men's during the approach to Equal Pay. However in fact, for full-time workers, male weekly earnings grew slightly faster than male-plus-female earnings in each April–April period, except from 1974–1975 when the all workers' pay increased 2·0 percentage points more than men's and in 1975–1976 when the difference was 0·8 percentage points. (The relative pay of women grew considerably, but women account for less than a quarter of all earnings.)

3. It is approximately correct to think of the policies as beginning and ending on the first of the month, while the actual data are recorded at some date during the month.

less than they would have been without the policies. Table 2 compares the prescribed rates of growth of average weekly earnings with the actual rates. Note that the policies were all either statutory or agreed with the TUC, with draft statutes on wages in reserve and actual statutory powers over prices available as a lever on employers. Virtually all pay *settlements* kept to the norms. But the actual rates paid for the job were in very many cases way above the norm. Many devices were used—especially regrading existing employees and hiring new employees onto higher scales.

The crucial question for redistribution is where the breaches occurred. Nearly all the policies were explicitly equalizing in that they included a lump-sum element. This would tend to produce more upward pressure on the formula wage, the higher-paid the group. So were the breaches greater for the higher-paid, so that the equalizing intentions of the formula were frustrated? Or were the breaches equiproportional, so that the equalizing effects were basically achieved?

Table 3 provides the best available data for an answer to this. Unfortunately the observations do not match exactly with the incomes policy periods. But we can get some casual insights from a rough inspection, before trying something more sophisticated. Consider for example the change from April 1975 to April 1976. In this period most people should have simply got £6 a week, except for the third of workers whose settlements fell between April and August 1975. But what actually happened? The man at the lowest decile got £7 a week (£1 'extra') and the man at the top decile got £17 a week (£11 'extra'). From casual inspection, it certainly looks as though the breaches were not equiproportional.

However we can investigate the question rather more systematically by performing the following experiment. Suppose that within some period there is a formula giving a fixed sum with or without a percentage element. If we know the overall average increase in wages which occurred, we can calculate a predicted wage in the second

Table 3. Dispersion of gross male weekly earnings: 1973–78.

	£s per week					As percentage of the corresponding median			
	Lowest decile	Lowest quartile	Median	Highest quartile	Highest decile	Lowest decile	Lowest quartile	Highest quartile	Highest decile
April 1973	25	31	38	48	61	66	80	125	159
April 1974	29	35	44	55	69	67	81	125	157
April 1975	38	45	56	70	88	67	81	125	158
April 1976	45	54	66	83	105	68	81	126	160
April 1977	49	59	72	91	114	68	81	126	158
April 1978	55	66	82	103	130	67	81	125	158

Note: The lowest decile means the man 10% from the bottom, the lowest quartile the man 25% up, and the median the man half-way up.
Source: New Earnings Survey, *Department of Employment Gazette*, October 1978.

period for each percentile group on the assumption that the breaches of the policy were equiproportional, i.e. that the equalizing effect of the formula was basically achieved. If we then express the percentile wage as a percentage of the median, this percentage must be predicted to rise for percentiles below the median, and to fall for percentiles above the median. In fact, between April 1975 and April 1977 the lower decile relative to the median should have risen by 2·7 percentage points as a result of the £6 a week. But it actually rose by only 1·1 percentage points. The upper decile relative to the median should have fallen by 4·5 percentage points, and in fact did not change. Thus the £6 a week had a negligible equalizing effect. By contrast, the more modest £1 lump-sum of the Heath period does seem to have had the predicted effects on wage structure between April 1973 and April 1974.

However, the overall picture from table 3 is of a remarkably stable structure, despite lump-sum incomes policies and threshold payments. This is confirmed in table 4 which looks at the movement of occupational differentials. White collar workers did nearly as well as manual workers—and even most of the professional groups did all right in relative terms. The popular mythology is of course quite different, for two main reasons. First the top (99th) percentile has indeed been clobbered relative to the median, and most journalists' friends are in the top percentile. Second, there have been a few very equalizing settlements, especially in engineering, which have produced notorious backlashes from the Leyland toolmakers and others. But in fact between 1975 and 1977, the spread of wages paid to a group of workers covered by a particular settlement actually increased for one third of the settlement groups covered by the national agreements listed in the New Earnings Survey. The engineering and mining settlements always receive great attention and it happens that together they account for nearly all the equalization that occurred among 'listed' manual workers over the whole period from 1970 to 1977.** Thus among the other two-thirds of workers the cases of disequalization almost exactly cancelled out the cases of equalization. I conclude that with few exceptions the forces of supply and demand have proved strong enough to get around policies that were explicitly equalizing, by paying more than the formula to the higher-paid workers.

** I refer to the contribution of the within-group variance in these two groups to the fall in variance of log hourly earnings among male manual workers covered by agreements listed in the New Earnings Survey (*see* Ashenfelter and Layard, 1979).

So much for the enforceability of wage maxima. What about the minimum wage? This may be more easily enforceable than a maximum. For most workers would prefer to be paid the minimum to being paid less. This is not always true, because some workers (as at Grunwick) may feel that their job is conditional on its low pay. But one might expect workers to report at least some of the cases where employers pay less than the minimum. By contrast, no workers would report an employer who paid more than the maximum, and many employers might also want to pay this much. However the enforceability of a minimum wage clearly depends on the number of workers affected. At present we have some 3 million workers covered by statutory Wages Boards or Councils, but it is not clear in how many cases the wage is higher than it would have been in the absence of the Wages Council. And there are a number of cases where the Wages Council rates are not observed. In the United States, Ashenfelter and Smith have done a detailed study of compliance with the Federal minimum wage law and conclude that it is enforced in respect of only about two thirds of the employed workers to whom is applies. There is no obvious reason to think that it would be much more successful here.

After this gloomy conclusion, at any rate about a general compression of relativities, I am in honour bound to revert to the experience of Equal Pay. As I have said, between 1973 and 1976 the hourly earnings of women workers rose by 15% relative to those of men. Suppose this *was* due to the Equal Pay Act. If legislation can affect the ratio of one sex's pay relative to another's, why should it not affect the relative pay of different occupations? The reason is simple. The Equal Pay Act says that women doing a particular type of work should be paid the same as men. It thus explicitly specifies a very visible relativity. A wages policy for occupations could perhaps specify relativities within various particular industries. But in general a wages policy would have to lay down absolute, rather than relative, levels of pay. These could then be eroded more in some cases than others, exactly as happened with the incomes policies.

INFEASIBILITY OF CONSENSUS

Finally I come to the question of consensus. The hope of most advocates of wages policy is that, by detached study and thought, one or both of the following objectives could be achieved:

(i) We should discover how people of the same abilities should be paid in occupations which differ in their attractiveness—roughly speaking the question of horizontal equity between occupations.

(ii) We should discover the appropriate vertical differential between occupations requiring different abilities.

Let me take these in turn. Consider two occupations, A and B, which require the same skill but where occupation A is nastier than occupation B—say sewage-worker and warehouseman. Presumably a fair differential in favour of the sewage-workers would be one which made existing sewage-workers feel as well off as they would have felt as warehousemen. But in a free society where people choose their jobs, the existing sewage-workers must feel better off than they would have felt as warehousemen, subject to one proviso. The proviso is that they could, if they wanted, get jobs as warehousemen. If some of them had wanted to become warehousemen but could not and became sewage-workers instead, then the sewage-workers' wage was not for them sufficient to compensate for not getting the warehouseman's job at the warehouseman's wage. So the test of whether the differential is fair in the sense defined is whether there is queueing for jobs in either of the markets. If there is queueing in market A then that occupation is relatively overpaid.†† And if there is queueing in both markets, then the occupation with the most queueing is relatively overpaid. This is *the* test of horizontal equity and should be the main basis of the work done by the Standing Commission on Pay Comparability.

There is however one important qualification. The principle only holds as a principle of equity in a static context. In a dynamic context there is always a problem of equilibrium wage changes for occupations where there are substantial costs of training or migration involved in gaining access to the occupation. If a worker decides to enter occupation A he is telling us that, on his forecast of the wages of A and B, the long-period benefits to him of being in A exceed any short-period costs. He then incurs the short-period costs. Some time afterwards, demand for A falls and the equilibrium wage falls to a level which, had he foreseen it, would have led him to reject A. What is now the equitable wage? Many people would consider there is a horizontal-equity case for preserving the wage level in A. The danger is of course that this would now produce queueing for jobs in A. However this can to some extent be avoided by lowering the entry wage, while preserving the wage of experienced workers. This would constitute an equity case for a steeper wage structure in declining than in expanding industries. Is university teaching an example of occupation A? I do not know, but it seems clear that the job-queueing test, softened to take account of historical relativities, should be sufficient to resolve most questions of inter-occupational comparabilities.

I have been advocating a behavioural approach to the measurement of compensating differentials—and one which, I should stress, can be used equally in socialist or capitalist countries, so long as there is no direction of labour. An alternative approach is the survey. Simply ask people what differential they would need. But different people will give different answers, and then whose answer should we use? The marginal man, of course. But unless people's answers are exactly consistent with their behaviour, the worker in A who most dislikes A will report a required differential that is higher or lower than the differential actually prevailing. In fact it will probably be higher since there is a strong incentive for workers to play up the ardours of their job. Do we then accept the survey differential or the one in the market? I would prefer the latter.

Another approach to the problem is job evaluation. Within a firm there has to be an acceptable institutional mechanism for establishing pay comparabilities, and job evaluation seems often to do the trick. It is of course not impossible to assemble at one place in a firm a good deal of relevant information about skill requirements, working conditions and the valuations which workers place on different dimensions of working conditions. But in a country it would be quite impossible to get together in one place even a tiny fraction of the relevant information and 'feel'. So national job evaluation would inevitably involve imposing on the wage structure the judgements of the job evaluators. By contrast the queueing test involves using the judgements of the workers concerned. Again I prefer the latter.

I turn now to the question of vertical equity. Loosely speaking, a part of the pay differential between skill levels is a compensating differential (which we have already discussed) and a part of it is a rent. A rent is a payment which exceeds what is needed to induce a person to supply the specified type of labour. So why not reduce the rent by reducing the pre-tax wage? The answer is of course an efficiency one and is well known. The pre-tax wage has an important function in rationing out the supply to

†† Not a bad test of queueing for a job is the proportion of new entrants whose fathers were in the occupation (at any rate among jobs in conurbations).

the highest value uses. If there are equity objections to the distributional effects of these rents (and I have strong objections to them), the right thing is to modify net incomes by taxes rather than to impose non-market-clearing pre-tax wages. Efficiency arguments also of course support the case for allowing compensating differentials, as well as rents, to reflect the influence of market forces.

This does not mean there is no role for public pay bodies—the public sector in particular needs to have an explicit method of rate fixing. But it does mean that the public sector should pay no more than is needed to attract the number of workers it wants, and recommendations made to the private sector should also aim to establish market clearing wages. Any attempt to abandon this objective criterion and to bring in ethical judgements will lead to the kind of see-saw we have observed recently. First, as in 1975, more equality is the objective; then, as in 1977, the restoration of differentials; and then as in 1978 the low-pay policy. This see-saw has itself added to the havoc already wrought by inflation in inducing a general obsession over pay.

THE IMPORTANCE OF FULFILLING EXPECTATIONS

This brings me to the final theme of this lecture. Where do we go from here? To tackle this, I want to start with some general thoughts about the relation between income and happiness. The following three facts have been fairly clearly documented by Easterlin (1972). First, Americans have not become happier over time despite economic growth. Second, at a point in time, richer Americans are happier than poorer Americans. Third (and a less hard fact) rich countries are not happier than poorer advanced countries. All these facts are based on self-reported happiness, but they are consistent with common observation. They suggest that happiness depends primarily not on absolute income but on income relative to something. The simplest hypothesis would be that what matters is one's income relative to the average income currently prevailing in one's country. Boskin and Sheshinski (1978) have recently shown how this would lead to a more equalizing optimal tax policy than would result if only absolute income mattered. However there is a problem here. For other evidence shows that people feel more hurt by the income gains of others if these others are near them in the income scale than if the others are far removed. This suggests that one should rather think of people as being concerned about status, where this may depend mainly on rank order in the income hierarchy but also perhaps on the relative income gaps between close rivals.

If people are mainly concerned about rank-order income, this would explain the four facts I have quoted so far. But there is an additional set of facts to be explained. When politicians consider any reform (e.g. of social security) they try desperately to avoid making anybody worse off. For they know that otherwise there will be no end of trouble, as occurred for example in 1934 when the proposed reform of unemployment benefit made nearly all better off, but a few worse off. Thus people behave as though they lose more in utility from a given loss of status than they gain in utility from an equal gain in status. In other words, utility depends not only on status but on expected status, as reflected in, say, status in the previous period. And the marginal utility for increases is less in absolute terms than the marginal disutility for decreases.‡‡

This story is consistent with my final fact: that as inflation proceeded in the early 1970s, people felt worse off despite unprecedented rises in average real wages. Obviously a part of the trouble was increased uncertainty. But higher inflation also

‡‡ The issues treated in the last two paragraphs are discussed more fully in Layard (1980).

brought about continual rearrangements in the income hierarchy. For example, consider two occupations, one settling in January and the other in July. Suppose that the January occupation has an annual average wage 5% above the July occupation. If wage inflation is at less than 10% a year the January occupation will always be paid more than the July occupation. But once wage inflation goes over 10%, there will be half the year when the July occupation is paid more than the January occupation. Such disturbances will have a very limited effect on the overall inequality of earnings. But they will bring about constant reordering of groups within a given income distribution—at great psychic cost.§§

By contrast, the pay policies of 1975–1977 passed off with remarkably little moaning, despite large falls in real income. People felt that the pay policy involved a common sacrifice and it probably did stabilize relative incomes. Since 1977, pay has once again become more volatile, and, despite increases in real income, most people are moaning.

THE WAY FORWARD: MONTH-BY-MONTH INDEXATION

What follows? Incomes policy cannot be the main weapon against inflation but it can be a useful adjunct to fiscal and monetary policy. But we do not want a policy which yet again tries to alter the relativities, with all the psychic cost that entails. In my view the ideal policy after the end of this wage round would aim to stabilize the wage structure. Let me begin by examining the consequences of a totally rigid pattern if such a thing could be imposed. If long-run supply curves are fairly elastic as seems likely, a stable wage structure might not be wildly inconsistent with long-run equilibrium in the face of quite a range of demand conditions. Many features of the wage distribution do in fact demonstrate a remarkable long-term stability. However, in the short-term a rigid wage structure would lead to a slower redeployment of labour from declining to growing sectors and hence to allocative losses and higher unemployment.

So this is where I put on my pragmatic hat. We know that a proportional incomes policy would be breached more in some places than others. But, if viewed as a semi-permanent institution, it could help to prevent some of the continual pointless reorderings which have been occurring. As table 4 shows, there is a strong tendency for a relative wage that rises in one year to come down soon after: what goes up must come down and vice versa. This tendency and the degree of movement that we have suffered would of course be more visible in a more disaggregated, and therefore larger, table of occupations. But my basic point remains: we want to cut out the pointless heart-ache engendered by the constant leap-frogging of workers caught in a Prisoner's Dilemma.

A proportional incomes policy would not, of course, be popular with some union leaders. The unions, as in Australia which has a proportional incomes policy, would have to devote more energy to their educational functions and to industrial democracy and less to their traditional function of wage bargaining. It follows that a proportional policy would only come about if it received massive popular support. Fortunately there is an instrument to hand. For people care not only about status but about the certainty attaching to their purchasing power. And the way to guarantee people's real incomes is by indexation. I would therefore suggest to whatever government is in power next summer that it adopt a pay policy where settlements are fully indexed from the start on a month by month basis. Thus the initial settlement could be quite

§§ These casual reorderings show clearly in the reduced explanatory power of earnings functions over the period. In multiple regression exercises done for men's log weekly earnings, the R^2s fell from 50% in 1971 to 41% in 1975.

Table 4. Average weekly earnings in each occupation as percentage of overall average weekly earnings (men).

Occupation	1973	1974	1975	1976	1977	1978
All non-manual	115	114	113	114	113	113
All manual	91	91	92	91	91	91
Non-manual						
Professional and related: supporting management and administration	139	139	131	131	132	132
Professional and related: education, welfare and health	121	120	122	127	124	118
Professional and related: science, engineering, technology and similar	121	118	119	115	120	119
Managerial (excl. general management)	119	115	111	112	112	113
Clerical and related	84	86	86	87	85	83
Selling	91	91	89	89	91	92
Security and protective service	101	98	102	102	100	99
Manual						
Catering, cleaning, hairdressing and other personal service	72	74	77	76	75	75
Farming, fishing and related	67	75	69	70	70	70
Materials processing (excl. metals)	90	92	89	90	91	90
Making and repairing (excl. metal and electrical)	97	95	91	90	91	90
Processing, making, repairing and related (metal and electrical)	99	98	98	97	98	98
Painting, repetitive assembling, product inspecting, packaging and related	91	90	89	89	90	90
Construction, mining and related not identified elsewhere	93	96	97	93	92	93
Transport operating, materials moving and storing and related	89	89	91	89	90	90
Miscellaneous	82	83	85	87	84	83
All public sector	100	102	106	107	105	102
All private sector	100	99	97	97	98	99

Note: The table relates to full-time men aged 21 and over whose pay was not affected by absence. Data relate to April.

low. To maintain a worker's real wage at its average level over the last 12 months the settlement would have to equal only half the rate of price inflation over the last 12 months. For example, if inflation had been at 10% the settlement could be for 5%, or a bit more to allow for real growth. This would have an excellent short-run effect on inflation, since the settlement levels early in the pay round would be much lower than they would otherwise be. Since we are not now in a boom (as we were when the threshold was introduced) it is likely that indexation would reduce the rate of inflation. But even if it did increase the rate of inflation, this might be acceptable since the consequences of inflation would be so much less bad.

My proposal also has the advantage that by eighteen months hence everybody's real wage at a particular date would be independent of when he last settled. So it should then be possible to move more easily to synchropay. At present synchropay is held up by the fact that at the first synchropay day there would have to be different levels of settlement for different groups. Once everyone is onto month-by-month indexation this problem disappears. But the basic argument for month-by-month indexation is that it will at last restore stability in relativities.

None of this takes us any further towards redistribution. That is the task of fiscal policy and it is a disgrace that more progress has not been made in developing an integrated policy which guarantees that every one automatically receives at least the present Supplementary Benefit levels. (The work test must of course remain.) The lack of such a system has left open one valid argument for a wages policy, namely the stigma attaching to means-tested benefits which have to be claimed. However it is possible to make the transfer system automatic. This requires essentially that National Insurance benefits and tax thresholds be raised to at least SB levels. Such a policy could be financed to some extent by abolishing the married man's extra tax allowance (in families without young children), by taxing short-term National Insurance benefits, and by reducing the tax threshold for the elderly. But there would inevitably be some increases in general taxation. In addition, if we are to continue to subsidize the actual rent payed by poor people, workers will have to notify the Inland Revenue of the amount of this rent and also of their spouses' earnings and their own supplementary earnings. But all these problems are superable. Most of the important changes are admirably discussed in the Meade Report (Meade, 1978), and I only mention them here to show that my heart is in the right place.

To conclude, I believe it is misleading to argue that policies on low pay would, if successful, have a major effect on income distribution. Moreover, they are unlikely to be successful. If adopted, they are likely to swing from year to year with the swings of fashion regarding equality. But see-saws in the wage structure are the last thing we need. Change is hurtful, and changes which are rapidly reversed are particularly pointless. Happy the country whose government can help it to stop thinking about money.

ACKNOWLEDGEMENTS

I am grateful for comments to T. Blackstone, P. Hammond, D. Metcalf, H. Phelps Brown, D. Piachaud, C. Pissarides, B. Roberts, A. Sen and P. Wiles. Much of the material presented stems from work with colleagues, especially D. Piachaud, as listed in the references.

REFERENCES

Ashenfelter O. and Layard R. (1979) *The Effects of Incomes Policy Upon Differentials.* Centre for Labour Economics, LSE, Discussion Paper no. 44.

Ashenfelter O. and Smith R. (1979) Compliance with the Minimum Wage Law. *J. Polit. Econ.* **87,** 2, 333–350.

Boskin M. and Sheshinski E. (1978) Optimal Redistributive Taxation when Individual Welfare Depends Upon Relative Income. *Q. J. Economics* **92,** 4, 589–602.

Easterlin R. A. (1972) Does Economic Growth Improve the Human Lot? In: David P. A. and Reder M. W. (ed.), *Nations and Households in Economic Growth.* New York, Academic.

Layard R., Piachaud D. and Stewart M. (1978) *The Causes of Poverty*, Royal Commission on the Distribution of Income and Wealth, Background Paper No. 5, HMSO; summarized in Layard R., Piachaud D. and Stewart M. (1979), The Causes of Poverty. *National Westminster Bank Quarterly Review*, February.

Layard R. (1979) Education Versus Cash Redistribution: The Lifetime Context. *J. Pub. Econ.* **12,** 377–385.

Layard R. (1980) Human Satisfactions and Public Policy. *Economic Journal* **90,** December.

Layard R. and Zabalza A. (1979) Family Income Distribution: Explanation and Policies. *J. Political Economy* **87,** 5(2), 133–161.

Meade J. E. (Chairman) (1978) *The Structure and Reform of Direct Taxation.* Inst. Fiscal Studies, 1978.

THE ANATOMY OF TAX AVOIDANCE

J. A. Kay

Institute for Fiscal Studies, London and St John's College, Oxford

At present, the top rate of tax on investment income in the UK is 98%. The top rate of capital transfer tax is 75%. Tax on earnings reaches a maximum rate of 83%. Rates of tax of this order of magnitude have now existed in the UK for 40 years. They are generally higher than those of other countries, and much higher than those of most countries with a comparable economic structure. If they had been effective, they would have brought about a transformation in wealth distribution. Yet the most casual empiricism suggests that this transformation has not occurred. Walk through Mayfair, drive through Surrey, or more prosaically consult the available statistics on the distribution of income and wealth, and ask—as foreigners do—how all this has survived what is, in its upper echelons, the most ostensibly redistributive tax system in the western world.

What then are the limits to redistribution? It is, after all, rather difficult to envisage significantly higher rates of tax than these—and in the case of the 98% rate it is literally impossible. Yet it is rather easy to envisage a more egalitarian society than modern Britain, even for those who would not necessarily think such an outcome desirable. Why is the redistributive capacity of the tax system apparently so limited?

The answer lies in tax avoidance. These rates of tax are unenforceable and unenforced. The stroller through Mayfair may know that the freeholds of most of the properties he passes form a part of the Grosvenor Estate. A little research will tell him that the Grosvenor family are Dukes of Westminster. A little more research will tell him that the last Duke died leaving an estate valued at £4m, on which duty payable amounted to about £1m. He may be surprised at the smallness of these figures, in relation to what is generally thought to be one of the richest families in England. He may be further surprised to learn that the estate did in fact pay no duty at all, it being ruled that the Duke (who died of cancer in 1967) was entitled to the benefit of an exemption for those who died from wounds received on active service. No doubt those who strolled around Constantinople in the days of the late Byzantine empire experienced a similar feeling. The central, and poorly understood, fact is that we have reached a stage where progressivity depends much more on the tax base than on the tax rates. 75%, 83%, 98% or indeed 101% of very little is in each case very little. This paper attempts to redirect attention from the rates to the base.

AVOIDANCE AND EVASION

Interest in tax avoidance is relatively new to economists. There has been some recent theoretical analysis of tax evasion (Allingham and Sandmo, 1972) and attempts to measure its extent (Frank and Deheyser-Meulders, 1977). But it is gradually becoming realized that it is avoidance activity which accounts for a high proportion of the economic effects of taxation, rather than the work/leisure or consumption/savings tradeoffs conventionally analyzed in public finance. In this paper, I attempt to identify the major avoidance opportunities in the UK income tax and to show how these arise from the lack of correspondence between legislative and economic concepts of what should be subject to tax. I use this approach to argue that expenditure based taxes—direct or indirect—are systematically less vulnerable to avoidance opportunities than income based taxes—direct or indirect.

English usage makes a conventional distinction between (legal) tax avoidance and (illegal) tax evasion. Moral and legal aspects of this dichotomy do not concern me much here but the general lines of the distinction are useful. Evasion is concerned with concealing or misrepresenting the nature of a transaction; when avoidance takes place the facts of the transaction are admitted but they have been arranged in such a way that the resulting tax treatment differs from that intended by the relevant legislation.

The incidence of evasion is therefore a function of the mechanisms by which tax is assessed and collected, and the extent to which they can be controlled or monitored; the incidence of avoidance is a function of the tax base and depends on the extent to which legislation is successful in expressing the underlying economic concepts. Avoidance depends on the base: evasion on the assessment procedures. There is still some area which lies in between the two, and this is where the tax treatment of a transaction depends on the reason for undertaking that transaction (as is the case, for example, with business expenditures). This is bound to prove difficult to police and offers scope for distorting and misrepresenting activities which gradually shade from tax avoidance into tax evasion. A tax system in which the burden of tax depends on motive rather than verifiable and objective fact is not very satisfactory, but such provisions arise in two main areas; in relation to business expenses and fringe benefits, where the problem is unavoidable, and in cases where legislators, unable to deal with avoidance in more appropriate ways, seek to inhibit it by passing laws which require taxpayers to observe the spirit as well as the letter of the code by means of very general anti-avoidance provisions. This means attempting to distinguish tax avoidance mechanisms from similar or identical actions which are bona fide commercial transactions. This type of provision is more common abroad than in the UK, and does not work well there either.

One source of divergence between legislative intention and actual outcome is simple error or oversight, in formulating or drafting tax legislation—where the rules do not say what those who wrote them intended them to say. This is a significant source of tax avoidance opportunities, but it is not really a matter for economists to discuss, except perhaps to note that the more complicated a tax structure becomes the more vulnerable to difficulties of this kind it becomes. In looking at tax avoidance, we are looking at ways in which the tax system induces people to modify their behaviour in order to pay less tax. But this is rather too broad, and to qualify for the label avoidance we imply that there is some element of artificiality involved, so that the effect of the untaxed or lightly taxed transaction is rather similar to what the effect of the taxed transaction would have been. The man who reacts to the tax system by drinking coca-cola instead of whisky is not engaging in tax avoidance, though he is reducing the amount of tax he pays; the man who reacts by staying at the office to drink the firm's whisky instead of his own is avoiding tax. (The man who responds by taking the firm's whisky home is engaging in tax evasion.)

The existence of a range of avoidance possibilities has a number of effects on a tax system. In a system such as that of the UK where there is an attempt to legislate absurd rates of tax on high incomes, it has an essential rôle as a safety-valve. It is quite obvious that one cannot reduce people's potential standard of living to 2% of what it would otherwise have been—and this is what a 98% income tax rate purports to do—without endangering social stability. It is only because reality does not correspond to the apparent legislative intention that the system 'works'—in the sense that it does not break down in some rather more dramatic way. If rates of tax of this kind cannot be avoided, they will be evaded, and if attempts are made to stop this then other forms of resistance will ensue.

If the effects of tax avoidance were simply to bring about a uniform reduction in the rate structure, then they would not be particularly serious. It would be possible to make some rough allowance for the fact that the effective rates were somewhat lower than the nominal rates, and set the nominal rates accordingly. But the importance of tax avoidance arises largely from the fact that opportunities for avoidance are not evenly distributed between individuals or across activities. The result of this is that even if the nominal tax structure is designed so as to be equitable between different groups of people and even-handed in its treatment of different sources of income, the effective tax structure will not be.

It is this problem which is at the centre of some of the most serious difficulties confronting the British tax system. Within the income tax system, avoidance possibilities are very much more limited in respect of employment incomes than in relation to incomes from business or from capital. Although the nominal rates are, if anything, more favourable to income from employment than from other sources, the effective outcome is the reverse. The practical consequence has been that differences in employment incomes are not a source of major inequalities in wealth distribution, which result overwhelmingly from the differential incidence of inheritance and capital gains. This outcome can give little satisfaction whatever relative weights any particular individual puts on efficiency and equity objectives; efficiency is sacrificed because high nominal rates of tax are left to bear principally on those engaged in productive activity and equity is not achieved because high but randomly effective nominal rates of tax are fair neither between rich and poor nor between rich and rich.

Opportunities for tax avoidance affect not only the distribution of resources between individuals, but also the distribution of resources between different activities and sectors. The most important example of this is the institutionalization of personal savings: the consequences of the different ways in which savings accumulated by individuals and savings accumulated by institutions are taxed, and the resultant effects on the channels of capital flows in the British economy. But it is important to recognize that it is often these avoidance possibilities, rather than the allocative effects discussed in traditional public finance theory, which are the source of the major economic effects of taxation.

AVOIDANCE AND THE DEFINITION OF INCOME

Avoidance possibilities are essentially products of difficulties in the definition of the tax base: in translating such concepts as 'income', 'expenditure', 'value-added' or 'whisky' into a legal definition for purposes of framing tax legislation. These problems are compounded in any tax structure that imposes multiple rates of tax on elements of the same tax base. These multiple rates can either be differentiated according to the identity of the individual involved in a transaction—as with income tax—or according to the nature of the transaction itself—as with value-added tax. The use of multiple rates increases the problems involved because it requires that each element of the base be allocated to some category or other within that base; for income tax, that each part of what is defined as income can be attributed to one, and only one, identified individual; for value added tax, that each output can be precisely allocated to some particular commodity group. If the conventional distinction between direct and indirect taxation is worth making, which is doubtful, then the question of whether rate differentiation is based on the identity of the individual or the nature of the transaction is perhaps the most helpful basis for it.

A natural place to seek a definition of what the 'income' that income tax is a tax on is in the relevant legislation. It is well known, however, that this is not very helpful. 'The Income Tax Acts nowhere define "income" any more than they define "capital"; they describe sources of income and prescribe methods of computing income, but what constitutes income they discreetly refrain from saying' (Lord Macmillan in Van den Berghs Ltd *v*. Clark, 1935, 19 TC 390 p. 428). The literature of economics and accounting, by contrast, provides a multiplicity of definitions. The best known, however, is that of Hicks:—'income is what a man can spend and still expect to be as well off at the end of the accounting period as he was at the beginning.' It is obvious that this is not an operational definition for tax purposes. There are three words in it that require elaboration; 'spend', 'expect', and 'well-off'. The vast majority of avoidance possibilities under an income tax regime arise from the difficulty of translating one or other of these three words, which form part of the principles of the measurement of income, into legislative reality.

'Expect': the problem of capital gains

We might begin with the word 'expect'. The impracticality of this as a guide to the tax inspector is obvious. One method of overcoming this is to delete it: to base tax liability not on what a man might have expected to consume, and still have been as well off at the end as he was at the beginning, but instead on what he could *in fact* have consumed and still have been as well off. This leads us to the Haig–Simons definition of personal income: 'personal income may be defined as the algebraic sum of (a) the market value of rights exercised in consumption and (b) the change in the value of the store of property rights between the beginning and end of the period in question'. Although the use of this income concept has been widely advocated by economists, especially in North America, and it has the merit of providing a relatively clear and operational definition, it has not won general acceptance and there appears to be no major country in which capital gains are treated on a par with income as the Haig–Simons definition would require.

The reason is that few non-economists are willing to accept that all capital gains are equivalent to income, either in the way in which they respond to receiving them or in the way in which they believe they should be taxed, and the Hicksian definition of income (and the permanent income model of consumption behaviour which is based on it) do provide support for this view. But the distinction they suggest is one between expected and unexpected gains. While the British legal position has been that some capital gains are income and should be taxed as such, while others are not and should be exempted, it is not surprising that it has not followed the expected/unexpected dichotomy: but instead, it has simply degenerated into a muddle over what the basis of the distinction actually is. In attempting to codify it, the 1955 Royal Commission suggested that taxable transactions were those which carried 'the badges of trade' and listed a number of characteristics which might enable one to recognize 'the badges of trade'; but as Kaldor's Minority Report noted, the list of characteristics had little coherence and was in certain instances self-contradictory.

Because of the difficulty of framing a rational distinction between taxable and non-taxable gains the conversion of income into non-taxable* gains is one of the central gambits in income-tax avoidance. The crudest forms of exchanging income for capital gain are the practices of 'bond-washing' and 'dividend-stripping'. These rely on the existence of taxpayers with different marginal rates of tax. Bond-washing exploits the fact that interest and dividends on securities are paid at intervals—typically six-monthly. Consider a bond which yields 10% and is priced at 100. As the six-monthly interest date comes closer, the price of the bond will rise—say from 100 to 104. For any such bond, there is a date on which it goes 'ex-dividend'—the person who holds it on that date is the person entitled to receive the coming interest payment, and a subsequent purchaser is not entitled to the dividend. When the bond goes ex-dividend, its price will therefore fall back to 100.

It is therefore efficient to ensure that a bond which is held by a (say) 50% taxpayer is held by a non-taxpayer on the day it goes ex-dividend. The holder of the bond sells the bond ('cum-dividend') the previous day for 104 and repurchases it a day ('ex-dividend') later for 100. Doing this every six months he obtains a tax-free return of 4 per six-monthly period, or 8%. The non-taxpayer makes a loss of 4 on each transaction, but this is more than offset by the interest payment of 5 which he receives. The bond-holder has raised his net annual return from 5% (after 50% tax) to 8%, so that the marginal rate he pays is not 50% but 20%: his associate makes a profit of 1, or 2%; the Revenue loses 2½ on each transaction. The scheme is advantageous for any price of the bond on the day before it goes ex-dividend which lies between 102½ and 105. Which level within these limits it reaches depends on the relative number of taxpayers and non-taxpayers. If the majority of participants in the market are taxpayers at 50%, then 'associates' will be in short supply and the rewards they gain bid up, so that the cum-dividend price of the bond will be close to 102½: if non-taxpayers are relatively numerous the price will approach 105. (Because indifference curves between income and capital gains are straight lines for sophisticated taxpayers, the limit theorem does not yield a determinate equilibrium even if the numbers of participants on both sides of the market are large).

Anti-avoidance legislation to deal with bond-washing began in 1927, with a provision (in relation to higher rates of tax only) which raised an additional charge to tax if liability had been reduced substantially below that which would have arisen if interest had been paid as it accrued. This provision proved insufficient; in particular, it reduced the attractions of the scheme to the higher-rate taxpayer but not to his associate. The position of associate was advantageous, not only to non-taxpayers but also to professional dealers in securities for whom capital losses are deductible against other income and who would therefore derive a (taxable) profit (of 1 in the example above) by holding the security for a day. A further strengthening of the legislation in 1937 therefore provided that if an agreement was made to sell and repurchase a security, and the outcome was that the interest payable on it accrued to someone else, then that interest would be treated as the taxable income of the original owner. However, this failed to cover the possibility that the original owner might simply sell the right to receive the interest, without selling the security itself. This loophole was closed in the 1938 Finance Act.

Imposing restrictions on agreements to buy and resell proved inadequate. It was possible to engage in bond-washing without an explicit agreement for purchase and resale, since there was in fact no difficulty in finding willing buyers and sellers at

* The following discussion ignores capital gains tax which (even when applicable) does not affect the central points of the argument.

predictable market prices. In 1959 more comprehensive rules were introduced for dealing with bond-washing which sought to identify situations where purchases and sales of securities were made within a short period during which an interest payment became due. Where these conditions are identified, a set of rules is prescribed, complex in both structure and application, for determining the relevant tax treatment. Finally, a number of transactions of this kind were brought within the scope of a very general 1960 provision which gave the Revenue power to undo the effects of some kinds of security transactions.

I have discussed bond-washing in some detail because it illustrates a number of general characteristics of tax-avoidance schemes and legislation. First, the source of the problem is the inability of the legislator to give effect to the underlying economic concept. In terms of the Hicksian definition of income, it is perfectly clear that capital gains which result from the accrual of predictable interest due but not yet paid have the character of income. If these gains *were* taxable income, the problem of bond-washing would disappear immediately. While it would not be impossible to achieve this result, there are some difficulties in distinguishing capital gains arising from this source from other capital gains which tax legislation treats differently, and for this or other reasons these gains are not treated as income. This creates the opportunity for tax avoidance. (For securities with less than 5 years to maturity, the UK practice is to quote the element of accrued interest in the sale or purchase as a component separate from the price. Even in these cases, accrued interest is treated as capital rather than as income).

Second, the legislative response is not to get to the heart of the problem, but to attack the mechanisms of the avoidance scheme. This is partly because the central problem is, in this example, genuinely difficult to solve, but also because the Inland Revenue is extremely reluctant to examine fundamental principles, preferring to make minimal responses to identified problems. Indeed this pragmatic approach based on the alleviation of symptom rather than the diagnosis of cause appears almost to be a matter of pride. The consequence is that the anti-avoidance provisions do not work very well. While one particular group of schemes is outlawed, it is often possible to construct more complicated if less efficient schemes that have similar effect.† A further set of anti-avoidance provisions is invoked, with slightly greater success and substantially greater complexity. The final exasperated outcome is the buttress of a rather vague and general provision which leaves doubt in the mind of honest and dishonest taxpayer alike: the sum of the resulting legislation is complex in appearance and uncertain in effect. The third characteristic of this saga which should be noted is that the anti-avoidance measures deal only with a small group of highly artificial schemes. In none of the cases discussed was there any shred of a motive other than tax avoidance attached to the activity. But in the much wider range of cases where the *principle* of this avoidance scheme is exploited but only in conjunction with a bona-fide commercial transaction nothing is done.

In consequence, the conversion of taxable income into tax-free capital gain remains a central device for reducing the tax-burden on investment income. On 8th September 1978 a potential investor in long-dated government stock had a choice between Treasury 12% Stock, 1995, priced at $97\frac{3}{4}$ to yield 12·5% and Gas 3% Stock, 1995, priced at $46\frac{1}{4}$ to yield 9·7%. The casual reader might wonder why, in an efficient market, anyone would be interested in buying a stock yielding almost 3% less than another stock so similar in redemption date and the security offered. The explanation

† Roy Tucker, a leading inventor of avoidance schemes, has commented that his principal source of ideas is existing anti-avoidance legislation.

is that one stock offers its returns principally in the form of (taxable) interest payments and the other provides them mainly in the form of (tax-free) capital gains. As a result, although the gross yields which are obtained on the two stocks are 12·5% and 9·7%, the net returns to someone who pays tax at the top marginal rate of 98% are 0·4% and 4·6% respectively. It can be assumed that the 12% stock is held predominantly by those who pay no tax or do so at low rates and that the 3% stock is held mainly by those liable to tax at higher rates.

I have estimated that the market value of securities like Gas 3% Stock, which are clearly unattractive to anyone who is not a higher-rate taxpayer, is in excess of £3000m (Kay and King, 1978). A rough estimate of the revenue losses which result from tax avoidance via these stocks can be obtained by supposing that the taxable yield on them is on average 5% lower than that on securities where the return is fully taxable and that the average of the marginal tax rates of the holders is 60%; this would put the annual loss of tax revenue from this source at about £100m. There can be little doubt that this annual cost exceeds the total amount of tax avoided by bond-washing over the whole history of the British tax system. This figure, however, overestimates the net cost to the Exchequer. This is because the Bank of England takes advantage of the attractiveness of low-coupon stocks to higher-rate taxpayers to issue such stocks on gross (i.e. before tax) yields lower than it would otherwise be obliged to offer. Thus there is a saving in debt financing charges to be offset against the losses of tax revenue: the loss of revenue is therefore less than the loss to the equity of the tax system.

'Well-offness': the problem of valuation

The transformation of income into capital gain represents the first major group of avoidance possibilities in the UK income tax system, which arise in essence from the difficulty of achieving practical application of the concept of expectations in the Hicksian definition of income. The second word in that definition which poses problems is the word 'well-off', and it is the difficulty of applying this in practice which leads to a second major group of avoidance opportunities.

Application of either a Hicksian or a Haig–Simons concept of income would in principle require an annual valuation of the assets of every taxpayer and a liability to a charge on any unrealized appreciation in the value of these assets. It is generally recognized that this cannot be done, for two major reasons. The first of these is the administrative burden involved in undertaking regular valuations, especially for the extensive range of assets in which there is no active market. The second is that even if taxes were levied on this basis a charge which resulted from an increase in value which had not been realized would in many instances prove impossible to collect; the owner of an asset which is not tradeable in practice or which is indivisible would normally not have the cash resources to make such payments.

General recognition of this has led to acceptance of the need to defer collection of tax until some receipt or realization takes place. But this raises new problems in the course of solving old ones. The difficulty of recognizing the moment at which a realization has occurred is the source of a good deal of complexity in income tax legislation. The opportunity for tax avoidance arises because the date of realization is frequently not fixed by nature but susceptible to control by the taxpayer. This allows the use of the device of the tax shelter, by which an individual arranges for his income to be received by an institution rather than by himself—by a corporation, trust, life insurance company or pension fund. As this list makes clear, the majority of tax shelters‡ exist for bona fide reasons that have nothing to do with tax avoidance. But this does not prevent their use for avoidance purposes.

Under an income tax regime which corresponded closely to an economic concept of income, it would be necessary to assign all income which accrued to an institution to the individual who was the ultimate beneficiary. This requires regular reassessment of the value of an individual's claims on the institution and for reasons already noted is a hopeless task. There are two alternatives. One is to defer collection of tax until payments are made to the ultimate beneficiary. This is the practice in relation to pension funds, and because it allows unlimited deferral it represents extremely generous treatment. Indeed by allowing tax liability to be postponed until income is finally required for consumption purposes it has the effect of transforming the income tax into an expenditure tax regime.

The alternative is to levy tax on the income as it accrues; but this implies that the rate of tax imposed must be related to the nature of the institution rather than the identity of the beneficiary. There are consequently special rates of income tax applicable to the income of corporations (52%), of life insurance companies and of discretionary (37½%) and accumulation trusts (48%). All these rates are substantially lower than the marginal rates of tax faced by high income individuals, and so such people have a substantial incentive to arrange for their income to be received by an institution rather than themselves. The use of a 'tax shelter' in this way is at the root of a wide range of avoidance schemes. To make them effective, however, it is necessary to be able to retrieve the income from inside the tax shelter. There are several ways of doing this. One is to ensure that the accumulated income is in due course distributed as capital rather than as income. Another is to arrange for the tax shelter to 'lend' money to the intended beneficiary. Even when these devices are restricted, it is impossible to prevent someone who knows that his capital is protected by the increasing value of his claims on an institution from achieving his desired balance of saving and spending by simultaneously dissaving offsetting amounts from his own other capital.

Anti-avoidance provisions fall into two main categories. One set is addressed to the central problem—the need for an income tax to impute all income to its ultimate beneficiary. These seek to identify the beneficiary and treat the income as his. This is done in cases where the operations of the tax shelter are very transparent—where a trust operates for the benefit of the individual who paid money into it or where a company, owned by a small group of people, exists mainly to receive investment income or retains profits much in excess of its trading requirements. Where these circumstances can be identified, the income of the trust or corporation is liable to be attributed to the settlor or to the shareholders in the company.

These provisions have not been found sufficient. Perhaps their most serious weakness is that although they attack cases where the tax shelter has no purpose other than tax avoidance, they put fewer difficulties in the way of shelters which have some other initial rationale being used as the basis of avoidance schemes. A second range of provisions therefore raises difficulties for those trying to get money out of tax shelters. There are elaborate restrictions on companies attempting to distribute their resources as capital rather than income payments, relating both to legal restrictions on what companies may and may not do and to the tax treatment of payments when they are made. Obstacles are put in the way of 'dividend-stripping', which is a version of 'bond-washing' applied to dividends rather than interest and generally to a whole company rather than a single security.

‡ In the US, the phrase 'tax shelter' has come to include almost any avoidance device, here I use it in a more limited sense.

The provision noted above, which gives the Revenue power to behave as though certain transactions in securities had not happened, is primarily intended to remedy weaknesses in this legislation. Loans from companies to their proprietors are treated for purposes of basic rate tax as distributions. The proceeds of certain life-insurance policies are in some situations and to some extent taxed as the income of the beneficiary. And so on.

These provisions are not, in the main, very effective against tax shelters which are located abroad and therefore not readily susceptible to control by UK tax authorities. There is therefore a very wide-ranging provision enabling the Revenue to treat income arising abroad as though it had been received by a UK resident. This very general provision is in contrast to the more usual British practice of directing specific legislation against particular mischiefs. This approach to tax avoidance is more common in other countries, but it is not clear that it is a more effective mechanism for dealing with the problem. It can only deal with highly artificial avoidance mechanisms, since the approach of treating one transaction as if it were another can only be followed if that transaction can be clearly identified and its effect separated from those of other transactions. They also create considerable uncertainty as to what the effect of the law is and whether particular transactions are or are not covered by it—and the 1936 legislation to deal with tax shelters abroad has been extensively criticized on this account.

Overall, however, legislation to deal with tax shelters has conformed to the pattern observed in relation to the shuffling of income and capital gains. It is directed mainly at the mechanics of avoidance schemes rather than the fundamental difficulty which gives rise to them. The outcome is more complicated forms of abuse and more complicated legislation to deal with them. Meanwhile, the device which is at the centre of the artificial avoidance schemes can be freely exploited as one aspect of more normal commercial transactions.

'Spend': the problem of perks

The third word in the Hicksian definition which was noted as a potential source of difficulty was the word 'spend'. The definition of expenditure might appear relatively straightforward. But it would normally be intended to exclude expenditure on intermediate goods; items which do not in themselves make the spender better off and which are incurred for the purpose of obtaining income. The difficulty of deciding what is a personal expense and what is a business expense is one of the most fruitful sources of opportunities for tax avoidance. Part of the difficulty arises because it is not easy to decide, in principle, what the distinction which we would like to make is. There is a continuous spectrum of expenditures ranging from redecoration of the office in which an employee works, to redecorating of his bedroom at home, all of which can be expected to contribute to the employee's utility. One most people would regard as a legitimate business expense, the other most people would regard as a fringe benefit; but the line that is drawn somewhere in between is inevitably arbitrary. There are good administrative reasons for drawing the line, as is normally done, in a rather restrictive way.

The line is drawn in UK tax legislation by the use of a test that an expenditure be incurred 'wholly and exclusively' (in the case of business activities) or 'wholly exclusively and necessarily' (in the case of employees) for the purposes of earning income. The difference between these tests is not easy to justify; but for present purposes the central point is that all of them relate to the motives of the person or organization incurring the expenditure. They are therefore open to exploitation by those who are in a position to alter, distort or conceal these motives. These opportunities are more readily available to the self-employed than to employees, and more likely to occur in the private than the public sectors; and the extent to which they are used is related to the honesty and truthfulness of the individuals involved. A tax which depends on the intention of the taxpayer can never be either fair or effective and it carries the necessary implication that the more candid an individual is about his reasons for acting as he does the more tax he is liable to pay.

The second, and much less important, problem in defining expenditure is the treatment of durable goods. In principle, the value of the services derived from the ownership of durables is a component part of individual income or expenditure. Until 1962, a somewhat desultory attempt was made in the UK to do this for owner-occupied houses, and provisions of this kind still exist in some other countries. The practical difficulties of applying the principle to other durables are obvious.

Differentiation and graduation

Finally, there is a set of avoidance problems which arise because of the differentiation involved in an income tax; because different individuals are charged tax at different rates. Actually, a number of tax shelter problems would disappear if there was no graduation in the rate schedule; it would be possible to obtain the appropriate amount of tax by charging the tax shelter tax at the universal rate, since it is then unnecessary to identify the individual who is the ultimate beneficiary. This does not work perfectly, since it is still necessary to identify the income of the shelter and there are always some beneficiaries who are not taxpayers (e.g. foreigners) and some tax shelters which cannot be treated in this way (e.g. ones located abroad) but there is no doubt that the problems would be eased considerably. It is also true that several devices for transforming income into capital gain depends on the existence of low-rate taxpayers who therefore do not mind receiving the income. (Bond-washing comes into this category.) This is true of gambits which depend on transferring the income to someone else rather than making it disappear altogether. Note, however, that the existence of some exempt taxpayers is sufficient to reintroduce problems—mere abolition of higher rates would not be enough.

An individual can only exploit the fact that other individuals are taxed at different rates from himself if he can arrange for his income to be received by someone who pays tax at a lower rate, while he himself still enjoys the benefit of it. I have noted how this can be done by exchanging the income for a capital payment. Other opportunities depend on the goodwill of the recipient of the income. The extent of opportunities of this second kind depends largely on the way in which the family unit is treated for tax purposes, since it is principally within a household that it is possible to be confident that one will continue to benefit from income which has been transferred to someone else. British tax law is such that there is no benefit to be obtained from transferring investment income to one's spouse, nor usually benefit in transferring it to dependent children. Employees are rarely able to persuade their employers to pay their salary to someone else; but it is a common practice for the self-employed and for small businessmen to transfer income by paying an earned income to their wives in return for modest services (or services of a kind which other workers would expect their wives to provide without explicit remuneration). If the tax were levied on a straightforward household basis (as in France), these opportunities would disappear; if on a straightforward individual basis (as in Australia) they would be increased.

The catalogue of avoidance opportunities discussed here has been available principally to those with income from investment and from self-employment. The availability of possibilities for tax avoidance in relation to employment incomes is very much more limited. Within the area of income from employment there is a close correspondence between income and receipts in any period. The areas of difficulty are those in which the correspondence breaks down—fringe benefits and payments in kind, and pension payments, where receipts occur much later than the performance of the related services. Where income is derived from trading or from capital, however, there is a much more tenuous relationship between income and receipts. The avoidance possibilities outlined arise either when a receipt occurs but there is doubt as to whether it is a receipt of capital or of income, or where income accrues but no receipt occurs. The profits obtained from bond-washing or dividend-stripping, or from selling a company whose assets have been derived from reinvested income, fall into the first category; the benefits derived from income accumulating in a tax shelter, owning durable goods, or having one's employer or business undertake one's personal expenditure, fall into the second category.

A common view is that tax avoidance is like disease; all tax systems are vulnerable to it, it is impossible to anticipate how or when it will break out and all that can be done is to wait and attempt to cure it when it arises. I have argued that this is not in fact the case and that avoidance possibilities in the UK income tax arise in a direct way from readily identifiable difficulties in turning the economic concept of income into a legislative reality. It would not be difficult for someone with no experience of the actual operation of an income tax system but who was equipped with a definition of income and a sense of what was likely to be administratively feasible to predict what the areas of difficulty in the operation of an income tax would be, and it is these areas which have posed major problems in practice. Moreover, it is also these areas which are responsible for much of the complexity of the income tax code. This complexity is aggravated by the ad hoc approach which is typically used in reacting to problems which arise. Because the emphasis is put on dealing with the manifestation rather than the underlying cause, the basic problem simply re-emerges in some different form, and the outcome is both complicated and limited in effectiveness.

AVOIDANCE AND THE DEFINITION OF EXPENDITURE

The other broad based tax currently applied in the UK—VAT—is much less subject to avoidance problems than is income tax. But is this because expenditure taxes are intrinsically superior to income taxes in this respect, or is it because the top rate of VAT is only 12½% whereas the top rate of income tax is 98%? (Indeed on a tax-exclusive basis comparable to that on which VAT rates are quoted the top rate of income tax is 4900%). The fact that rates of VAT are very much lower is undoubtedly a major element in the explanation. For example, VAT legislation attempts to differentiate between house repairs, which are standard-rated, and house improvements, which are zero-rated. The nature of this distinction is not easy to specify in principle, far less to identify in practice. But because the difference in rates is only 8%, the difficulty is not very acute; § if the standard rate of VAT were 50% the problem would be very different.

But this is not the only reason why VAT poses fewer avoidance problems. While income is defined as the amount an individual can expect to spend and still remain equally well-off, the expenditure base is simply what individuals do spend on certain commodities. Thus two of the three words which pose difficulty in applying an

§ Though it is the most important single source of dispute.

income definition—'expect' and 'well-off'—disappear, and only 'spend' remains. We would therefore expect that VAT would avoid the first two groups of problems described above but would have to face analagous problems to the third group, and this is indeed the case. The difficulty of disentangling business and personal expenditure reappears as the problem of deciding whether a particular business expenditure should or should not be allowed as an item on which input tax is to be refunded—when a company buys racehorses for 'advertizing purposes', for example. Again, this is not a very acute problem with a basic rate of VAT of 8%, and appears to be met by a rather generous interpretation of what are admissible as taxable inputs. It would become a very substantial problem with a basic VAT rate of 50% (corresponding to a basic income tax rate of 33%—the distinction between tax-exclusive and tax-inclusive rates again). Difficulties also arise in relation to durables, but again of a rather minor nature. Tax is normally levied on durable goods by charging it when the durable is purchased, rather than on the flow of services which the good generates. Imputed rent on owner-occupied houses is ignored.

The existence of different rates of income tax applied to different people allowed opportunities for avoiding tax by changing the identity of the person who received the income; the analagous opportunity under VAT is that of transferring the commodity from one rate-band to another. This can be done either by the consumer—who avoids VAT on his lunch by buying it from a take-away restaurant and eating it on a park-bench, or by the producer distorting the nature of the commodity—by siting his take-away restaurant next to the park bench. The difficulty of distinguishing 'repairs' from improvements has already been noted, but in general these problems do not seem very acute (possibly because the rate differences are rather small). These difficulties of classification raise different kinds of problem for the two taxes, but otherwise the avoidance possibilities under VAT are a strict subset of those which arise under an income tax. For every problem which arises under VAT there is an analogous difficulty for an income tax, but the converse is not true.

The problems of defining expenditure for the purposes of a direct personal expenditure tax are essentially the same as those of defining expenditure for VAT. Indeed this must be so; although a VAT is collected from the expenditure side of the national income accounts and an expenditure tax on the income side, national accounting identities imply that one base must be equal to the other, and so definitional problems encountered in one area must be matched by definitional problems in the other. There is an apparent dissimilarity in that transactions undertaken by firms are dealt with under VAT by levying tax on the difference between outputs and inputs; these are not brought into account under the personal expenditure tax, which instead levies tax on the net amount paid from the corporate sector to the personal sector. But since the accounts of firms also balance, and sources of funds must be equal in total to uses, the two tax bases are the same.

It follows that just as two of the three main groups of avoidance problems confronting an income tax disappear under VAT, so also these problems disappear with the introduction of a personal expenditure tax. There is no distinction between income and capital receipts required, and the use of tax shelters confers no advantage. The difficulties which remain are those involved in the definition of expenditure—some problems in the taxation of durables and the major difficulty of distinguishing personal and business expenditures. But these problems arise in essentially the same form under both income tax and VAT.

As with VAT, the avoidance problems faced by a direct personal expenditure tax are a strict subset of those arising for a personal income tax. This may seem surprising to those brought up in the traditional view that expenditure is harder to measure than income, though it is somewhat puzzling how this view ever gained currency, (*see* Andrews, 1974). But the central reason why avoidance opportunities are much reduced is that an expenditure tax is a tax on net receipts. I have already noted that the area in which the personal income tax is relatively impervious to avoidance problems is in the taxation of employment incomes, where there is a close correspondence between income and receipts. The expenditure tax operates by applying this receipts basis to all forms of personal income—to investment incomes and business and self-employment incomes also. (*See* Kay and King, 1978, and Meade, 1978, for further explanation of how this works).

The description of the tax base is therefore substantially easier to handle under a personal expenditure tax than under a personal income tax. How serious are the problems which arise from graduation? This requires that taxable expenditure should in all cases be attributed to some identifiable individual. It is much easier to misrepresent the attribution of expenditure than the attribution of income: it is easier to persuade someone else to do one's spending than to persuade payers of income to transfer the payment to another person. But what are the mechanics of successfully implementing this type of operation? If personal gifts could be deducted from receipts in computing taxable expenditure, the simplest device would be to make regular 'gifts' to some individual or organization in the hope that he or it would undertake beneficial expenditures on one's behalf. But it does not seem likely that gifts would be deductible in any practical implementation of an expenditure tax. Avoidance of this kind, then, would depend on inducing payers of income or capital receipts to divert these flows towards others in the hope that they would then act in ways which would make (taxable) personal expenditure less necessary.

It is hard to imagine that this would be a substantial problem. In respect of income receipts, this opportunity exists under an income tax, and some use is made of covenants of income to others for purposes of tax avoidance. It would be necessary to maintain restrictions on this. Because it is receipts, rather than income, which provides the tax base under an expenditure tax, there would be additional scope for those who presently covenant the *whole* of their income to dispose of capital in a similar manner. It does not seem probable that this is a frequent occurrence. Broadly speaking, the opportunities for avoidance using these devices are the same under both income and expenditure taxes.

CONCLUSION

In this paper, I have tried to identify the major sources of avoidance opportunities in tax systems and to relate these to difficulties in implementing the economic concepts which underlie tax legislation. It is widely believed that tax avoidance is an inevitable product of high tax rates, the unscrupulousness of taxpayers and the ingenuity of their advisers. All this is true, and is likely to remain true however the tax system is reformed. But it is not the whole truth, and in particular it is not true that all taxes and all tax systems are equally vulnerable to avoidance. Income tax is especially subject to avoidance because income has proved a particularly difficult concept to turn into acceptable legislative form. If we are concerned—as I believe we should be—about the widespread economic and social effects of the consequences of large scale tax avoidance, we should heed the warning of the minority in their Report for the 1955 Royal Commission; 'The existence of widespread tax avoidance is evidence that the system, not the taxpayer, stands in need of radical reform.' (Para. 33.)

REFERENCES

Allingham M. and Sandmo A. (1972) Income tax evasion—a theoretical analysis, *J. Pub. Econ.* **1.**

Andrews W. O. (1974) A consumption—type or cash flow personal Income Tax, *Harvard Law Review*, **87.**

Frank M. and Deheyser-Meulders D. (1977) A tax discrepancy coefficient resulting from tax evasion or tax expenditures, *J. Pub. Econ.* **8.**

Kay J. A. and King M. A. (1978) *The British Tax System*, Oxford Univ.

Meade J. E. (1978) *The Structure and Reform of Direct Taxation*, Report of a Committee chaired by Professor J. E. Meade. Allen and Unwin.

DISCUSSION

by **G. Whittington,** *Department of Economics, University of Bristol*

The main theme of this paper is that tax avoidance is the result of ambiguity in the definition of the tax base, exacerbated by high tax rates (which give an incentive to exploit avoidance opportunities) and by differences in rates between taxpayers (which facilitate avoidance by switching the tax liability from high-rate to low-rate taxpayers). The main body of the paper is devoted to elaborating this theme using the United Kingdom income tax system as an illustration, which leads to the conclusion that income compares unfavourably with expenditure as a tax base.

Three broad criticisms of the theme of the paper are as follows:

(i) The author's case for expenditure taxation, on the grounds that expenditure is a less ambiguous tax base than income, is a weak one if considerations of equity and efficiency suggest that we should tax income rather than expenditure. In this case, expenditure taxation would imply that *all* forms of saving be allowed as tax avoidance devices, which would be inequitable as between net savers and net dis-savers. Of course, the author wishes to include gifts in the expenditure tax base (p. 147), so that nobody would be a net saver, for tax purposes, over his whole life-time. But bringing gifts into the expenditure tax base introduces the problem that we no longer have a simple transactions base like that of Value Added Tax: gifts will need to be valued and liquidity problems may arise (e.g. for family businesses), as they do with an accruals-based income tax.

(ii) The author has failed to produce a clear definition of tax avoidance which distinguishes it from the other substitution effects of taxation. We are told in the early part of the paper that 'an element of artificiality' is necessary for a transaction to be classified as avoidance. In the extreme, avoidance may lead to doing things which have *no* utility to the individual (other than reducing his tax bill), but it is not clear that even this extreme case is qualitatively different from an ordinary substitution effect which involves doing things which have *less* utility than the taxed alternatives: in both cases there is a loss of utility to the individual which he incurs in order to reduce his tax burden. Moreover, some of the examples of avoidance quoted in the paper do not imply doing things which have no utility to the individual, e.g. the man who responds to the tax system by drinking the firm's whisky in the office rather than his own at home is regarded as a tax avoider: the man who substitutes coca-cola for whisky is not regarded as a tax avoider, although he too is presumably sacrificing some utility in order to reduce his tax bill. Finally, some of the tax-induced distortions quoted in the paper as avoidance, particularly the institutionalization of savings, might be justified as being socially desirable, e.g. the encouragement of private pension funds and life assurance.

(iii) The relationship between avoidance and evasion is neglected in the paper. If high tax rates have created a demand for tax avoidance, then an unambiguous tax base which prevented avoidance, might lead to more evasion, as a substitute for avoidance. This would involve an undesirable discrimination against the honest taxpayer who is unwilling to practise evasion. It might well be the case that certain taxes which are difficult to avoid are relatively easy to evade. For example, VAT, which is quoted with approval towards the end of the paper certainly has a relatively unambiguous base, and is therefore difficult to avoid, but it has suffered from serious evasion problems, despite its modest rates.

Some criticisms of particular points in the paper are as follows:

(i) At the beginning of the paper, it is asserted that Britain has 'the most ostensibly redistributive tax system in the western world', but the evidence provided for this is merely the highest *marginal* rate of income tax, whereas redistribution results from the progressivity of *average* rates of tax.

(ii) In the discussion of the treatment of capital gains in the income tax base it is suggested that the distinction between expected and unexpected gains is important, the former being taxed as income and the latter not being taxed. A more relevant distinction is that between recurrent and non-recurrent gains, the former being entirely available for potential consumption and therefore taxable if we adopt a consumption maintenance (Hicks number 2) definition of income, and the latter being only partially treated as income (to the extent that the gain and its subsequent interest yield could produce a permanent rise in consumption) on the same definition. Of course, there is an element of expectation involved in assessing whether a gain is recurrent or non-recurrent, but it is the extent of recurrence which is the fundamental criterion for separating income from capital.

(iii) In the discussion of 'bond-washing' it is stated that 'Because indifference curves between income and capital gains are straight lines for sophisticated taxpayers, the limit thereon does not yield a determinate equilibrium . . .'. This is true in the very simple case stated in the paper, in which there are only two tax rates, but in practice the degree of indeterminacy will be reduced substantially by the multiplicity of tax rates.

(iv) In the discussion of VAT it is correctly stated that (with one qualification) 'For every problem which arises under VAT there is an analogous difficulty for an income tax, but the converse is not true'. However, it should be borne in mind that the problems do not necessarily carry the same weight under the two taxes, for example if an Income Tax were replaced by a VAT but the latter, because of its narrower base, were levied at a higher rate, the problems common to the two taxes would be more serious under VAT.

(v) In the discussion of the equivalence of the bases of personal expenditure tax and VAT it is claimed that 'although a VAT is collected from the expenditure side of the national income accounts and an expenditure tax on the income side, national accounting identities imply that one base must be equal to the other, and so definitional problems encountered in one area must be matched by definitional problems in the other'. This is true of strictly *definitional* problems but not of *measurement* problems in general. For example, it is well known that there is, in practice, a discrepancy between the two sides of the national income accounts. Such errors of measurement may, of course, be classified by the author as being the equivalent of evasion rather than avoidance, but their possible occurrence does detract from his argument for the administrative attractions of a personal expenditure tax.

TAX COMPLIANCE COSTS, EVASION AND AVOIDANCE

C. T. Sandford

Centre for Fiscal Studies, University of Bath

The object of this paper is to explore the relationships between compliance costs, evasion and avoidance and to indicate how these may constitute, or relate to, limits of redistribution. The reader should be warned that little in-depth research has been undertaken in this field and that much of the paper is tentative and speculative.

Let us begin by trying to define our terms—by no means an easy task.

DEFINITIONS

The term 'tax compliance costs' may be used in at least two ways: as enforcement costs i.e. costs incurred by the administration in securing taxpayer compliance with tax legislation; or as costs incurred by taxpayers or third parties (such as employers) in meeting the requirements of the tax legislation, over and above the revenue actually handed over by taxpayers to the authorities, and apart from any costs of distortion arising from the tax.

This paper follows the general practice of public finance literature in using compliance costs in the second sense as costs to the taxpayer or third parties. The total of compliance costs and administrative costs together make up what may be called the 'operating' costs of a tax.

For personal taxpayers compliance costs may involve fees to advisers, the time they spend in completing returns, filing the necessary data and acquainting themselves with the regulations; and as Muller (1963) points out, for third parties, such as firms, 'The burden of compliance involves more than just the cost of physically collecting the tax, accounting for the tax, preparing the tax returns and paying the tax to the taxing authorities. It also includes the duty to understand the nature and requirements of the legislation, the appreciation of the risks inherent in penalties which may be assessed and the planning and organizing required to perform the function of collection'.

The compliance costs of both personal taxpayers and firms may take the form of money costs, time costs and psychic costs, and the compliance costs of firms may arise from taxes on their employees, their products or their profits. We can usefully distinguish between temporary and permanent compliance costs. Temporary compliance costs are associated with a new tax or a change in a tax and include commencement costs (once-and-for-all costs associated with the introduction of a tax, e.g. the cost of attending a conference to learn the legal requirements of the tax) and costs which arise from unfamiliarity. Permanent compliance costs are the continuing costs after the taxpayer or third party has developed what seem to him the most suitable methods of complying with a tax.

Another important distinction is between 'discretionary' and 'non-discretionary' costs. Discretionary costs are avoidable, expenses which taxpayers or third parties deliberately incur in the hope of reducing the total size of their tax bill (e.g. fees for 'tax planning' advice). Non-discretionary costs are necessarily incurred in meeting the requirements of the tax system. It can be argued that discretionary costs ought not to be included as a part of compliance costs at all, but probably practice should depend on purpose: if our concern is the overall resource costs arising from a particular tax or tax system, we ought to include the real costs incurred by taxpayers' efforts to reduce their tax bills.

Evasion is the least ambiguous of our terms; it means illegal tax-dodging. But we can distinguish evasion by commission and by omission. Evasion by commission, or positive evasion, consists of deliberate action to evade tax, e.g. falsely claiming a child or dependent relative. Evasion by omission, or negative evasion, is evasion by non-action, e.g. failing to inform the Inland Revenue of casual earnings or tips. These two kinds of evasion differ in at least three (related) ways: the moral opprobrium attached to them; the willingness of taxpayers to engage in them; and the likelihood of detection and punishment. A second distinction is between intentional and unintentional evasion. Evasion may be deliberate, or it may result from ignorance or incompetence, e.g. a failure to realize that a particular form of income was taxable and should have been declared; or a muddled and incorrect VAT return. The borderline between the deliberate and the unintentional can be a grey one—for example, the return of a personal valuable for purposes of a wealth tax or death duty, at a, knowingly, 'conservative' value; or 'muddles' that always work to the taxpayer's advantage.

Avoidance is the term which creates the most problems of definition. It has been generally defined as any *legal* method of reducing one's tax bill, in contrast to the *illegality* of evasion. But this definition does not take us far; by it, I 'avoid' tax if I marry; have children; buy a house on a mortgage; make a gift and live for three years; decide, as a result of income tax, to substitute leisure for work and income, or as a result of capital transfer tax, to consume my wealth instead of giving it or leaving it to my children. For operational purposes avoidance needs to be defined much more narrowly. We can approach the issue from two points of view—that of the government and the tax avoider.

From the government point of view we can distinguish at least four categories of tax saving:

(i) Tax savings arising from actions which the government wishes to encourage, such as capital allowances for certain kinds of investment, tax reliefs for home ownership, or lower rates of capital transfer tax for life-time gifts to encourage early transfers.

(ii) Tax savings resulting from action about which the government is neutral, but where it recognizes a welfare obligation, e.g. allowances under income tax for a wife, children, or dependent relative.

(iii) Tax savings in ways which the government dislikes, but which it may feel bound to accept for administrative reasons—the difficulties and costs of policing the preventive measures. Into this category may come the UK tardiness in adopting a general gifts tax to support its death duty; some *de minimis* exemptions; and the wealth tax exemptions accorded by some countries to personal chattels (e.g. Denmark's dictum: 'the tax stops at the door'). The scope for avoidance by conversion of 'income' to 'capital gains' may come into this category. Because of the administrative difficulty of taxing accrued gains, in practice all capital gains taxes are charged on realized gains; but because realized gains may be bunched and represent the accumulated gains of many years, it would seem unfair to tax them at progressive rates akin to income tax. Hence capital gains taxes tend to be proportional or only mildly progressive; conversion of 'income' to 'capital gain' then becomes an attractive method of avoidance which a government cannot wholly block.

(iv) Tax savings arising from taking advantage of technical loopholes in the law because of inadequate draughting. Governments are likely to seek to block such methods once the loophole has been officially recognized.

Tax savings coming under categories (4), and probably also under (3), might be thought of as constituting avoidance proper. But both the conclusions and the distinctions are not free from difficulty.

Thus, take the example of tax concessions to owner occupiers in category (i). The end of the practice of imputing income to owner occupiers in the UK, combined with the relief for the interest on house mortgages encourages not only home ownership *per se*, but also encourages wealthy taxpayers to go in for more expensive houses or expensive extensions, up to the limit of mortgage relief, to reap the benefits from the mortgage interest concession at their marginal tax rate. Is this what the government intended? Should home extensions by wealthy taxpayers count as avoidance proper? Is this an instance in which the ad hoc way in which the situation arose, with the government responding to pressures to abolish schedule A income tax on home owners, has led to a result which was inadequately foreseen. If so, then some tax saving from the concessions to owner occupiers should perhaps be classified under category (iv) rather than category (i).

Or take the third example under category (i)—lower rates of CTT on life-time transfers. When the Labour Government changed its mind and decided (contrary to the proposals in its White Paper) to charge lower rates on life-time gifts, the official reason given was the desire to encourage the owners of businesses and farms to part with them earlier to guard against gerontocracy. However, the concession applied not only to gifts of farms and businesses but to *all* gifts. Where gifts other than productive assets benefit from the lower rates for life-time transfers under CTT, does this really come under category (iii)—tax savings disliked but permitted by the government for administrative reasons?

Or again, take category (iii). Unless a government has made its reasons explicit, it is difficult to be sure whether tax-saving opportunities arise from administrative difficulties, or from intention, or from a failure to appreciate the results. Thus a *de minimis* exemption on gifts (per recipient or per annum) may be thought desirable by a government or merely be accepted for administrative reasons.

We seem to be moving towards a definition of avoidance which focuses on government intention: that avoidance is an action in accordance with the letter of the law, but not its intention. But here we meet a major difficulty. As Shenfield (1968) puts it: 'The spirit of the law is elusive'. As individuals we may feel that a particular action is contrary to the intention of the law, but the only *objective* interpretation of that intention is to be found in the words the law uses.

Nor is it much more help to try to define avoidance by reference to taxpayer behaviour. In his paper to this symposium, John Kay characterizes avoidance as tax saving by actions in which there is some element of artificiality implied; but this is not free of ambiguity. If I react to investment incentives by investing, as the Government hopes, that might be regarded as an artificial action—I would not have done it but for the tax concession; but should it then be classed as avoidance? I doubt it. But to extend my house and take advantage of the mortgage interest concession is no more 'artificial'; yet, it could more readily be regarded as avoidance.

It seems to me that, in deciding what constitutes avoidance, we need to distinguish whether the taxpayer, in reacting to a tax, has substantially attained his original objective, despite the operation of the tax. If so, there has been avoidance. If, however, he abandons the original objective for another, then there has been no avoidance. Thus, if in the face of a heavy death duty, a man who wished to pass on his property to his heirs abandons the intention and reduces the death-tax bill by taking his family on a round-the-world spending spree, this is not avoidance proper. If, on the other hand, he maximizes opportunities for tax-free giving to them, establishes trusts, takes out insurance policies and the like, all with the object of seeing that they do receive as large a post-tax inheritance as possible, this is avoidance.

If pushed to offer a general definition of tax avoidance I would thus say that it was legal actions undertaken to save tax, which would not have been undertaken but for the tax, which enabled the actor to achieve substantially what he would have achieved in the absence of the tax, and which actions are contrary to the intention of the Government. But I realize that in using words like 'substantially' and 'Government intention' I beg almost as many questions as have been answered.

INTER-RELATIONSHIPS

There are a series of inter-relationships between compliance costs, evasion and avoidance.

First, 'discretionary' compliance costs (*see* page 151) are essentially costs of obtaining advice on tax avoidance (as we have now defined it) or of implementing tax avoidance schemes, e.g. the costs of incorporation or of changing one's asset portfolio.

Secondly, and less precisely, the existence of heavy compliance costs may alienate those on whom they fall, reducing their reluctance to engage in avoidance or evasion (*see below*).

Evasion and avoidance are related to each other in various ways. First, some avoidance measures merge into evasion—the border-line between them is somewhat fudged—particularly in the area of 'business expenses' of the self-employed. For example, I can legitimately save tax by employing my wife on secretarial or cleaning services, so that we gain the benefit from her married woman's earned income relief; but if I am generous in counting the hours I attribute to her work or in the rates I pay her, an element of evasion enters. It is not surprising, in these circumstances, that many members of the public appear to adopt the same moral stance on avoidance as on evasion (Lewis, 1979) and make no clear distinctions between the two.

Another link is that, as well as according with introspection and economists' assumptions about personal behaviour, such little empirical evidence as exists suggests that reduction in avoidance opportunities increases willingness to evade (Spicer and Lundstedt, 1976).

RELEVANCE TO REDISTRIBUTION

Compliance Costs

The total compliance costs of a tax depend on three main features: the number of persons affected; the complexity of the tax; and the balance struck by fiscal legislation between the responsibility of the revenue authorities and that of the taxpayer or third parties.

To illustrate these points: the compliance costs of VAT are very much higher than were those of purchase tax primarily because VAT is collected by some $1\frac{1}{4}$ million 'traders' as against some 75 000 for purchase tax; this difference is not so much because VAT covers a wider range of goods and services, but because it is collected at every stage in the chain of production and distribution, not just at the wholesale stage as with purchase tax.

The more complicated a tax, the higher the compliance costs are likely to be. Complication relates both to the tax base, the number and form of exemptions, and to the rate structure. For example, the UK income tax is complicated by many and complex reliefs (Sandford, 1973); and the multi-rate structure of VAT substantially increases compliance costs (Sandford et al., 1979).

Finally the size of compliance costs depends partly on the distribution of tax-operating costs. Most taxes offer scope for adjusting the balance between administrative and compliance costs, with more of one implying less of the other. For example, whatever the difference in total operating costs, the USA system of self-assessment of income tax imposes relatively heavier compliance burdens on the taxpayer than the UK system of revenue assessment.

There are severe conceptual and practical problems involved in trying to measure the compliance costs of a tax and little has been published on this topic in the United Kingdom. Some tentative estimates by the author (Sandford, 1973) suggest that the total operating costs (administrative plus measurable compliance costs) of personal direct taxes in England and Wales in 1970–71 may have amounted to between 3·8% and 5·8% of tax revenue, plus up to 4% more for tax work not billed as such. Measurable compliance costs (consisting of fees to tax advisers, the value of the time costs of taxpayers and unpaid advisers, miscellaneous expenses like postage and travel and the costs to firms of operating PAYE) were at least 180% of total administrative costs. Allowing for all tax-generated work not billed as such, might have increased this figure by a factor of six.§ Provisional work on VAT suggests that here too, at least for small traders, the compliance costs can be very high as a proportion of tax liability (Godwin, 1976).

The relevance of compliance costs to redistribution can be seen in at least four ways:

(i) Compliance costs themselves directly affect income distribution in a way which is often inequitable and generally regressive. Personal compliance costs tend to fall with disproportionate weight on certain categories of the taxpaying population, especially the self-employed, many of whom are amongst the low earners in the population (Sandford, 1973). Low income groups with high compliance costs include small farmers, small self-employed retailers and retired persons.

Several inherent features in the make-up of the compliance costs of personal taxes make for regressiveness. There are economies of scale in the provision of tax advisory services, e.g. it takes the same time and skill to value, for CGT or CTT, a holding of 50 shares in a private company as to value a holding of 1000 shares in the same company. Hence tax advisers' fees will usually be a higher proportion of liability for small liability cases than for large liability cases (and liability will often be related to income or wealth). Similarly, the existence of a tax threshold may generate regressiveness in compliance costs. Thus the Green Paper on Wealth Tax (1974) suggested a possible threshold for wealth tax of £100 000 with the proviso that persons whose wealth constituted a certain minimum percentage of £100 000 should be required to file returns. Thus a £90 000 wealth holder would have to value his possessions and submit a return to establish a nil liability. A wealth holder of £110 000 would have to

§ These figures include both discretionary and non-discretionary costs, which it was not found possible to separate.

incur similar costs for a very low liability.|| Someone with considerably more wealth, say £300 000 would typically have to incur very little more trouble and expense than either of the others, although his liability would be substantially more.

Evidence on the compliance costs of firms all points in the same direction: that the costs of collecting taxes from employees and the compliance costs of profits taxes and sales taxes are all relatively larger for the small firm than the large (e.g. Bryden (1961) Yocum (1961) and Sandford et al. (1979)). Moreover, because the burden is differential rather than uniform, it is unlikely that market conditions will permit the small firm to shift the compliance cost to the consumer.

(ii) Compliance costs together with administrative costs comprise tax-operating costs. There is some level of tax-operating cost which might render unattractive a tax designed for redistributive purposes. The proposals for a wealth tax in the UK might be held to constitute such a case. The Inland Revenue estimated the administrative cost of the wealth tax proposed in the Green Paper, with £100 000 threshold, at between 3% and 7% of yield, depending on tax rates, the proportion of property annually audited and the frequency of valuations for unquoted shares (Select Committee, 1975). This figure may be compared with the cost of administering other Inland Revenue taxes, which, for many years has been between 1 and 2%.¶ But this is far from the whole picture. This estimate of the administrative cost of a wealth tax was acknowledged in the Inland Revenue memorandum, to be 'conservative' (Select Committee, 1975), whilst there are also reasons to believe that the revenue yield on which the percentage was calculated was optimistic (Sandford et al. 1975). Further, while no figure can be placed on the compliance costs, it is universally recognized that they would be exceptionally high because of the self-assessment basis proposed, with the taxpayer responsible for valuing his own property.

Moreover, the Inland Revenue proposed such a high threshold partly because of their calculation that a lower one would mean still higher administrative costs as a percentage of yield (Select Committee, 1975). Yet it could be argued that serious measures to reduce inequality in the distribution of wealth in the UK require a lower threshold: the proposed threshold of £100 000 would affect only a fraction of the top 1% of wealth holders, and moreover the very group whose holdings of wealth have been most markedly reduced during the present century (Royal Commission, 1977).

(iii) Compliance costs (like administrative costs) grow with the complexity of the tax. One contributor to complexity is the number of rates of tax; yet a multiple rate structure may be a prerequisite to secure a desired progression. This feature can be illustrated from the UK tax system. The establishment of a zero rate of VAT (on products other than exports) and the subsequent introduction of a higher rate of tax, were both intended to lessen the regressiveness or increase the progressiveness of VAT. Such limited evidence as is available (Sandford et al., 1979) suggests that multiple rates of VAT raise compliance costs significantly. It is particularly doubtful if the uncertain distributional benefit from having a higher rate of 12½%, against a standard rate of 8%, justifies the additional compliance (and administrative) cost. A standard rate of 10% as formerly would yield more revenue with lower operating costs.

(iv) High compliance costs may generate an anti-tax mentality and an antipathy to the tax system which in turn generates avoidance and, more particularly, evasion.

|| It could be argued that vertical equity is improved if the £90 000 wealth-holder (who pays no wealth tax) has to incur some compliance costs. On the other hand it was presumably the government's intention in setting the threshold that no-one below it should be burdened with the tax.

¶ The latest cost/yield ratio for the Department as a whole was 1·92%. The tax with the highest ratio was CTT at 3·57% (120th Report, Board of Inland Revenue, January 1978).

Compliance costs may have this effect partly because they are uneven in their incidence and hence felt to be unfair and partly because, at any rate in the UK, they are not explicitly recognized as tax-deductible (though in practice, especially for companies, they are often deducted along with general accounting costs). The personal taxpayer may feel that it is bad enough to have to pay taxes; to have to meet further bills, or spend precious time, for the privilege of paying them is to have insult added to injury. Similarly, the proprietor of a small firm may strongly resent the costs he incurs in acting as an unpaid tax collector for a government which he may consider to be 'wasting' the money anyway.

It is significant that the small self-employed business man may face high compliance costs both as a personal income taxpayer and as a third party deducting PAYE from his employees' wages and collecting VAT. Not only will such a person be under the strongest pressure to develop an anti-tax mentality, his situation is likely to give him maximum opportunities for avoidance and evasion.

It is widely held that evasion is most rife amongst the self-employed (Sandford, 1973). How far that evasion is a result of resentment at high compliance costs is debatable. The fact of resentment is not open to question, but some would argue that the same entrepreneurial mentality which leads people into self-employment inherently generates antipathy to taxation and public spending. However, resentment at high compliance costs can hardly fail to be a contributory factor.

Evasion

Willingness to evade and the extent of evasion may be influenced by a complex of factors, about which our ignorance is more notable than our understanding. The following list derived from introspection, casual empiricism and what limited data are available, is believed to contain the most relevant factors.

(i) The gains to be made from evasion—or the level of marginal tax rates. (It should be recognized, however, that marginal increments of income not only generate higher tax rates under a progressive income tax but also carry a diminishing marginal utility. The unambiguous situation is where marginal tax rates are increasing over time on the same level of real income).

(ii) The opportunities to evade in a manner likely to escape detection; e.g. the scope for the self-employed to put their hands in the till, the receipt of income in the form of tips or casual earnings.

(iii) The effectiveness of the enforcement procedures—covering the likelihood of detection, the ease of proof of intent to evade, the nature and severity of punishment (including the use of publicity about convicted evaders).

(iv) The taxpayer's own perception of the fairness of the tax system and the perceptions of his reference groups—friends, relatives, work associates, acquaintances. The more unfairness is perceived, the more the willingness to evade.

(v) Perceptions of the fairness of the 'exchange relationship' between the taxpayer and the government and the perception of this relationship by one's reference groups. The exchange relationship may embrace not only views on the benefits of government expenditure, but also the perceived fairness of other government policies; for example, someone who perceives himself as the victim of an anomaly under a government's incomes policy, may react by seeking to recoup by means of tax evasion, which the anomaly has 'justified'; or, similarly, someone caught in the 'poverty trap' might react by evading.

(vi) The behaviour of reference groups with respect to evasion.

(vii) The degree of ignorance and incompetence—which may lead to unintentional evasion.

(viii) Opportunities for avoidance.

In addition to these more specific points, it is generally true that economic and financial pressures, however caused, increase the likelihood of evasion.

The 'natural' tendency for economists, thinking in terms of income-maximizing individuals, is to concentrate on the first three aspects listed; as Spicer and Lundstedt (1976) put it: 'Some economists have seemed content to view tax evasion as a special form of gambling: gambling for extra income in the light of the likelihood of detection and penalties imposed on detected tax evaders'. Models of tax evasion along these lines have been evolved by Allingham and Sandmo (1972) and Srinivasan (1973). Apart from criticisms which can be made of such models within their own framework, such as how taxpayers are to measure the risk of detection, this approach treats taxpayers as amoral and ignores the psychological and sociological influences. Some recent empirical work in the USA and the UK, following in the tradition of Schmölders (1970) who sought to establish the 'tax mentality' of the public, suggests that the psychological and sociological factors may be the more important and carry important implications for policy. It must be stressed, however, that the three empirical studies to which we refer all suffer, as the investigators readily admit, from methodological defects: small, geographically restricted samples and non-random selection, as well as the inherent difficulties of investigating such sensitive matters by survey methods. The findings of the studies must be regarded as tentative and indicative rather than conclusive.

Spicer and Lundstedt, (1976) using survey data from the United States, sought to test hypotheses concerning the relationship between tax evasion and (i) the perceived severity of sanctions; (ii) the perceived likelihood of detection; (iii) the perceived terms of trade of taxpayer and government, including within the terms of trade the perceived equity of the tax system and (iv) the number of evaders known to the respondent. Perceptions of tax equity and the influence of reference groups (the number of tax evaders known personally to the respondent) emerged as the most significant features in their indices of tax resistance and tax evasion. The perceived severity of sanctions appeared to have no significance.

Of the recent studies on United Kingdom data, Dean et al. (1980) and Lewis (1979), the former is the more comprehensive both in size of sample and range of questions. Dean and his colleagues established by a series of general questions relating to the exchange relationship that the vast majority of their respondents considered that the level of income taxation in the United Kingdom was too high; and more significantly, a majority thought that they paid too much in relation to other people in general, and a majority also considered that they paid too much in relation to those with similar earnings; thus the system was perceived as lacking in both vertical and horizontal equity. A large majority did not consider that, on the whole, the Government spent taxpayer's money wisely.

In response to more specific questions on attitudes to evasion, salient conclusions were that respondents considered that opportunities for small evasions were widespread and were widely exploited; and that, given more opportunities, the preparedness to exploit them would be even more widespread. Few respondents (only 4%) considered small tax evasions 'good'; nearly 40% held that they were 'neither good nor bad'; around 37% considered small tax evasions 'quite bad' or 'very bad'; whilst nearly 20% held that it would depend on the circumstances. 'Tax levels too high' was the reason most frequently given by respondents (25%) for why they thought people might decide to evade tax, whilst unfairness in the tax system accounted for another 12%. General economic considerations (covering greed, financial hardship or other financial pressures) accounted together for 33% of the responses. Only 6% gave wasteful government expenditure as a reason.

Lewis' findings are derived from a factor analysis of respondents views on a series of Likert matched statements. The different questions and approach restrict the scope for direct comparison between the findings of Lewis and those of Dean et al. But where questions are comparable, Lewis' findings tend to support those of Dean; sometimes they reinforce inferences which may be drawn from Dean's study; and they add some new evidence. Thus, Lewis' respondents were largely unsympathetic to tax avoidance; attitudes to evasion were dependent on the amount of money involved rather than the ethics of the practice; the view was widely held that a similar number of people would evade tax even if taxation were reduced; the relationship between taxation and services received through public expenditure was not a major part of tax mentality. Lewis concludes: 'Clearly items concerned with personal taxation liabilities are amongst the most salient aspects of tax mentality as are items concerned with the ethics of tax avoidance'.

In applying conclusions from this empirical research we need to be cautious, not only for the reasons already given but also because the direction of causation could flow in either of two ways: for example, people may evade because of perceived inequities in the tax system or, having decided to evade, they may justify their actions by reference to such inequities. With that warning the following conclusions may be suggested concerning the relationship between evasion and income distribution and the relevant policy implications.

(i) If there is evasion, the common assumption would be that tax rates need to be set higher to finance a given level of government expenditure. Evaders are free riders: their evasion reduces their tax bill but does not reduce their benefits from public expenditure. Thus evasion generates its own redistribution of income and wealth—a redistribution from the honest to the dishonest (or from these with less opportunity to evade to those with more opportunity). Apart from moral considerations, this redistribution is undesirable in that it is unrelated to any equity considerations. However, not everyone would accept the 'common' assumption. Some economists (e.g. Bracewell-Milnes, 1977) argue that evasion can be economically desirable if it results in economic activity which would otherwise have been stifled by high taxation—and such activity may conceivably result in an increase in tax revenue (if only from indirect taxes) as compared with a situation in which legitimate activity is being curtailed by high taxes. Be this as it may, it does not gainsay the inequitable distributional effect of evasion. Further, evasion may result in economic loss through distortions arising from attempts to utilize opportunities for evasion (e.g. by 'artificial' self-employment) and may engender an atmosphere favourable to further law-breaking in other forms.

(ii) If evasion becomes rife it undermines a policy of redistribution based on rational criteria. A vicious circle may be created such that high tax rates intended to achieve a desired redistribution generate evasion, which then necessitates still higher tax rates in order to achieve the desired redistribution, thus generating more evasion.

Because of the behavioural aspects there are particular dangers. Evasion feeds on itself—the more people evade taxes, the more inequities there are in the operation of the tax system to drive taxpayers towards evasion, and the more people whose reference groups evade taxes, the more there are who are themselves so influenced. Moreover, the situation may not be amenable to simple remedy; contrary to the assumptions of the economists' model, the relationship between tax evasion and tax rates is probably asymmetrical: a rise in marginal tax rates may increase evasion but a subsequent reduction may not reduce it to its previous level. This conclusion, in line with one of Lewis' findings (above), follows from the influence of reference groups on evasion; and in particular, it reflects the moral reluctance to evade still felt by many people; once that moral barrier is broken it cannot be re-erected simply by a reduction in these rates.

A recent increase in evasion in the UK is suggested by casual empiricism; and the Commissioners of Inland Revenue have themselves stated that there are 'a number of indications' that the scale of *undetected* evasion is rising (119th Report). One disturbing feature of the findings of Dean et al. was that younger respondents were much more inclined to believe that people would commit evasions than older, a result for which confirmation can be found in Spicer and Lundstedt (1976). This difference between the young and the old could reflect a difference in norms dependent on age, which would imply that as the young grew older they would acquire the norms of their elders; or it could reflect a declining tax morality over time.

(iii) There is another way of looking at the significance of psychological and sociological factors in evasion. By appropriate educational policy it might be possible to create a tax mentality unfavourable to evasion and the process might be cumulative, reinforced by the attitudes and behaviour of reference groups. Thus a virtuous circle would be created. The more powerful are such influences, the less the significance of the *level* of tax rates on evasion and the weaker becomes that constraint to redistributive policies.

(iv) On one feature relevant to policy all three surveys provide supporting evidence —that perceived inequities in the tax system generate evasion and that avoidance appears as a critical factor in evoking perceptions of inequity. The point is most explicit in the United States study by Spicer and Lundstedt (1976): of their respondents who considered the distribution of the tax burden to be unfair, 75% (in open-ended responses), gave tax avoidance by affluent tax payers or corporations as a major reason for the unfairness. Lewis' respondents showed strong antipathy towards tax avoidance; whilst Dean et al. surmized that the differential incidence of avoidance was a possible explanation why a majority of their respondents considered the tax system of the United Kingdom to be horizontally inequitable. As Spicer and Lundstedt write: 'If unfavourable attitudes toward the fiscal system are an important factor underlying tax evasion, then it follows that efforts should be made to isolate that part of the tax system which stimulates such attitudes. It seems therefore that tax compliance could be improved in the United States by closure of certain tax avoidance routes'. However, as they point out, it would be necessary to consider any economic effects of such closure before implementing it.

Avoidance

We defined avoidance, rather inadequately, as action which resulted in legal tax saving, where the actor substantially achieved the objective to which the tax was intended as an obstacle, and acted in ways contrary to the intentions of the government. More specifically, we indicated two ways in which government taxing intentions might be frustrated: loopholes because the law was badly framed and opportunities for avoidance which the government considered it necessary to tolerate for administrative reasons.

Whilst the sociological and psychological influences are different and less pronounced, there are similarities between the factors affecting evasion and avoidance.

The extent of avoidance is influenced by the level of tax rates; high marginal tax rates will encourage taxpayers to look for avoidance opportunities because the gain from successful avoidance will be more. Additional expenditure on tax-planning advice and implementation will be more worthwhile. Also something akin to likelihood of detection and 'punishment' is applicable to some extreme and artificial avoidance devices, where the avoider takes the risk that the government will discover the 'trick' and legislate against it retrospectively or in such a way that the avoider loses some or all of the advantage of his avoidance device, having suffered losses in the form of advisers' charges and possibly economic distortion. Perceptions of the fairness of the system and the perceptions of reference groups may influence a taxpayer's readiness to search for avoidance devices and willingness to accept the more artificial ones, as may the behaviour of reference groups with respect to avoidance. Opportunities for avoidance will be affected by the thoroughness with which the tax legislation is framed and drafted and the implications thought out.

On the relationship of avoidance to redistribution and relevant policy measures, the following comments can be made.

(i) As with evasion, the initial assumption is that avoidance narrows the tax base and requires higher tax rates than would otherwise be necessary to achieve a desired revenue for redistribution. Avoidance involves its own redistribution of income and wealth as between avoiders and non-avoiders (the sophisticated and the unsophisticated). Furthermore the rich, who can afford the 'best' advice, are those best placed to take advantage of avoidance possibilities, so that redistribution as a result of avoidance is regressive in its incidence.

(ii) Again, as with evasion, there are those who argue that, where marginal tax rates are very high, avoidance is a desirable phenomenon because it may prevent more economically harmful consequences, e.g. saving takes place in particular, tax-saving ways, which is better than it not taking place at all. On the other hand, the costs of tax avoidance to the economy are high both in terms of the resources applied to providing advice on tax minimization and of the distortion to the economy resulting from avoidance. Clearly the existence and utilization of widespread opportunities for avoidance may frustrate a rational policy on redistribution.

(iii) As already discussed in the context of evasion, the existence of avoidance opportunities generates feelings of inequity about the tax system, leading to evasion. The essence of the problem is that avoidance opportunities are both unevenly distributed—e.g. one man has the opportunity of a firm's car, even though it has little to do with the nature of his job, whilst another does not—and tend to favour the rich.

(iv) In so far as avoidance opportunities arise because the law is badly framed, two directions of improvement are indicated—one a matter of drafting, the other of policy-making. Let us take drafting first. The views of Philip Vineberg (1969) on the Canadian situation may well be applicable to the UK and elsewhere. He has deplored 'The failure of draftsmen, notwithstanding their obvious prowess and ingenuity, to find a suitable way in tax matters to express what is really meant' and continues 'We must learn anew to make tax laws say what they mean . . . . Exposure of projected amendments to legal talents closer to the market place would be helpful. Errors should be corrected as soon as they are discovered instead of waiting to see what some court may make of it five years hence. Just as businessmen must learn about the tax laws the makers of tax laws must learn about business'. Speed of action against avoidance is important for its deterrent effect on those artificial forms which require a major rearrangement of a taxpayer's affairs and are expensive to implement; the prospect that the tax-saving gain may be short-lived will discourage would-be tax avoiders.

(v) More important, however, in giving rise to avoidance opportunities are defects of policy-making. Sometimes governments may lack the will or integrity to take action. Some politicians, one suspects, may want to play it both ways—to please the egalitarians by pointing to high tax rates whilst satisfying the opposing faction by leaving avoidance opportunities. Sometimes avoidance opportunities may arise from a tax concession, with some social or economic objective, the implications of which have not been thought through, like agricultural concessions under CTT or measures to promote home ownership under income tax. Such results are the more likely when governments give way to pressure groups.

(vi) These deficiencies of policy-making lead on to and are interlinked with policy about tax base. First, an appropriate choice of tax base will reduce opportunities for avoidance by switches as between, for example, income as generally defined for tax purposes and capital gains. This argument is central to John Kay's case for an expenditure tax (*see* previous paper) and I need say no more about it. Second, once a tax base has been determined, maintaining its integrity minimizes avoidance opportunities; the more the exemptions, concessions, reliefs, etc accorded within a tax, the more opportunities for avoidance are created and the less it is possible to assess the distributional effects of the tax. The American terminology for such reliefs, 'tax expenditures', is salutory and where there are good reasons why 'tax expenditures' cannot be abolished or replaced by explicit expenditures, we would do well to follow United States practice and publish a tax expenditure budget indicating, as far as possible, the distributional incidence (Willis and Hardwick, 1978).

GENERAL CONCLUSIONS

Three overall conclusions suggest themselves.

(i) There is enough evidence to make it clear that high compliance costs, evasion and avoidance may each represent significant barriers to a policy aimed at redistribution of income and, indeed, that each may generate its own form of redistribution running counter to that sought by the policy-makers. The undoubtedly high compliance costs and high level of tax avoidance in the United Kingdom, allied to signs of growing tax evasion, are serious causes for concern.

(ii) A less ambitious target may reduce inequalities more than a more ambitious target which generates high compliance costs and extensive avoidance and evasion.

(iii) There is a vital need for more research in this badly under-researched field of tax compliance—compliance costs, avoidance and evasion. To this classic response of the academic, two riders can be added about the nature and direction of the research. As to nature, it is clear that all aspects of compliance need to be considered together, because of the links between them and that the research needs to be multi-disciplinary. As to direction, a number of pointers can be given. There is a particular need to obtain an operational definition of avoidance which can carry wide acceptability. Some estimates of the magnitudes of compliance costs, and of the loss of tax revenue from evasion and avoidance, need to be attempted which are more comprehensive and reliable than anything at present existing. Ideally such estimates would also indicate the distributional effects. Finally there is a need to supplement attitude studies with behavioural studies of evasion and avoidance if we are to have a sound basis for policy.

REFERENCES

Allingham M. G. and Sandmo A. (1972) Income Tax Evasion: A Theoretical Analysis, *J. Pub. Econ.* **1,** 323–28

Bracewell-Milnes B. (1977) The Fisc and the Fugitive: Exploiting the Quarry, *The State of Taxation*, London Inst. Economic Affairs

Bryden M. H. (1961) *The Cost of Compliance*, Canadian Foundation Papers, No. 25.

Dean P. N., Keenan A. and Kenney F. (1979) *Taxpayers' Attitudes to Income Tax Evasion: An Empirical Study. British Tax Review*, forthcoming.

Godwin M. (1976) VAT—Compliance Costs to the Independent Retailer, *Accountancy* **87,** 48–55

Lewis A. (1979) An Empirical Assessment of Tax Mentality (forthcoming), *Public Finance* **34/2,** 245–57.

Muller F. J. (1963) *The Burden of Compliance*, Seattle Bureau of Business Research, Univ. Washington.

Sandford C. T. (1973) *Hidden Costs of Taxation*, London, Inst. Fiscal Studies

Sandford C. T., Willis J. R. M. and Ironside D. G. (1975) *An Annual Wealth Tax*, London, Inst. Fiscal Studies/Heinemann Educational Books

Sandford C. T., Godwin M., Hardwick P. J. W. et al. (1979) *Compliance Costs of VAT—A Pilot Study*, Centre for Fiscal Studies, Bath

Shenfield A. A. (1968) *The Political Economy of Tax Avoidance*, London, IEA Occasional Paper No. 24

Schmölders G. (1970) Survey Research in Public Finance: A Behavioural Approach to Fiscal Policy, *Public Finance* **25/2,** 300–306

Spicer M. W. and Lundstedt S. B. (1976) 'Understanding Tax Evasion'. *Public Finance* **2,** 295–305

Srinivasan T. N. (1973) *J. Pub. Econ.*, **2/4,** 339–346

Vineberg P. F. (1969) The Ethics of Tax Planning, *British Tax Review* **1,** 31–48

Willis J. R. M. and Hardwick P. J. W. (1978) *Tax Expenditures in the United Kingdom*, London, Inst. Fiscal Studies/Heinemann Educational Books

Yocum J. C. (1961) *Retailers' Costs of Sales Tax Collection in Ohio*, Ohio State University

Royal Commission on the Distribution of Income and Wealth (1977) *Third Report on the Standing Reference*, London, HMSO

Select Committee on a Wealth Tax (1975) Volume 11, *Minutes of Evidence*, HMSO, 187–220

Wealth Tax (1974), Cmnd. 5704, London, HMSO

DISCUSSION

by **J. A. Astin****, *Inland Revenue, London*

Sandford's paper starts by providing definitions of the three terms 'compliance costs', 'evasion' and 'avoidance'. Of these, easily the most difficult concept is the last, and the author is himself not entirely happy with his definition. Kay's paper also tackles this problem, and if a general definition is needed, his may be the better one—'in looking at tax avoidance we are looking at ways in which the tax system induces people to modify their behaviour in order to pay less tax'. But in reality tax avoidance covers a wide range of activities, and the best approach is to discuss the various types separately.

Sandford states that the effect of compliance costs on income distribution is 'often inequitable and generally regressive', illustrating the point by reference to the 1974 wealth tax proposals, despite the fact that these proposals were not enacted and in any case do not relate to income. Recognition of the burden of compliance costs *has*, on the other hand, been made in the legislation on capital gains tax with the switch from a small gains exemption to a small disposals exemption in 1970 followed by the much more wide-ranging exemption of gains up to £1000 introduced in 1978.

One relevant fact which is often overlooked is the deductibility of compliance costs by businesses in computing their income tax or corporation tax liability. The costs of, for example, operating PAYE schemes, preparing business accounts, collecting national insurance contributions and complying with VAT requirements are all part of the operating costs of a business and are deductible in arriving at taxable profits.

** The author is a statistician with the Board of Inland Revenue. Any views expressed are purely personal, although factual statements may be taken to have official approval.

One of Sandford's conclusions on compliance costs is that more up-to-date research needs to be done. Sandford's own work in 1973†† was a milestone, but it is now considerably out of date. The Inland Revenue is conscious of the need to quantify the total resource costs of the tax system and in 1978 the Chairman of the Board of Inland Revenue said, in evidence of the House of Commons Public Accounts Committee, that efforts were to be made to measure these costs. Work has since then been continuing in the department on the planning of a major survey of compliance costs in two fields: the costs to the individual of complying with the income and capital gains tax requirements; and the costs to firms of operating PAYE systems. At the time of writing a ministerial decision had not yet been taken on whether to go ahead with these surveys, but if they are carried out a valuable updating of Sandford's earlier research will be achieved.

Turning to tax avoidance, my feeling is that avoidance is bound to accompany any system of taxation which has any semblance of equity or progression about it. High marginal tax rates may be imposed in order to achieve redistribution or in order to achieve a desired total revenue from a progressive structure, or both. The highest marginal rate of income tax in the UK is currently 98%; and although Kay in his paper says 'one cannot reduce peoples' potential standard of living to 2% of what it would otherwise have been without endangering social stability' (and thereby confusing average rates with marginal rates) the fact is that in 1976–77 about 25 000 people paid tax at this rate‡‡. Nonetheless, clearly the importance of the higher rates to the taxpayers concerned provides an incentive for them to find ways of re-arranging their affairs so as to bring about a lower effective tax rate. The artificial conversion of income into capital gains is one way of achieving this and, although the re-distributive purposes of the legislation may be thwarted, it could be that the channelling of funds into high risk (and hence high capital-growth, low income) enterprises is beneficial to the economy in general—although one cannot of course be sure of the broad economic importance of this. Professor Sandford may have this idea in mind when he says that 'avoidance through saving in tax-saving ways may prevent more economically harmful consequences.'

In explaining that tax avoidance may involve not only the transformation of income but the exploitation of reliefs and allowances, the author calls for the publication by the government of 'a tax expenditure budget, indicating, as far as possible, the distributional incidence'. Some steps in this direction have already been taken. A comprehensive list of all the reliefs for the direct taxes, together with the assumptions on which they are based and their approximate cost (where known) was published by the Board of Inland Revenue in its latest annual statistical report§§ and annual publication is planned for the future.

As the author points out, speedy anti-avoidance legislation is important, for a deterrent effect on those artificial forms which require a major re-arrangement of a taxpayer's affairs. Although the Inland Revenue has specialized staff working in this field, there has been a considerable increase in the marketing of highly artificial avoidance schemes: a single scheme sold to a small number of taxpayers can put the Exchequer at risk of losing hundreds of millions of pounds before the Revenue even becomes aware of its existence. Thus, practical difficulties can prevent the achievement of the most desirable goals.

Tax evasion, being an unlawful activity, is an area in which it is extremely difficult to obtain facts, either as to the methods used or as to their impact on the economy,

†† Hidden Costs of Taxation (CT Sandford, Inst. Fiscal Studies, 1973).
‡‡ Inland Revenue Statistics (1979), Table 1.7 HMSO.
§§ Inland Revenue Statistics (1979), Tables 1.10 and 1.11, HMSO.

although the generally accepted view is that such activity has been increasing in recent years. As regards evasion by the self-employed, the Inland Revenue's new system of accounts examination, under which a small number of specially selected accounts are subjected to detailed examination, has produced significant results, the total yield from investigation work having increased from £23m to around £60m in two years without any increase in manpower.

The economic effects of evasion are complex. There is a re-distributive effect—from the honest to the dishonest—which however 'economically desirable' the activity evading tax may sometimes be, clearly could not be tolerated on a large scale. On the other hand, it is probably true to say that net revenue is maximized at some level of enforcement below 100%. Not that revenue maximization necessarily maximizes social welfare. For example, failure to tax economic activity in the home leads to, say, professional people spending more time decorating their houses and less time devoted to their own skills—to the probable detriment of both the appearance of their houses and of their professional achievements. The Inland Revenue's task is, of course, to maximize net revenue in the prevailing circumstances, and it is not official policy to permit pockets of evasion activity to grow where effective anti-evasion activity is possible.

Sandford's paper is a valuable exposition of a subject which is not widely discussed in the economic literature, and which admirably interlinks the three strands of avoidance, compliance costs and evasion in ways which are by no means obvious. It has been all the more valuable for being presented at a time when the subject is under wide public discussion.

SUMMARY OF THE GENERAL DISCUSSION ON THE PAPERS BY KAY AND SANDFORD

There was a wide-ranging discussion on the difficulties of defining tax avoidance. Brown remarked that the authors seemed to be trying to define avoidance as a subset of the effects of taxes, but there did not really seem to be a clear boundary. Collard agreed, but felt that the alternative of taking in all income and substitution effects made the concept useless. Todd pointed out that some taxes were introduced clearly aimed at producing distortions (e.g. smoking). But the basic problem was the definition of the tax base. One would like a non-substitutable base, but it just wasn't possible. Clarke added that some tax concessions also seemed directed at encouraging avoidance. Kay felt that avoidance really occurred where the elasticity of substitution between the base activity and the avoiding activity was very high—but that still left the problem of how high. Forward commented that one could not define avoidance without knowing what the government's intention was with regard to the tax. Davies asked whether there was any point in defining avoidance. Did it matter whether actions were called avoidance or substitution effects? Perhaps what we really meant by avoidance was *unanticipated* substitution effects. Lecomber wondered whether a definition should take account of morality. Davies disagreed. In a legal environment where businessmen were supposed to look after their own interests, one could hardly call avoidance immoral.

Pond said that the British tax system combined low average rates of taxation with high marginal rates, thus producing large substitution effects and low income effects—the worst possible combination from the point of view of avoidance and evasion. Seade added that the incentive to avoid depended not only on the marginal rate, but on how far the marginal rate applies. King felt that this association of avoidance with marginal rates was not really correct. The tax with most avoidance problems was Capital Gains Tax, which had a low marginal rate. The problem here was that the tax was a one-off event with a large total payment.

O'Hagan asked whether there were any countries that treated capital gains on a par with income. Sandford replied that Norway did.

Layard asked whether, from a strict marginal revenue point of view, avoidance and evasion really did constitute a limit. Astin felt that it was really impossible to answer that question, through lack of information. Kay said there would be many offsetting effects if tax rates were reduced, but executive salaries would probably go down, so the revenue would not lose too much. Sandford said that the only clear figure on this was the revenue currently gained from the very top rates of taxation, which was very small.

Layard asked where the real weight of evasion lay. Astin replied that there were probably two large components:

(i) totally unrecorded incomes, which would be mainly taxable at basic rate;

(ii) understatement of self-employed incomes, which would probably be taxable at higher rates.

It was impossible to estimate accurately the amount of this evasion, but one estimate put it at 7·5% of GNP. Evasion of Capital Gains Tax would be over and above this figure.

Lecomber noted that Kay had argued very strongly for a simpler structure, e.g. expenditure tax, as a solution to these problems. King questioned whether the alleged advantage of an expenditure tax was merely semantic—that what was now thought of as avoidance would appear quite alright under an expenditure tax system. Kay agreed that there was some truth in this, e.g. in the treatment of pensions, but savings would only remain untaxed so long as they were unrealized—money-boxes were not very useful if you couldn't take the money out. Pond said that both Kay and King and the Meade Report had argued strongly that there was distortion in the treatment of different types of savings. Either you should exempt them all, or you should tax them all.

Heald asked how tight was the VAT system of collection. A progressive expenditure tax would have the same problems of under-reporting if direct assessment were used. Kay agreed. Avoidance was a matter of the tax base, but evasion was more concerned with the method of collection. Sandford replied that one of the hoped-for advantages of the Cascade system of VAT collection was that it might prevent evasion, by reducing the level of individual bills and by providing a means for cross-checking returns. But in practice cross-checking had proved unmanageable. There was no published evidence on the strictness of VAT collection relative to purchase tax collection.

In conclusion, Sandford said that he was not entirely convinced by the Inland Revenue's recognition of the importance of compliance costs. They were not deductible from individual taxes, although they could get slipped in against income tax, if that were possible.

LABOUR SUPPLY AND REDISTRIBUTION

C. V. Brown

Department of Economics, University of Stirling, Stirling, Scotland

INTRODUCTION

My object is to survey some empirical work on labour supply and to explain some of the ways in which it is relevant to the discussion of income redistribution. I will suggest that all of the following views are wrong, outdated or seriously incomplete:

(i) Empirical evidence suggests that the effect of taxation on labour supply is so small that it can be safely ignored.

(ii) Empirical evidence on labour supply is so inconsistent that it can be safely ignored.

(iii) If the price effect is negative there is no limit to the amount of redistribution that is possible because raising taxes will cause those taxed to work harder.

(iv) That all we need to know about labour supply is the elasticity of substitution.

The meaning of (iv) may require a little elaboration. Optimum tax theory (*see* Brown and Jackson, 1978, or Meade, 1978, for non-technical introductions), suggests that the ideal amount of redistribution depends on various factors such as the distribution of wages (which is assumed to depend on the distribution of ability); society's views about the extent to which equality is desirable; and the elasticity of labour supply. Typically, elasticity of labour supply is measured by the elasticity of substitution.

Because of space limitations I have restricted the survey in several ways. First, I have confined consideration to cross-section analysis. This omission of the other main methodologies (Brown, 1977; Brown and Jackson, 1978; Godfrey, 1975; and Holland, 1977), the interviews approach and the experimental approach, may be justified as these techniques usually have not, at least to date, led to elasticity estimates—which are a necessary, though not a sufficient, condition for deciding on the limits of redistribution. (There are exceptions, such as Burtless and Hausman (1977).) Second, I have confined myself to studies of men. Third, the emphasis has been placed on the improvements in technique that have occurred rather than on the enumeration of results from many studies. This is because it is the improvements in technique that have occurred which offer the main explanation for the recent findings that labour supply elasticities are high enough to be important for policy purposes.

Views (i) and (ii) above both derive from empirical studies which are both theoretically and econometrically unsound. It will be argued that as theoretically correct models have been developed and econometric difficulties reduced, it has become increasingly apparent that people will respond to changes in the tax/transfer system. I will then suggest some of the difficulties involved in applying the results of this work to a study of redistributive taxation. Early econometric work and, to my knowledge, all optimal tax work suffers from the same limitation: failure to take into account the complications caused by non-linear budget constraints.

ECONOMETRIC WORK ON LABOUR SUPPLY

When Godfrey (1975) surveyed work in labour supply he found little variance in the way in which the models were specified. He wrote (p. 54):

> As well as the general agreement about the appropriate theoretical basis, researchers have also differed very little in their specification of labour supply functions. The model established by Kosters (1966) has been the standard framework for almost all of the published work. . .

Type I Studies

The Kosters' model, which I will refer to as a Type I model, is an application of the elementary theory of labour supply, in which it is assumed that individuals are faced with a choice between a composite consumption good (represented by net income) and leisure. The individuals have an endowment of non-employment income, say rental income or welfare benefits which are *independent* of earnings, as well as an endowment of time—say 168 hours a week, and the individual also faces a given wage rate. The consumption possibilities open to the individual can then be represented by a budget constraint such as ABC in figure 1. In this figure income is measured on the vertical axis and leisure on the horizontal axis. The initial endowment of time is represented by the horizontal distance OA and non-employment income is represented by the vertical distance AB. The slope of segment BC is determined by the extra net income that can be exchanged for giving up an hour of leisure. This is the wage rate w. The individual is also assumed to have a given set of preferences between income and leisure which can be represented by a set of well-behaved indifference curves. The individual is said to be in equilibrium when his budget constraint is tangential to the highest attainable indifference curve. Thus, in figure 1, equilibrium occurs at E, the point of tangency between I I, and CB. It may be noted that in equilibrium the individual consumes OH hours of leisure and works AH hours.

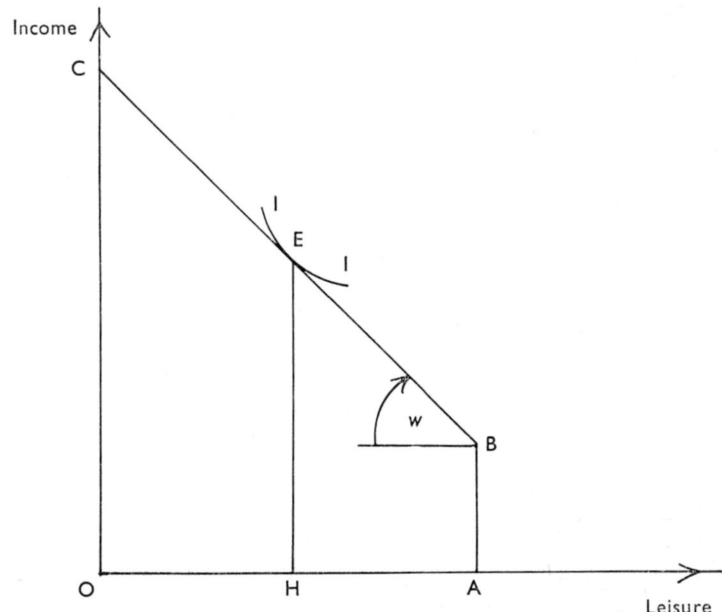

Fig. 1.

In his model a change in non-employment income will give an income effect. A change in the net wage rate will give a price effect and the substitution effect can be found from the Slutsky equation.

There have been a large number of Type I studies and they have varied in a number of respects such as data source, measure of labour supply, preference variables included, definition and measurement of non-employment income, functional form estimated etc. Despite this variation they all employ the same theoretical framework and a similar specification.

I will argue that the distinguishing feature of the Type I studies is this common framework and that this framework is fundamentally defective. That being the case, the detailed differences in approach are not of great interest and are largely ignored, the studies being represented by a single example discussed in some detail.†

A recent Type I study is the book by Masters and Garfinkel (1977). This study is taken to represent the Type I studies because it is recent and in general very carefully done. Masters and Garfinkel employ a large number of alternative measures of labour supply, two measures of non-employment income, and two measures of the wage rate. They do their estimates on two different data sets and for a variety of demographic groups. Space precludes reporting all their results, and those reported here are confined to one data set (that from the Survey of Economic Opportunity), one measure of labour supply (hours worked in the survey week) and one definition of the wage rate (the log normal wage rate) of prime age males.

In the regression that is reported here, hours worked in the survey week were regressed on non-employment income, the earnings of other household members, the log of the gross average wage rate, a constant and a further 11 variables to control for preferences. They found a price elasticity of $-0{\cdot}16$, an income elasticity of $0{\cdot}10$ and a substitution elasticity of $-0{\cdot}8$.

It may be noted that the income elasticity should be negative if income and leisure are normal goods and that the substitution elasticity should always be positive. (Other results not reported have different signs and in some cases these other signs conform to the predictions of theory.)

The wage rate employed is a gross average wage rate found by dividing gross income by hours. As the fundamental defect of the Type I studies derives from the use of this variable it is worth quoting extensively from Masters and Garfinkel's discussion (1977, p. 41). In the quotation that follows they explain how the wage rate is defined and the problems that arise from measurement errors.

> The hourly wage rate in the SEO is constructed by dividing normal weekly earnings by actual hours worked during the survey week. This wage rate variable presents two major problems. First, it is missing for all individuals who did not work for wages during the survey week. Thus for demographic groups in which most members do not work, such as men 72 or older, no measure of the hourly wage exists for large portions of the sample. Even for groups like prime-age married men in which almost everyone works, however, dividing normal earnings by actual hours worked may create serious measurement errors in the wage rate variable. The hourly wage rate is too low for all individuals who worked fewer hours than their normal work week. This kind of measurement error will normally bias the wage rate coefficient toward zero. When hours worked during the survey week is the dependent variable, however, the wage rate will be negatively correlated with the error term and a negative bias will result. . . .
>
> . . . There are some other, less important, sources of measurement error. Perhaps the most important of these stems from the confusion between gross and net earnings. Although interviewers were instructed to obtain normal gross weekly earnings, there is undoubtedly some error due to confusion between gross and net, since many individuals know only their take-home pay. Experience in the

† Other Type I studies are discussed in Cain and Watts (1973). It may be noted that one study in the Cain and Watts volume, that of Hall (1973), is a Type II study according to the terminology used here.

New Jersey Income-Maintenance Experiment suggests that it takes many interviews for families to learn the distinction well and to report gross earnings consistently. *See* Watts and Mamer (1973).

Masters and Garfinkel thus believe that their estimate of price elasticity is too large a negative number.

It will be noted in the passage quoted above that the researchers went to a great deal of trouble to insure that their income measure was *gross*: Masters and Garfinkel 1977, p. 45) state that it would have been better to use net income.

Next let us consider the effects of using gross income rather than an income measure that is net of taxes and working expenses. Let us start with the relatively simple case of a proportional income tax. In this case, a given percentage change in the gross wage will be equivalent to the same percentage change in the net wage. Therefore, when a logarithmic form of the wage variable is used, . . . a relatively small proportional tax will not bias our results. To the extent that our tax structure is progressive, however, our wage rate coefficients will be smaller in absolute value than they should be. Moreover, our estimates of the income effect will be a little too small in absolute value even if the tax is proportional, since these estimates are based on linear coefficients. . . .

If there is a proportional tax rate of t, our income effect estimates should be increased by a factor of $1+t$. Although we would have preferred to use data on each source of income after taxes, such information was not reported in our data sets. Making detailed tax rate adjustments is beyond the scope of this study. Rather than making a simple, inaccurate adjustment we prefer to make no adjustment at all.

While Masters and Garfinkel's study is careful, the authors taking considerable care to point to possible biases in their results, they fail to recognize two interrelated fundamental difficulties with their analysis. Other Type I studies have the same problems.

The first problem is that the theoretical model they use is improperly specified when budget constraints are non-linear. The argument is illustrated with reference to figure 2. Suppose there are two individuals who have the same non-employment income (AB), the same tax threshold (OX), and who face the same tax rate (t) for incomes above the threshold. Individual 1 has a job where he is paid extra for hours in excess of the standard working week (AS). In the absence of tax, his budget constraint is ABCD. With tax his budget constraint is ABFGH and he is in equilibrium at E_1. Individual 2 is not paid extra for overtime. In the absence of tax, his budget constraint is ABI; with tax the budget constraint is ABJK and he is in equilibrium at E_2. The Type I models would assign both of these individuals the same non-employment income (AB: which is correct) and the same gross average wage (which leads to difficulties). It will be remembered that the wage rate is defined as gross income divided by hours. For individual 1 this is

$$w_1 = \mathrm{LM}/\mathrm{AH}_1 = \mathrm{LM}/\mathrm{BL}$$

and for the second individual

$$w_2 = \mathrm{PN}/\mathrm{AH}_2 = \mathrm{PN}/\mathrm{BN}.$$

Thus

$$w_1 = w_2 = \mathrm{LM}/\mathrm{AH}_1 = \mathrm{PN}/\mathrm{AH}_2.$$

It is thus clear that gross average wage and non-employment income do not uniquely determine labour supply.

Masters and Garfinkel argue in the quotation above that it would have been better to have used net income rather than gross income. While there may be some advantages in using a net average wage rate rather than a gross average wage rate, it does not solve the theoretical problem outlined in the previous paragraph, as Brown et al. (1974a) have explained.

In addition to the theoretical problem just outlined, the Type I procedure suffers from endogeneity bias. This endogeneity bias exists in addition to the bias caused by measurement error mentioned by Masters and Garfinkel. If budget constraints are non-linear both the gross and the net average wage depend upon hours worked (rather than hours depending on the wage). The problem is illustrated for two different types of non-linear budget constraints in figures 3 and 4 which for simplicity are drawn on the assumption that non-employment income is zero. In figure 3 the only non-linearity is caused by the tax (t) on incomes above the exemption level. If equilibrium is at E, Type I models using a gross wage would use the slope of AB as the wage and those using a net wage would use the slope of AE_1 as the wage. Suppose that, from the random error in the model, someone works H_1+U hours. In this case the net wage would be given by the slope of line from A to J, which is less than the slope of AE_1. The random error in the model would thus cause the wage rate to change, which

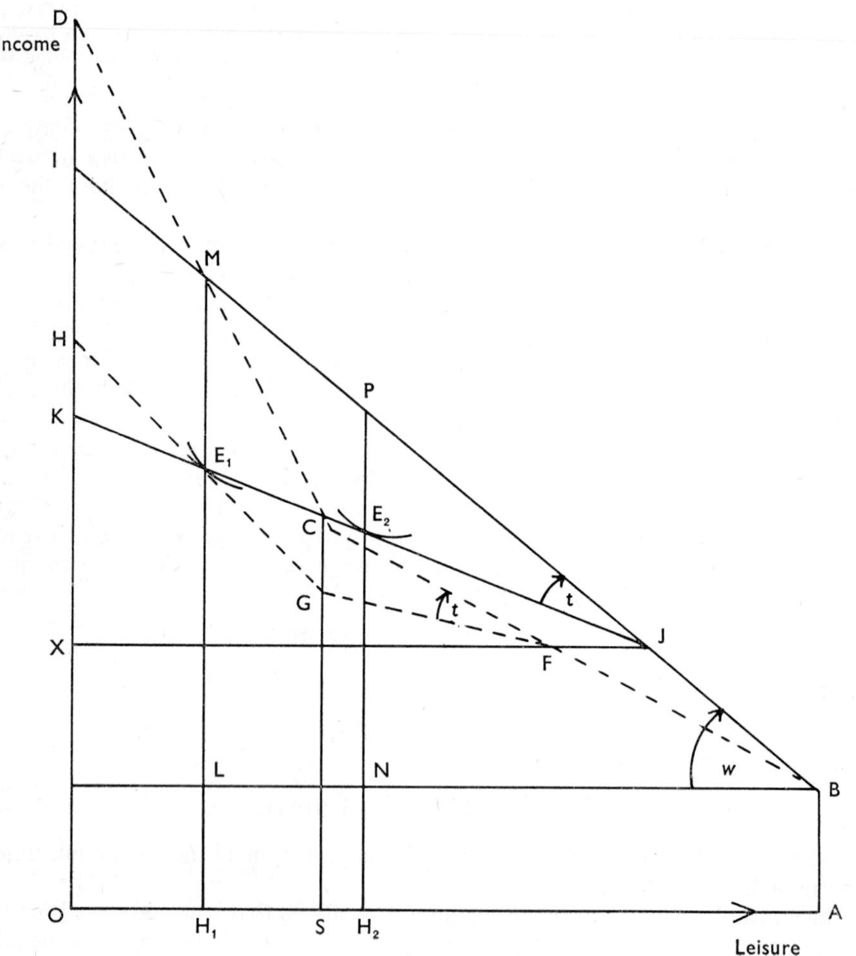

Fig. 2.

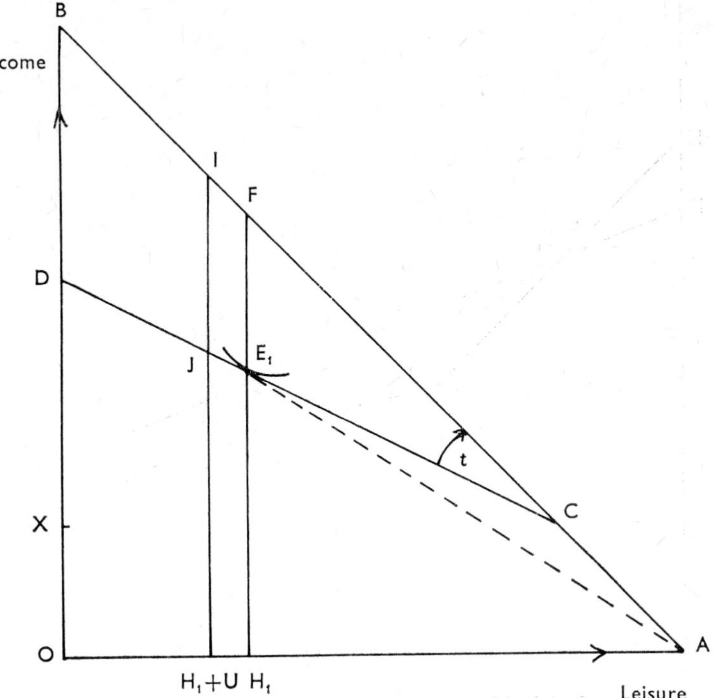
B
Income
I
F
D
J
E1
t
C
X
O
H1+U H1
A
Leisure

Fig. 3.

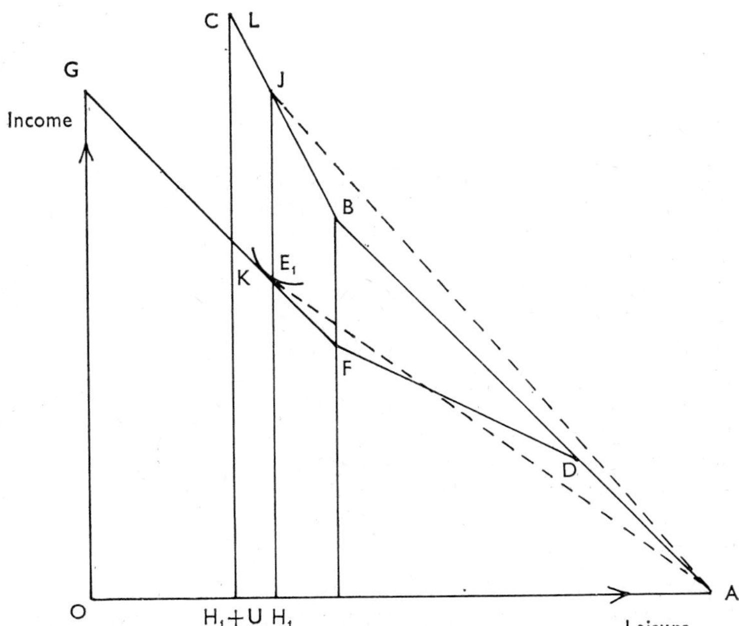
C L
G
J
Income
B
E1
K
F
D
O
H1+U H1
A
Leisure

Fig. 4.

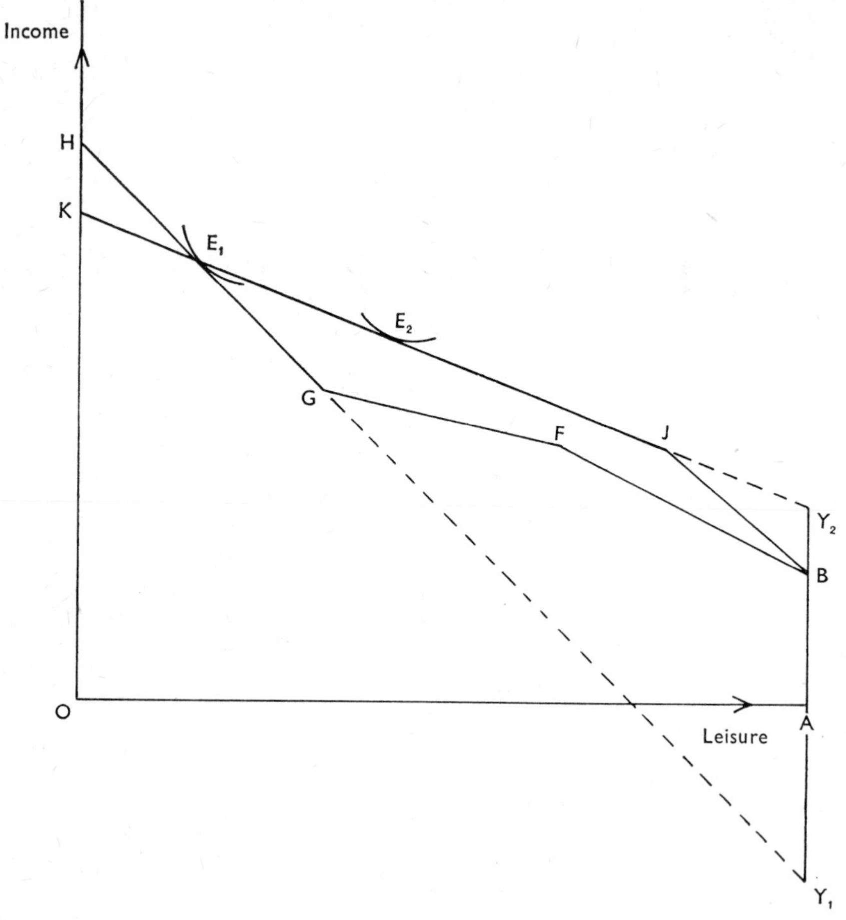

Fig. 5.

means that the wage rate has become endogneous. It may be noted that with the gross average wage rate the problem does not arise in this case because the gross average wage is AB irrespective of whether hours is H_1 or H_1+U.

This advantage for the gross average wage disappears when overtime premia are paid‡ and in these circumstances the gross average wage rate suffers from endogeneity bias, as can be explained with reference to figure 4. The pre-tax budget constraint is ABC (the top of the segment BC is omitted to save space), the post-tax constraint ADFG and equilibrium is at E_1. The gross average wage rate is given by the slope of AJ and net average wage rate by the slope of AE_1. With random error, hours might again be H_1+U. This would make the net average wage *rise* to equal the slope of a line connecting A to K. It may be noted in figure 3, where the budget constraint is concave (from the origin), that endogeneity bias caused the average wage to be inversely related to the error term; but with the convex budget constraint in figure 4, endogeneity bias is directly related to the error term. With convex budget constraints, the gross average wage rate suffers from endogeneity bias. Thus random error,

‡ It is often suggested that overtime is uncommon in the US. If this were true the deficiencies of the Type I studies in the US might be considerably less. However, Dickinson (1975) in a study discussed below has found very common overtime working in the US.

causing hours to be H_1+U rather than H_1, would mean that the gross average wage would be computed as the slope of a line from A to L, which is greater than the slope of AJ.

The combination of the theoretical indeterminancy of the Type I model and the particularly acute form of endogeneity bias have led to searches for models which avoid these problems.

Type II studies

The distinguishing feature of what are here called Type II studies are that they employ a linearized budget constraint which solves the theoretical problems outlined above and which reduce endogeneity bias. [Levin developed a model employing both an average and a marginal wage rate which solved the theoretical problem. This model is discussed in Brown et al (1974a)]. The way in which the theoretical problem is solved can be illustrated with reference to figure 5, which is similar to figure 2. In figure 5 the after-tax budget constraints of 1 (ABFGH) and of 2 (ABJK) are reproduced from figure 2 and the two equilibria are shown as E_1 and E_2. The crucial element in the linearization procedure is to note that E_1 would be the equilibrium position if the budget constraint were Y_1H and E_2 the equilibrium for the budget constraint Y_2K. In the Type II studies a linearized budget constraint is used and frequently the method used involves calculating hypothetical intercepts—sometimes termed 'as if non-employment income' such as Y_1 and Y_2 in figure 5. [Hall (1973) was the first person to use a linearized budget constraint but instead of calculating an intercept at zero hours of work, he used a concept he termed 'whole income after tax' which is in effect an 'as if' intercept calculated at 2000 hours of work per year.]

Labour supply is then assumed to depend on this hypothetical intercept and on the slope of the linearized budget constraint. Thus individual 1's labour supply is assumed to depend on Y_1 and the slope of the line Y_1H and 2's labour supply on Y_2 and the slope of Y_2K. This solves the theoretical problem, because the two individuals no longer have a common intercept (AB) and a common wage (the slope of BJ = slope of BI in figure 2), but instead are recognized to have distinct budget constraints which uniquely identify their equilibria.

Type II models also reduce endogeneity bias. Any random error in the model leading to individuals working more or less hours than those indicated will not matter, *provided that the individual remains on the same segment of his budget constraint.* The italicized proviso in the last sentence is important. It is the failure of Type II models to deal with this element of the endogeneity problem that has led to the development of Type III models. However, before examining these it is worth looking at some of the results from Type II models and to compare results from Type I and Type II models to examine what difference in the estimates is made by the theoretical and econometric improvements.

Type II results

I propose to report on the findings of two Type II studies: one American and one British. These two studies are selected from the relatively small number of Type II studies because they are the only two, that I am aware of, where a comparison of Type I and Type II is available on a single data set.

In the British study, Brown et al. (1976) use a model in which labour supply is assumed to depend on calculated intercepts such as Y_1 and Y_2 in figure 5 and on a net marginal wage rate which measures the slope of the linearized budget constraint.

They also use a term 'other income', which includes mainly the income of other household members and state transfer payments, but which also includes in principle rental and dividend income. If this other income were true non-employment income it obviously should be included in the intercept. However such income, especially the earned income of other household members and means tested transfers, is not independent of the individual's labour supply. To include this other income in the intercept would thus bias the estimate of both income and substitution effects. To omit it altogether would be to ignore an important element of income. It was therefore included as a separate variable. The equation estimated was

$$H = a_1 + a_2 MW + a_3 (MW)^2 + a_4 I + a_5 I^2 + a_6 (MW)(I) + a_7 OY + a_8 N + a_9 JS$$

where H = hours worked last week; MW = net marginal wage rate; I = the calculated intercept, OY = other income, N is a preference variable to control for need and JS is a preference variable to control for job satisfaction.

The data was derived from a specially commissioned survey carried out from Stirling University in 1971. The population studied was weekly-paid workers in Great Britain. To be eligible for inclusion in the equation reported here, the respondent had to be a married man under 65 who worked at least eight hours 'last' week and who reported that he was free to work his desired number of hours (i.e. was not constrained by demand factors to work an amount different from the amount he wished to work). He had to come from a household where either he was the only worker or where he and his wife alone worked, he had to provide enough information to allow the variables to be constructed and he had to have a positive net marginal wage rate.

'Hours' were hours worked in all paid jobs 'last week'. The marginal wage made appropriate allowances for income taxation, overtime premia (which varied considerably between individuals) and second jobs. It did not take into account loss of means-tested benefits. The intercept was calculated using hours worked at a previous kink rather than using actual hours of work, in order to prevent bias in the intercept being associated with measurement error in the dependent variable.

Brown et al. found the following elasticities: price elasticity −0·18, income elasticity −0·1, substitution elasticity 0·18, elasticity of substitution 0·25. It may be noted that these elasticities are all consistent with economic theory. Brown et al. (1974b) have also run a Type I model on this data. With this improperly specified model both the income and substitution effects have the 'wrong' sign and the negative price effect appears considerably larger. These differences strongly suggest that the improvements in the Type II studies are important.

The other Type II model that I will report on in some detail is an American Study by Dickinson (1975). Like Brown et al., Dickinson studies married men (between 25 and 60 in Dickinson's case) who are free to vary their hours and who have a positive net marginal wage rate. He also uses a calculated intercept (which he terms 'non-wage income, effective level') and a functional form that allows for interactions between the wage rate and the intercept.

There are however many differences in the details of the way the variables are defined—e.g. hours are annual hours. In the version of the model reported here, which is Dickinson's preferred version, the gross marginal wage is defined with a uniform overtime premium of 1·5 times the basic wage rate. The net marginal wage is the gross marginal wage less the marginal tax rate which is estimated separately.

The intercept is calculated on the assumption that the basic wage rate is paid for the first 2000 hours per year and overtime wage rate for hours over 2000. [It is assumed that the standard week is 40 hours and that 50 weeks are worked. If either the number of hours or the number of weeks differ then there will be error in the calculations.] Dickinson proceeds by summing gross non-employment income and the estimated value of gross employment income of both husband and wife. Estimated tax is then subtracted from this total and the whole is then brought back to zero hours.

Dickinson tries to minimize the endogeneity problem by splitting his sample into three groups depending on the value of the net marginal wage rate. In his justification for this procedure he notes that the direction of the endogeneity bias depends on whether the kinks are concave or convex. He argues that within each of the bands the bias from overtime premium will roughly cancel out the bias from the change in tax rates.

In his regressions Dickinson employs large numbers of control variables many of which are interacted with the wage rate and the intercept. As a result there are nearly 30 variables in the regression. Table 1 shows the resulting elasticity estimates.

Dickinson's results which are reported here are from his preferred specification. Like Brown et al., he has experimented with Type I models. However Dickinson finds much smaller differences between the alternative specifications than those found by Brown et al. Dickinson (1975, p. 182) concludes:

> Most previous estimates of labour supply functions have thus been based on the assumption of a constant wage rate, at least before taxes, and on the assumption of effective freedom of choice of work hours at that wage rate. In the above comparative exercise we have controlled on the second factor and explored the sensitivity of our estimates to alternative budget specifications. If no wage–income interactions are allowed, the estimates are relatively insensitive to changes in the marginal wage specification. When this restriction is dropped, however, failure to account for overtime premiums in the wage specification leads to an apparent strengthening of the income effect for low wage workers relative to that for high wage workers. While such a differential is theoretically plausible, the empirical result must be viewed as a consequence of misspecification unless a convincing argument can be made that the effective gross marginal wage rate is closer to the straight time rate than to the overtime rate.

Table 1. Estimated labour supply parameters preferred specification.[a]

Wage rate	Expected work hours[b]	Wage effect	Income effect	Substitution effect
	White males, no second job			
Under \$3·25 (w=\$2·60)	2307	−109·4	−0·101	124·7
		(70·4)	(0·042)	(107·7)
\$3·25–\$4·99 (w=\$4·30)	2183	−50·5	−0·101	170·0
		(36·7)	(0·035)	(78·9)
\$5·00–\$9·99 (w=\$6·10)	2106	−38·8	−0·080	130·3
		(24·6)	(0·033)	(63·7)
	Black males, no second job			
Under \$3·25 (w=\$2·60)	2197	−122·7	−0·065	20·0
		(64·2)	(0·052)	(123·0)
\$3·25–\$4·99 (w=\$4·30)	2050	−63·8	−0·065	68·4
		(45·8)	(0·048)	(92·6)
\$5·00–\$9·99 (w=\$6·10)	1949	−52·1	−0·044	33·3
		(43·9)	(0·048)	(83·6)

a Married male workers, no second job, wives not working, select equilibrium sample. Net overtime wage specification, all preference control variables included.

b Assumes the following standard characteristics: age 40, 4–9 years on job, 1 week sick time, 190 hours commuting time, children in family, mean values on preference control variables.

Source: Dickinson (1975).

It is not clear why Dickinson's estimates should be much less sensitive to model specification than those of Brown et al. It is frequently stated that overtime is less common in the US than in the UK and this could be the explanation were it not for Dickinson's finding that most of his sample (like the UK sample) did work overtime. The difference might lie in details, such as Dickinson assuming a constant overtime premium and a constant number of hours paid at basic rate while Brown et al. put in separate figures for each individual. It could be simply that various errors in the Type I models happened to cancel out with Dickinson. Brown et al.'s findings suggest it would be unwise to assume that this will always happen.

Type III studies

The major drawback of the Type II studies is that they do not fully solve the endogeneity problem. Type III studies solve the endogeneity problem by estimating each segment of the budget constraint separately and then have the individual choose that segment which gives him the highest utility.

The Type III approach appears to have been evolved quite independently by three separate groups of authors. Ashworth and Ulph (1977) and Burtless and Hausman (1977) both state they became aware of the work of Wales and Woodland (1977) after they had worked out their own approaches. While it would appear that Wales and Woodland were the first to produce a discussion paper, it is interesting that several people saw more or less the same answer at more or less the same time. Once again there are differences in the detailed approach followed and again it is convenient to choose one study to explain the principles involved. In this case Ashworth and Ulph is taken as the example because it is then possible to compare Type II and III studies on a single body of data.

The Type III procedure can, in principle, be used for budget constraints with any number of linear segments. The budget constraint may be concave throughout, as in figure 6*a* which could be generated by an income tax with two marginal rates. Or the budget constraint could be convex throughout, as in figure 6*b*; such a constraint could arise if there were a means-tested benefit giving ABC, an ordinary income tax giving a net wage equal to the slope of HI and an overtime wage rate in the final segment of figure 6*b*. Or the constraint could contain alternating convex and concave segments as

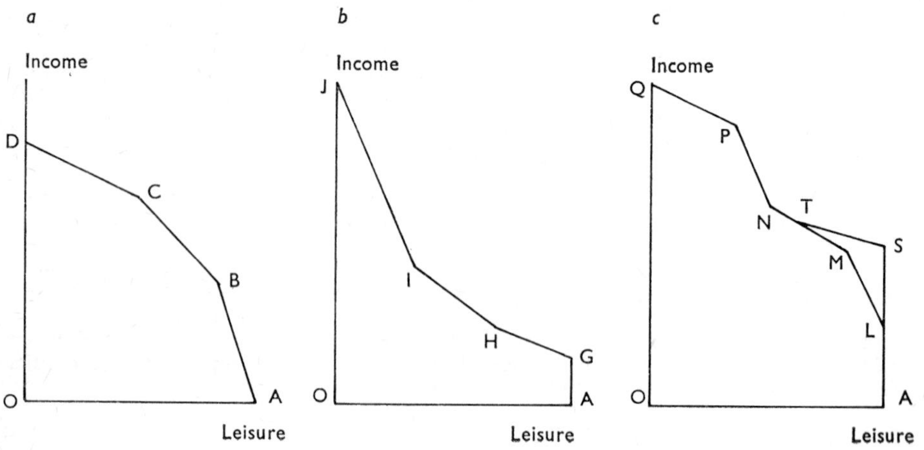

Fig. 6.

in figure 6*c*. Individuals might be in equilibrium on any of the segments shown. An unconstrained individual would not choose convex points such as H, I or N but might well choose concave points such as B, C, M and P.

In their preferred specification Ashworth and Ulph find the following elasticities: price elasticity −0·06, income elasticity −0·004, substitution elasticity 0·56, elasticity of substitution 0·78. [It is important to note that these are provisional estimates.] Although these results are from same data sample as those of Brown et al. the change in elasticities is not entirely due to the change from Type II to Type III models. Other reasons (with their effects on the elasticity of substitution given in brackets) include (i) the reduction in numbers resulting from additional data requirements (which appears to increase the elasticity of substitution, perhaps because those knowing most about their budget constraints are most sensitive to tax changes), (ii) the incorporation of other income into the intercept (which reduces the elasticity of substitution, perhaps because of simultaneity bias), (iii) a change in functional form—from a quadratic labour supply function to an indirect utility function (which increases the elasticity of substitution, particularly when the most generalized utility functions are employed), and (iv) the change from Type II to Type III (which also increases the elasticity of substitution).

Clearly this is an important advance but there are problems remaining which may be listed. The data requirements restrict numbers. Other income is treated as if it were non-employment income. To date it has proved impossible for Ashworth and Ulph (1977) to incorporate preference variables into Type III procedures. [Work on this problem is, however, underway.] As work by McGlone and Ruffell (1978) has shown, this may lead to biased estimates. The results are sensitive to functional form.

There is a final problem caused by data limitations. Type III studies can in principle handle any number of budget segments but in practice data limitations may restrict the set estimated. The problem may be illustrated with the Ashworth and Ulph study and figure 6*c*. It is very likely that the Ashworth and Ulph procedure will locate some people at M, the kink caused by the tax threshold. However, point M may not exist in reality. The reason for this is that people may become eligible for various income-maintenance benefits before their income drops below the tax threshold. This is because the tax and social security systems overlap in the UK. However, the Stirling data set has incomplete information on means-tested benefits which, as a result, have not been modelled by Ashworth and Ulph. These implications are explained with the aid of figure 6*c*. The budget constraint as modelled by Ashworth and Ulph is ALMNPQ and they might find someone at M. However the true budget constraint with means-tested benefits is ASTNPQ and, if this had been modelled, equilibrium would have been found at some point on the segment ST. The policy implications of the two positions may be very different, as we will see.

These findings by Ashworth and Ulph are in general in line with the findings of Wales and Woodland (1977) that, to use my terminology, Type II studies have under-estimated the elasticity of substitution, due to their failure completely to solve the endogeneity problem.

Conclusions

Clearly there has been very considerable progress in the dozen years since Kosters' pioneering work. The present state of evidence suggests very strongly that it would be a mistake for policy makers to assume that labour supply is not responsive to tax changes. The evidence suggests both that people are responsive and that modelling

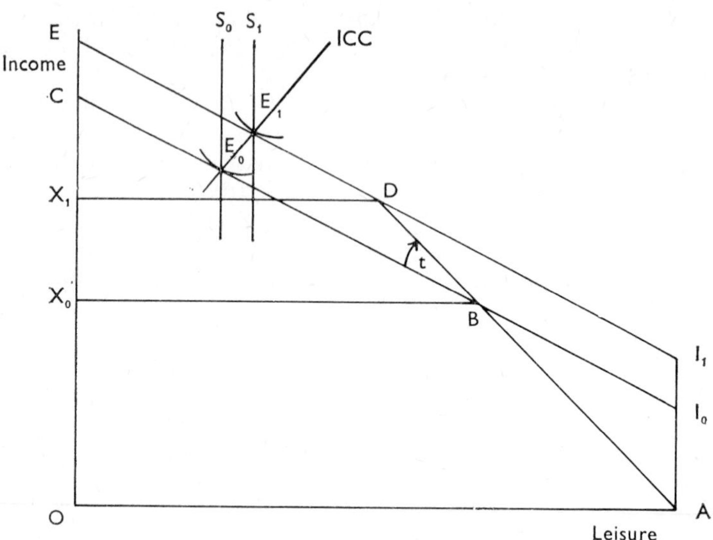

Fig. 7.

this response very carefully is important. Precisely how responsive people are is still an open question, but it does seem well established that the price elasticity for men is low and negative and it seems likely that the elasticity of substitution is between 0·5 and 1·0.

IMPLICATIONS OF LABOUR SUPPLY ESTIMATES FOR REDISTRIBUTION

At the start of this paper I suggested that it was a mistake to assume that, if the price elasticity is negative, people will necessarily work more if taxes are raised. This is a variant on the view that all we need to know about labour supply is the sign of the price effect.

The sign of the price effect would be sufficient to predict whether a change in income tax would increase or decrease labour supply if there were no non-employment income, if the tax were proportional and there were no other non-linearities in the budget constraint. When there is no non-employment income a change in the rate of a proportional income tax results in a pure price effect causing a movement along the labour supply curve. Indeed the labour supply curve can be defined as the locus of such points.

However, when taxes are non-proportional most tax changes will cause the labour supply curve to shift and there may be movement along the labour supply curve as well. In these circumstances the sign of price effect can only tell us about the direction of movement *along* the labour supply curve. It cannot tell us in which direction the supply curve will shift. In considering the predicted effects of tax changes on labour supply, it is necessary to distinguish between cases where equilibrium occurs on a linear segment of the budget constraint and where it occurs at a kink. I will take the case of a linear segment first and I will assume that the person does not change segments. I will also assume that the price elasticity is zero.

The problem may be illustrated with the simplest possible example of a proportional tax with an exemption as in figure 7. Suppose the tax system exempts the first OX_0

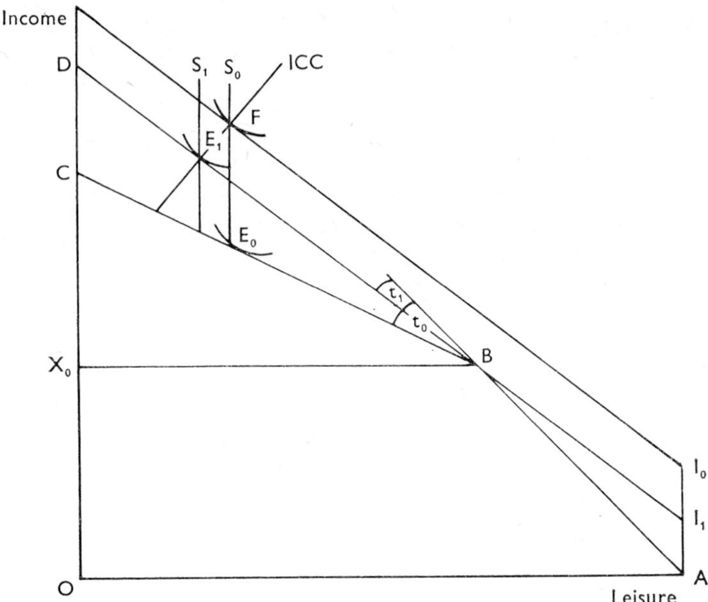

Fig. 8.

units of income and taxes the remainder at rate t. The budget constraint will be ABC, with equilibrium at E_0. Suppose a decision is then made to cut taxes. This might be achieved either by *increasing* the exemption level or by *reducing* the tax rate and the predicted labour supply effects would be rather different. If the exemption level were raised from OX_0 to OX_1 the actual budget constraint would change from ABC to ADE and the linearized budget constraint would shift from I_0C to I_1E. The new equilibrium would be at E_1 which is assumed to lie on the segment DE. It is evident that this is a pure income effect involving a movement along the ICC curve and shifting the labour supply curve in the direction of more leisure/less work.

Reducing the tax rate would shift the labour supply curve in the opposite direction, as can be seen from figure 8. Reducing the tax rate from t_0 to t_1 changes the linearized budget constraint from I_0C to I_1D. [An intuitive explanation of this reduction in the intercept is that the original intercept represents the value of the tax exemption to the taxpayer. As the tax rate is reduced the value of the exemption is correspondingly reduced.] The new equilibrium position is at E_1; the change can be broken down into a price effect (E_0 to F) resulting from the change in the slope of the budget constraint and an additional income effect (F to E_1) associated with the reduced value of the allowance. The additional income effect will lead to additional work, shifting the supply curve to the left. If the price effect is nil then the overall effect will be to increase work. The contrast between those two examples suggests that it is important to consider the labour supply results of alternative tax strategies at the macroeconomic level. [A start in this direction has been made in Brown and Jackson, (1978) Chapter 13 Appendix.]

Turning to the position when equilibrium occurs at kinks, such as B in figure 9, it is again necessary to consider both changes in tax rates and the position of the kink. At concave kinks the slope of the budget constraint is not defined and equilibrium might be unaffected by quite substantial changes in the slope of the budget constraint.

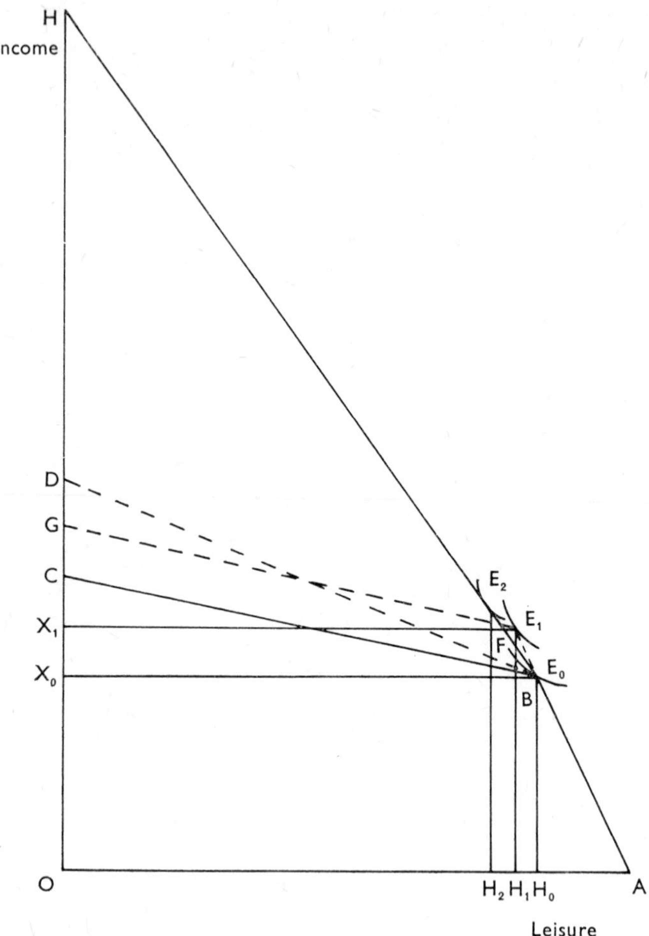

Fig. 9.

Thus an individual working to the point where tax starts (i.e. who is at B) could be unaffected by quite substantial changes in tax rate. [As the tax rate falls it becomes increasingly likely that hours of work will rise, as there will be a pure substitution effect in the direction of more work. The higher the elasticity of substitution, the more likely it is that this will occur and, if it does occur, the larger the effect will be.]

While changes in the slope of a budget constraint may sometimes have no effect on behaviour when an individual is at a kink, changes in the position of the kink may be important. The argument may be illustrated with figure 9. The individual is in 'equilibrium' at E_0 on the budget constraint ABC where he works until his income reaches the tax threshold. If the tax rate is reduced so that his budget constraint becomes ABD, his behaviour is unaffected.§ However, if the tax threshold (the exemption level) were increased from OX_0 to OX_1, the budget constraint would become AFG and the individual would increase his hours of work up to the amount determined by the

§ If the tax falls far enough this may not be true. Thus, if the tax rate fell to the point where the budget constraint was ABH, the new equilibrium would be at E_2 where hours would have risen from AH_0 to AH_2.

new threshold, that is from AH_0 to AH_1. It is thus necessary to note that the predicted effects of an increase in the threshold are not always the same. Someone in equilibrium on CB who moves to a new equilibrium on FG will *decrease* work, while we have seen that someone on the kink will *increase* work. [If the segment changes from BC to BF no *a priori* prediction is possible.] This means that even if all individuals have the same preferences an increase in allowances may cause some to work less, others more.

The fallacy in view (iv) (that all we need to know about labour supply is the elasticity of substitution) is now easy to see. Suppose we confidently believe that we know not only the elasticity of substitution but also the distribution of ability and the weight we wish to place on equality. In these circumstances it might be quite tempting to look at one of the simulation studies that has been done (e.g. by Stern, 1976) and to read off the optimum tax rate(s). However no accurate estimate of labour supply response could in fact be made in these circumstances.

It should be clear that not only do we have to know the elasticities and the distribution of abilities but we also have to know in considerable detail the distribution of individuals relative to their budget constraints. We have to know what segment of their constraint they are on and if they are at or near kinks. This is of course true not only in the discussion of optimal tax structures but also in the more mundane job of trying to estimate the redistributive effects of routine changes in tax rates and tax bands.

ACKNOWLEDGEMENTS

This paper draws heavily on a forthcoming report to the Commission of the EEC and I am grateful for their permission to make use of the material. I am grateful to K. Glaister, A. McGlone and R. J. Ruffell for comments.

REFERENCES

Ashworth J. and Ulph D. (1977) *Estimating Labour Supply with Piecewise Linear Budget Constraints.*

Brown C. V. (1977) Survey of the Effects of Taxation on Labour Supply of Low Income Groups. In: *Fiscal Policy and Labour Supply*. London, Inst. Fiscal Studies.

Brown C. V. and Jackson P. M. (1978) *Public Sector Economics*. Oxford, Martin Robertson.

Brown C. V., Levin E. and Ulph D. T. (1974a) *On Taxation and Labour Supply*, Univ. Stirling Discussion Paper in Economics, No. 30.

Brown C. V., Levin E. and Ulph D. T. (1974b) *Inflation Taxation and Income Distribution* (evidence submitted to the Royal Commission on the Distribution of Income and Wealth), Univ. Stirling Discussion Paper in Economics, No. 33.

Brown C. V., Levin E., and Ulph D. T. (1976) Estimates of labour hours supplied by married male workers in Great Britain. *Scottish J. Political Economy* XXIII, **3**, 261–277

Burtless G. and Hausman J. (1977) *The Effect of Taxation on Labor Supply: Evaluating the Gary Negative Income Tax Experiment.* Discussion paper no. 211, MIT.

Cain G. G. and Watts H. W. (ed.) (1973) *Income Maintenance and Labor Supply*. Chicago, Markham.

Dickinson J. G. (1975) *The Estimation of Income-Leisure Structures for Prime Age Married Males:* Doctoral Dissertation, University of Michigan.

Godfrey L. (1975) *Theoretical and Empirical Aspects of the Effects of Taxation on the Supply of Labour.* Paris, OECD.

Hall R. E. (1973) Wages, Incomes, and Hours of Work in the US Labor Force, chapter 3 in Cain and Watts, (1973).

Holland D. M. (1977) The Effect of Taxation on Incentives of Higher Income Groups. In: *Fiscal Policy and Labour Supply*. London. Inst. Fiscal Studies.

Kosters M. H. (1969) Effects of an Income Tax on Labour Supply. In: Harberger A. C. and Bailey M. J. (ed.), *The Taxation of Income from Capital*. Washington, Brookings Inst.

McGlone A. and Ruffell R. J. (1978) *Preferences and the Labour Supply of Married Women*, Univ. Stirling Discussion Paper in Economics, No. 62.

Masters S. and Garfinkel I. (1977) *Estimating the Labour Supply Effects of Income-Maintenance Alternatives*. London, Academic Press.
Meade J. E. (Chairman) (1978) *The Structure and Reform of Direct Taxation*, London, Allen & Unwin.
Wales T. J. and Woodland A. D. (1977) *Labour Supply and Progressive Taxes*, Discussion paper no. 77–105, Univ. British Columbia.

DISCUSSION

by **J. Le Grand,** *Department of Economics, London School of Economics and Political Science*

If it weren't too cumbersome, this paper might well have the title 'The effects of non-linear budget constraints on (a) econometric studies of labour supply, and (b) theoretical predictions concerning the effects of tax changes on labour supply'. For Brown is arguing that most of the widely-quoted theoretical and empirical results concerning, in particular, the effects of taxation on labour supply, are based on the assumption that budget constraints are linear. If we regard that assumption as implausible (and Brown implies that we should, though he doesn't actually say so), then all these results are largely worthless.

Overall, Brown is to be congratulated on producing a useful addition to the important work he and his associates have been doing on the incentive effects of taxation. It is clearly argued and makes some important points. I shall comment on the various sections in turn.

I have little to add on the Type I studies. Brown's discussion of the difficulties they involve seems to me to be admirable. So far as the Type II studies are concerned, I have a philosophical unease with their Friedmanite 'as if' assumption. In fact people are not making their work/leisure choices under the 'as if' linear constraint, and I feel dubious about results based on the assumption that they are. Professor Brown

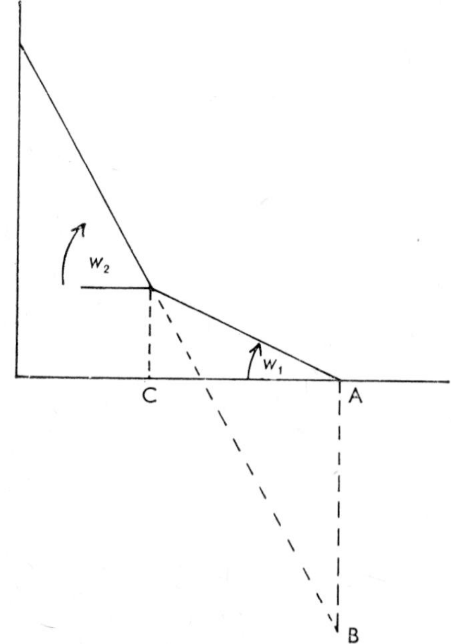

Fig. 10.

obviously does not share this unease (except in the case where individuals may change segments) and I must confess that I find it difficult to specify precisely why it should make a difference: nonetheless I remain sceptical. A possibly more serious econometric difficulty is that the hypothetical intercept used in the regression equation is a linear function of the wage rate. In figure 10 below, for example, the hypothetical 'non-employment income', AB, is equal to $(w_2 - w_1)H_1$, where H_1 is the number of hours that can be worked at wage rate $w_1(=\text{CA})$. This will create multi-collinearity problems if H_1 is the same for any substantial body of workers in the sample.

Brown reviews the Type III studies relatively sketchily, and from his review I don't fully understand how they work. (Nor have I been able to check with the originals, since they are all unpublished). So I will confine myself to the comment that so far as I can tell they do indeed seem to be theoretically superior.

However, there is one point concerning all three types which Brown does not mention. This is the difficulty that any kind of linear regression involves some assumption about the form of the underlying utility function, for which there is no independent justification. For example, Type I regressions are presumably generated by some form of Klein–Rubin type of utility function;|| but we have no reason to believe that utility functions do in fact take that form. Deaton, in a recent unpublished paper, has pointed out the dangers of drawing conclusions about tax policy from econometric studies incorporating unsupported assumptions about the underlying utility functions: a criticism to which all these studies are open. In fact, it seems to me that our best hope of obtaining reliable estimates of the effect of taxation on labour supply come not from those types of study but from the experimental approach, typified by the New Jersey Negative Income Tax experiments. However, these are not reviewed by Brown.

Finally, the theoretical section. I have a terminological problem here. Brown seems to interpret the 'price' effect as the movement from E_0 to F in his figure 8; and if indeed this is what it means then his point stands. However, I would have thought it could be more consistent with the general use of the term to mean the movement from E_0 to E_1 (this being presumably the discrete analogue of $\mathrm{d}H/\mathrm{d}t$—Koster's definition of the price effect). In that case, knowledge of the price effect would be sufficient to predict the effects of, at least, a tax rate change on the supply of labour.

On balance, therefore, I do not feel that Brown has fully succeeded in his aim of refuting all the four propositions with which he starts the paper. In particular, I find an expanded version of (ii) acceptable: viz. that the empirical evidence on labour supply derived from even the most sophisticated cross-section studies made to date is based on too many unjustified assumptions to be very useful for policy purposes.

SUMMARY OF THE GENERAL DISCUSSION

Brown opened by saying that it should not be thought that he was trying to reduce all problems into the framework of multi-segment budget constraints. His colleague,

|| Assume income comes from wages only and is all spent on one good, X, offered at price $P=1$. A Klein–Rubin utility function defined over the good and leisure, L, would have the form:

$$U=A(X-c)^{1-\beta}(L-d)^{\beta}$$

where A, β, c and d are parameters. Maximizing this subject to the constraint:

$$T=L+H=L+X/w$$

where T is total time available, H is hours worked and w is the wage rate, yields standard first-order conditions which in turn can be solved to give the linear regression equation.:

$$H=a_0+a_1/w_1$$

where a_0 and a_1 are functions of the parameters of the utility function.

Ruffell, had evolved another method of looking at the problem which suggested that Type III studies were not all that different from Type II. Turning to some of Le Grand's specific comments, he did not think there was a great problem of multicollinearity (Le Grand, p. 183); there was in fact quite a lot of variation in standard hours and the position of the kink. He had nothing against experiments of the New Jersey type, but they did have their own problems (Hawthorne effects, truncation bias in sampling). A similar survey in the UK would cost £5–10 million. He did not feel that Le Grand's pessimistic conclusion was justified. What after all was the alternative for a policy-maker? Presumably to assume that the substitution effect was zero, which was surely not true.

Zabalza queried the definition of wages rates on p. 170, and whether the work of Ashworth and Ulph (1977) cited had sufficiently controlled for tastes.

Todd expressed doubts about the narrowness of the treatment of tax changes. One could normally devise all sorts of combinations of average and marginal tax-rate changes by altering personal allowances etc; one wasn't in practice confined to simple marginal changes. Also, perhaps more important than short-run adjustments were the much longer-run decisions such as life-time career choice. Mirrlees agreed with Todd's emphasis on the long run. Were the kinks as important in the long run? Also one would need to make some assumptions about how utility functions differed. If people were identical then 'hours worked' could be simple a proxy for career choice. Brown replied that in principle his method could handle complicated tax changes, but long-run job choice was more difficult. Layard said he did not know of any studies of long-run job choice, but studies on the demand for education were an important pointer. They showed an elasticity of demand with respect to 'earnable' wage of between 1 and 2.

Sheshinski commented that Brown's methodology was directed at marginal adjustments while other studies have emphasized the importance of the initial participation/non-participation decision. In reply, Brown said he felt that the participation/non-participation decision was more important for women than for men.

Gregory noted that the sample comprised people who were able to work their desired hours. Could this be legitimately aggregated up? Brown thought that the Type III procedure could get around the problem of constrained hours, but it was not easy. Layard thought that male manual workers were constrained more downwards than upwards. 40% of manual workers work normal hours, the rest work overtime.

Heald asked Brown what, having disposed of his four propositions, his own advice to policy-makers would be. Brown replied that it would be simply not to assume that the elasticity of substitution was zero; 0·5 might be closer to the truth.

WHAT LIMITS AND WHAT KIND OF REDISTRIBUTION?

F. Field*

Child Poverty Action Group, London and Low Pay Unit, London

INTRODUCTION

The debate on 'the limits to redistribution' is likely to be changed fundamentally by the Yom Kippur war. The slowing down of the world economy is beginning to have major political repercussions, not least on the question of distribution of income. Entry into what is generally agreed will be a period of slow economic growth brings to an end a chapter in post-war British politics. Until the 1973 oil crisis most discussion centred on redistributing newly created wealth. The first section of this paper looks at those forces which are beginning to emphasize the importance of redistributing existing wealth towards the poor.

This changing debate will need to be accompanied by widespread understanding of the current distribution of personal incomes. Since the Second World War, and particularly during the last ten years or so, there has been a powerfully orchestrated campaign asserting that the limits to redistribution have been reached. The second section of this paper looks critically at those assertions, to show that while changes have occurred, the gains for those at the bottom end of the distribution have been very modest.

Living standards are not only affected by vertical changes in the distribution of incomes. The horizontal distribution is of equal importance, although it has hardly featured in the current debate. The final section of this paper looks at the extent to which households with children—whatever their level of income—have been losing out over the past 20 years or so and questions those who assert that welfare provisions have adequately compensated for this trend.

THE END OF POST-WAR CONSENSUS

Central to the post war political consensus has been a set of beliefs stemming from the role performed by economic growth. The agent for lowering the political temperature, while at the same time removing the stains left by society's grosser forms of poverty, was a steadily rising national income.

As on so many issues, the clearest exponent of how to achieve simultaneously these two apparently contradictory goals was Anthony Crosland. Crosland believed growth provided the formula for leaving the rich rich, while also lessening the poverty of the poor. Writing after the 1970 election defeat, Crosland began with a frank admission; he'd been wrong on the question of growth: 'I was too complacent about growth in the *Future of Socialism*' (Crosland, 1971, p. 2–3). He continued by listing

* The author is now MP for Birkenhead, and so is no longer with the CPAG.

the objectives to which Labour was still committed; the abolition of poverty, massive increases in public spending on education, housing and health, as well as mounting a major attack on environmental pollution. He continued his argument by adding 'Certainly we cannot even approach our basic objectives with the present state of growth. For these objectives . . . require a redistribution of resources; and we shall not get this unless our total resources are growing rapidly.'

By developing this theme Crosland expressed one of the key premises of post-war consensus politics (emphasis added):

> I do not of course mean that rapid growth will automatically produce a transfer of resources of the kind we want; whether it does or not will depend on the social and political values of the country concerned. But *I do assert dogmatically that in a democracy low or zero growth wholly excludes the possibility*. For any substantial transfer then involves not only a relative but an absolute decline in real incomes of the better off half of the population . . . and this they will frustrate.

Crosland concluded by saying that in a utopia, or a dictatorship, it might be possible to transfer resources of a near or static GNP to the have nots, but 'In the rough democratic world in which we live, we cannot.'

New World

Slowly people are becoming aware that the current recession is different from previous swings in economic activity. Not only is unemployment higher than at any time during the past 35 years but neither government nor opposition holds out the prospect of returning to full employment in the near future. And, while people puzzle over the economic indicators, little or no time is given to plotting the political consequences to our society of the loss of an ever rising national income.

One reason why we are so unprepared is that the scenarios presented by the revisionists excluded consideration of the world in which we now find ourselves. Crosland's argument is nothing if not comforting. Radicalism could be put on ice while awaiting a return to a high level of economic activity. The one possibility which was not discussed by Crosland, or subsequently by any of his disciples, was that a period of slow growth could result in real cuts in the living standards of the poor. But this is the future we may now face.

Powerful forces are at work increasing the numbers of poor. Slow growth will increase the numbers made poor by unemployment while demographic changes are adding daily to the welfare roles. Real cuts in the poor's standard of living may therefore occur if the current period of slow growth is not accompanied by a redistribution of existing income to the poor (Field, 1979).

Unemployment

The first challenge to those arguing that the limits of redistribution has already been passed is being mounted from the dole queues. Today the unemployed number almost 1·5 million and the latest estimate from the Department of Employment projects a rise in the labour force of about half a million by 1982. On the assumption that the current job market is unaffected by technological change, it is estimated that a growth rate from between 3% and 4% per annum is required to match the projected increase in the labour force, let alone reduce the current record post war level of unemployment.

It is on the basis of a growth rate below the level required to match the expected increase in labour supply that practically all forecasting organizations project a rise in the numbers of unemployed. For example, the Cambridge Group has estimated the level of unemployment at 2·25 millions in 1982. How will this growth in the ranks of the unemployed affect the social security budget?

Increasing unemployment will affect the amount spent on the social security budget in two ways. In the first place more claims will be made on the insurance benefits scheme as a greater number of people draw unemployment benefit. Many of the projected 2·25 millions will be eligible for national insurance benefits. Secondly, larger numbers of the unemployed will also be drawing supplementary benefit. If the Cambridge Group predictions are right, and the proportion of the unemployed drawing supplementary benefits remains the same as at present (which is unlikely because the proportion is increasing as the recession worsens), then by 1982 the numbers made poor by unemployment will have risen to over a million.

Demographic Changes

At a time when the numbers of unemployed are likely to increase, demographic changes are taking place which will also increase the number of households on low income. The major change on this front is the increase in the numbers of single-parent families. Recently one-parent families have been increasing at a little over 6% a year. If this rate of increase is maintained over the next five years one-parent families will grow from a total of 798 000 in 1977 to 1053 400 in 1982. The corresponding increase in the numbers of children cared for in these families will rise from 1436 000 to 1896 000 over the same period of time. This increase in the number of one-parent families will have a major effect on the social security budget.

At the present time, 60% of one-parent families depend on supplementary benefit. If the same ratio is maintained we can estimate that by 1982 there will be 632 040 single-parent families drawing supplementary benefit.

In making estimates about the future size of the social security budget, another group that must be taken into account are retirement pensioners. Although the number of retirement pensioners will not increase greatly in the next five or ten years (their numbers will in fact have declined by the turn of the century) expenditure on retirement pensions and supplementary pensions now accounts for over 50% of the total social security budget.

It would be possible to continue these projections across the whole field of welfare-state provisions. However the full range of calculations have been excluded, partly because it is more difficult to estimate their likely financial consequences, but also because an analysis limited to those three groups of claimants—the unemployed, one-parent families and pensioners—clearly illustrates the challenge to the 'limits-to-redistribution' thesis which will be brought about by an increasing number of the poor if national income fails to grow at above the average post-war rate.

If the living standards of the poor are to be maintained at a time when the number made poor by unemployment, as well as the numbers of one-parent families in poverty, are growing, the social security budget will need to rise from the current level of £13·2 billion to £14·5 billion by 1982.

At the present time, 10·8% of GNP is spent on social security payments. In considering the effects of increases amongst the unemployed and one-parent families only, we see that if the living standards of all beneficiaries are to be maintained without a policy of redistribution, GNP will need to grow by 9·7% in the years up to 1982. Failure to achieve this rate of increase will not just mean, as Crosland predicted, a freezing of radical intent, but a cut in the living standards of the poor. It is this prospect which gives a renewed urgency to the issue of redistribution and those sweeping generalizations which support the claim that we have already reached the limits to redistributing from the rich to the poor.

A VERTICAL DISTRIBUTION OF INCOME

The most popularly presented view about changes in the distribution of income in this country is of an inexorable move towards greater equality. To what extent have variations between incomes diminished in the recent past, have these changes affected all or only part of the distribution, and what role has the direct tax system played in this process? These are the questions to which we now turn.

The two main sources of data on the distribution of personal incomes are the Survey of Personal Incomes and the Blue Book tables. The Survey of Personal Incomes was only occasionally carried out in the early post-war years, but annually since 1962. The Blue Book tables begin in 1938 and were published for each year from 1949 except for a gap from 1967 to 1972–3. One of the useful tasks completed by the Royal Commission on the Distribution of Income and Wealth (referred to hereafter as Royal Commission) was to fill this gap, so that complete data for recent years now exist for both series. What pattern of income distribution do they show?

First, a word of warning about the data. In the initial report on its standing reference, the Royal Commission summarized what are generally agreed to be the reasons why the Survey of Personal Incomes presents an inaccurate picture of total personal incomes (see p. 37–38 Royal Commission, 1975). Here it is necessary to emphasize the main reservations which stem from the fact that the data are derived from tax returns. As not all income is subject to tax, a survey based on tax returns cannot give a complete picture of the distribution. And, even where the definition of income is more in line with a 'command-over-resources' approach, the Revenue doubt whether returns about fringe benefits are reported with complete accuracy.

A second disadvantage of using tax returns to construct data on income distribution is that by definition those below the tax threshold are excluded. As we will see later, the tax threshold has changed dramatically during the post-war period. The Royal Commission observed that the exclusion of those with incomes below the tax limits has considerable implications for the conclusions which can be drawn from the data, particularly when making comparisons during the pre- and post-war periods, when the number of tax payers doubled.

A third main distorting factor is that the Revenue is uncertain about the scale of tax evasion. Changes in the extent of evasion will place further limits on the use to which the data can be put in making comparisons over time.

The Blue Book tables (summarized in table 1) are based on the Survey of Personal Income (SPI) tables of the distribution of total net income, supplemented by data from other sources, notably the DHSS and the Family Expenditure Survey (FES). Commenting on the Blue Book data, the Royal Commission listed the advantages of using this source of information. They were the 'only official statistics compiled solely for the purpose of presenting information about the distribution of personal income' and 'we regard these CSO tables as the most valuable income statistics available' (Royal Commission, 1975, p. 43). But the Commission added an important rider: 'they retain many of the defects of the SPI data'.

Official Surveys

Bearing in mind how incomplete any snap-shot of the personal distribution of income from official data must be, let alone the hazards of presenting changes over time, what can be said about the changes in the personal distribution of income charted by these official sources of data? Is the popularly held view about the diminishing differences

Table 1. Distribution of personal income—Survey of Personal Incomes 1938–9 to 1974–5.

		1938–39	1949–50	1954–55	1959–60	1964–65	1965–66	1966–67	1967–68	1968–69	1969–70	1970–71	1971–72	1972–73	1973–74	1974–75
		%	%	%	%	%	%	%	%	%	%	%	%	%	%	%
Pre-tax																
Top	1%	17·1	10·6	8·8	7·9	7·7	7·8	7·2	7·0	6·9	6·7	6·2	6·1	6·0	6·2	5·9
	2–5%	14·4	12·5	10·9	10·8	10·6	10·7	10·4	10·4	10·4	10·4	10·4	10·3	9·9	9·9	9·9
	2–10%	23·4	21·5	19·5	19·5	19·3	19·5	19·2	19·2	19·1	19·1	19·5	19·2	18·7	18·7	18·9
	2–20%	35·3	34·7	33·3	33·3	33·2	33·3	33·1	33·2	33·5	33·3	33·7	33·7	32·9	32·8	33·5
	2–30%	44·1	45·3	44·7	44·9	44·9	45·0	45·0	45·2	45·5	45·3	46·1	45·9	44·9	44·9	45·8
Bottom	10%	—	—	—	—	3·4	3·3	3·2	3·2	3·1	3·2	3·3	3·2	3·7	3·5	3·1
	20%	—	—	—	—	7·9	7·7	7·7	7·6	7·4	7·6	7·8	7·6	8·4	8·1	7·6
	30%	13·8	13·8	13·4	13·4	13·5	13·3	13·3	13·2	13·0	13·2	13·4	13·2	14·2	13·9	13·3
Post tax																
Top	1%	11·7	5·8	4·8	4·8	5·0	4·8	4·7	4·6	4·5	4·3	4·1	4·2	4·0	4·2	3·8
	2–5%	13·6	10·9	9·8	9·7	9·5	9·5	9·4	9·4	9·4	9·3	9·3	9·4	8·9	9·1	9·1
	2–10%	22·9	19·9	18·4	18·3	18·0	18·0	17·8	17·9	18·0	17·9	17·9	18·1	17·4	17·6	17·9
	2–20%	35·6	33·6	32·5	32·5	32·2	32·2	32·1	32·2	32·3	32·1	32·4	32·7	31·7	31·9	32·6
	2–30%	45·2	44·7	44·6	44·7	44·5	44·6	44·4	44·5	44·8	44·5	44·9	45·2	44·0	44·2	45·1
Bottom	10%	—	—	—	—	3·8	3·7	3·7	3·6	3·5	3·7	4·0	3·7	4·3	4·0	3·8
	20%	—	—	—	—	8·7	8·6	8·5	8·4	8·3	8·6	8·9	8·5	9·6	9·0	8·7
	30%	15·4	15·9	16·0	14·5	14·8	14·5	14·7	14·4	14·3	14·7	15·0	14·4	15·9	15·2	14·8

Key: not available.
Source: Reworked from Royal Commission (1977), Table D5 and D7.

Table 2. Distribution of Personal Income—Blue Book 1949 to 1974–5.

	1949	1959	1964	1967	1968–69	1969–70	1970–71	1971–72	1972–73	1973–74	1974–75
	%	%	%	%	%	%	%	%	%	%	%
Pre-tax Top											
1%	11·2	8·4	8·2	7·4	7·1	7·0	6·6	6·5	6·4	6·5	6·2
2– 5%	12·6	11·5	11·3	11·0	10·7	10·8	11·1	11·0	10·8	10·6	10·6
2–10%	22·0	21·0	20·9	20·6	20·0	20·2	20·9	20·8	20·5	20·3	20·4
2–20%	36·1	36·1	36·4	35·8	35·4	35·7	36·8	36·7	36·3	35·9	36·2
2–30%	47·3	48·7	49·0	48·4	48·3	48·7	50·0	49·9	49·4	48·8	49·3
Pre-tax Bottom											
10%	—	—	—	2·2	2·3	2·2	2·5	—	—	2·7	2·6
20%	—	5·3	5·2	5·6	5·7	5·5	5·6	5·6	5·8	6·2	6·2
30%	—	9·7	9·5	10·4	10·4	10·2	10·2	10·1	10·6	10·9	10·8
Post-tax Top											
1%	6·4	5·3	5·3	4·9	4·6	4·7	4·5	4·6	4·4	4·5	4·0
2– 5%	11·3	10·5	10·7	9·9	9·8	9·7	10·0	10·0	9·8	9·8	9·7
2–10%	20·7	19·9	20·6	19·4	19·0	18·9	19·4	19·5	19·2	19·1	19·2
2–20%	23·9	35·6	36·7	34·6	34·5	34·5	35·3	35·4	35·0	34·6	35·0
2–30%	47·1	48·5	49·6	47·6	43·6	47·8	48·6	48·8	48·2	47·8	48·2
Post-tax Bottom											
10%	—	—	—	—	—	—	—	—	—	3·2	3·1
20%	—	6·0	6·5	7·1	6·6	6·4	6·7	6·6	6·8	7·4	7·5
30%	—	11·2	11·6	12·0	11·9	11·6	11·9	11·7	12·3	12·8	12·8

Key: not available.
Source: Reworked from Royal Commission (1977), Tables D1 and D3.

in personal incomes supported from this data? Of particular importance are the more recent changes, for it was after the election of the Labour Government in 1964 that the most recent debate about high levels of taxation and the growing equality of income was initiated.

In one sense the pre-tax data (shown in the top half of table 1) support the view of a move towards greater equality in income. The Survey of Personal Incomes shows that since 1964–5 the share of pre-tax personal incomes going to the richest 1% fell from 7·7% to 5·9%. A reduction in pre-tax income is also recorded for the following top 4% in the income distribution, but the change is much smaller. If the richest 2–20% are taken as a group, we find that their share of pre-tax income remains almost unchanged throughout the period since 1964–5. Not surprisingly, therefore, the data shows that the share going to the poorest 30% remains fairly constant throughout the 10 years following 1964–5.

A similar picture emerges from the data on the post-tax distribution of income shown in the bottom half of the table. Again there is a marked reduction in the share going to the top 1% but the richest 2–10% in the income distribution commanded almost the same share (17·9%) in 1974–5 of total personal incomes as they did back in 1964–5 (18%). Again the share of total personal incomes going to the poorest, 30% remains almost the same throughout the period since 1964–5, although it is important to bear in mind the qualifications, cited earlier, about changes in the tax threshold affecting the data on low income earners.

To what extent does a different picture emerge from the Blue Book statistics? Table 2 presents the relevant information in a similar way to the data from the Survey of Personal Incomes.

The years since 1964 record a similar reduction in the share of pre-tax income going to the richest 1%. But, as with the Survey of Personal Incomes, the share of personal incomes commanded by the richest 2–10% in the income distribution remains almost the same. During the same time the poorest 30% share rose from 9·5% in 1964–5 to 10·8% in 1974–5.

The post-tax data from the Blue Book show a reduction in the share of total personal incomes commanded by the richest 1% during the years since 1964, their share falling from 5·3% after tax to 4% in 1974–5. But the share of the following 9% in the income distribution again shows a much smaller reduction of 0·6 percentage points. The poorest 30% in the income distribution again record a small increase with their share rising from 11·6% in 1964 to 12·8% eleven years later.

The official data do not therefore support the broad generalization about the extent to which personal incomes have been redistributed from rich to poor in the post-war period, particularly over the years since 1964. Both series of data show a reduction in the share of the richest 1% but with the richest 2–10% of the population maintaining their share of personal incomes. The redistribution has been from the super rich to the very rich and the total personal income going to the poorest 30% show an increase significantly smaller than the reduction witnessed by the richest 1% of the population.

While this conclusion does little to support the view that we have reached the limits to redistribution with respect to levelling down top incomes, it leaves unexplained why most people regard the British tax system as a powerful engine grinding ever relentlessly towards a greater equality in personal incomes. To understand the basis of this misconception requires a discussion of what has been called the welfare state for the rich—or the growth of the tax allowance system.

Tax Changes

One of the key changes in the British system of direct taxation occurred in 1923. Until then the income of the poor was protected from taxation by the operation of an exemption system. Tax allowances could be claimed up to a certain level of income but beyond this point all income became liable to tax. The budget of 1920 changed the British tax system at a stroke; from the exemption to an allowance system (Field et al., 1977). In that year tax payers were allowed to set the tax allowance against their income no matter how large.

One major effect of changing from the exemption to an allowance system has been to decrease the size of the tax base. The most comprehensive study so far on the effects of tax allowances on the size of personal income subject to tax has been compiled by researchers at the Centre of Fiscal Studies at Bath University. In their book *Tax Expenditures in the UK*, Willis and Hardwick (1978) show that largely because of tax allowances 'only 45% of total gross income is taxed at the present time'. They also make a distinction between structural allowances, which are the main personal allowances, and non-structural allowances, such as mortgage interest relief. In the year 1973–4 Willis and Hardwick calculate that non-structural tax relief accounted for 15% of gross personal income. Had this sum been taxed at the then standard rate, total income tax revenue would have increased by 32%, allowing a reduction in the standard rate of 7p in the £.

Growth in the tax-allowance welfare state has reduced significantly the amount of personal income subjected to tax. But, because the post-war period has been characterized by increasing public expenditure, it has been necessary to widen the tax base by increasing the proportion of the workforce required to pay tax. This process has continued to such an extent that tax is now levied on those levels of income which are below the supplementary benefit poverty line and the eligibility threshold level for the family income supplement.

Governments have also tried to compensate for the loss of revenue entailed in granting tax allowances by subjecting that income which is liable to tax at high marginal rates. It is these higher marginal rates which make most of the running in the current debate on the supposed redistributional impact of direct taxation. But high marginal rates of taxation are necessary partly because of the loss of revenue from tax allowances, which have themselves resulted in a reduction in the total of personal incomes subjected to tax.

A few examples show the difference between the marginal and average rates for tax payers on different levels of income. A single person on £1000 a year faces a marginal tax rate of 25% on each £1 increase in earnings, but has an average tax rate of 6·9%. Likewise, while a single person on £20 000 a year faces a marginal tax rate of 75%, this same tax payer's average tax rate is below 50%. But while it is the average tax rate which is the more important in determining net income, it is the marginal rates which are quoted in public debate to support the 'unacceptable-face-of-taxation' thesis.

Both marginal and average rates of tax are further reduced below the nominal rates quoted by the claiming of non-personal tax allowances and, as we can see from table 3, these tax allowances are of greater cash and percentage value to higher income groups. The average deduction in the tax year 1974–5 for the richest 1% of tax payers amounted to £648. In stark contrast, the average deduction in the sixth decile amounted to £34.

Table 3. The value of deductions for mortgage and other allowable interest payments and charges and retirement annuity premiums, 1975.

United Kingdom Quantile group	Deductions as a proportion of average income	Income unit i.e. tax unit Average value of allowance, £
	%	
Top 1%	4·6	648
2– 5%	4·7	286
6–10%	4·2	187
Top 10%	4·5	274
11–20%	3·8	138
21–30%	3·5	105
31–40%	3·2	81
41–50%	2·9	62
51–60%	2·0	34
61–70%	1·7	22
71–80%	1·0	10
81–90%	0·8	7
Bottom 10%	2·0	12

Source: Derived from Tables E4, E5 and E6, Appendix E: Reworked data from Royal Commission (1977), table 9.

Table 4. Income tax as a percentage of income: percentage change between 1964–5 and 1977–8.

Income w.r.t average earnings	Single person	Married couple	Married couple and two children
	%	%	%
$\frac{2}{3}$ ×	88	177	235[a]
1 ×	47	72	306
2 ×	33	49	122
5 ×	42	40	51
10 ×	31	32	33
20 ×	15	14	15

a From 1970–71: no tax paid in 1964–65.
Source: Reworked from T&GWU (1976), updated.

Taxation of various groups

The emphasis given to the high marginal rates of tax has been important in creating the image that the increasing burden of tax has been borne by higher income groups. In deciding which income groups have reached the limits of redistribution, it is important to look at changes in the incidence of taxation, not only between individual tax payers on different levels of income, but also at changes between different income groups. The changing incidence on individual tax payers is presented in table 4.

A single person tax payer on two-thirds average earnings at the beginning and end of the period under study faced an increased tax bill of over 88%. The single person remaining on five times average earnings over the same period of time also faced an increase in the percentage of income paid in tax, but it was only half that of the low-wage earner on two-thirds average earnings. Similar increases occurred for workers on 10 and 20 times average earnings for the periods 1964–5 to 1977–8 but their increases amounted to a little over 31% and less than 15% respectively.

Some might argue that the very highest income earners experienced smaller percentage increases in the incidence of taxation because they are already paying too high a percentage of their income in tax in the first place. This argument is weakened when an examination is made of the changing incidence of taxation on different income groups and table 5 gives the changes in the percentage of total revenue raised from each decile group over the past 20 years.

When considering changes in the total revenue contributed by different decile groups over a period of time, it is also necessary to bear in mind changes in the share of pre-tax income going to each of these groups. It is possible for the richest 10% to be contributing less of total revenue now than they did in 1959–60 because they now command a smaller percentage of total pre-tax personal income.

The Blue Book data show the share of personal incomes going to the top 10% in the income distribution fell by 9·5 percentage points during the period from 1959 to 1974–5. Part of the explanation of why the richest 10% pay a smaller total share of all revenue raised now than 20 years ago is that their share of total pre-tax income has fallen. But as the Blue Book data makes clear, the change in pre-tax income is only one reason for the changing incidence in taxation between income groups. During the 20-year period covered by the table, the percentage of total tax paid by the top decile fell from 57% to 37%, a fall much greater than the fall in pre-tax income. One important reason, therefore, for the richest 10% contributing less to total revenue now is that over these years the tax system has become less progressive.

Table 5. Percentage shares of tax paid by different income groups 1959–60 to 1974–5[a b].

	1949–50	1959–60	1970–71	1971–72	1972–73	1973–74	1974–75	1975–76	1976–77[c]
Top 10%	72	57	41	39	40	38	37	35	34
10–20%	9	12	15	15	14	14	15	15	14
20–30%	5	7	11	12	11	12	11	12	12
30–40%	3	6	9	9	9	9	10	10	10
40–50%	3	5	7	8	8	8	8	8	8
50–60%	3	4	6	6	6	7	7	7	7
60–70%	2	4	5	5	5	5	5	5	6
70–80%	1	3	3	3	4	4	4	4	5
80–90%	1	1	2	2	2	2	2	3	3
Bottom 10%	1	1	1	1	1	1	1	1	1
Total Tax (£m)	1101	1735	6158	6356	6572	8045	11 846	15 987	18 300

a Years up to and including 1972–3 take income tax and surtax together. Subsequent years relate to income tax (including higher rates and the additional rate on investment income).
b Married couples are counted as one tax payer. Only tax paid by individuals (i.e. excluding trusts etc) is included.
c Provisional estimate.
Source: House of Lords Hansard, vol. 388 cols. 739–40. January 31, 1978.

Data presented in this section do not support the thesis that we have reached the limits of redistributing from those at the upper end of the distribution. The Survey of Personal Incomes and the Blue Book data show that while the shares of pre- and post-tax income going to the very richest 1% have shown a marked reduction, this reduction is less marked amongst the richest 10% and that most of the redistribution which has taken place has been amongst the top 20 or 30% of the distribution. The share going to the poorest 30% of the population shows very little change over the last 15 years. Indeed, far from reaching the limits of redistribution from the rich, the data on the incidence of taxation suggests that their burden has lessened somewhat in the recent past. For example, the share of total tax revenue contributed by the richest 10% has fallen to a significantly greater extent than has their share of the total pre-tax income. Not surprisingly, therefore, the burden has increased for those lower down the distribution. But this has been only one change in the incidence of taxation. We now turn to examine the second fundamental shift in the incidence of taxation which has occurred in the post-war period.

THE HORIZONTAL REDISTRIBUTION OF INCOME

Vertical changes in the distribution of the tax load are only part of the total change in the incidence of taxation through the past 20 years. At the same time there has occurred a major change in the horizontal incidence of taxation: from the childless to those households responsible for children. This second trend can be illustrated in a number of ways. Table 6 looks at the tax threshold for different households expressed as a percentage of average earnings.

For each household group, whether it is a single person or married couple, or family with children, tax payments now begin at a level below average earnings. While more poorer people are now paying tax than in the immediate post-war period, households with children have been singled out for particularly harsh treatment. The

Table 6. Tax thresholds as a percentage of average earnings.

Year	Single person	Married couple	Married couple with 1 child under 11	Married couple with 2 children under 11	Married couple with 3 children (2 under 11, 1 between 11 and 16)	Married couple with 4 children (2 under 11, 2 between 11 and 16)
1949–50	39·4	62·8	83·0	99·7	115·4	130·0
1950–51	37·3	59·6	78·8	94·8	109·8	124·0
1951–52	33·8	56·9	77·1	94·6	110·9	126·5
1952–53	35·3	60·3	83·8	103·4	121·6	138·5
1953–54	33·3	56·9	79·1	97·1	113·8	129·1
1954–55	30·9	52·7	73·3	90·3	106·0	120·7
1955–56	32·9	55·2	77·4	96·0	113·6	129·8
1956–57	31·0	51·9	72·7	90·3	106·6	121·6
1957–58	29·4	49·1	68·8	85·7	105·5	123·7
1958–59	28·9	48·3	67·6	84·2	103·7	121·7
1959–60	27·4	45·7	64·1	79·9	98·6	115·9
1960–61	25·5	42·6	59·7	74·5	92·2	108·6
1961–62	25·6	41·6	57·8	71·9	88·8	104·5
1962–63	24·7	40·2	55·9	69·6	86·0	101·4
1963–64	32·8	50·5	67·5	82·5	99·8	116·1
1964–65	30·4	46·7	62·4	76·4	92·6	108·0
1965–66	27·8	43·0	57·4	70·5	85·7	100·1
1966–67	26·8	41·5	55·4	58·1	82·8	96·8
1967–68	25·5	39·4	52·7	64·8	78·9	91·3
1968–69	23·7	36·6	48·9	55·5	63·8	71·5
1969–70	25·4	37·4	48·8	54·1	61·2	67·7
1970–71	28·6	41·0	51·1	55·8	62·0	67·8
1971–72	26·0	37·2	49·6	57·0	65·6	73·7
1972–73	31·8	41·4	52·1	58·4	66·0	73·0
1973–74	28·0	36·4	45·8	51·3	67·9	64·3
1974–75	24·7	34·2	43·7	50·2	57·7	64·9
1975–76	21·8	30·8	38·6	43·5	49·4	54·9
1976–77	21·1	31·2	39·8	45·9	52·7	59·2
1977–78	24·9	38·4	44·3	49·8	55·9	61·8
1978–79	23·6	36·8	41·1	45·1	49·7	54·0

In order to produce a consistent series of figures over this period, average earnings have been taken to be the annual equivalents of average weekly earnings of full-time male manual workers aged 21 and over in manufacturing and certain other industries at October of each year, excepting 1978–79 for which this information is not available and the October, 1977 figure has been increased by 10%. Family allowances and child benefits have been included in average earnings where appropriate, and the November, 1978 increase in child benefits has been taken into account. Where appropriate, the tax thresholds used take account of the effect of unearned income relief and of the family allowance deduction—'clawback'. For the sake of comparability, the thresholds in 1977–78 and in 1978–79 include any tax-free child benefit received.

Sources: Hansard Vol 935, col 579–81, 20 July 1977 and Vol 954, col 37–8, 19 July 1978.

tax thresholds for a single person and for married couples without children have fallen as a proportion of average earnings by 40·1% and 41·4% respectively. In contrast, falls of 56·9% and 58·5% are recorded for married couples with three and four children.

We gain a clearer picture of changes in the tax burden for different households by looking at the percentage of income paid in tax and national insurance by households who are childless and by those who are responsible for children. Information on this question for selective years since 1960 is set out in table 7. Again the two trends in the changing incidence of taxation are illustrated. The tax burden has increased for all

Table 7. Tax and national insurance contributions as a percentage of average earnings, plus family allowance/child benefit where appropriate.

Year	Single person	Married couple	Married couple with 2 children aged under 11	Married couple with 4 children aged under 11
	%	%	%	%
1960–61	19·0	14·0	6·8	3·2
1964–65	23·4	18·4	9·7	5·1
1973–74	28·2	25·8	21·6	18·6
1977–78	32·2	28·1	24·4	21·1
1978–79	31·3	27·4	24·6	22·0

Source: Hansard, Vol 950, col. 735–8, 25 May, 1978.

groups, but it has increased fastest for those households with children. Single persons and married couples on average earnings in both 1960–61 and 1978–79 experienced increases in their tax bills of 65% and 96% respectively. On the other hand, for married couples with two and four children, also on average earnings, the tax burden rose by 262% and 588%.

It would be wrong to assume that these changes have occurred evenly for all groups during the post-war period. The most recent period since 1974 illustrates how short-term gains can be chalked up for some groups which are not substantial enough to offset the long-term trend. Early on in the life of the 1974 Labour Government it became clear that the Chancellor was unwilling to increase child tax allowances, as the Government was committed to the introduction of the child benefit scheme which entailed the phasing out of child tax allowances (CTAs). The Chancellor was likewise disposed against increasing family allowances as this was viewed as a rise in public expenditure. Instead, the married man's tax allowance was raised as the way of helping families with children. But it is a very indiscriminate way of lessening the tax burden of working people with children, for half the households claiming this allowance are childless. The result of such a policy has been that the tax threshold has fallen for all groups bar one. Those whom the policy was designed most to help, families with children, saw, for example, falls in the tax threshold as a proportion of average earnings, of 4·8% and 8·2% for households with one and two children. Only for a married couple without children has the tax threshold risen. The tax threshold for a childless couple expressed as a percentage of average earnings rose by 6·9% in the years since 1973–4.

It is possible to show the combined effects of the changes in the vertical and horizontal incidence of direct taxation. The data in table 8 shows that the tax burden has both increased fastest for those on low incomes and, especially, rapidly for households with children. Households on a low income who are responsible for children have suffered the greatest increase.

The same trend can be seen from the data in table 4, and particularly for those on lower incomes. For example a single person on average earnings saw his tax burden rise by 47% over the period 1964–5 to 1977–8. But the tax burden of a married couple with two children, also on average earnings, increased by 306% over the same period.

A further distinction needs to be made between households with one and two earners. The best guide to the substantial changes in tax-allowance relativities is to be found in Hermione Parker's work (Parker, 1978). This study details the changing relative value of each of the main tax allowances.

Table 8. Income tax as a percentage of income by family size and income.

Income: proportion of average earnings	0·67				0·80				0·90				1·00				1·30			
Household composition[a]	s	m	2c	4c	s	m	2c	4c	s	m	2c	4c	s	m	2c	4c	s	m	2c	4c
1954–5	7	2	0	0	9	4	0	0	11	6	0	0	12	7	1	0	16	11	4	0
1964–5	12	6	0	0	15	9	1	0	17	11	3	0	18	13	5	0	21	17	10	3
1970–1	18	12	4	0	21	16	9	4	22	18	10	6	23	19	15	9	25	22	18	15
1973–4	17	14	7	4	20	16	11	8	21	18	13	11	22	19	15	12	24	22	18	17
1974–5	21	16	9	4	23	19	13	8	24	21	15	11	25	22	17	13	27	24	21	18
1977–8	23	17	13	10	25	20	17	14	26	21	19	16	26	22	20	17	20	25	23	21

Income: proportion of average earnings	1·50				2				5				10				20			
Household composition[a]	s	m	2c	4c	s	m	2c	4c	s	m	2c	4c	s	m	2c	4c	s	m	2c	4c
1954–5	19	13	6	1	23	19	12	—	35	34	31	—	50	49	48	—	65	65	64	—
1964–5	22	19	12	6	24	22	16	—	28	27	25	—	40	39	37	—	59	59	58	—
1970–1	26	23	20	17	28	26	23	—	37	36	34	—	54	53	52	—	72	72	71	—
1973–4	24	23	20	18	26	25	22	—	38	37	35	—	52	52	51	—	64	63	63	—
1974–5	28	26	22	20	29	27	25	—	44	43	41	—	60	59	58	—	71	71	70	—
1977–8	29	26	25	23	31	28	27	25	50	48	47	46	66	65	64	63	75	74	74	73

a s=single-person household, m=married couple, 2c=married couple with 2 children, 4c= married couple with 4 children.
Key: not available.
Source: T&GWU, (1976) updated.

Since 1938–9, there have been major changes in the differences in value of each of the main personal tax allowances. A single person's tax allowance has risen by 885% and the married man's tax allowance by 726%. The biggest change, however, has occurred in the wife's earned income relief. Before the last war it was valued at 25% of the married person's tax allowance while today it has risen to 65%. As a result, this allowance has increased by over 2000% in the period since 1938–9. In stark contrast, the child tax allowance, together with cash benefits, has risen least of all, by 189%.

Here then is yet another dimension to the changing incidence of taxation in the post-war period. The poor, and families with children, have seen their tax burden increase faster than for other groups, and for poor families with children the incidence of taxation has increased even faster. But even within families with children the tax burden has not increased uniformly. The group which has lost out the most in the post-war period is low income families with children who have only one earner.

One possible reason why the incidence of taxation has moved horizontally against households with children with so little public discussion is the widespread belief that the provision of the welfare state favours households with children. But the CSO evidence from 'The effects of taxes and benefits on household income 1976' suggests that this assumption needs to be viewed cautiously.

There are dangers in using this data to illustrate the redistributionary effect towards low income groups of the welfare state. Writing in 1968 Peacock and Shannon argued that no reliable conclusions could be drawn about the overall effect of combining tax payments and social security benefits when the analysis was based on a little over a third of government expenditure and only a half of tax revenue (Peacock and Shannon, 1968). The most recent analysis from the CSO covers 60% of Government receipts and 44% of all Government expenditure (Stephenson, 1978).

Since 1968, a number of attempts have been made to include in analysis of redistribution a higher percentage of the taxes levied and the benefits conferred by the welfare state. This work shows the allocation of the missing tax revenue and social benefits as having an important impact on the level of redistribution. Pioneering work on this front has been carried out by Nicholson. Reporting recently, Nicholson and Britton (1976), made two sets of assumptions about allocating the residual. These were that benefits of all unallocated expenditure, and the cost of unallocated taxation, fell equally on each individual, or that the net benefit from unallocated expenditure less tax fell on households in proportion to their final income. Their conclusion was that 'The extent of vertical redistribution is rather crucially dependent on the treatment of the residual.'

The allocation of the residual tax and benefits in the CSO's studies is even more important to an analysis of the extent to which the overall effect of taxes and benefits favours households with children. (Peretz no date.) Peretz also added back a large proportion of the public expenditure which is excluded from the CSO analysis. Her findings were that 'the general effect of including these additional categories have probably been to reduce somewhat the degree of redistribution to some households which is implied. This is because these categories of expenditure are mostly on services etc., used by the whole population or, in some cases, used more by the better-off'. Moreover the 'net effect of having better information about the uses of the various services could be to make a further reduction in the degree of redistribution implied'.

This conclusion needs to be borne in mind, since the main cluster of benefits which are allocated in the CSO analysis are the payment of cash allowances and the use of the main welfare state services such as schools and hospitals. Those benefits and services which are easiest to allocate in the analysis are predominantly used by pensioners and families with children. Both Nicholson's and Peretz's work shows that to include some of the residual lessens the redistributionary effect, and Peretz also suggests that to include other forms of unallocated public expenditure will lessen still further their redistributionary gains marked up to the poor and to households with children.

The belief that the welfare state redistributes generously towards families, to such an extent as to offset the rising burden of taxation amongst this group, is undermined still further by the pioneering study conducted by Muriel Nissel.

Taxes and Benefits begins by emphasizing the relative increase in the burden of taxation for families with children—already been commented upon in this paper. Nissel then uses the CSO data to look at the redistribution brought about by the welfare state. It is important to remember that Nissel is using data which has not been adjusted for the large percentage of taxes and benefits which remain unallocated and which the work both of Nicholson and Britton and of Peretz suggests lessens what redistribution there has been to low income groups and to families.

As well as presenting CSO data, Nissel (1978) reworks the material on the basis of adult equivalent scales, adding that these calculations are 'admittedly rough and ready but they are sufficient to bring home the point that the income available to individuals and households varies considerably at different stages of the life cycle and that it matters a great deal how many types of people live in these households'.

CSO data on disposable household income after tax and benefits for a four-child family on a household basis shows this group faring in 1976 very slightly better than other groups. However, once the data is reworked on an adult equivalent basis, a four-child family is shown to be slightly worse off than the average retired couple, and having only about half as much income as a non-retired couple without children. On the basis of the reworked data Nissel (1978) concludes that 'For the average household with children . . . cash benefits (including indirect benefits such as housing and food subsidies) were small and substantially outweighed by taxes'.

Nissel's pioneering study shows that it is not possible to argue that the tax burden for families with children is offset by their being awarded a disproportionate share in what has become known as the social wage. In addition we do not as yet have the reworked information along the lines of *Taxes and Benefits* to know whether the overall position of households with children has improved or deteriorated over time.

Limits to Redistribution

This paper has discussed three reasons for scepticism when considering the assertion that the limits of redistribution from the rich have been reached. What available data there are illustrate how limited has been the redistribution away from the top 20 or 30% of the income distribution, particularly during the period since 1964. On the basis of published evidence, the carefully guarded conclusion is that there has been some redistribution from the very rich to the rich both before and after tax but that little of the resources lost by the very rich have found their way into the pockets of the poorest 30%. The Blue Book tables show the bottom 30% of the income distribution commanding only 12·8% of total personal incomes after tax in 1974–5.

This argues powerfully against the view that the limits of redistributing from the rich have been reached. But a second front in the campaign needs to be simultaneously opened up. The horizontal distribution of income likewise has an important effect in determining relative living standards. And this debate will entail a move away from a weekly or monthly view of income to a lifetime's command over resources. Such a change of perspective will show the two periods of relative deprivations suffered by most households in their lifetime, whatever their level of income. Households are most vulnerable when they are responsible for children and when the breadwinner's themselves move into retirement (Field, 1978).

The debate about the vertical and horizontal redistribution of resources is taking on new significance as we become more aware of the effects of moving into what might possibly prove to be a period of relatively slow economic growth. Slow growth will itself give rise to an increasing number of people made poor by unemployment, while at the same time demographic changes will increase the numbers of poor. Whether or not the limits to redistribution have been reached (at least for the rich), this second period of the post-war world marks the beginning of a new ball game for all of us.

ACKNOWLEDGEMENT

I would like to thank Louie Burghes who prepared some of the material for this paper and Chris Pond for checking the calculations.

REFERENCES

Crosland C. A. R. (1971) *A social democratic Britain*, London, Fabian Society.
Field F. (1978) *Priority for Children*, London, Child Poverty Action Group.
Field F. (1979) Poverty, growth and the redistribution of income. In: Beckerman W. (ed.) *Slow growth in Britain: Causes and Consequences*, London, Oxford University Press.

Field F., Pond C. and Meacher M. (1977) *To Him Who Hath*, Harmondsworth, Penguin Books.
Nicholson J. L. and Britton A. J. C. (1976) The Redistribution of Income. In: Atkinson A. B. (ed.) *The Personal Distribution of Incomes*, London, Allen & Unwin.
Nissel M. (1978) *Taxes and Benefits: Does Redistribution Help the Family*? London, Policy Studies Inst.
Parker H. (1978) *Who Pays for the Children*? London, Outer Circle Policy Unit.
Peacock A. and Shannon R. (1968) The Welfare State and The Redistribution of Income, *Westminster Bank Review*, August.
Peretz J. (no date) *Beneficiaries of public expenditure: an analysis for* 1971/1972.
Royal Commission on the Distribution of Income and Wealth, (1975) Report No. 1, *Initial Report on the Standing Reference*, Cmnd. 6171, London, HMSO.
Royal Commission on the Distribution of Income and Wealth, (1977) Report No. 5, *Third Report on the Standing Reference*, Cmnd. 6999, London, HMSO.
Stephenson G. A. (1978) The effect of taxes and benefits on household income, 1976, *Economic Trends*, February.
T&GWU, (1976) *Inequality*, Spokesman Books.
Willis J. R. M. and Hardwick P. T. W. (1978) *Tax Expenditure in the UK*, London, Heinneman Educational Books.

DISCUSSION

by **F. A. Cowell,** *London School of Economics.*

Field's piece is a campaigning paper. This is quite appropriate in view of the importance of the topic of income redistribution. However, my comments will be of a more mundane nature, and will deal with two issues—the basis on which Field's campaign is mounted, and the direction in which it takes us.

The basis of the campaign consists of four propositions, which I have reordered a little from the paper. (*a*) Such redistribution of incomes pre- and post-direct taxes as there has been in recent years has not benefitted the bottom 30% of the distribution very much. (*b*) The 'taxable capacity' of the non-poor has not yet been reached. There is here the consequent proposition that a change in the structure or rates of taxation would provide considerably more benefit for the worst off. (*c*) Particularly awkward problems are raised by recent economic and demographic shifts: notably the reduction in the rate of growth and the changing composition of the poor. (*d*) The structure of allocated benefits does not tell the whole story in regard to the support provided by the state for society.

Proposition (*a*) is undoubtedly true on the evidence of income distribution before and after direct taxes. Changes in UK income distribution, though decidedly equalizing at the upper end have not been particularly exciting elsewhere. There are one or two mitigating circumstances—without the post-war change in the age-composition, for example, the slight downward trend in inequality would probably have been a little more impressive—but these do not change the general picture. On the other hand, the implication of this is not quite as obvious as Field seems to suggest—a point to which I shall return.

I have put proposition (*b*) in a rather vague form, although it is evidently central to the whole paper. We are given two principal pieces of evidence on this—the discussion on allowances on pp. 191–2 and the discussion relating to table 5. In each case the argument seems to me to be incomplete. On non-structural allowances, certainly, we find the upper quantiles benefiting in absolute terms and, to a lesser extent in proportional terms (*see* table 3). This is a valuable point, and in part can be seen as part of a wider discussion on the appropriate balance between personal and commodity taxation which the author has, in my view, rather strangely neglected. The mortgage allowance is really part of haphazard policy of public subsidy to housing. Moving from this to other non-structural allowances we find an argument not so much about rich versus poor as about the choice of base—expenditure or income—for a personal tax system. It seems to me that this issue ought to be settled in its own right, and the progressivity of the rate structure of the personal tax system treated as a separate issue.

This brings me on to the issue of 'structural' or personal allowances. The discussion here, which follows the author's earlier joint work (Field et al., 1976) seems to verge on the misleading. This is a pity because there are two important issues concealed in there. One is the exemption *vs.* allowance point which is *purely* an administrative one, in that if you give me a system with exemptions of which you approve then, if I am allowed to have multiple tax bands, I can give you an equivalent system with allowances. Where the argument comes into its own, it seems to me, is the ease with which progressivity is administered by the Inland Revenue (which on the whole is not discussed), and in the automatic shifts in tax incidence from year to year as the income distribution changes with economic growth, inflation and the like. But what Field seems to do, is to use this as a thin cloak for an argument about progressivity of the rate structure. It may be that we regard an average tax rate of less than 50% for a single person on more than £20 000 p.a. as unacceptable. Very well then, we had better bring up the marginal rates lower down the income scale—but we might as well come straight out with it as complicate it with the exemptions *vs.* allowances issue. As an example of this, take the proposed reform in Field et al. (1976). This proposed an exemption of £1000 which was progressively withdrawn up to an income of £4000 at which point it vanished. The m.t.r. on non-exempt income increased by 10% at every £1000 step. What this implied was much larger *effective* m.t.r.'s on middle income receivers. In particular, at the assumed 'average wage', the m.t.r. was 50% under the author's scheme compared with 35% under the existing scheme. It seems to me that even if one is sceptical of disincentive effects in practice, one would have to accept that such a reform would effectively involve a substantial increase in the m.t.r. with comparatively little or no change in the a.t.r. for a large number of middle income receivers, and that the potential effect on labour supply and consequently upon the total product to be distributed cannot be ignored.

The other point, of course, was on the 'burden of personal taxation' argument presented in table 5. This shows that the proportion of income tax paid by the top 10% consistently declined from 1949–50 to 1976–77, that (over 59–60 to 76–77 at least) the proportion of tax paid by the next decile was roughly constant and that for all other decile except the bottom, the proportion rose. However, to assert, as was done on p. 193, that the tax system was therefore becoming less progressive is not valid without much more careful discussion because the overall volume of taxation as a proportion of total personal income (TPI) was simultaneously increasing. TPI was approximately £19 900 million in 1959–60 and £79 600m† in 1974–75, and so the proportion of personal income surrendered by the top decile *increased* from about 18% to about 22%. Well of course the proportion of personal income surrendered increased for everyone else too; but that takes us to the central point. Does this evidence mean (as Field suggests) that we have retrogressed and that we are now further from the limits of redistribution? Or, on the other hand, does the same evidence mean that we are *closer* to the limits of redistribution? The reasoning here is simple: as the social wage rises along with the ratio (total tax)/(TPI) we find 'taxable capacity' being reached first on the top decile, then on the next, then on the next, . . . where taxable capacity is now related not to proportionate tax burden, but to the above ratio. Let me say that I do not think this alternative view tells the whole story

† Source: *Econ. Trends*, An. Supp. (1975).

either. However, you *cannot* use table 5 to support the author's argument without a much more careful discussion of the incidence of the growing tax burden.

Let me move on to proposition (*c*) which I consider to be the most interesting: the late 1970s have raised special problems. Rising unemployment at a time of near zero growth will among other things, put a great strain on the system of income support. Also, changing demographic factors will mean that not only are the numbers of the poor expected to rise, but that their composition will change significantly. This 'horizontal redistribution of income' consists of a worsening of the relative after-tax position of families with children, and a growth of single parent families which are in the main dependent on Supplementary Benefit. I think the evidence on this speaks of itself from tables 6 to 8, but at the same time I am not sure that the author makes clear the implications of this horizontal shift for the 'limits to distribution' argument.

Proposition (*d*)—which emerges from pp. 197–9 and is used as a support for (*c*)—appears to be much less satisfactorily argued. The gist of it seems to be this: you cannot explain away the horizontal redistribution implicit in the tax burden by saying that incidence on the *expenditure* side is biased in favour of the family; there is a large component of public expenditure the distribution of benefits from which is far from clear. The danger in this switch of the argument is this. On the tax side we have been looking at *trends* over recent history—but the same procedure has not been applied to the expenditure side. To get a fair appraisal of what is going on I think two things ought to be done. (i) Examine the trends not just in the distribution of income after tax, but in the distribution of total disposable income defined as income-taxes + direct benefits. The direct benefits play the symmetric role of negative *personal* taxes. This exercise might be worth repeating with indirect taxes and allocable indirect benefits included as well. (ii) To examine the *change in the composition* of the social wage. Not only has expenditure on social security risen as a proportion of total public expenditure, but also the expenditure on family benefit and supplementary benefit has risen as a proportion of total public expenditure. Even within the category of unallocable expenditure I should expect this trend to be maintained—we probably spend proportionately more on skateboard parks now in relation to ballistic missiles than we did 10 years ago. Moreover, as Field acknowledges (pp. 186–7) this trend is expected to continue over the immediate future. While I would agree that the 'unallocable' component of public expenditure is unlikely to be neutral in its true incidence, it also seems that the shift in the composition of total public expenditure to some extent offsets the trends in the allocable tax burden to which the paper draws our attention.

Let me turn to the direction in which all this takes us. One of the difficulties I find with the paper is that it does not deal with one of the central questions at all—what are the limits of redistribution? To do this we should need to do two things: determine the effect of policy proposals on the potential size of the total product; describe the institutional framework within which we envisage reforms to be effected. This paper does neither, which is a pity because it would be nice to answer the question: 'What could be done if we tried?' I am going to assume that we retain roughly the same sort of socioeconomic institutional framework within which to discuss this issue. What might be achieveable by revolution is another question.

The analysis of the equity/efficiency tradeoff has been discussed earlier in the conference so I shall not repeat it, though it is totally misleading to suppose that national income is some fixed scale from which we may redistribute at will. One particular problem strikes me though. An important feature of recent history is the rising number of households headed by women and of women in the labour force. Now, even though

Table 9.

	Employment income as % TPI	Entrepreneurial income+interest dividends rent as % TPI	Social security and other trans. as % TPI	Direct taxes and social sec. contributions % TPI	Indirect taxes as % TPI
Sweden, 1974	68·8	12·1	19·1	39·4	15·1
UK, 1974	72·2	16·3	11·4	21·5	15·4

Source: Stark (1977), Tables 130, 131.

Table 10.

Distribution of Post-Tax TPI by Households 1972: Quintile Shares

	Top	*2nd*	*3rd*	*4th*	*5th*
Sweden	37·0	24·8	18·5	13·1	6·6
UK	38·1	23·9	18·2	12·8	6·7

Source: Stark (1977), Table 143.

much of the work incentives evidence is ambiguous, for women the effect of higher marginal tax rates is clearly negative, so that there may be considerable practical difficulties in the way of raising marginal tax rates lower down the income scale.

One alternative method of approaching this question which is fairly popular in the field is that of international comparisons. This is always a tricky exercise, but there seems to be a reasonable case for it if the comparison is with economies not too unlike the UK. In this respect the recent study by Stark for the Royal Commission on the Distribution of Income and Wealth (Stark, 1977) is rather useful since it surveys the facts for a number of Western economies plus Japan. Now one of the conclusions which I am tempted to draw from Field's paper is that the observed unsatisfactory trends in income distribution (on which part of his case rests) might have been avoided had our tax structure been rather different. In particular, might we have done better if we had a larger proportion of social security transfer incomes financed by a greater reliance on progressive personal taxation rather than indirect taxation? In this respect Sweden makes rather an interesting comparison (table 9). I am not claiming that Sweden is an ideal, but it is an example of what might be attainable within the same broad social framework. We should perhaps expect Sweden to have a significantly more equitable distribution of income both pre- and post-tax than the UK, especially in view of the lower proportion of 'profit' income and the higher proportion of transfer income. This does not at first sight appear to be the case from table 10. Of course the household composition in Sweden will modify the result so that per capita income be less unequal in Sweden. Overall I am struck by the general similarity between the two pictures. Neither is the particular comparison I have chosen atypical—indeed I chose Sweden because it generally exhibits the smallest degree of inequality in the countries considered.

So, have we reached the limits to inequality on principle? The analytical argument is not supplied. Have we reached them in practice? Comparison with other similar economies to see what might be possible within the kind of social framework we now have gives an answer not very favourable to Field's campaign.

REFERENCE

Stark T. (1977) *The Distribution of Income in Eight Countries*. Background Paper to Report No. 5, of the Royal Commission on the Distribution of Income and Wealth, London, HMSO.

SUMMARY OF THE GENERAL DISCUSSION

In reply to Cowell, Field said that in his view many of the other papers presented had also been campaigning papers. There was a well-orchestrated political campaign against redistribution, and the economics profession as a whole was lending its support to this campaign while pretending to be politically neutral. But despite this, there was no real evidence of limits; people kept coming up with evidence about high tax rates, but high tax rates simply arose because of high allowances. Unfortunately policy seemed aimed at reducing tax rates by either reducing expenditure, or shifting to indirect taxation, both of which were regressive. Collard doubted the existence of an orchestrated campaign among economists. In his opinion many of the papers had been aimed at *pushing back* the limits to redistribution. Certainly the tone of discussions had not been anti-redistributive.

Astin wondered whether Field was losing sight of reality. If the top decile were to maintain its 1949–50 share of 72% of the tax bill (table 5) their average tax rate would have to increase from 33% to 67%. This group included people with incomes of £5–6000 p.a.

Layard felt that it was misleading to discuss the share of different groups in the *tax burden*; more important were their shares in *after tax income*. He gave a simple example: if there were two individuals A and B, and A's pre-tax income was £200 while B's was £100; suppose that in one year A paid £20 tax and B paid nothing, while in a second year A paid £40 and B £1. Clearly A's share in the total tax burden had gone down from the first to the second year, but did that mean that the tax system was less progressive in the second year? Looked at in terms of *retention rates*, originally A had been keeping 90% of his income, and now he kept only 80% B's retention rate had decreased only from 100% to 99%.

Layard also said that he had not understood the exemption *vs.* allowances argument. Where did Field want the jump to occur? There might be a very high marginal tax rate somewhere. Pond replied that the aim of the proposal was twofold: to exempt the poor from taxes altogether and to introduce more progressivity into the system. He admitted that there was a problem with poverty traps. Exemption would be gradually withdrawn, but this was really a matter of administration. Field explained that the figures in Field et al. (1977) were purely illustrative. Forward said he still wanted to know at what point the jump in tax rates would occur. He felt that the use of terms like 'rich, 'very-rich' and 'super-rich' was not helpful as they appeared to cover people on £50–£110 p.w. The line had presumably to be drawn below these people, but one should realize that there were a large number of occupations concerned.

Whittington felt that the exemption rate was an important feature of progressivity—it caused average tax rates to rise with income even if the marginal tax rate was constant. Sandford drew attention to the long standard-rate band in the UK tax system; in other countries the marginal tax rate began to rise earlier, so he did not find the idea of marginal tax rates of 50% at average incomes that surprising. Lecomber stressed again the importance of *average* rates in regard to progressivity. He felt that lessening progressivity was due to the fall in real values of tax thresholds, which was an easy political option. Brown did not think that the real value of tax thresholds had altered very much, although perhaps their relation to the average wage had. Nicholson noted that in future tax thresholds were to be indexed, which would solve this particular problem.

Layard referred to Cowell's Swedish comparison. He noted that Cowell's figures were in household terms, but figures quoted by Wiles in per capita terms suggested greater equality in Sweden. Sawyer suggested that Sweden might argue that she had achieved substantial redistribution over a long period, say from 1930. He noted that the Swedish tax system acted on a more unequal initial distribution of income. Also, high social services expenditure did not necessarily indicate a great effort at redistribution. In fact, the higher the level of social services expenditure, the less equalizing it would be, because there would be a greater proportion of earnings-related benefits.

Sandford doubted that a switch from direct to indirect taxation would necessarily be regressive. The zero-rated band in VAT produced some progressivity in indirect taxation, and the net effect would depend on exactly where the cuts in income tax would occur. Champernowne agreed with Sandford. He thought that the question of the relative regressivity of direct and indirect taxation was a very interesting and intricate one, but on the whole he thought indirect taxes were less regressive. However, he felt that the situation called less for changes in *general* taxation; what was needed was more government expenditure on removing *particular* kinds of inequality. McAuley pointed to the implications of Le Grand's work. If that were correct, then it would suggest that indirect taxes were indeed more progressive.

Clarke said that the discussion had largely been about vertical distribution whereas Field had rightly emphasized the problems of horizontal distribution. There was great discrimination on the grounds of family size and housing tenure. Field agreed, and felt that this supported his earlier remarks. It was vertical distribution that concerned the rich, and seemed to concern economists. He felt that it was unhealthy that the debate about distribution, which was essentially a moral one, should be dominated by economists and their claims to 'objectivity'. Economists should contribute to the debate, but not dominate it.

LIMITS TO REDISTRIBUTION: THE HUNGARIAN EXPERIENCE

G. Szakolczai

Research Institute for Applied Computer Sciences, Budapest

INTRODUCTION

The conventional analysis of income redistribution generally starts from the assumption that the primary distribution of income corresponds more or less—at least in the developed industrial countries—to marginal efficiency ratios, or at least can be considered as given, so that the problem of redistribution can be dealt with separately. The most important instrument for redistributing this given income is taxation, especially direct taxation, because this latter has a greater weight in absolute terms and a greater direct impact upon incomes. Thus the problem of redistribution becomes a part of the theory of optimal taxation.

This way of thinking has its weaknesses even under present Western institutional conditions, but is definitely unsuitable for the analysis of the problems of the Eastern-European socialist countries. Here, primary incomes can be influenced directly by the central authorities, and there is therefore no given primary income distribution unaffected by redistributive endeavours that could be considered as a given starting point for the analysis. Furthermore, direct taxation is of secondary importance in most of these countries, its level being low and its progressivity small, the brunt of taxation being borne by indirect taxes and by taxes paid by state enterprises and co-operatives. The problems of redistribution are therefore inseparably interwoven with the problems of determining primary incomes, which also depend on state intervention, while even in the context of genuine fiscal redistribution indirect taxes predominate. That is why the problem of redistribution through indirect taxes, or rather through the price system appears as the central element of this paper.

The paper presents a broad survey of problems and policies, concentrating less on theory than on practice. While much of the discussion is applicable to all or most East European countries, consideration is here confined to Hungary. For the benefit of a predominately West European audience it will be useful to begin by detailing the institutional background.

The first two sections of the paper describe the level and structure of consumption in Hungary in international perspective, as well as the distribution of income and the system of prices. The next two sections demonstrate that the price system which generates the present situation is a very inefficient tool of income redistribution, and cannot be defended on allocational grounds. The very short fifth section deals with the impossibility of introducing an extended form of direct taxation in Hungary; this leads to the conclusion that, under present conditions, the only practicable way of increasing redistribution is to raise family allowances and some of the lowest pensions, the limits to such a policy being given by the determination of the government that real income must continuously increase in all major sections of the population. The paper starts therefore from the instruments of redistribution, but—after a survey of all the instruments—arrives at definite conclusions also as to its limits.

NATIONAL INCOME AND STRUCTURE OF CONSUMPTION IN HUNGARY

The conclusions of this paper depend very much on the level of national income and the structure of consumption already attained. In order to delimit therefore, at least roughly, the range within which these conclusions are valid, the level of Hungarian national income must be indicated in a form which makes international comparison possible. This can best be done by using the figures of the United Nations International Comparison Project (Kravis et al., 1978).

According to the findings of the above research (summarized in Hungarian, in *Tizenhat ország ...*, 1968), the per capita GDP of Hungary—as reproduced in table 1—represented in 1970 about 2043 international dollars i.e. 42·7% of the US level. This figure represents 86·7 and 71·8%, respectively, of the same year's Italian and Japanese figures. Thus Hungary's per capita GNP was comparable to that of the poorest Western industrialized countries, and rather more than double that of Iran, the next country shown in the Kravis et al. sample. By 1973, the picture changed somewhat: Hungary's GDP per head rose to 45·1% of the US and 95·9% of the Italian

Table 1. Per capita gross domestic product in US dollars, 1970 and 1973.

Country	1970				1973			
	In US dollars converted at official exchange rates		In international dollars		In US dollars converted at official exchange rates		In international dollars	
	US dollars	US=100	International dollars	US=100	US dollars	US=100	International dollars	US=100
United States	4790	100·0	4790	100·0	6192	100·0	6192	100·0
Germany, FR	3072	64·1	3747	78·2	5535	89·4	4791	77·4
France	2790	58·2	3504	73·2	4777	77·2	4709	76·1
Belgium	2639	55·1	3449	72·0	4618	74·6	4663	75·3
Netherlands	2431	50·8	3289	68·7	4402	71·1	4234	68·4
United Kingdom	2190	45·7	3039	63·5	3136	50·6	3750	60·6
Japan	1908	39·8	2835	59·2	3738	60·4	3962	64·0
Italy	1722	36·0	2356	49·2	2525	40·8	2913	47·0
HUNGARY	1036	21·6	2043	42·7	1619	26·2	2793	45·1
Iran	401	8·4	972	20·3	914	14·8	1809	29·2
Malaysia	388	8·1	915	19·1	633	10·2	1180	19·1
Colombia	347	7·2	869	18·1	440	7·11	1106	17·9
Korea, Republic of	258	5·4	580	12·1	366	5·91	904	14·6
Philippines	185	3·9	576	12·0	259	4·18	755	12·1
India	99	2·1	331	6·9	129	2·08	394	6·37
Kenya	143	3·0	303	6·3	184	2·97	379	6·12

Source: Kravis et al. (1978), p. 10.

level, while its rate of growth was somewhat slower than that of Japan, the above ratio sliding to 70·5%. The relative difference decreased much more in comparison with Iran, due of course to very special circumstances.

The above authors show also the per capita consumption of food as a percentage of the US consumption, expressed in international dollars. Some of the figures are reproduced in table 2; these suggest that Hungary's nutritional position is practically the same as that of the more developed Japan, but rather worse than that of Italy. These latter findings seem to be contrary to some general impressions, and it is therefore worth comparing them with other international comparisons of economic development levels.

Table 2. Per capita consumption of food, 1970.

Indices, US = 100

	Bread and cereals	Meat	Fish	Milk, cheese and eggs	Oils and fats	Fruits and vege-tables	Coffee, tea and cocoa	Spices, sweets and sugar	Total of food
United States	100·0	100·0	100·0	100·0	100·0	100·0	100·0	100·0	100·0
Germany, FR	128·5	64·9	36·0	69·2	131·3	49·4	66·4	53·7	69·6
France	122·2	113·2	135·5	107·7	113·7	75·2	49·0	39·7	93·1
Belgium	117·1	112·1	80·6	73·2	129·4	71·7	52·8	53·3	87·8
Netherlands	107·2	62·8	74·2	106·7	72·4	69·3	76·6	59·7	75·6
United Kingdom	162·7	88·7	62·4	78·9	83·9	57·0	86·0	76·8	84·3
Japan	194·1	20·0	328·1	41·4	20·3	53·0	25·2	64·9	60·9
Italy	133·6	92·7	87·7	70·6	112·3	107·4	18·8	31·4	85·1
HUNGARY	143·5	45·4	22·7	57·3	103·8	58·5	15·5	56·0	60·9
Iran	164·8	24·2	9·8	48·3	32·1	34·2	18·6	20·8	41·2
India	134·0	1·5	29·9	13·5	28·4	16·3	5·5	15·3	22·3

Source: Kravis et al. (1968), pp. 94–95.

Table 3. Per capita consumption of basic foods, 1970.

Country	Cereals	Animal protein	Milk[a]	Sugar	Coffee
	kg/head	g/head/day	cal/head	kg/head	kg/head
United States	64·2	71·5	384	51·1	7·43
Germany, FR	68·0	54·5	285	34·7	7·31
France	79·9	64·0	358	34·3	5·55
Belgium–Luxembourg	79·9	54·0	271	39·1	7·83
Netherlands	66·8	53·5	387	50·0	17·79
United Kingdom	73·0	53·4	375	49·6	7·27
Japan	128·5	31·8	81	26·6	2·12
Italy	128·8	38·3	210	27·0	3·91
HUNGARY	128·2	43·4	206	33·6	2·58
Iran	—	—	—	—	—
India	140·2	5·6	97	6·9	0·48

Source: Ehrlich (1978).
[a]Milk and dairy products expressed in calories per head per day.

The most easily accessible data to be used here are presented by Ehrlich (1978), and are reproduced in table 3. Ehrlich bases her study on elementary comparisons in terms of physical units. Her data show that in 1970 the Japanese, Hungarian and Italian consumption of cereals was practically the same in physical units, while the Hungarian consumption of animal protein and sugar was well above the level of the other two countries; Hungary's consumption of milk was practically the same as Italy's, but again well above the Japanese level. Considering that comparisons of physical units avoid the problems of repricing and revaluation associated with comparisons of values, it seems justified to build the conclusions of this paper on the findings of Ehrlich. This is all the more interesting as the difference between the general level of economic development of Japan and Italy, on the one hand, and Hungary, on the other, is—according to Ehrlich—of the same direction but of a much greater order of magnitude (see Ehrlich, 1979).

It would be inappropriate to embark here on a more detailed discussion of the intricacies of international comparisons, and it seems therefore justified to conclude that Hungary's position is more favourable from the aspect of the nutritional value of its food consumption—with regard to both level and composition—than from the aspect of general economic development. This means, of course, that there are differences in the opposite direction, for instance the much lower level of car ownership, particularly in comparison with Italy, and the inferior supply of many industrial goods. Some reasons for these differing patterns of development will be given in the next section.

Table 4. Decile distribution of personal income[a] and total income[b], and the coefficients of distributional inequality[c], 1972.

	Decile distribution											Coeff.
	1	2	3	4	5	6	7	8	9	10	Highest 5%	of inequality[c]
Personal income[a]												
White-collar	4·9	6·4	7·3	8·1	8·6	9·5	10·5	11·8	13·7	19·2	11·0	1·84
Blue-collar	4·4	6·3	7·3	8·4	9·0	9·9	10·9	12·0	13·6	18·2	10·2	1·80
Families with dual income[d]	4·9	6·6	7·7	8·5	8·9	9·8	10·8	11·8	12·9	18·1	10·5	1·74
Peasants[e]	4·0	5·9	6·9	7·9	8·7	9·8	10·7	11·9	14·2	20·0	11·7	1·99
Self-employed	3·9	5·7	6·7	7·7	8·6	9·6	10·4	12·0	13·9	21·5	13·5	2·05
All families with active earners	4·3	6·1	7·0	8·1	8·8	9·8	10·6	12·0	13·8	19·5	11·4	1·89
Families without active earners ('inactives')	3·9	5·4	6·5	7·4	8·3	9·5	10·6	12·1	14·4	21·9	13·2	2·14
Total population	4·0	5·9	7·0	8·0	8·9	9·8	10·8	11·9	13·8	19·9	11·6	1·96
Total income[b]												
Total population	4·1	6·2	7·4	8·2	8·8	10·0	11·3	11·9	13·6	18·5	—	1·85

Source: A családi jövedelmek szinvonala . . . (1975).
a Excluding social benefits in kind.
b Including social benefits in kind.
c Average of the upper half/average of the lower half.
d At least one member of the family working in an agricultural co-operative, and at least one other member working in some other line of activity, in practically all cases as a blue-collar worker.
e Active members of the family working in agricultural co-operatives.

INCOME DISTRIBUTION AND PRICE SYSTEM IN HUNGARY

It has been shown that the level of basic food consumption in Hungary was already in 1970 almost as high as that of leading Western industrial countries and it can be assumed that the relatively small difference has decreased further in the last few years. Apart from the occasional influence of historical factors difficult to analyze, this special feature of the Hungarian consumption structure is mainly due to two factors, the distribution of income and the structure of consumer prices. The first of these factors can be analyzed quite simply, while the second needs a little more elaborate analysis.

The Hungarian income distribution in 1972—the last year for which quinquennial income-survey data are available—is shown in table 4. Personal income represents money income paid out to all members of families, while total income includes also social benefits in kind, e.g. part of the costs of nurseries not covered by the payments of the families utilizing them.

The data reveal a very egalitarian distribution of income both within and between the main social groups. The greatest dispersion can be found in the category of families without active earners (hereafter 'inactives'), due mainly to the large difference in the pensions paid out both under the former, less advantageous, and under the present, much more advantageous, system. The similarly great dispersion found among self-employed persons is the result of the fact that this category contains some rather poor elderly persons sticking to their old way of life, and also some very prosperous

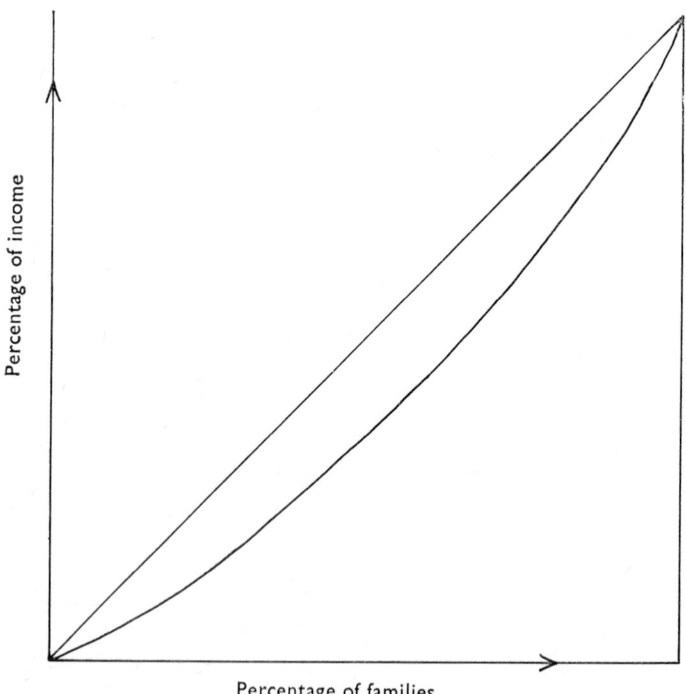

Fig. 1. Lorenz chart of the Hungarian income distribution[a], 1972.
Source A családi jövedelmek szinvonala . . . (1975)
a Calculated from the personal income of the total population, *see* table 4.

elements; the actual dispersion may be even greater than that shown here. The relatively great dispersion among peasants has a similar explanation. Finally, the dispersion within the other social categories, though similar, is less pronounced. Certain incomes not appearing in the statistics will increase the real dispersion, but their impact is probably small.

A comparison of the last two rows of the table shows that social benefits in kind decrease the dispersion of income, but only very slightly. In other words, the central element of income policy in Hungary is the determination of the incomes themselves, and not their redistribution. Finally, the coefficients of inequality, defined as the average of the five upper deciles divided by the average of the five lower deciles, reveal again the relatively great equality both of the incomes themselves, and of their dispersion within the main social groups.

This structure of incomes is also depicted as the Lorenz chart (figure 1) derived from the personal income data in table 4. An international comparison of the income distribution would be difficult and is not therefore attempted, but it seems evident, even without such a formal comparison, that the income structure of Hungary is strikingly egalitarian, indeed one of the most egalitarian of our time.

Something should also be said about the historical development of this income structure. The income distribution during and before the two great wars was excessively unequal, due largely to the high incomes of some narrow social groups, and to the very impoverished condition of some sectors of the peasantry, notably landless agricultural workers. Because of this vast impoverished stratum within the peasantry in an overpopulated agriculture, even the wage differentials between the agrarian and industrial labour were very high: the average agricultural wage amounted to only about 40% of the wage rate of unskilled labour in industry (Csikós-Nagy, 1975).

The first great step towards equalization—apart from abolishing very high incomes—was taken on the occasion of the 1946 stabilization. At this time, owing mainly to the tremendous destruction caused by the war, only about 40–50% of the commodity supply of the last pre-war year, 1938, was available for the population (Jávorka, 1967; Csikós-Nagy, 1975). Wages of white and blue collar workers were fixed therefore at about 35 and 50% of their 1938 levels, respectively, and wage differentials between skilled and unskilled manual workers were also reduced. The differences between the earnings of these categories were decreased further in the forthcoming years (Jávorka, 1967), but the relative poverty of the agrarian population persisted and was even showing a sharp increase in 1952, furthering a mass migration into industrial and building activity. However, the differential between industrial and agrarian incomes was constantly and deliberately reduced after the ending of collectivization of agriculture in the late fifties; the present approximate parity of agricultural and industrial earnings was attained in the early seventies (Csikós-Nagy, 1975). This historical survey, given primarily to explain the evolution of the present income distribution has a further purpose: it shows most clearly that incomes were shaped directly, and that the *re*distribution of incomes already paid out was of only secondary importance.

However, consideration must be given to another vehicle of redistribution—through consumer price policy. To begin again with the historical development, food prices were always relatively low, and prices of industrial consumption goods relatively high. This was due not only to the predominantly agrarian character of the country but also to the rapid development of heavy industries (especially engineering)—compared with consumer goods industries—since the beginning of industrialization in the second half of the nineteenth century. This price disparity became sharper in the years of the Great Depression, and was maintained at this level—using price-control measures—

even in the war years. Thus Hungary emerged from the war with a price disparity between (low) food prices and the (high) prices of other consumer goods.

This initial price disparity was increased further by the post-war stabilization of 1946. Food prices (as expressed in the new unit of the currency, the Forint) had increased to 348% of their 1938 level compared with an increase to 656% in the case of textiles. The prices of heating and lighting increased to 358% while those of house rents and some public utilities such as health, social and cultural services and also travel increased to only 126% of their 1938 value. These developments expressed the needs of a very impoverished country striving to increase the rate of accumulation. It was most important to avoid starvation and ensure at least a moderate level of nutrition, while even the most simple industrial goods were considered more or less as luxuries. At the same time the prices of services had to be fixed at a level well below cost to make possible the utilization of what was available.

The forthcoming years brought some sharp changes, but the basic structure of the price system introduced in 1946 did not change. Food prices rose markedly in 1947 and 1948, but in the 1949 price adjustment increases were concentrated on industrial goods, while service tariffs, which remained practically unchanged since 1946, were actually reduced. Food prices rose again in 1950, but the 1951 price readjustment raised industrial prices, together with consumer incomes. As a result, the price relatives introduced in 1946 were re-established in 1951—apart from house-rents which remained unchanged despite the very pronounced rises in all other prices and also incomes.

Thus, the consumer price policy of the years 1946–1952, although characterized by a series of large changes, led in the end to a price structure very similar to that originally introduced in 1946. These hectic years were followed—owing mainly to political considerations—by 16 years of virtual stability in consumer prices. From 1968, absolute prices have increased, but still without much change in price relatives. So, even now, the basic structure of the consumer prices system is much the same as that introduced in 1946. Thus, as emphasized by Csikós-Nagy (1971), the current price system has strong historical roots and expresses the conditions of the early post-war years, or even earlier.

However, the redistributive character of the price system does not depend solely on the development of consumer prices—the evolution of producer prices must also be taken into account. These two sets of prices are distinct in Hungary, such a system being made possible by the existence of separate 'trade' enterprises supplying raw materials and semi-finished products to the production enterprises. To understand the role of the producer prices in the redistribution of incomes through the price system it is best to trace their historical development.

The basic character of the system of producer prices was shaped by the 1951 price reform (which, as already shown, determined also the later development of consumer prices). Producer prices were fixed thereafter by the authorities on the basis of effective costs supplemented by a small margin of calculated enterprise profits. Producer prices were thus made independent of both consumer prices and foreign trade prices, and lived a more or less independent life. But later, as prices, once fixed, tended to remain stable while costs inevitably changed—at a varying pace and in either direction—the system of producer prices tended to differ more and more from calculated costs. This price system expressed the view prevalent at the time that prices have no role in the allocation of resources or in the shaping of revenues. According to this view, prices were simply technical means of economic accounting, while planning was carried out in terms of physical units.

Table 5. Approximate number of turnover tax rates, 1947–1978.

Year	State industry	Co-operatives, services, local industries	Total
1947			30
1950			400
1951			720
1952			1500
1958	2500	750	3250
1959	3100	2050	5150
1968			2000
1978			900

Source: Erdei (1978).

The disadvantages of such a price system became obvious very soon. For example, it became clear that enterprises should pay for the imported means of production whatever their procurement costs and obtain for their exports whatever their selling brings to the national economy. These and similar views had some impact on the 1959 price reform, but did not become really influential until 1968. The price system was then made much more flexible: locally-determined prices were introduced along with prices fixed by the authorities, while many of the centrally-fixed prices were modified in 1975, 1976 and 1978 to take into account changes in world prices in and after 1973–74. The conformity of costs and prices, on the one hand, and producer, consumer and foreign trade prices, on the other, could not, however, be attained to the degree generally held desirable, and it seems that this dichotomy will persist, at least partially, in the future. In short the price system prevailing now and probably in the future has very definite historical roots (*see* Csikós-Nagy, 1971).

Until 1968, the technical problems arising from the divergence between prices and costs were solved by means of the turnover taxes. The spread of these taxes constantly increased owing to the stability of prices and the variability of costs combined with the increasing efforts of the authorities to translate all differences in enterprise profits into differentiated turnover taxes. This led to a continuous increase in the number of turnover tax rates as shown in table 5.

At the height of the system, in 1967, the number of turnover tax rates surpassed ten thousand (Juhász, 1978).

The above considerations show quite clearly that the present Hungarian system of turnover taxes is very unlikely to have a definite normative character. Some normative influences are undoubtedly present—thus food is subsidized and alcoholic beverages taxed—but these normative elements of the system are greatly blurred by the dominating historical and technical elements. This is why this paper uses the expression 'redistribution through consumer prices' or 'redistribution through the price system' rather than 'redistribution through turnover taxes and subsidies' or 'redistribution through indirect taxation': the dominant element is clearly the almost totally independent life of consumer prices; taxes and subsidies playing here mostly a secondary, technical role.

In 1968, turnover taxes on productive consumption were abolished for the reasons discussed earlier. But, in practice, price flexibility could not be introduced to the extent originally considered desirable, largely because greater flexibility tends to go hand in hand with greater price rises. New financial instruments had therefore to be found to bridge new gaps arising between prices and costs. These were found in an intricate system of uniform and non-uniform production taxes, in exemptions from the uniform taxes, and in production subsidies. The effects of such fiscal interventions are not confined to the industries directly affected but, through inter-industry linkages, are more widely felt; hence the effective real production costs can only be determined by input–output-type analysis. Thus, it is preferable to think in terms of 'the differences between producer prices and calculated real costs of production' rather than 'taxation of enterprises': the whole system of taxation is so intricate that it is almost impossible to delineate the effects of its isolated elements.

The specific, and very important case of foodstuffs can only be considered with these general issues in mind. It has been explained how consumer prices of food were originally fixed at a very low level, low even in relation to the low level of agrarian earnings prevailing at the time. The income parity of the agrarian and non-agrarian population was, however, established by the early seventies; this had repercussions on costs, but could not be reflected in the development of producer and consumer prices. Relative costs changed heavily, too, leading to a very intricate system of (i) agricultural subsidies, bridging the differences between producer prices and costs, and (ii) food price subsidies (or in some isolated cases, taxes), dealing with the differences between consumer and producer prices. The historical character of the price system can therefore be felt particularly strongly in the case of agricultural and food prices, which express to a certain extent even now the political considerations of the late forties and early fifties, and even perhaps the relative income of the agrarian population in the interwar period. This shows particularly clearly how the redistributive character of the Hungarian price system cannot be studied by considering only the turnover taxes and subsidies on consumer goods—the differences between production costs and producer prices must also be taken into consideration. This was already recognized in the mid-fifties, in the course of preparatory work on the 1959 price reform.

The most important results of the calculations made at this time are summarized in table 6. The data presented in this table were obtained by input–output methods, material inputs were valued at their calculated real costs, wages, capital values and amortization were entered without modification, the calculated rate of return on capital was estimated at 10% of the capital value and labour costs were complemented by a hypothetical uniform pay-roll tax of 26·6%. This assumed tax rate brought the cost of total private consumption of goods and services into equality with its value as calculated using actual consumer prices. The data show enormous dispersion; it is quite clear that no rational justification can be given for such discrepancies between costs and prices. The situation is made worse by the fact that this dispersion was present not only between but also within the main categories of consumption goods. These discrepancies were subsequently reduced but are still substantial; it is therefore essential to analyze the redistributive character of the present Hungarian price system in a similar way. This will be done in the next section.

EFFICIENCY OF REDISTRIBUTION THROUGH THE PRICE SYSTEM

As has just been shown, the analysis of the producer and consumer prices must be combined in order to determine the redistributive effect of the price system as a whole. This is made difficult by some statistical problems, the structure of production and producer price statistics differing from the subdivisions of turnover taxes and subsidies, this latter differing again from the subdivisions used in consumption statistics. The first task is therefore to reconcile these conflicting classifications.

Table 6. Differences between consumer prices and calculated real costs of production[a], 1955.

	%
Cotton goods	142
Haberdashery	118
Woollen and worsted	94
Household chemicals	86
Paints	82
Ready-made clothing, hosiery	70
Leather clothing and footwear	49
Linen, hemp and silk	43
Sugar, sweets and coffee products	38
Paper	35
Pottery and glass	33
Mass-produced articles of iron and other metals	28
Telecommunication and vacuum products	26
Building and construction	18
Bricks and tiles	12
Furniture	9
Lime and cement	7
Hides and skins	−2
Canned, tinned and frozen foods	−4
Flour and bakery products	−15
Electricity	−18
Meat and milk	−19
Agricultural products	−29
Transport and communications	−41
Coal	−56
Rents	−86

Source: Jávorka (1967).
a Expressed in percentages of calculated real costs.

Fortunately, this difficult task was made somewhat easier by the coincidence in timing of the relevant statistical surveys, so that all these calculations could employ current price data for the same year (1976).

The problem was tackled in the following way. First, a 77 sector input–output type producer price calculation was conducted using a subdivision corresponding to input–output and national accounting statistics. The main characteristics of this calculation were the following:

(i) Only current inputs were revalued;

(ii) Wages and depreciation allowances were not changed;

(iii) The rate of return on capital was set to provide sufficient funds to finance net investment, a condition for optimality on a golden-age path. The calculation was performed separately for industry and agriculture, yielding rates of 8 and 4·15% per annum, respectively. Capital in waterworks, water regulation, transport, communications and services was largely ignored;

(iv) The assumed rate of profits on wages, i.e. the starting point of the profit-sharing system, was again 8%, corresponding to an incentive system leading to maximization of the returns on capital;

(v) Wages were complemented by a uniform 35% pay-roll tax, according to the actual system of 1976; except that a rate of only 24% was used, in agriculture, to allow for the exemption granted to small producing units, and the direct financing of some social expenditures by the agricultural co-operatives themselves;

Table 7. Calculated real costs of production,[a] 1976.

	%
Mining	105·2
Electric energy	101·2
Metallurgy	95·0
Engineering	79·0
Building materials	97·1
Chemicals	78·2
Light and other industries	82·9
Food products	99·9
Building materials	85·4
Agriculture	106·0
Forestry	107·6
Waterworks and water regulation	100·0
Transport and communications	98·7
Domestic trade	71·4
Foreign trade	57·0
Personal services	85·8
Housing	90·9
Public health	119·0
Cultural services	114·8
Science and scientific services	83·7
Public administration and other services	106·7
All sectors	91·9

a As percentages of producer prices in the sectoral breakdown used in national accounts and input–output tables.

Table 8. Balance of turnover taxes on consumption (+) and consumer price subsidies (−)[a], 1976.

	%
Food (excluding catering)	−18·4
Drink[b] and tobacco (excluding catering)	36·9
Catering	−3·7
Clothing, footwear, and household textiles	9·6
Furniture	−6·6
Other durables and metal goods	7·7
Fuel and power	−39·0
Gasoline and chemicals	6·6
Books, stationery and other non-durables	−16·4
Dwellings and real estate[c]	0
Services	−34·9
All goods and services	−3·3

a As percentages of consumption valued at consumer prices, in categories used in tax statistics.

b Including alcoholic and non-alcoholic drinks, coffee, tea etc.

c Excluding some special taxes, e.g. duties on conveyancing.

Table 9. Differences between consumer prices and calculated real costs of production,[a] 1976.

	%
Food	−19·9
Drink[b] and tobacco	42·1
Clothing and footwear	24·8
Durables	21·7
Miscellaneous industrial articles	1·8
Dwellings and real estate	10·0
Services	−34·2
All goods and services	2·6

a Combined effect of differences between consumer prices and producer prices, and between producer prices and calculated real costs of production, expressed as percentage of consumption, valued at consumer prices, and in the categories used in consumption statistics.

b Including alcoholic and non-alcoholic drinks, coffee, tea etc.

(vi) Imports were valued using official exchange rates and including import duties; imports from socialist countries are duty-free;

(vii) The calculated rent in mining corresponds to the difference between import prices and home production costs; land-rent was set at zero in agriculture.

Three of the above assumptions need further elaboration. The lower rate of return on capital in agriculture (v) and the omission of the land-rent corresponds to a situation where agriculture finances its own accumulation but provides no funds for financing the accumulation of other industries. Such an assumption may have some theoretical support but, more fundamentally, it seems clearly impossible to introduce agricultural prices higher than those computed in this way. Dikes, dams, railway substructures and similar edifices (iii) need not be extended if their system is once established. Hence, it may be argued, no returns are needed in this case as these structures need finance only their maintenance, not their extension. Similarly, in the case of services (iii) it is possible to argue that their capital inputs may rather be considered as current, mostly collective, consumption, and thus the rate of return on capital may be omitted. All these arguments are questionable, but one thing is certain: a price system where agricultural prices include land-rent, or the compensations for social and cultural services include a rate of return on capital would not be possible in Hungary.

The results of these calculations are shown in table 7. It can clearly be seen that the differences between prices and real costs are much smaller now than they were twenty years ago. This is due partly to the higher level of aggregation and partly to the efforts made to develop a more rational system of prices. The direction—if not the magnitude—of differences persisted, however, in the years that have elapsed since 1955.

Let us now turn to the turnover taxes on consumption and consumer price subsidies. While the calculations used a 101 sector breakdown, the results were aggregated into the eleven groups shown in table 8. In spite of differences in classification it is clear that the two kinds of price differentiation tend to work in the same direction:

Table 10. Number of persons appearing in the various categories of the household census, 1976.

Income[a]	White-collar workers	Blue-collar workers	Dual income[b]	Peasants[b]	Inactives	Total
– 9 600	—	1 022	—	423	197	1 913
9 601–12 000	—		—		271	
12 001–14 400	243	1 022	188	259	268	4 573
14 401–16 800		1 636	264	398	295	
16 801–19 200	388	1 862	359	372	260	6 533
19 201–21 600	482	1 899	284	388	239	
21 601–24 000	507	1 558	326	360	256	5 434
24 001–26 400	587	1 244	298	298		
26 401–28 800	446	1 556	260	385	306	7 564
28 801–31 200	350		163			
31 201–36 000	580	917	228	192		
36 001–45 600	541	863	196	235		
45 601–	346					
Total	4470	13 579	2566	3310	2092	26 017

Source: Háztartásstatisztika 1976 and 1978.
a Per capita personal income p.a. expressed in current Forints.
b See notes to table 4.

producer prices of foodstuffs and services are lower than calculated real costs, and their consumer prices are again lower than their producer prices; the contrary is true for industrial consumption goods. Some definite exceptions to this rule are apparent even at this level of aggregation (and the exceptions no doubt increase with disaggregation), but the general tendency is beyond doubt.

The combined effect of both kinds of price differentiation was analyzed using a transformation matrix of 77 × 101 sectors; this shows the industrial origin of the goods appearing in the various entries of the turnover tax statistics. Linearity was generally assumed, implying that the ratio of producer prices to costs depends only on the producing industry and not at all on the turnover tax category. This certainly led to distortions, the most important of which were corrected, for instance by subdividing the sectors. Finally, the data obtained in such a way were transformed into the 117 sectors of the consumption (household) statistics. This latter transformation caused no great problems owing to the similarity of the subdivisions.

The cumulative effect of the above two forms of price differences is shown in aggregated form in table 9. The subsidization of foodstuffs and services stands out, together with the taxation of industrial goods, and of drink and tobacco. The variability of the differences between groups is reduced by the high level of aggregation.

Before turning to the reallocation of incomes resulting from this price system something must be said about the income and consumption statistics used here. They are based on the Household Census of 1976; the composition of the sample is shown in table 10. The data were obtained by stratified random sampling, and the sample covers all social groups apart from the unimportant category of self-employed persons. For further details of the methodology see the original source, *Háztartásstatisztika* 1976. It seems only necessary to mention here that ratios of the social groups within the sample are not proportional to the ratios of the social groups within total population: inactives are under-represented, while peasants and families with dual income

Table 11. Redistribution through the price system[a]: all goods and services, 1976.

Income[b]	White-collar workers	Blue-collar workers	Dual income[c]	Peasants[c]	Inactives	Total population
Redistribution through consumer prices						
– 9 600	—	898	—	589	1337	966
9 601–12 000	—		—		1544	
12 001–14 400	1965	1110	419	961	1788	1223
14 401–16 800		1262	774	760	2036	
16 801–19 200	1528	1344	942	806	2344	1375
19 201–21 600	1577	1455	809	682	2596	
21 601–24 000	2202	1382	908	666	2888	1524
24 001–26 400	2287	1561	1012	515		
26 401–28 800	2215	1613	733	424	3473	1852
28 801–31 200	2661		382			
31 201–36 000	2755	1924	849	769		
36 001–45 600	3170	1793	424	378		
45 601–	2785					
Total	2346	1421	771	652	2291	1488
Redistribution through consumer and producer prices						
– 9 600	—	357	—	–216	858	370
9 601–12 000	—		—		977	
12 001–14 400	960	353	–431	125	1216	380
14 401–16 800		389	–98	–276	1245	
16 801–19 200	284	291	–190	–607	1361	206
19 201–21 600	179	255	–506	–486	1652	
21 601–24 000	855	–37	–491	–660	1611	97
24 001–26 400	803	192	–749	–1181		
26 401–28 800	649	–40	–972	–1226	1786	–187
28 801–31 200	857		–1454			
31 201–36 000	744	64	–1224	–1313		
36 001–45 600	517	–811	–1588	–2190		
45 601–	–714					
Total	534	138	–695	–727	1355	112

a By social groups and income categories.
b See table 10, notes.
c See table 4, notes.

are over-represented. (Of course, the sample accurately reflects the ratios of income categories within each social group.)

The data presented here make possible, as already mentioned, two different kinds of analysis: (i) the appraisal of the redistributive effect of turnover taxes and price subsidies alone—or redistribution through consumer prices—and (ii) the above analysis complemented by the similar effect of the differences between calculated real production costs and producer prices—or redistribution through consumer and producer prices. Table 11 shows both for all goods and services as well as for all social groups subdivided by income categories as shown already in table 10.

The upper half of the table shows that consumer prices have a very poor redistributive effect within the total population and within most of the social groups appearing here. In fact, as income increases, subsidies generally increase, but less than proportionately, so that the ratio of subsidies to income shows a modest fall. (The

Table 12. Redistribution through the price system[a]: food, 1976.

Income[b]	White-collar workers	Blue-collar workers	Dual income[c]	Peasants[c]	Inactives	Total population
Redistribution through consumer prices						
– 9 600	—	679	—	591	732	707
9 601–12 000	—		—		973	
12 001–14 400	817	732	618	670	1113	792
14 401–16 800		803	643	625	1203	
16 801–19 200	894	835	732	677	1251	863
19 201–21 600	903	878	712	715	1319	
21 601–24 000	975	909	780	724	1399	932
24 001–26 400	976	1006	772	760		
26 401–28 800	1059	1069	860	815	1482	1117
28 801–31 200	1098		802			
31 201–36 000	1205	1180	887	826		
36 001–45 600	1261	1322	891	877		
45 601–	1361					
Total[b]	1064	923	767	715	1202	928
Redistribution through consumer and producer prices						
– 9 600	—	824	—	651	876	820
9 601–12 000	—		—		1029	
12 001–14 400	1092	903	701	763	1224	954
14 401–16 800		1010	719	702	1334	
16 801–19 200	1205	1077	861	746	1362	1085
19 201–21 600	1244	1144	812	813	1491	
21 601–24 000	1379	1191	917	807	1567	1202
24 001–26 400	1376	1328	882	889		
26 401–28 800	1499	1412	1008	869	1681	1479
28 801–31 200	1562		933			
31 201–36 000	1721	1588	1012	920		
36 001–45 600	1816	1788	999	979		
45 601–	1992					
Total[b]	1504	1200	882	798	1338	1181

a By social groups and income categories.
b See notes to table 10.
c See notes to table 4.

ratios themselves are not shown here for lack of space.) This small redistributive effect is the least pronounced in the cases of white collar workers and inactives, while somewhat greater redistribution takes place within the social groups of families with dual income and peasants. All this shows clearly that this form of indirect taxation—where negative taxes dominate—is very inefficient: greater absolute amounts are paid out to the more well-to-do half of the population to make the distribution of income a little bit more even. Payments to the highest income brackets (especially among white-collar workers and inactives) must be considered as mere losses from the point of view of redistributive efficiency, especially if we take into account the resulting distortions of the price system which involve further losses of efficiency.

Things are made worse if we look at the differences not within but between the main social groups. This system of prices is clearly benefiting white- and blue-collar workers,

Table 13. Net direct food subsidies in percentage of food purchases, 1974–6[a].

Annual per capita income	White-collar workers	Blue-collar workers	Dual income[b]	Peasants
– 9 600	—	34·3	33·1	33·3
9 601–14 400	32·4	32·4	33·3	32·0
14 401–19 200	32·9	33·0	32·8	32·5
19 201–24 000	32·7	33·5	33·0	32·3
24 001–28 800	32·9	32·6	33·4	32·6
28 801–	32·2	32·6	32·0	32·6

Source: Juhász (1978).

a 1974 consumption data combined with turnover taxes and subsidies of the first half of 1976.

b For definitions see notes to table 4.

Table 14. Redistribution through the price system[a]: drink[b] and tobacco, 1976.
Redistribution through consumer and producer prices

Income[c]	White-collar workers	Blue-collar workers	Dual income[d]	Peasants[d]	Inactives	Total population
– 9 600	—	–427 [rows 1–2]	—	–435 [rows 1–2]	–286	–394 [rows 1–2]
9 601–12 000	—		—		–286	
12 001–14 400	–412 [rows 3–4]	–419	–492	–391	–351	–476 [rows 3–4]
14 401–16 800		–534	–608	–488	–447	
16 801–19 200	–486	–585	–531	–598	–418	–572 [rows 5–6]
19 201–21 600	–566	–586	–664	–607	–544	
21 601–24 000	–571	–709	–711	–645	–602 [rows 7–8]	–679 [rows 7–8]
24 001–26 400	–599	–745	–693	–640		
26 401–28 800	–684	–869 [rows 9–10]	–889	–835 [rows 9–10]	–812 [rows 9–13]	–1007 [rows 9–13]
28 801–31 200	–752		–955			
31 201–36 000	–863	–1085	–1085	–812		
36 001–45 600	–1050	–1514 [rows 12–13]	–1128 [rows 12–13]	–1130 [rows 12–13]		
45 601–	–1359					
Total	–740	–709	–751	–638	–479	–691

a By social groups and income categories.

b Including alcoholic and non-alcoholic drinks, coffee, tea etc.

c See notes to table 10.

d See notes to table 4.

and, particularly, inactives, to the detriment of peasants, and of families with double income. Possibly this is best seen as a hangover from the peasant policy of bygone times, reflected in the historical elements of the present price system. The government has deliberately raised peasant incomes to the general national level, and has maintained them there by an elaborate system of production subsidies and other fiscal means of a redistributive character. The parallel existence of two redistributive systems working in opposite directions can only be explained in historical terms.

To turn now to the lower half of table 11, it can clearly be seen that the redistributive character of the price system as a whole is much greater than that of turnover taxes and consumer price subsidies alone. The sums paid out to the highest income brackets

Table 15. Redistribution through the price system[a]: clothing and footwear, 1976.
Redistribution through consumer and producer prices

Income[b]	White-collar workers	Blue-collar workers	Dual income[c]	Peasants[c]	Inactives	Total population
– 9 600	—	−237	—	−352	−232	−267
9 601–12 000	—		—		−276	
12 001–14 400	−454	−343	−435	−324	−324	−395
14 401–16 800		−420	−427	−409	−439	
16 801–19 200	−466	−505	−542	−501	−396	−538
19 201–21 600	−627	−576	−597	−574	−506	
21 601–24 000	−648	−633	−747	−589	−579	−682
24 001–26 400	−719	−726	−864	−696		
26 401–28 800	−745	−870	−925	−786	−817	−986
28 801–31 200	−869		−921			
31 201–36 000	−982	−1023	−944	−832		
36 001–45 600	−1153	−1275	−1143	−969		
45 601–	−1345					
Total	−814	−633	−736	−579	−458	−635

a By social groups and income categories.
b See notes to table 10.
c See notes to table 4.

represent even in this case clear losses in terms of redistributive efficiency, but their relative importance is much smaller. The reasons for this state of things will be elucidated by the following tables.

Table 12 shows the redistributive effect of food prices; its structure is the same as that of the previous—and also of the following—tables. It clearly depicts the most important and obvious reason for the above tendencies: a great part of subsidies is included in food prices; food consumption—owing to the egalitarian distribution of income, and to low food prices—is not much influenced by social status and income level; redistribution tends therefore to increase everybody's income by a very similar absolute amount. This tendency emerges very clearly from the figures of Juhász (1968), reproduced in table 13. These show the ratio of net direct food subsidies (consumer prices subsidies minus turnover taxes) to food purchases. The uniformity of these data is striking, showing the similarity of consumption structure, but also the problems connected with this system of subsidies.

The most obvious problem is that such a system favours in absolute amount those who buy more: on the one hand the rich (or perhaps even the heavy eaters), and on the other those who buy and do not produce food (*see* Ládanyi 1975a). The first of these categories needs no further comment; the second leads to the conclusion that the system is working against those who—having some private plots, gardens or animals—provide at least some part of their own food consumption, or even sell food to others. The disadvantages of this situation are also fully discussed by Juhász (1978) who sees in this system of prices one of the main reasons why, in spite of the strenuous efforts of the government to the contrary, private production of food has actually decreased. This must lead to social losses, since the social costs of producing food in one's spare time or as a secondary occupation are clearly lower than those in the so-called organized activities. To return to the main topic of this paper: this is the first important reason why this system works against peasants and families with dual income, in a way that cannot be considered rational, either economically or socially.

Table 16. Redistribution through the price system[a]: consumer durables, 1976.
Redistribution through consumer and producer prices

Income[b]	White-collar workers	Blue-collar workers	Dual income[c]	Peasants[c]	Inactives	Total population
- 9 600	—	−159	—	−271	−100	−171
9 601–12 000	—		—		−115	
12 001–14 400	−291	−295	−395	−259	−67	−278
14 401–16 800		−295	−326	−346	−115	
16 801–19 200	−492	−380	−490	−411	−289	−437
19 201–21 600	−671	−471	−530	−405	−113	
21 601–24 000	−727	−666	−505	−660	−235	−652
24 001–26 400	−822	−649	−452	−843		
26 401–28 800	−737	−729	−714	−874	−401	−891
28 801–31 200	−599		−958			
31 201–36 000	−811	−785	−747	−744		
36 001–45 600	−1303	−1124	−785	−832		
45 601–	−2132					
Total	−870	−532	−566	−541	−185	−567

a By social groups and income categories.
b See notes to table 10.
c See notes to table 4.

Table 14 shows redistribution through the prices of drink and tobacco. Here, producer prices are somewhat higher than calculated real costs; and there is some private production of beverages. It is evident that this system as a whole works in a desirable way. One might however criticize the grouping of coffee and tea with alcoholic beverages and tobacco; the former are no longer luxuries, nor are they particularly detrimental to health.

Redistribution through the prices of industrial consumption goods is represented in tables 15 and 16. In the case of clothing and footwear (table 15), taxation dominates everywhere, but the redistributive effect is small, because tax payments increase roughly in proportion to incomes. Nevertheless, it is clearly true that more well-to-do people pay higher taxes in this way. In the case of consumer durables (table 16), the redistributive effect is very definite among workers due mainly to the spread of car ownership. The differences in consumption structure and, therefore, in taxation are much less pronounced in case of peasants and families with dual income; in the latter case this form of taxation is even regressive, if only slightly. The weight of consumer durables is very small in the consumption structure of the inactives, and the result of this can also be seen in these figures. Finally, it is very difficult to say anything specific about the very heterogeneous category of miscellaneous industrial goods, and this table is therefore omitted. In the cases of peasants, of families with dual income and of blue-collar workers, these purchases consist largely of building materials, but in the case of white-collar workers, luxuries are also important. Fuels also appear here, and coal, purchased mainly by lower income groups, is heavily subsidized.

To turn to the remaining categories, dwellings and real estate are taxed, but the redistributive effect, though favourable, is slight and the figures are not reproduced here. However, services, shown in table 17, are of very great importance from the point of view of redistribution. It can clearly be seen that their subsidization tends to

Table 17. Redistribution through the price system[a]: services, 1976.

Income[b]	White-collar workers	Blue-collar workers	Dual income[c]	Peasants[c]	Inactives	Total
Redistribution through consumer prices						
– 9 600	—	339	—	198	275	289
9 601–12 000	—		—		253	
12 001–14 400	1069	474	275	345	353	530
14 401–16 800		625	517	322	526	
16 801–19 200	796	758	585	310	814	762
19 201–21 600	1071	887	562	333	975	
21 601–24 000	1565	969	672	446	1327	1074
24 001–26 400	1709	1163	727	494		
26 401–28 800	1698	1314	763	586	2014	1661
28 801–31 200	1998		723			
31 201–36 000	2221	1686	909	649		
36 001–45 600	2879	2057	756	519		
45 601–	3237					
Total	1859	978	649	400	847	**1013**
Redistribution through consumer and producer prices						
– 9 600	—	332	—	196	264	282
9 601–12 000	—		—		243	
12 001–14 400	1003	465	283	346	323	509
14 401–16 800		597	518	308	485	
16 801–19 200	691	715	573	296	707	710
19 201–21 600	914	840	581	339	870	
21 601–24 000	1432	895	676	455	1141	996
24 001–26 400	1564	1087	697	451		
26 401–28 800	1531	1197	765	603	1745	1506
28 801–31 200	1791		701			
31 201–36 000	1980	1551	900	607		
36 001–45 600	2528	1867	738	385		
45 601–	2996					
Total	1669	910	644	385	748	934

a By social groups and income categories.
b See notes to table 10.
c See notes to table 4.

favour white-collar and, to a certain extent, blue-collar workers, while families with dual income, and particularly peasants receive relatively little benefit. There is, moreover, an important geographical aspect not revealed in these figures—this form of subsidization gives most advantage to those who live in cities and are better supplied with services. Services are utilized if, when, and where they are available, and their use does not depend on the working of the price system. These subsidies would seem even larger if a return on capital had been included in costs.

The following considerations are however very important. First, the wage differentials between white- and blue-collar workers are definitely much smaller in Hungary than in the Western countries. This great equalization was introduced—as already mentioned—in 1946, and has been maintained ever since. The subsidization of cultural and some other services was therefore—and is to a certain extent even now—an absolute necessity counteracting the efforts to equalize incomes, but serving also very definite social purposes: the raising of the general public health and cultural level. Nevertheless, it is widely held that this price system gives excessive benefits to families with flats in state-owned buildings, children in state nurseries or access to the other social benefits in kind that are in short supply. It follows that the further equalization of the standard of living, considered as desirable everywhere in Hungary, depends not on the redistribution of income, but on the wider availability of services.

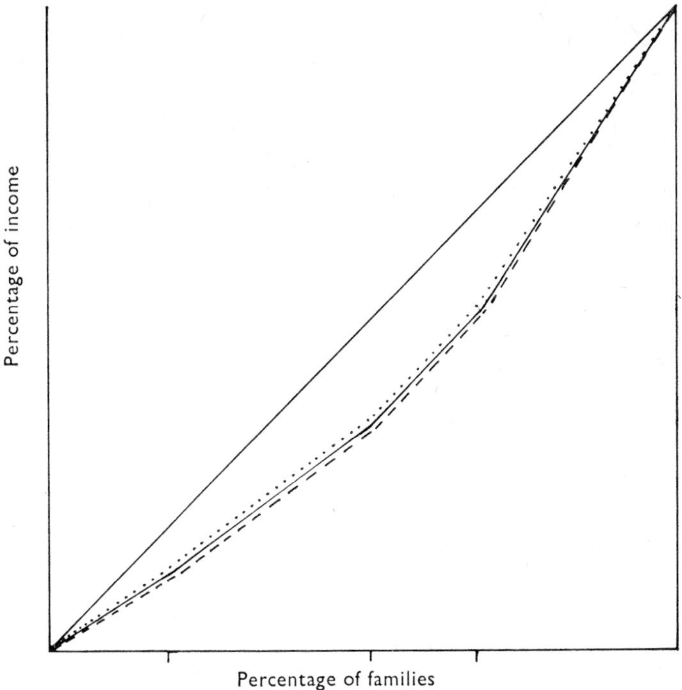

Fig. 2. Chart of the Hungarian income distribution[a] before and after redistribution through the price system[b], 1976

a Calculated from consumption expenditures appears in table 10.

b ---- Before redistribution through the price system.

—— After redistribution through consumer prices.

········ After redistribution through consumer and producer prices.

The equality of opportunities, so important from the socialist point of view, can therefore be served much better by the rapid development of the tertiary sector and a more equal access to its services than by any other form of redistribution policy.

To conclude this section, some skeleton Lorenz curves are drawn to indicate the overall effect of price policy on income distribution in Hungary (figure 2). These curves have been drawn from three points only, and show the original distribution of incomes, as well as its modification after redistribution through consumer prices, and through consumer and producer prices, respectively. It can clearly be seen that the three curves almost coincide, as is confirmed by table 18.

Table 18. Cumulative income distributions, before and after redistribution.
Income of the first *n* percent of the population as a percentage of total income.

n	19·0	46·1	68·8
Before redistribution	12·0	34·2	56·4
After redistribution through consumer prices	12·2	34·5	56·7
After redistribution through consumer and producer prices	12·3	34·6	56·8

The figures differ somewhat from those of figure 1 owing to differences in data, but the effect of these differences is not significant. The data show that—under conditions currently prevailing in Hungary, i.e. with the present level and dispersion of income—consumer price policy is a very inefficient method of income redistribution. These findings support the view of the overwhelming majority of economists here that this system should be discontinued. Nevertheless, before summing up these final conclusions, certain welfare arguments will be considered.

WELFARE EFFECTS OF REDISTRIBUTION THROUGH THE PRICE SYSTEM

This section is devoted not to advanced welfare theory, but to certain practical problems. Specifically, consideration is given to the claims put forward by some Hungarian economists that the prevailing system of turnover taxes and subsidies, together with the differences between producer prices and calculated real costs, promote the development of a consumption pattern favourable from social, cultural and public health considerations. The validity of these considerations in relation to cheap or free cultural and medical services is undisputed in this country, but the extension of this reasoning to the whole of consumption, though advocated by Hoch (1972), has been rejected by most Hungarian economists concerned with price policy (Csikós-Nagy, 1974; Jávorka, 1967; Vincze, 1971).

It is easy to demonstrate that many elements of the present system of turnover taxes and subsidies are contrary to nutritional and health considerations. As shown by Ladányi (1975a,b), edible oils and margarine were taxed in 1973, while lard, bacon fat, and butter were heavily subsidized. Nutritional considerations would obviously require discrimination in the opposite direction. Similarly, no nutritional arguments could support the differing degree of subsidies given to different kinds of meat (and no subsidies to eggs), or the fact that cereals are subsidized while fruits and vegetables are not. Similar remarks are made by Érsek (1976) and Juhász (1977). It is clear (p. 212) that the actual system of taxes and subsidies is a consequence of the historical character of the price system, and of certain other practical considerations, while the task of basing a price system directly on nutritional and similar considerations would be very difficult or even impossible.

Let us turn now to another, much more important aspect that deserves serious attention. As shown in the first section, policies towards prices and incomes have generated a pattern of food consumption closely resembling that of much more well-to-do countries; it can even be assumed that the food consumption pattern of lower income groups compares particularly well with that of similar groups in much more developed countries. This seems to be one of the greatest successes of Hungarian economic policy, and this achievement must clearly not be sacrificed for the sake of some theory such as that turnover taxes should be either inversely proportional to price elasticities or else uniform (cf. Sandmo, 1976, and the literature given there). The consequences to be expected from abandoning the present consumer price policy must be studied very thoroughly. The remaining parts of this section will be devoted to the most important results of this research.

The methodological aspects of this study were published by Hulyák and Losonczy (1978), and Muszély (1978), while the methods and results were summarized by Szakolczai et al., (1979a,b). Three models were used in this empirical study: the 'constant elasticity' model, the Stone model, and the 'cross-section' model.

The form of constant elasticity model used was originally developed by Houthakker (1965), and later employed by Goldberger and Gamaletsos (1970). The model consists of independent loglinear equations of the type

$$\log q_i(t) = \alpha_i + \eta_i \log \bar{Y}(t) + \delta_i \log \bar{p}_i(t) \tag{1}$$

where q_i represents consumption of commodity group i (at constant prices), $\bar{Y}$ the deflated total consumer expenditure, $\bar{p}_i$ the price of the ith commodity group relative to the general index of consumer prices, and t time.

The Stone model was used in the original form developed by the above author (Stone 1954a,b; *see also* Stone 1978, for an account in Hungarian). The model can be written in the form.

$$v_i(t) = \bar{p}_i(t)\gamma_i + \beta_i Y^* \tag{2}$$

where v_i represents expenditures at current prices, γ_i 'committed or necessary consumption' at constant prices, Y^* 'residual or supernumerary' consumption at current prices, and β_i the proportion of residual consumption devoted to commodity group i. The parameters have been estimated by the original iterative procedure developed by Stone (1954a); further developments of this model (cf. Barten, 1969; Pollak and Wales, 1969; Zellner, 1962) have not been used.

The time series employed in both the above models were taken from income and consumption statistics (*A lakosság jövedelme* ... 1960–1970 and 1960–1974), as well as from the Statistical Yearbook (*Statisztikai Évkönyv* 1960, 1961, 1962, 1963 and 1974). The methodological details are dealt with in these statistical publications, and also by Szakolczai et al. (1979a).

The 'cross-section' model was adapted from Frisch (1959, 1974), and Theil (1967, 1970). The starting point of this model is the equation

$$\frac{\Delta q_i}{q_i} = E_i \frac{\Delta Y}{Y} + \sum_j E_{ij} \frac{\Delta p_j}{p_j} + u_i \tag{3}$$

which states that proportional changes in constant-price consumption (q_i) from one year to another depend on proportional changes in current-price income (Y), changes in relative prices (p_j) and a stochastic term (u_i). Considering the large number of parameters (the model determines also the cross-elasticities), an additional assumption was needed: a specific utility function was introduced and maximized. Assuming the additivity of the utility function, equation (3) can be re-expressed

$$\frac{\Delta q_i}{q_i} = E_i \frac{\Delta Y - \sum_j q_i \Delta p_j}{Y} - E_i\varphi \left(\frac{\Delta p_i}{p_i} - \sum_j \frac{E_j q_j p_j}{Y} \frac{\Delta p_j}{p_j}\right) + u_i. \tag{4}$$

Table 19. Square roots of coefficients of determination and income elasticites of demand obtained from constant elasticity analysis[a], 1960–74.

	Food	Drink[b] and tobacco	Clothing and footwear	Fuel and power	Durables	Other industrial goods	Services
Square roots of coefficients of determination							
White-collar workers	0·919	0·913	0·933	0·938	0·936	0·782	0·932
Blue-collar workers	0·997	0·990	0·996	0·996	0·982	0·828	0·970
Families with dual income[c]	0·996	0·986	0·996	0·995	0·989	0·992	0·982
Peasants[c]	0·994	0·986	0·998	0·976	0·994	0·984	0·985
Total population	0·998	0·997	0·989	0·990	0·997	0·993	0·993
Income elasticities of demand[d]							
White-collar workers	0·36	1·12	0·68	0·72	0·50	0·87	0·59
	(7·07)	(5·85)	(5·45)	(4·86)	(1·61)	(2·62)	(3·52)
Blue-collar workers	0·55	1·77	1·08	1·15	1·09	1·21	1·44
	(38·97)	(27·69)	(24·57)	(24·74)	(2·78)	(2·97)	(7·45)
Families with dual income[c]	0·71	1·15	0·96	0·96	1·88	1·21	1·44
	(38·02)	(11·98)	(38·56)	(28·73)	(7·47)	(19·56)	(7·67)
Peasants[c]	0·69	1·12	0·91	1·01	2·35	1·44	1·60
	(31·32)	(11·73)	(59·05)	(35·20)	(10·34)	(15·44)	(7·92)
Total population	0·57	1·34	0·86	1·25	1·87	1·66	1·12
	(44·95)	(27·53)	(17·13)	(16·51)	(17·69)	(14·39)	(13·32)

Source: Szakolczai et al. (1979a).
a By social and commodity groups.
b Including alcoholic and non-alcoholic drinks, tea, coffee etc.
c See notes to table 4.
d *t*-values in parentheses.

Passing over further theoretical problems (see e.g. Muszély, 1978), the following estimation procedure was adopted. The empirical Engel-curves of all commodity groups were first determined, and these were used to estimate the income elasticities. From these values and from the relative changes in consumption, prices and incomes, the income flexibility parameter φ can be estimated by ordinary least squares. Having found φ, price and income elasticities can be determined.

The data used in this model were taken from household statistics (*Háztartasstátisztika* 1972, 1973, 1974), and consumption price statistics (*A fogyasztói árak* … 1972, 1973, 1974).

After this very short survey of methods, let us reproduce some of the most important findings, first of all those of the constant elasticity model. These computations were based on the 1960–74 time series obtained from household budget statistics (*A lakosság jövedelme* …, 1960–1974), and the square roots of the coefficients of determination as well as the income elasticities of demand are shown in table 19. The model fits the data well, and the values obtained correspond to general expectations. It seems that the main determinant of consumption is always the level of incomes; the connection is the closest in the case of peasants and families with dual income, the consumption of blue-collar and, particularly, white-collar workers being somewhat less influenced

Table 20. Price parameters and direct non-compensated and compensated price elasticities of demand obtained from constant elasticity analysis[a], 1960–74.

	Food	Drink[b] and tobacco	Clothing and footwear	Fuel and power	Durables	Other industrial goods	Services
Price parameters[c]							
White-collar workers	0·46	−0·86	−1·15	−1·16	−4·46	−0·12	2·12
	(0·82)	(0·80)	(1·91)	(2·61)	(2·59)	(0·07)	(2·37)
Blue-collar workers	−0·19	−1·11	−0·51	−0·64	−3·33	1·06	−0·70
	(1·44)	(4·06)	(2·64)	(5·12)	(1·90)	(0·57)	(0·65)
Families with dual income[d]	−0·09	−0·73	0·20	−0·69	−0·85	−0·51	−0·98
	(0·41)	(1·90)	(0·72)	(5·93)	(0·33)	(0·59)	(1·01)
Peasants[d]	0·12	−0·93	0·60	−0·43	0·31	−0·20	−0·72
	(0·45)	(2·22)	(3·24)	(3·99)	(0·14)	(0·12)	(0·78)
Total population	−0·21	−0·64	−0·13	−0·46	−1·75	−0·04	−0·76
	(1·67)	(2·82)	(0·44)	(1·94)	(1·18)	(0·05)	(1·76)
Non-compensated price elasticities							
White-collar workers	0·21	−0·88	−1·08	−1·14	−4·03	−0·23	1·66
Blue-collar workers	−0·31	−1·16	−0·60	−0·66	−3·12	0·76	−0·80
Families with dual income[d]	−0·31	−0·81	0·03	−0·70	−0·98	−0·60	−1·03
Peasants[d]	−0·20	−0·95	0·41	−0·46	0·07	−0·37	−0·81
Total population	−0·35	−0·76	−0·22	−0·49	−1·76	−0·25	−0·81
Compensated price elasticities							
White-collar workers	0·32	−0·80	−0·99	−1·11	−3·97	−0·10	1·77
Blue-collar workers	−0·12	−1·02	−0·43	−0·61	−3·02	0·91	−0·60
Families with dual income[d]	−0·06	−0·71	0·17	−0·66	−0·74	−0·44	−0·88
Peasants[d]	0·07	−0·84	0·53	−0·41	0·28	−0·17	−0·65
Total population	−0·14	−0·53	−0·11	−0·44	−1·60	−0·03	−0·65

Source: Szakolczai et al. (1979a).
a By social and commodity groups.
b Including alcoholic and non-alcoholic drinks, coffee, tea etc.
c *t*-values in parentheses.
d See notes to table 4.

by their income situation. Consumption of food, as well as of clothing and footwear, tends to depend much more on the level of income than does the consumption of other industrial goods, and, more particularly, consumer durables.

These results are, however, of secondary importance as regards our present problem, and have been shown here in order to demonstrate the reliability of the model. However, the price parameters, as well as the non-compensated and compensated price elasticities of demand, presented in table 20, lead to some very important conclusions concerning the viability of a consumer price system which reflects costs more accurately. In the Hungarian case, such a system would imply higher prices for food, and lower prices for industrial goods.

Table 21. Limits of income categories[a] used in cross-section analysis, 1972–4.

	1972	1973	1974
White- and blue-collar workers			
Category 1	–15 000	–16 000	–17 500
Category 2	15 001–19 000	16 001–21 000	17 501–22 000
Category 3	19 001–24 000	21 001–25 500	22 001–28 000
Category 4	24 001–	25 501–	28 001–
Families with dual income and peasants			
Category 1	–13 500	–14 700	–15 500
Category 2	13 501–17 000	14 701–18 400	15 501–19 700
Category 3	17 001–22 000	18 401–23 600	19 701–25 400
Category 4	22 001–	23 601–	25 401–

a Personal income per head per year expressed in current Forints.

First, as to the reliability of the results, it can easily be seen that the *t*-values are much lower here, indicating that the price effects are much more difficult to detect than the income effects. This is just what one would expect, considering the high degree of price stability in Hungary. Nevertheless, very definite price effects can be found in many cases: it seems that dependence of consumption on prices is greatest among white-collar and, particularly, blue-collar workers, and somewhat less in the other two social groups. It can also be seen that dependence on prices tends to be higher or lower according as dependence on incomes is lower or higher. For instance, the purchases of durables and other industrial goods—mainly building materials—seem to depend, in the case of peasants and families with dual income, on the level of incomes, and not at all on prices. Again this can easily be understood, because such purchases represent to a large extent a kind of property accumulation, a motive of particular importance among peasants. All these considerations confirm the reliability of these findings.

The most important feature of the results, however, is the insensitivity of food consumption to prices (see the coefficients and *t*-values in the first third of table 20). The positive values obtained for white-collar workers and peasants, together with the relevant *t*-values, must be interpreted as signs of an almost complete independence of food consumption of food prices—at least at this very aggregated level and within the very narrow limits of price changes observed. It also seems, not surprisingly, that food prices exert most influence among blue-collar workers.

Let us consider next the differences between the non-compensated and compensated price elasticities; while the latter are, of course, smaller everywhere, the difference is insignificant for industrial goods, but very important for foodstuffs. These findings tend to support the view that a given level of food consumption once attained subsists even in spite of adverse changes in relative prices, or decreases only slightly. Our calculations lead therefore to the conclusion that price rises of food—if compensated by adequate changes in incomes—exert their effect mainly by changing the pattern of incremental consumption, having very little effect on the level of food consumption. With due allowance for all the uncertainties of such calculations we may therefore argue that a more rational system of consumer prices would not endanger the achievement mentioned before, namely the high level and advantageous structure of food consumption already attained. To put it otherwise: it seems that the inefficient system of redistribution may be changed without any very damaging effects on welfare.

Table 22. Income elasticities obtained from cross-section analysis[a], 1972–4.

	Food	Beverages, tobacco, coffee, tea	Clothing and footwear	Fuel and power	Durables	Other industrial goods	Services
White-collar workers							
Category 1	0·68	0·94	1·24	0·63	1·50	0·90	1·63
2	0·67	1·03	0·87	0·66	1·68	1·21	1·49
3	0·59	1·07	0·80	0·66	1·60	1·14	1·39
4	0·56	0·96	0·40	0·83	1·57	0·93	1·17
All categories	0·58	1·02	0·79	0·67	1·54	1·11	1·27
Blue-collar workers							
Category 1	0·80	1·06	1·19	0·58	1·45	1·12	1·38
2	0·88	1·21	0·85	0·66	1·18	1·03	1·45
3	0·79	1·14	0·75	0·69	1·23	1·02	1·31
4	0·51	0·88	0·59	0·69	1·22	1·03	1·22
All categories	0·75	1·12	0·89	0·67	1·21	1·05	1·32
Families with dual income[c]							
Category 1	0·77	1·10	1·10	0·61	1·80	1·34	1·10
2	0·55	0·72	0·90	0·64	1·35	1·16	1·32
3	0·53	0·46	0·52	0·73	1·29	1·07	1·14
4	0·48	0·56	0·60	0·85	1·20	1·14	1·50
All categories	0·56	0·68	0·82	0·69	1·37	1·20	1·27
Peasants[b]							
Category 1	0·35	0·66	1·20	0·45	1·45	1·45	1·20
2	0·41	0·63	0·88	0·63	1·24	1·36	1·30
3	0·38	0·56	0·61	0·67	1·24	1·22	1·31
4	0·42	0·50	0·33	0·50	1·54	1·16	1·40
All categories	0·40	0·62	0·82	0·59	1·30	1·25	1·35

Source: Szakolczai et al (1979a).

a By social groups and income categories, as well as by commodity groups. Income categories were defined in table 21.

b Including alcoholic and non-alcoholic drinks, coffee, tea etc.

c See notes to table 4.

As to the other models referred to above, the results of the Stone model are not reproduced here. These calculations were based on the same data, and they largely reinforce the findings obtained from the constant elasticity model. The differences between the calculated parameter values are similar, but it seems that this model tends to decrease the differences in order to ensure the consistency of the computed values. These aspects of the results are exhaustively dealt with in the publications cited above, and cannot be discussed further here.

Some very interesting results have been obtained, however, from the cross-section model, estimated from the 1972–4 household budget data. The very detailed processing of these data made it possible to determine parameters not only for the four main social groups, but also for four income categories within each. The limits of the income categories for the three years in question are shown in table 21. It can be seen that the

Table 23. Non-compensated direct price elasticities of demand obtained from cross-section analysis[a], 1972–4.

	Food	Drink[b] and tobacco	Clothing and footwear	Fuel and power	Durables	Other industrial goods	Services
White-collar workers							
Category 1	−0·86	−1·12	−1·41	−0·77	−1·75	−1·08	−1·70
2	−1·06	−1·57	−1·35	−1·06	−2·46	−1·81	−2·02
3	−0·90	−1·50	−1·17	−0·99	−2·18	−1·59	−1·77
4	−0·69	−1·09	−0·48	−0·96	−1·66	−1·06	−1·25
All categories	−0·78	−1·20	−1·02	−0·85	−1·41	−1·20	−1·34
Blue-collar workers							
Category 1	−1·21	−1·57	−1·75	−0·71	−2·17	−1·70	−1·97
2	−1·05	−1·37	−1·03	−0·81	−1·39	−1·21	−1·62
3	−0·87	−1·16	−0·81	−0·74	−1·04	−1·06	−1·29
4	−0·61	−0·95	−0·65	−0·74	−1·27	−1·09	−1·24
All categories	−0·98	−1·37	−1·14	−0·88	−1·51	−1·32	−1·56

Source: Szakolczai et al. (1979a).

a By social groups and income categories, as well as by commodity groups. Income categories were defined in table 21.

b Including alcoholic and non-alcoholic drinks, coffee, tea etc.

limits of these categories are moved upwards from year to year in order to ensure a comparatively even distribution of the sample.

The income elasticities obtained from these calculations are presented in table 22. They are numerically different from those obtained from the constant elasticity model, but there is no reason to expect time-series and cross-section analyses to lead to identical results. It can be seen that, in the cases of clothing and footwear and also durables and other industrial goods, income elasticities tend to be higher with lower incomes. There is only one exception—the case of durables in the highest income category of peasants—but in this case the purchase of just a few private cars can distort the results. On the other hand, it can be seen, particularly in cases of white- and blue-collar workers, that the income elasticities of food and drink and tobacco tend to be highest not in the first, but in the second income category, indicating that the families in the lowest income brackets tend to increase their consumption of food, as well as of drink and tobacco only slightly, in order to attain the level of consumption of industrial goods that seems already necessary, in relation to the consumption patterns of the higher income brackets.

These findings are very relevant to the welfare effects of redistribution through the price system as now practised in Hungary. Even if it is true that the more well-to-do sections of the population buy more industrial goods, the practice of taxing these latter articles seems to exert a very unfavourable effect, in that it hinders the families in the lowest income brackets in catching up with the other social groups in these important fields of consumption. This is another and even more important reason for believing that the welfare effects of the redistribution through the price system are of highly questionable value, and that welfare considerations suggest that this system should be abandoned.

The price elasticities of demand appearing in table 23 add another argument for this case. These parameters—owing to the insignificant sensitivity of peasants and families with dual income to price changes—could only be determined for blue- and white-collar workers. It seems that with blue-collar workers the lowest, and with white-collar workers the second lowest income bracket has the highest price elasticity: in both cases the computed values of elasticities decrease quickly in the higher income brackets. This leads to the conclusion that poorer people are more able and willing to comply with, or even gain additional benefits from changing prices.

The preliminary nature of the above analysis cannot be too strongly emphasized. While the results tell an apparently consistent and convincing story, much more empirical work needs to be done to provide a really firm foundation for the policy recommendations developed here.

POSSIBILITIES OF REDISTRIBUTION THROUGH DIRECT TAXATION: LIMITS TO REDISTRIBUTION BY OTHER MEANS

The bulk of this paper has been devoted to the problem of redistribution through the price system, and has led to very negative conclusions as to its rationality, at least under present Hungarian conditions. Now—for the sake of completeness—two additional problems will be considered: the advisability of introducing direct income taxation in Hungary and the limits to the possible other instruments of income redistribution.

The proposal to introduce direct income taxation was made by Farkas (1977) and endorsed by Szántó (1977). Strong criticisms were, however, advanced by Weitz and Molnár-Venyige (1977) and, more thoroughly, by Ferge (1978). The following paragraphs present a brief summary of this debate.

Farkas (1977) begins by demonstrating that differences in the ratio of earners to dependents are the main source of differences in family income; thus income per head depends much more on the number of children than on the social status or the level of earnings of the active members of the family. Low incomes/head may also arise if some members of a family are elderly persons with low pensions obtained according to the old pension system, or perhaps with no pensions at all. The solution proposed by Farkas is the introduction of a family income tax, based on the per capita income of the family. This tax would comprise family allowances and some other social benefits paid now. A guaranteed minimal per capita income would be set and income tax would be negative if the per capita income of the family did not reach the guaranteed level. This system would therefore raise all incomes at least to the subsistence (guaranteed minimum) level without decreasing earnings directly and thus, according to Farkas, without decreasing the material incentives to work, taxing—in a progressive way—only families where per capita income ensures a standard of living above or well above this minimum level.

The critics of this proposal point out first that the absolute guarantee of a minimal income, and very progressive taxation of the higher incomes would decrease incentives to work, already very feeble in Hungarian society. They emphasize that money illusion —working for nominal pay even if it is taxed away—cannot be as strong as supposed by the supporters of this proposal. Moreover, the really high incomes and the sources of conspicuous consumption (which undeniably exists) are not wages and salaries that could be taxed in such a way, but other kinds of income where tax evasion is possible. To add another counter-argument to the case against extending the income tax, the proposal involves the taxation of all wage and salary earners, without solving the problem of tax evasion so important with regard to the other sources of income. However, both the present pay-roll tax and the present form of enterprise taxation are much cheaper and simpler. The answer of the professional public to this proposal is therefore definitely negative.

The way out is seen by practically everybody in Hungary in terms of raising family allowances, and the lowest pensions. These measures would give most help to those families with lowest income per head, so that their redistributive efficiency would be high. At the same time, their application would not entail direct assessment of the conditions of individual families, which tend to be difficult and expensive and therefore should be avoided whenever possible. Apart from this, central control of wages can be used to correct some obvious disproportionalities. The limits to using these methods are set by the determination of the political leadership that the real incomes of all major sections of the population must constantly grow, and should never be allowed to fall, even for a transitional period. This very serious limitation makes any major redistribution impossible, particularly under the present conditions of the world economy. However, it has proved possible to raise the lowest pensions and to correct certain outstanding anomalies in the wages structure.

ACKNOWLEDGMENTS

The author is indebted to Mr András Fiala, Mrs Eszter Hamza, Mrs Sára Losonczy and Mr György Muszély for their help with the calculations.

REFERENCES

Barten A. P. (1969) Maximum likelihood estimation of a complete system of demand equations. *European Economic Rev.*, **1**, 7–73.

Csikós-Nagy B. (1971) *Magyar gazdaságpolitika* (Hungarian economic policy), Budapest, Kossuth.

Csikós-Nagy B. (1974) *Szocialista árelmélet és árpolitika* (Socialist price theory and price policy), Budapest, Kossuth.

Csikós-Nagy B. (1975) *A magyar árpolitika történeti áttekintése* (Historical review of Hungarian price policy), *Gazdaság.*

Ehrlich É. (1978) *Fejlettségi szintek, arányok, szerkezetek* (Levels, ratios, and patterns of development), Budapest, Planning Inst. Central Planning Board.

Ehrlich É. (1979) 'Comparison of development levels; inequalities in the physical structures of national economies', in *Proceedings of the Seventh International Economic History Congress.* London, Macmillan, (in press).

Erdei J. (1978) *Forgalmi adórendszerünk* (System of turnover taxes), Budapest, Ministry of Finances. (Mimeographed.)

Érsek T. (1976) Az árrendszer jövedelem- és fogyasztásszabályozó szerepérõl (The role of the price system in controlling incomes and consumption), *Pénzügyi Szemle*, **XX**, 263–275.

Farkas I. (1977) A családi jövedelmek kiegyenlitésére alkalmas eszközök felmérése—az egy före jutó személyi jövedelem adóztatása (Survey of suitable means of equalizing family incomes—taxation of personal income per head), *Pénzügyi Szemle*, **XXI**, 390–400.

Ferge Zs. (1978) Keresetek, jövedelmek, adózás (Earnings, incomes, taxation), *Valóság*, **XXI**, 27–41.

Frisch R. (1959) A complete scheme for computing all direct and cross demand elasticities in a model with many sectors, *Econometrica*, **27**, 177–196.

Frisch R. (1974) *Kvantitativ és dinamikus közgazdaságtan, Válogatott tanulmányok* (Quantitative and dynamic economics, Selected studies), Budapest, Közgazdasági.

Goldberger A. S. and Gamaletsos, T. (1970) A cross-country comparison of consumer expenditure patterns, *Eur. Econ. Rev.*, **3**, 357–400.

Hoch R. (1972) *Fogyasztás és ár* (Consumption and prices), Budapest, Közgazdasági.

Houthakker H. S. (1965) New evidence in demand elasticities, *Econometrica*, **43**, 277–288.

Hulyák K. and Losonczy S. (1978) Keresleti modellek számszerüsitése idõsoros adatok alapján (Estimation of consumption models from time-series data), *Szigma*, **XI**.

Jávorka E. (1967) *A fogyasztói árak és a dotációk.* (Consumer prices and subsidies), Budapest, Kossuth.

Juhász J. (1978) Fogyasztói árrendszerünk hatása a jövedelem- és fogyasztási struktúrára (The impact of the (Hungarian) consumer price system on the structure of income and consumption), *Pénzügyi Szemle*, **XXII**, 813–827.

Kravis I. B., Heston A. and Summers R. (1978) *International comparisons of real product and purchasing power.* UN Int. Comparison Project: Phase II, Pub. for the World Bank, Baltimore and London, Johns Hopkins Univ.

Ladányi J. (1975a) *A fogyasztói áreltéritések hatása az egyes régetek jövedelmére és fogyasztására* (The impact of turnover taxes and subsidies on the income and consumption of the various social groups), Budapest, Szövetkezeti Kutató Intézet.

Ladányi J. (1975b) Fogyasztói árak és szociálpolitika (Consumers' prices and social politics), *Valóság*, **XVIII**, 16–29.

Muszély Gy. (1978) Egy fogyasztási modell számszerüsítése keresztmetszeti adatok alapján (Estimation of a consumption model from cross-section data), *Szigma*, **XI**.

Pollak R. A. and Wales T. J. (1969) Estimation of the linear expenditure system, *Econometrica.*

Sandmo A. (1976) Optimal taxation. An introduction to the literature, *J. Pub. Econ.*

Stone R. (1954a) Linear expenditure systems and demand analysis: An application to the pattern of British demand. *Econ. J.*, **64**, 511–527.

Stone R. (1954b) *The measurement of consumer's expenditure and behaviour in the UK 1920–1938.* vol. 1. Cambridge, Cambridge Univ.

Stone R. (1978) A cambridge-i növekedési modell fejlödése (The development of the Cambridge Growth Project), *Statisztikai Szemle*, **56**, 236–249.

Szakolczai Gy., Hulyák K., Losonczy S. et al. (1979a) Klasszikus fogyasztás-elemzési modellek felhasználása a fogyasztói árpolitika megalapozására (Use of classical models of demand analysis to determine consumer price policy), *Közgazdasági Szemle*, **XXVI**.

Szakolczai Gy., Hulyák K., Losonczy S. et al. (1979b) Use of classical models of demand analysis to determine consumer price policy, *Acta Oeconomica*, **22**.

Szántó A. (1977) A személyes jövedelemadózásról az életszinvonal szabályozás részeként (On personal income taxation as a means of controlling the standard of living), *Pénzügyi Szemle*, **XXI**, 548–560.

Theil H. (1967) *Economics and information theory*, Amsterdam, North-Holland.

Theil H. (1970) *Közgazdaságtan és információelmélet.* (Economics and information theory), Budapest, Közgazdasági.

Vincze I. (1971) *Árak, adók, támogatások a gazdaságirányítás reformja után* (Prices, taxes and subsidies after the reform of economic management), Budapest, Közgazdasági.

Weitz T. and Molnár-Venyige J. (1977) Megjegyzések Farkas István: A családi jövedelmek kiegyenlitésére alkalmas eszközök felmérése—az egy fõre jutó személyi jövedelem adóztatása cimu cikkéhez. (A note on the paper written by I. Farkas on the survey of means suitable to equalize family incomes —taxation of personal income per head), *Pénzügyi Szemle*, **XXI**, 950–995.

Zellner A. (1962) *An efficient method of estimating seemingly unrelated regressions and tests for aggregation bias*, Vienna, IIASA.

Basic Statistical Sources

A családi jövedelmek szinvonala és szóródása 1972-ben. Az 1973. évi reprezentatív jövedelmi felmérés összefoglaló adatai (1975) (The level and dispersion of family incomes in 1972. Summary results of the 1973 representative income survey), Budapest, Central Statistical Office.

A fogyasztói árak alakulása a lakosság egyes rétegeinél. (The development of consumer prices for the various strata of the population) 1972, 1973 and 1974 (1973, 1974 and 1975), Budapest, Central Statistical Office.

Háztartásstatisztika (Household statistics) 1972, 1973, 1974 and 1976 (1974, 1975, 1976 and 1978). Budapest, Central Statistical Office.

A lakosság jövedelme és fogyasztása (Income and consumption of the population) 1960–1970 and 1960–1974 (1972 and 1976), Budapest, Central Statistical Office.

Statisztikai évkonyv (Statistical yearbook), 1960, 1961, 1962, 1963 and 1974 (1961, 1962, 1963, 1964 and 1975), Budapest, Central Statistical Office.

Tizenhat ország bruttó hazai termékének nemzetközi összenhasonlitása, 1973 (1978), (Comparison of sixteen countries' gross national product) 1973 (1978), Budapest, Central Statistical Office.

DISCUSSION

by **A. Deaton,** *University of Bristol*

So far in this symposium, and indeed in general, distribution and redistribution have been discussed in terms of income or of wealth. However, if consumers differ in their tastes, or if different consumers have different incomes, then changes in relative prices, even with unchanged endowments, will produce changes in the pattern of welfare between individuals. Such effects have attracted a good deal of attention in Western industrial economies in recent years as high rates of inflation have carried with them marked changes in relative prices so that the impact of the inflation has often been markedly different for poor and for rich households. The problem in Hungary takes a rather different form. Because of an elaborate system of 'subsidies' and 'taxes', consumer prices bear little relationship to the real transformation possibilities between goods in production. In consequence, these 'wedges' alter the distribution of real income or welfare compared with what it otherwise would be if consumers were to be faced with 'economic' prices. Indeed, some at least of the subsidies (e.g. on food) undoubtedly owe their existence to recognition of these distributional effects. However, most economists would argue that such distortions have deleterious consequences for economic efficiency, so that it is a vital question as to how important these price distortions are in guaranteeing distributional aims. Such is the object of Szakolczai's study.

The first step in the calculation is to evaluate the correct 'economic' prices. This cannot be done by the mere removal of consumer taxes and subsidies since at no stage in the production process are 'correct' prices used. Consequently, Szakolczai has gone back to the input–output table to calculate real production costs given import prices and existing wages. Of course, these latter may themselves be heavily distorted but nevertheless seem an appropriate basis for calculation in this context. The resulting Leontief prices can thus be compared with the actual consumer prices (table 9) and then used to 'reprice' the consumption bundles of different individuals so as to compute the distributional value of the distortions to various groups in society. Tables 11 to 19 summarize the results of this exercise and contain the major findings of the study. Notably, the system of distortions is only very mildly progressive, it favours white-collar workers and 'inactives' at the expense of other groups, and it favours the city at the expense of the countryside—the latter largely because the lack of provision of services in the countryside. The conclusion would thus seem to be that there are few distributional grounds for preserving an inefficient and uneconomic system of prices in Hungary.

One possible reservation provides the topic for the last part of the paper: if economic prices are established, might not the resulting substitution effects in consumption patterns have deleterious effects? Of course, much of the efficiency case for the changes rests precisely on allowing such substitution. Nevertheless, Szakolczai attempts to quantify the substitution responses by estimating a complete system of demand functions for Hungary. This is a brave exercise indeed. There are very few observations available and, for much of the period, price changes were very severely limited or prohibited. In consequence, strong *a priori* restrictions have to be imposed, as for example in the linear expenditure system, and these are likely to guarantee that very little substitution is found. Hence, I feel that the conclusions of this part of the study, that price elasticities are generally low, so that the reforms could be accomplished without dramatic changes in consumption patterns, are not really established. And if this were so, presumably the deadweight loss associated with the current distortions is correspondingly low and there is a good deal of (at least casual) evidence that this is not in fact the case.

In conclusion, it is worth returning to the starting point. Clearly, prices are important in determining the distribution of real income. But why are the 'limits to redistribution' in Hungary so crucially tied to prices alone? How are wages and incomes determined? And is it so much harder to alter them in Hungary than it is in the West? And if price reforms can be carried out so painlessly in theory, why has there been so much difficulty in those socialist countries where major price reforms have been instituted?

SUMMARY OF THE GENERAL DISCUSSION

In reply to Deaton, Szakolczai said that he felt the system of primary income determination in Hungary had many similarities to the picture painted in Layard's paper. Differentials were fairly sticky, and the principal aim of wages policy seemed to be simply the avoidance of cost inflation.

He felt that any price reform would have to be gradual, with compensating income variations. In fact price changes were more frequent and hence more moderate than Deaton had suggested. Although there was great difficulty with drastic price changes, as for example occurred recently in Poland, such cases were rare; the Hungarian population has seemed able to tolerate price changes which amounted to a creeping inflation of about 4% p.a., accompanied by compensating benefits. Education helped, and a general confidence that the government would keep its promises. He agreed with Deaton that the consistency conditions required by the linear expenditure system tended to reduce the apparent price effects. He was now trying to find less restrictive conditions.

Forward asked about the data sources for income distribution. Szakolczai explained that data came from stratified sample surveys. The income-receiving unit was considered to be the household, i.e. members of a family living in the same dwelling.

Hare queried the treatment of housing in Szakolczai's paper. He felt that the assumption that all consumers faced the same prices would not be correct here, since there were considerable differences between town and country, and between owned, public-sector rented and private-sector rented accommodation. Also he felt that supply problems and waiting lists might distort measurements of price elasticities. Szakolczai agreed that there were noticeable differences in the structure of consumption between house-owners and non-house-owners. However, supply problems were important in very few commodities, probably only housing and cars.

Hare also suggested that world prices might be a better reference point for calculating price distortions. Szakolczai agreed that this had much to recommend it in principle, but there were practical difficulties of matching international trade classifications with industrial classifications.

SOCIAL WELFARE UNDER SOCIALISM: A STUDY OF SOVIET ATTITUDES TOWARDS REDISTRIBUTION

A. McAuley

Department of Economics, University of Essex

INTRODUCTION

This paper contains an account of recent Soviet discussions on the distribution of income, on the proper limits and objectives for government policy and on the scope for redistribution in a socialist society. For perhaps a quarter of a century, under Stalin, these issues enjoyed a low priority in official thinking and were largely neglected by the academic community. Since the 1960s there has been a revival of interest—both among policy-makers and economists—new initiatives have been undertaken, a number of books and articles have been published and there have been several public discussions of related topics in the correspondence columns of the national press. The ideas put forward in these different contributions are of interest, not only for the insight they provide into developments in the USSR, but also because they cast some light on the more general question of equity in the distribution of income—the topic of this conference.

The (Soviet) Marxist framework for analyzing income distribution identifies three areas of state policy: (i) wage and salary determination, (ii) transfer payments and (iii) state expenditures on particular goods and services; recent Soviet speculations about objectives and constraints in each of these are discussed in the three middle sections of this paper. The final section contains an analysis of the implicit concept of equity that emerges from these discussions and also deals with the question of their relevance to government policy in this area. By way of background, I begin with a brief account of the main trends in income, inequality and government policy in the USSR since 1950.

WELFARE AND INEQUALITY IN THE USSR SINCE 1950

For all its shortcomings, the following extract from a recent popular pamphlet provides a reasonable summary of the changes in the Soviet standard of living that have taken place since the early 1930s (Kostin, 1976, p. 14).

> ... during the period when the foundations of socialism were being laid [1917–1936], the possibilities for growth in popular welfare were limited. Society was forced to devote the major part of its resources to the development of heavy industry, to strengthening defensive capacity, to creating the necessary economic potential of the country.
>
> Under conditions of developed socialism [1965 . . .], when the scale of production of gross social product and national income had attained significant proportions, it was possible to embark upon a

more rapid, consistent and all-embracing solution to the problem of raising popular welfare, 'it was possible to do what we had always wanted: to place the growth of the standard of living of the Soviet people in the centre of the practical policy of the party.'

(The quotation is from Brezhnev.)

In fact, the real wages of Soviet state employees were very little higher in 1952 than in 1928 and the evidence suggests that the living standards of the mass of peasantry were lower than they had been before the collectivization of agriculture (Gordon et al., 1974, p. 59; J. Chapman, 1963, p. 170). For this early period, figures are difficult to come by, but in 1958 the decile coefficient* of the distribution of state employees and their dependents by per capita income was 4·1 and, given the trends in earnings, it was probably higher in the early 'fifties (McAuley, 1977a, p. 228). Similarly, in 1958 some 20–25% of non-agricultural state employees and their dependents lived in families with per capita incomes below the official (and somewhat niggardly) poverty line; again, earnings data suggest that the proportion would have been greater in the early 'fifties (McAuley, 1977b, p. 9). Thus, at the time of Stalin's death, Soviet living standards were low; there was substantial inequality and extensive poverty, urban as well as rural. Further, the lack of importance attached to questions of distribution on the part of the authorities and the lack of interest in them evinced by academic economists meant that little was known about the sources of such social problems as poverty—there was even considerable ignorance about their extent. There was little understanding about the impact of the Soviet state upon the distribution of income, about its potential for redistribution, about the limits to such a policy (McAuley, 1978, ch. 8, 11).

Party propagandists now ascribe the changed priority accorded to consumer welfare to the Brezhnev government and it is true that living standards and redistribution received a certain prominence in the resolutions of the XXIV Party Congress and in the ninth five-year plan (1971–75). But the record shows that this increased preoccupation with questions of welfare and equality occurred somewhat earlier—in 1955–56 if not immediately after the death of Stalin (McAuley, 1978, ch. 1; Rzhanitsyna, 1971, p. 12).

At all events, between 1950 and 1975 the real wages of state employees in the USSR more than doubled; *kolkhoznik* living standards showed even greater gains†. There was also a marked reduction in inequality—at least as measured by the decile coefficient of per capita incomes (McAuley, 1978, ch. 2, 9–10). The period was also characterized by a sevenfold increase in nominal expenditures on social consumption—transfer payments, subsidies and expenditures on services like health and education. (This increase refers to expenditures on Soviet official definitions. Both Soviet and western economists believe that these leave something to be desired; nevertheless, all would agree that there has been a significant expansion in the scale of state provision.) This increase in state expenditures reflects the fact that a start has been made on solving certain pressing social problems—poverty, the plight of the elderly, the position of children in deprived families and so on. But, as I have suggested elsewhere, the

* The decile coefficient, used here as a crude measure of inequality, is defined as the ratio of the first to ninth deciles of the relevant distribution. For a more extended discussion of its properties and of various methodological and empirical problems associated with the measurement of inequality in the USSR *see* (McAuley, 1978, ch. 1).

† Members of collective farms, *kolkhozniki*, are not considered employees of the state by Soviet economists and statisticians. Consequently, their money receipts are not classified as wages (nor are they reported as such) and little attempt is made to integrate official data on their living standards with statistics relating to the rest of the population. This is why state employees and *kolkhozniki* are mentioned separately in the text. For an extended discussion of the implications of this distinction as reflected in Soviet policy (*see* McAuley, 1978, ch. 2).

effectiveness of policies in this area has been reduced by ignorance about the underlying social and economic processes and, possibly, by disagreements about the desirability of specific policies (McAuley, 1977b).

It would be wrong to conclude that the greater importance attached to personal welfare and the increased preoccupation with the state's role in determining the distribution of income are solely the result of a spontaneous change in party attitudes after the death of Stalin (or even the forced removal of Khrushchev). In part it has been forced upon the Soviet leadership by demographic evolution and by wider changes in Soviet society (Lantsev, 1976, p. 57, 151).

Whatever the causes, however, the increased emphasis on welfare and equality as official objectives, the enormous increase in state expenditures in this area and the general increase in economic sophistication in the USSR have resulted in pressure for clarity and consistency in the formulation of policy and in the demand for a better understanding of the economic and social processes involved. There has been an upsurge of interest in these matters by academic economists, by sociologists and by those who work in government research institutes. A number of articles and monographs dealing with distribution and the role of the state have been published; it is to the analysis of the main ideas in this literature that the remainder of this paper is devoted.

THE DISTRIBUTION OF EARNINGS UNDER SOCIALISM

Recent Soviet discussions of inequality and redistribution have been formulated within a Marxist analytical framework; because this may not be familiar and because the Soviet version may contain its own peculiar glosses, it is desirable to set this out briefly. Marx's own views on the distribution of income in a socialist society are set out clearly and succinctly in the *Critique of the Gotha Program*. (References given here are to the International Publishers ed., New York 1967). In it, Marx distinguishes between two phases of post-revolutionary society; these are now commonly called socialism and communism although Marx himself refers to them as the lower and higher phases of communism, a source of some confusion. The distinction between these two stages is important but it is often neglected in popular comment and criticism in the west.

Under communism, labour productivity is sufficiently great for there to be an abundance of material goods; also, labour itself confers utility or, in Marx's own words '...labour, from a mere means of life, has become the prime necessity of life.' (p. 10) At this stage, the problem of income distribution will disappear, it will be possible for '...society to inscribe upon its banners: from each according to his ability, to each according to his needs.' (p. 10) Socialism, on the other hand, is characterized by relatively low labour productivity; material goods are still scarce so that some form of rationing is required. Also, individuals still work to live rather than live to work—incentives and coercion are still needed to elicit the necessary supply of labour. At this stage '...the right of producers should be proportional to the labour they supply... this equal right is an unequal right for unequal labour.' (p. 9) Soviet economists refer to this as the socialist principle of distribution: from each according to his ability, to each according to his labour. And, since the USSR is still only a *socialist* society, only this second principle applies: thus, there should clearly be earnings differentials; the issue is how large should they be and what role should the state play in modifying them.

In the *Critique*...Marx also suggested that a future socialist society would set up, *inter alia*, a centrally-administered fund for the support of those unable to work and another to finance communal satisfaction of needs, such as schools, health services etc. (p. 7). Soviet economists refer to these as Social Consumption Funds and discussions of the principles governing their use reveal much about Soviet attitudes to inequality and redistribution.

This framework of analysis is accepted by all Soviet economists; it identifies three areas of state policy that bear upon the question of distribution: wage and salary determination, transfer payments and the provision of specific goods and services by the state, either free of charge or at subsidized prices. Soviet ideas about the principles that should determine government policy in each of them are examined here; a more extensive account of actual measures may be found in my book (McAuley, 1978, ch. 8–11)‡.

Soviet economists, then, start from the proposition that, under socialism as under capitalism, individuals are unequal—they are unequal in their capacity for work, in their skills and abilities, in their needs, tastes and preferences; they should be unequal in their incomes. The sole gain from the revolution (but, they would argue, it is a crucial one) is that the elimination of private ownership of the means of production and hence of exploitation, imposes upon all an equal obligation to work, to be judged by their work (Rakitskii, 1966, p. 171). Certainly such a state is to be preferred to capitalism. But no particular ethical claims are made for the socialist principle of distribution; rather, it is forced upon society by the 'level of productive forces', and by individual attitudes to work (Rabkina and Rimashevskaya, 1972, p. 13). And, it is universally asserted that any attempt to eliminate earnings differentials or even to reduce them prematurely would undermine the main objective of socialist society—the building of communism (Kulikov, 1972, pp. 58–59).

In the context of this view of socialism, what determines the extent of earnings differentials and what is the role of the state? According to the labour theory of value, all work, whatever its concrete form, whatever the skills involved, the conditions in which it is undertaken and so on, can be 'reduced' to a greater or smaller amount of simple labour. It is this reducibility that permits labour to act as a rationing device under socialism. But it also implies that (Rabkina and Rimashevskaya, 1972, pp. 18–19):

> the sources of differentiation are to be found in the quantitative and qualitative inhomogeneity of labour... [that] the differentiation of earnings in its broadest sense is the result of the existing relationships between the quantity and quality of labour at the disposal of a socialist society. Its extent is at each moment objectively determined.

The role of the state, of government wages policy, is to specify wage relativities that will encourage workers to acquire relevant skills, that will encourage those with special abilities or training to exercise them (Kuprienko, 1976, p. 44). If the authorities select the 'right' set of differentials, the growth of productivity and the smooth operation of the economy is facilitated; if they choose a wrong set, bottlenecks in the supply of particular types of labour will occur, turnover will be high and wages policy will be contravened, leading to the possibility of inflation or other undesirable phenomena (ibid., p. 17; *see also* Kulikov, 1972, p. 51). Much recent empirical work by Soviet

‡ The Marxist framework provides little scope for using personal taxation as an instrument of redistribution. There is little discussion of taxation from this point of view among Soviet economists and, indeed, little evidence to suggest that income tax in the USSR performs this role; tax rates are low and tax schedules are virtually proportional. Questions of taxation and tax policy will not be pursued here (*but see* McAuley, 1978, ch. 11 *for some further analysis*).

labour economists is devoted to demonstrating that relativities are wrong in one or other respect and elucidating the consequences. However, in the absence of formal specification of the relationships implied and some more-or-less rigorous estimation of the parameters involved, much of this reduces to *obiter dicta* and ad hoc assertions by so-called experts that this or that wage should be higher or is too high (*see for example*, Kuprienko, 1976, pp. 63, 65–66, 67–68).

At the same time, the socialist principle of distribution is taken to imply that Soviet wage and salary structures should be characterized by 'equal pay for equal work'—a principle of equity that appeals far beyond the specifically Marxist framework of analysis. However, the doctrine of the reducibility of labour gives this principle a specific interpretation in the USSR. Since all jobs, all work, can be reduced to more or less 'simple labour' it implies more than that all doing the same job should receive the same pay; it means that all jobs containing the same amount of labour should pay the same rates. This is seen to justify, if not to necessitate the widespread use of job-evaluation procedures (not only within particular plants or industries but on an economy-wide scale) and the introduction of centralized, bureaucratic wage-determination procedures (McAuley, 1978, ch. 8; Sukharevskii, 1974, p. 216 ff).

This emphasis on the objective determinants of earnings differentials, on the limited scope for state intervention and on the dangers associated with ignorant or short-sighted actions should be seen in large part, I think, as a reaction to the incompetence of the Stalinist period. It constitutes an affirmation of the need for information, for calculation, for theoretical understanding. At the same time, it implies a particular view of an appropriate distribution of income and attempts to relate it to the wider objectives of government policy.

First, a majority of Soviet economists are opposed to formal equality in wage structures, to too great an emphasis on the equalization of consumption opportunities: '...all that bears the stamp of social security, that is not connected with production, should be separated from wages.' (Rabkina and Rimashevskaya, 1972, p. 26). Or, again, 'in determining the wage rates of workers with various skills, office staff, technical and higher administrative personnel all thought of egalitarianism, *uravnitelnost*, should be rejected.' (Kapustin, 1974, p. 259)§ To quote one more judgement (Kulikov, 1972, pp. 58–59):

> Any form of payment for labour is in no case compatible with egalitarianism, *uravnilovka*. All such tendencies are harmful, in conflict with the rapid development of productive forces and the creation of conditions necessary for the continuing growth in workers' welfare. Egalitarianism undermines material incentives and, in the last analysis, causes irreparable harm to the building of communism.

This attitude has led some economists to suggest that the degree of equality attained after the 1968 increase in the minimum wage was excessive—although they are quick to point out that the position would be rectified during the 1971–75 wage-round (Sukharevskii, 1974, p. 226; Kapustin, 1974, p. 266. *For empirical details, see* McAuley, 1978, chaps. 9–10).

Second, most Soviet economists appear to advocate what one might call a meritocratic structure of wages (Maier, 1968, p. 19):

> Labour has still not become a necessity of life for all members of society. It is possible to guarantee the participation of the majority in work only if the possibility of receiving a share of society's output is made conditional upon undertaking socially useful labour and if the size of this share depends upon the importance, *vesomostyu*, of the contribution made.

§ This statement was originally made by Lenin in 1921 and it has been cited more than once to add authority to this point of view (*see, for example*, Sukharevskii, 1974, p. 204). For a different quotation from Lenin expressing a similar attitude, *see* Kulikov (1972, p. 50).

Or again (Kulikov, 1972, pp. 53–54),

> Under socialism, greater rewards are given to those workers who create more value, whose contribution to the fulfilment of plans and the development of production is larger. This is achieved by paying higher wages to skilled workers, to those requiring longer training. Work undertaken in dangerous or harmful conditions is also better paid. If this were not so, there would be no incentive to acquire education, to raise skills, to undertake more complex and responsible work.

Again, the authority of Lenin is invoked in support of the assertion that such work does not constitute its own reward (Kulikov, 1972, p. 48).

Finally, it is argued that in the short term at least, there should be little further reduction in differentials—if anything they should be increased (Rzhanitsyna, 1971, pp. 13–14). It is claimed that existing levels of wages, in particular of the minimum wage, are sufficiently high to eliminate the category of low-paid workers (Rzhanitsyna, 1971, p. 13). Future reductions in earnings inequality should come 'not so much from direct increases in the minimum wage as from reductions and, in time, the complete elimination of unskilled and low-skilled work.' (Kuprienko, 1976, p. 14; *see also* Kunelskii, 1971, pp. 7–8).

The opinions outlined in the preceding paragraphs represent what one might call the orthodox Soviet view of the distribution of earnings in a socialist society. On the one hand, it reveals a (perhaps naive) belief in the efficacy of wage differentials to act as an allocation device. It is taken as self-evident that workers will select preferentially those occupations and industries in which wages are high; that the acquisition of desirable skills can be encouraged by wage differentiation; that in the absence of such pecuniary signals developmental priorities are likely to be obscured. But there is little empirical work to substantiate this belief. On the other hand, in the analyses of many Soviet economists there is something more, a sense that wage differentials are equitable; that those, whose contribution to the goals of the state is greater, deserve and are morally entitled to enjoy greater rewards. There is some doubt, however, about how widely this orthodox view is held. Although neither the workers themselves nor dissenting economists have expressed themselves in print, their views have left traces in the words of official spokesmen (Kostin, 1976, pp. 49–50):

> There exists an opinion about the necessity of further reductions in differences in the pay of workers, specialists, managerial and scientific staff, about imposing some maximum wage, about not providing higher salaries for those with academic qualifications or honours, *zvaniya*, and so on. However, at the present time such proposals are inappropriate. In the first place, the differences between the earnings of a skilled worker, a specialist and a scientist are not all that great. And second, wages and salaries in our country are based on the quality and quantity of labour; the quality of labour supplied by a specialist is, on average, greater than that by a worker, that by a member of the scientific staff greater than that by a specialist. The amount of time necessary for training is different also.

In the early post-revolutionary years there was a party ordinance laying down that party members should not earn more than the wage of a skilled worker (the so-called *partmaksimum*.)|| The reference to the introduction of a maximum salary for administrative and managerial personnel might be taken to indicate that some Soviet citizens have long memories.

On the other hand, too much should not be made of this apparent egalitarian strand in popular Soviet opinion. Even a Soviet Marxist as critical of government policy as Roy Medvedev suggests that disparities of the order of 7·5–10 : 1 are quite acceptable (Medvedev, 1975, p. 226):

|| Matthews, (1978, pp. 67–68) provides a detailed discussion of the regulations governing the earnings of higher party officials in the early 1920s. This shows that the position was rather more complicated than indicated in the text. But the simple view given here corresponds more closely to the ordinary Soviet citizen's recollection of the *partmaksimum*, insofar as he has one.

> When ordinary workers receive 200 rubles [a month], those more highly skilled should be paid 400–600 rubles. But top specialists and administrators should never be allowed to get more than 1,500–2,000 rubles a month, no matter how many posts they hold.

This would seem to imply that Soviet socialism has more in common with the meritocratic views of a social democrat like Crosland than the radical egalitarianism of a thinker like Tawney.

At the same time, among those most interested in social problems, those concerned with the position of the elderly or of deprived families, there is a note of resigned bitterness that I am sure will strike a chord among their British counterparts (Rzhanitsyna, 1973, p. 83):

> One often still encounters the opinion that there exists some sort of watershed between policies in the area of social consumption funds and policies to do with wages. Wage-policy measures are seen as a powerful engine of production while those to do with social consumption are thought of as akin to an inevitable tax on production, diverting resources from the needs of economic development.

Just how Soviet economists view the relationship between earnings and social welfare programmes and what they take to be the appropriate objectives of government policy in this area will be described in the next section.

SOCIAL WELFARE EXPENDITURES UNDER SOCIALISM

The Marxist analytical framework within which Soviet discussions of income distribution take place identifies two sets of instruments that a socialist government might use in the interests of redistribution, given the structure of earnings. These are associated with the two social consumption funds mentioned in the *Critique*. Recent Soviet ideas about the principles governing the provision of goods and services are discussed in this section; transfer payments are dealt with in the next section

The idea that the state or government should provide certain goods and services either free of charge or at subsidized prices has a long history in socialist thought; it also has the authority of Marx himself although the brief remarks in the *Critique of the Gotha Program* provide little guidance about which goods and services should be allocated in this way, how the consumption of these by various individuals should be regulated and how this activity can be reconciled with the differentiation implied by 'distribution according to labour.' It is upon these issues that much recent Soviet discussion has focussed and it is upon them that I shall concentrate here.

In the 1940s and 1950s, little thought was devoted to any of these questions; it was common for economists to advance the rather facile claim that expenditures from the state's social consumption funds were governed by the communist distribution principle and, indeed, these claims can still be found today (Maier, 1977, p. 222). As a result, it was claimed, such goods and services were made available according to need, thus tending to reduce the degree of inequality generated by the distribution of earnings; further, it was suggested, with continued economic development, as society gradually approached the phase of communism, the share of such programmes in total consumption would increase and the distribution of income would become more equal (*Politicheskaya*, 1959, p. 643). But there was little rigour in these discussions, little attempt to show why specific goods and services should be allocated in this way, little attempt to derive constraints on government action or prescriptions for future policy. Economists usually mentioned education and health as categories for 'free' allocation, perhaps because these were mentioned by Marx or perhaps because they were services that the state allocated through non-price mechanisms at the time. But no serious attempt was made to justify their inclusion. Nor was there any theoretical analysis of the way that the area of 'free distribution' would expand with the approach to communism. The Party Programme of 1961 simply listed a number of goods and services (urban transport, bread etc.) whose provision would become free in the next twenty years or so, but no reasons were given for their selection.

In the last twenty years these views have been extensively criticized by a number of Soviet economists on both empirical and theoretical grounds. First, as a matter of fact, doubts were raised about the extent to which existing programmes reduced inequality. On the basis of a number of studies, conducted for the most part in the period 1956–64, it was shown that cash transfers tended to increase with the living standard of the recipient household and access to free services offset this only partially. It has also been suggested that this situation remained basically unchanged at least until the middle 'seventies (Mamontova, 1973, p. 80; Mamontova, 1975, p. 298). Since it is not my intention to examine the actual policies pursued by the Soviet government in this paper no more will be said about this empirical literature here (*but see* McAuley, 1978, ch. 11 *for more details*).

Second, it is suggested that the claim that distribution of 'free services' is according to need implies that individual demands for these items are completely satisfied. But, it is pointed out, under socialism resources are limited and access to goods and services must be rationed; this applies as much to social as to individual consumption (Khabibi, 1975, p. 274). Thus the concept of need implicit in the traditional view is inadequate. It should be replaced by a formulation that emphasizes the criteria which determine access. Khabibi himself favours participation in the labour force, 'the socialist character of social consumption funds is demonstrated by the fact that...participation in social labour—past, present or future—is a condition for participation in the distribution of social consumption funds...' (Khabibi, 1975, p. 273). And he criticizes those who advocate that the state should restrict itself to the provision of minimum consumption for all—leaving the balance of demand to be satisfied through the market (Khabibi, 1975, p. 272). His opinion is widely shared.

A more detailed rationale for the existence of social consumption funds under socialism (and one that contains more explicit policy constraints) has been put forward by Lantsev (1974, p. 129):

> ... the necessity for a social security system is derived from two groups of causes. First of all there is loss of earnings as a result of temporary or permanent loss of working capacity through sickness, old age or injury, *invalidnost*. Consequently the first task of a social security system is to provide some measure of compensation for loss of earnings in the form of a pension or allowance.
>
> The second group of causes is connected with disease, family circumstances, *mnogodetnost*, [i.e. having many children] or other factors which impose an additional burden on the worker and his family and do not depend on either the level of earnings or on whether such groups are employed at all. For this reason forms of social security connected with this group of causes, like free medical care or child allowances, have in our country from its very beginning been made available to the population as a whole. Their objective has been, by means of free services, allowances and subsidies to prevent the imposition of such additional expenses on the family or to reduce their burden, *tyazhest*.

Thus, the possibility of interruptions in earnings gives rise to the development of income-maintenance schemes, while the possibility that certain households will be called upon to meet substantial and perhaps unanticipated demands upon their resources is used to justify the development of a network of free or subsidized services. Although the point is not made explicitly, the justification for both components is in terms of risk-spreading; it also suggests a certain lack of faith in the effectiveness of decentralized mechanisms or personal provision. The concept of need implicit in this argument is similar to that found in the social welfare programmes of many other countries.

The state undertakes to indemnify the household against certain extraordinary expenses because the incidence of these is fortuitous, does not depend upon individual choice. In this way, it is suggested, the distribution of real consumption will be closer to the distribution of earnings; the existence of such social welfare programmes reinforces the socialist distribution principle. This conception, it seems to me, fails to recognize the satisfaction that parents derive from the education of their children (or the benefits that they derive from their own training), it presupposes that there is a clear distinction between sickness and health and, arguably, underestimates the extent to which fertility is under the conscious control of the family. Thus, it does not provide as clear guidelines for policy as Lantsev perhaps believes. But I shall not pursue these issues here. Rather, I shall simply point out that it does provide answers to the questions raised at the beginning of this section; it does provide an operational definition of need, it indicates the conditions under which individuals are entitled to assistance. What is lacking, however, is any justification for the use of non-market mechanisms in the allocation of particular services (instead of an expanded system of child allowances, for instance). This issue is taken up by Rakitskii, perhaps the most perceptive Soviet economist to write on these questions recently.

Rakitskii attempts to demonstrate that the nature of socialist society necessitates the introduction by the state of a range of specific, *tselevye*, programmes designed to modify patterns of consumption—and hence, the distribution of income. He starts from the proposition that individuals are unequal in their skills and capacity for work; therefore, as a result of the socialist distribution principle they will receive unequal earnings. This has two consequences (Rakitskii, 1966, pp. 18–19):

> If distribution according to labour was the *sole* form of distribution under socialism, the whole personal consumption fund would be distributed according to the quantity and quality of labour. In such circumstances, producers with more ability would be awarded larger quantities of consumer goods and would always enjoy much more favourable conditions for the reproduction of their labour power than those whose abilities were less developed. In other words, those capable of using more productive and more complex means of production, those capable of undertaking scientific research or management, that is, fulfilling more complex functions would always enjoy significant advantages in the development of their capacities and would develop them more rapidly than workers, *trudyashchiesya*, more backward than themselves in the development of their abilities for reasons of a socio-economic kind. In such circumstances, socio-economic differences in productive skills, *sposobnosti k trudu*, would not diminish but, on the contrary, would become more pronounced.

This situation is undesirable, not only because the achievement of communism requires the greatest possible increase in labour productivity but also because socialism presupposes the gradual elimination of socio-economic differentiation. Thus, the wider objectives of socialism require that the socialist distribution principle be supplemented.

But, Rakitskii claims, the above argument does not in itself imply that the state should provide specific goods and services through non-market means. This follows from the second conclusion drawn from the assumption of individual inequality under socialism (Rakitskii, 1966, p. 29):

> This differentiation, *neodnorodnost*, involves not only differences in the volume of needs but also structural differences, that is different relationships between the elements that make up the sum total of the needs of different members of society.

Here Rakitskii, like most Soviet economists, uses needs, *potrebnosti*, in a way that is similar to the western concept of tastes or preferences. He suggests that individual preferences (and hence the satisfaction derived from a particular level and structure of consumption) are determined by individual experience and that, in general, is mediated by income. As a result (p. 121):

if the whole of the social consumption fund were distributed among members of society in cash and if consumption goods and services satisfying intellectual and social needs were paid for, the money at present allocated from social consumption funds for, let us say, the education of children or for physical culture and so on might be partially or wholly spent by consumers on the satisfaction of needs that they regarded as more important, on goods like clothing, footwear, food etc.

Thus it is recognized that planners' preferences and those of individuals may not coincide. Indeed, it is suggested that individuals will tend to attach a lower weight than do the authorities to the consumption of such services as education and health; it is also claimed that the divergence is likely to be most marked among those with lowest incomes (Maier and Rakitskii, 1976, pp. 192–93). It is for this reason that a socialist society should 'actively intervene in the process of exchange, in the process of forming the structure of consumption funds.' (Rakitskii, 1966, p. 119) That is, the state should provide specific goods and services either free of charge or at subsidized prices¶ (*see also* Maier and Rakitskii, 1976, p. 197).

Although initially put forward by Rakitskii in the mid 'sixties, the ideas developed in the preceding paragraph have been repeated by a number of other Soviet economists; they now enjoy a measure of general acceptance (*see, for example* Basov, 1967 *or* Kulikov, 1972). These ideas also show considerable similarity to Musgrave's concept of merit wants and the government's obligation to supply merit goods (Musgrave, 1959, ch. 1). In some ways they are superior; for instance, Rakitskii is more explicit in his ascription of priority to the preferences of the state and, I think, more convincing in his explanation of why individual tastes might be found wanting. (But I have long felt the assumption of exogenous preferences to be unsatisfactory (*see* McAuley, 1967, p. 354)). Finally, it should be noted that Rakitskii is aware of some of the social and political implications of his theory.

These ideas about the nature and function of social consumption expenditures in a socialist society have specific implications for the development of Soviet government policy, implying a definite limit to redistribution. They conflict in a number of ways with the rather superficial views advanced in the 'fifties. First, the primary objective of these programmes is to modify individual consumption and preferences in the interests of economic development; this is achieved through the provision of specific goods and services. There is no reason to suppose that the array of services provided will increase with time or with increasing affluence; there is no reason to suppose, therefore, that the share of such expenditures in total consumption will increase indefinitely, that gradually the state will extend non-market distribution to a widening range of goods, or that such programmes constitute the beginnings of a 'communist distribution'. In neither the short term nor the long term are such expenditures intended to bring about mechanical reductions in the inequality generated by the 'socialist principle' (Rakitskii, 1966, p. 43). With this Lantsev would agree, although for somewhat different reasons. Hence the new view, if one can call it that, conflicts with the principles implicit in the 1961 Party Programme.

Of course Rakitskii and his adherents would not deny that the distribution of real incomes (or real consumption), when allowance is made for the value of state expenditure on health and education, is likely to be more equal than when these are excluded. Indeed, on more than one occasion they have pointed out this reduction in inequality (Rakitskii, 1966, p. 43; Maier and Rakitskii, 1976, pp. 192–93). Their point is, rather, that such programmes should be designed to supplement and not

¶ In principle, state subsidization of both housing and pre-school child care in the USSR are income-related; but failure to adjust the relevant schedules in line with increases in earnings means that the overwhelming majority of families now pay the top rates for both services. (For more details, *see* McAuley, 1978, ch. 11).

supplant distribution according to labour. The purpose of such a distribution policy should be 'to ensure that all individuals enjoy a real possibility of acquiring the highest qualifications and, as a result, can conceivably occupy any position in production or in society' (Maier and Rakitskii, 1976, p. 192). It is this provision of equal educational (and, to a lesser extent, medical) opportunity that, through its effects on the distribution of skills will in the long run lead to reductions in the inequality of earnings and income (Mamontova, 1975, p. 297).

But equality of educational opportunity has a wider role to play. It is invoked by Maier and Rakitskii (p. 192) as the mechanism that counters tendencies towards elitism that are still to be found under socialism:

> The tendency towards exclusivity, *zamknutost*, among social groups that arises as a result of the social significance still ascribed to the division of labour and the higher earnings of the more highly skilled is to a large extent neutralized by the intervention, *vmeshatelstvo*, of a socialist government in the process of forming the structure of consumption.
>
> The formation of a group of highly skilled cadres (including specialists) proceeds under socialism as a deeply democratic process, open to all.

I do not believe that elitism can be overcome as easily as this. I also feel that Rakitskii and Maier are over-sanguine about the possibilities for social mobility through educational opportunity in the USSR, perhaps because they attach too much importance to the experience of the 'thirties and 'forties. But it is refreshing to see these problems acknowledged.

The ideas described in this section do not suggest that a socialist government (at least as Soviet economists understand that term) should embark upon any radical egalitarian programme. On the contrary, they emphasize the importance of differentials, the primacy of the 'socialist principle' of distribution. Market mechanisms should be supplemented only to ensure 'equality of opportunity' according to Rakitskii or possibly (according to Lantsev) as a form of insurance. Further, the range of programmes needed to achieve this end is narrowly conceived; it is limited to education (including vocational training) health and possibly housing. There is little awareness of the possibility that other factors might affect an individual's chances of success, and little awareness of cultural deprivation or the cycle of poverty. The underdeveloped state of empirical sociology in the USSR is apparent. As a result, recent Soviet work displays an almost naive belief in the rationality of social processes.

The emphasis on equality of opportunity combined with payment according to merit raises another problem: that of alienation among those who do not succeed. But there is little to suggest that Soviet economists are aware of these issues and I shall not discuss them further here.

TRANSFER PAYMENTS UNDER SOCIALISM

Although Marx sanctioned the use of transfer payments in a socialist state, his discussion of them was brief—at least in the *Critique of the Gotha Program*. He does little more than suggest that they should provide the same range of benefits as the poor relief of his day. Lenin was more explicit: he advocated an all-risks, no-fault, non-contributory state insurance scheme covering all employees and providing benefits at a level equal to lost earnings (Lenin, 1961, vol. 21, p. 146). But his discussion too leaves a number of questions unsettled. In any case his scheme proved too generous and social security in the USSR has developed on somewhat different lines.

Some of the earliest legislation adopted by the Soviet government was concerned with the establishment of a social security system, but the resources available for such purposes in the 1920s were meagre. Social security continued to receive low priority after the inception of central planning and, in the early 1950s, the old and the incapacitated were among the worst off in Soviet society. Since the death of Stalin however, there have been significant increases in both total expenditure and average benefit levels. This growth in expenditure has been accompanied—and, to some extent, occasioned—by legislative change. The present system dates from 1956 for state employees and from 1965 for collective farmers although both rules of entitlement and benefit levels have been changed since these laws were passed. The 1956 law recodified a number of industry-based schemes that had grown up in the preceding thirty years and reintroduced the principle of unified coverage for all state employees. The 1965 law for the first time extended state support to *kolkhozniki* in sickness or old age; previously the bulk of the rural population in the USSR had been forced to rely upon their own resources, those of their families or some, usually limited, assistance from individual *kolkhozy*.

In this section I shall concentrate upon the issues raised by *old-age pensions* but it is important to realize that the Soviet social security system also provides invalidity and survivor pensions, sickness benefits and a number of specific grants (e.g. for burials). In addition, the state pays child allowances, student stipends, a 'family income supplement' and a niggardly system of public assistance for those without relatives obliged by law to support them. Finally, published statistics on transfers also include holiday pay. (*For a discussion of these programmes see* Madison, 1972 *or* McAuley, 1978, ch. 11).

The question of pension provision has not received much attention from Soviet economic theorists and there is no analysis of the issue like Rakitskii's discussion of educational expenditures. But pensions are the largest single category of transfer in the USSR and the changing demographic structure of the country has given a certain prominence to the problem of fair treatment for the old. This topic has been extensively discussed by lawyers and applied economists. For the most part, they have focussed on the following issues: who should be entitled to support and in what circumstances? What should be the relationship between the pension and previous earnings—if any? How should pensions be adjusted to take account of subsequent changes in the cost or standard of living? Answers to these questions clearly affect the equity of any particular scheme and its impact upon the distribution of income; it is around them that the discussion in this paper is organized.

Pension Entitlement

In the USSR, the formal linking of benefits to prior contributions is ruled out on theoretical grounds. In Marxist economic theory the idea that current savings can be invested to yield a claim on income in the future is rejected; hence contributory pension schemes are impossible and actuarial calculations are irrelevant. The formulation in the *Critique of the Gotha Program* makes it quite clear: pensions are financed through a levy on the income generated by the currently employed. The existence of a social security system under socialism reflects the voluntary assumption by society (and thus by present workers) of an obligation to care for the old, the sick, all those not able to support themselves. The incapacitated have and can have no right to a pension, no claim to a share of society's output; they must rely upon the 'charity' of the currently employed.

Since prior contributions cannot be used, some other criterion of entitlement is necessary. It is claimed that immediately after the revolution this was *need*, previous employment record being used only to exclude socially alien groups (Acharkan, 1974,

p. 122). However, in keeping with more general attitudes, from the 1930s, if not before, '...the pension increasingly acquired the character of assistance in return for labour in the past'. It was generally agreed that '...the principle of each according to his labour should operate in the field of social security as well' (Acharkan, 1974, p. 122). Thus, although the right to a pension is enshrined in the 1936 Constitution (Acharkan, 1967, p. 44):

> ... analysis of the legislation on social security leads to the conclusion that this right arises in the main out of the fulfilment by citizens of two constitutional obligations: the obligation to work and the obligation to defend one's country.

(*See also* Andreev, 1974, pp. 53–54). In practice, the conditional nature of pension rights are maintained by laying down a minimum number of years previous employment, *stazh*, necessary for the receipt of an old-age pension and specifying a sliding scale of minima (depending on age) for entitlement to invalidity or survivor benefits. Those who fail to satisfy these criteria either receive partial pensions at much lower rates or receive nothing at all.

There is, I think, widespread acceptance of this principle in the USSR, both among specialists and among the population at large. Criticism has centred on the plight of certain (deserving) categories deprived of support through a rigid interpretation of the regulations or because of the existence of two independent schemes. The most frequently quoted anomalies are ex-*kolkhozniki* who, in spite of substantial work records have insufficient *stazh* to qualify under either system (*see, for example* Acharkan, 1974, p. 124) and women, many of whom 'on reaching the age that entitles them to a pension do not possess the necessary twenty-year *stazh* since, in fulfilling their family obligations and bringing up children, they have interrupted their work in production'. (Lantsev, 1976, p. 122) I estimate that, in 1970, some 20–25% of those of pensionable age were not in receipt of a pension as a result of these lacunae (McAuley, 1978, ch. 11).

Although there is general acceptance of the idea that prior employment should be a necessary condition for pension support, there is less agreement about whether it should also be sufficient. Most specialists would argue (Acharkan, 1971, p. 122):

> If pensions were awarded solely on the basis of work, they would not be pensions. The basis of pension support is incapacity in conjunction with employment, with useful activity in the past. The support of the able-bodied is not the objective of the pension system.

On the other hand, among the population at large (and possibly among government officials and policy-makers) there are other views. Lantsev (1976, p. 121), is critical of:

> ... the widespread opinion that the old-age pension constitutes a specific reward, an acknowledgement of services to society, a right to well-earned rest acquired after the attainment of a certain age.

Both Lantsev and Acharkan are here responding to suggestions in the press that pensions should be payable to all with the necessary *stazh*, irrespective of whether they continue to work or not; and both find the idea objectionable.

Yet this has been a feature of Soviet pension schemes for most of the time since the early 1930s. It was true of most of the industrial schemes in operation before 1956 and amendments to the pension law of that year have made it possible since 1964 for more and more state employees to retain their pensions while in full-time employment. The authorities have adopted this policy in an attempt to persuade more of those of pensionable age to stay at work in the face of a worsening labour-supply situation. It is not surprising that people have come to regard it as normal. But it has been criticized as costly and ineffective in the short run (Lantsev, 1976, pp. 121, 129–131,

139) and also because it diverts resources from other, more deserving groups (Acharkan, 1971, p. 122).

A number of alternative policies have been proposed. These range from raising the retirement age, either generally or for selected occupational groups, to the abolition of old-age pensions and their replacement by assistance for those whose loss of working capacity has been attested by a panel of experts (Acharkan, 1973, p. 147, 148–149; Lantsev, 1974, p. 136; Kuprienko, 1976, p. 39; Lantsev, 1976, p. 120). These discussions are interesting not so much for the details of the proposals they contain, but for the relative frankness with which they admit that the interests of different groups in Soviet society can conflict, for their implicit criticism of the doctrine of social harmony. I believe that they may also presage some increase in the retirement age in the next decade.

Earnings and Benefits

It is possible to distinguish between two related issues under this heading: first, there is the question of the relationship between pensions and previous earnings, if any; secondly, there is the question of the levels of benefit provided. On both of these there is general acceptance, by specialists at least, of the principles upon which the Soviet system operates, although a number of authors are critical of the way that particular regulations work.

It might be thought that in circumstances where available resources are limited, as they have been over much of the Soviet period, the fairest system to adopt would be one in which all received the same pension, especially in a system that lacks any notion of an actuarially based payments flow. But such is not the Soviet view. Flat-rate pensions were provided in the USSR only in the immediate aftermath of the revolution. The principle of earnings-related benefits was introduced soon after the end of the Civil War (1921–22) and has been retained ever since. Opposition to uniform pensions is based on two grounds. First, it is argued that such schemes must inevitably result in low levels of support (Lantsev, 1976, p. 100). This follows because it is generally accepted that the pension a person is entitled to cannot exceed his earnings while in employment without undermining labour incentives and adversely affecting participation rates (Livshits, 1972, pp. 241–242). Thus the pension would have to be set at or below the minimum wage. Second, the differentiation of benefits is regarded as a desirable reinforcement of the socialist distribution principle, as providing added incentives for people both to participate in the labour force and to acquire desirable skills (Zaitsev and Rashchikov, 1972, pp. 43–44):

> the socialist distribution principle 'from each according to his ability, to each according to his labour' operates in pension provision as well. The observance of this principle is intended to increase the material interests of *kolkhozniki* in the results of their work, to strengthen labour discipline and to ensure further increases in the volume of agricultural production.

(*See also* Acharkan, 1967, p. 58). To this purely instrumental justification of differentials, some would add an equity argument: it is only fair that those who have worked harder, whose contribution to society and social production has been more valuable while able-bodied, should receive a larger share of social output when incapacitated or retired. 'The state's evaluation of the past activity of those no longer capable of work is shown in [their] pensions.' (Acharkan, 1967, p. 58; *see also* Lantsev, 1976, p. 92 *and* Zaitsev and Rashchikov, 1972, pp. 46–47).

Under the various industrial pension schemes in force during Stalin's lifetime, the value of the pension depended not only upon earnings but also upon occupation, conditions of work and, for invalidity benefits, the cause of disability. Although it introduced some rationalization, the 1956 law retained many of these provisions. As a result, the relationship between earnings and benefits is complicated and frequently seems arbitrary. For instance, it is claimed that the same prior earnings can generate as many as thirty or fifty different rates of invalidity benefit depending upon other circumstances (Lantsev, 1976, p. 91). Specialists and others have extensively criticized the horizontal inequities that the detailed application of these regulations generate (*see*, *for example*, Lantsev, 1976, pp. 92, 105–110, 114–115). And, one should add, many of the amendments introduced in the past decade have been designed to overcome some of these shortcomings (*for details see* McAuley, 1978, ch. 11).

Turning now to the question of benefit levels: it is universally agreed that the average level of pensions paid under the pre-1956 industrial schemes was too low—at least in the post-war period—and some commentators have ascribed this to the formulae used in calculating benefits (*see*, *for example*, Lantsev, 1976, p. 102). But there seems little point in going into this issue since the 1956 law introduced new principles. Briefly, according to the present system, the pension is calculated as not less than 50–55% of average earnings in the last twelve months before retirement, subject to a maximum and minimum limit. In 1956, the minimum was set at 30 rubles a month (roughly equal to the minimum wage at the time) and this was raised to 45 rubles a month in 1971. The maximum was laid down as 120 rubles in 1956 and has not been raised since (*for further details see* McAuley, 1978, ch. 11). There has been little discussion of the adequacy of the formulae embodied in the act; attention has been focussed rather on the appropriateness of the maxima and minima. I too shall concentrate on these issues.

In 1956, the minimum pension coincided with the minimum wage, but the link between them is seen as indirect (Lantsev, 1976, p. 96):

> ... the minimum pension should be lower than the minimum wage. Their relationship can be considered rational if it corresponds to the relationship between the cost of subsistence, *stoimost minimalnogo normativnogo byudzheta*, for unskilled workers and that for those no longer able to work, *netrudosposobnykh*.

And this proposition has widespread support (*see*, *for example* Acharkan, 1967, pp. 137–138). Although Lantsev himself gives no figures, other evidence indicates that, since 1971 or so, this relationship has been secured (*see* Maier, 1977, p. 108). But, since the minimum wage is now substantially above the subsistence level for unskilled workers (70 rubles a month as opposed to 56 rubles, neglecting inflation since 1965), this means that the minimum pension is substantially less than the minimum wage. This has significant implications for the older pensioner and for those in receipt of disability benefits (*see below*).

Similarly, it has been suggested that the maximum pension should not exceed average earnings (a position reached in about 1970) or, alternatively, it should correspond to the cost of a budget-basket (Acharkan, 1967, p.138)

> guaranteeing the full satisfaction of the rational, *razumnykh*, needs of a non-working pensioner from the point of view of current perceptions and bearing in mind the economic possibilities of the state.

(*See also* Lantsev, 1976, p. 95.) Thus, the criterion used in setting limits to differentiation among pensioners is need; but it is need as determined by the authorities rather than by the individuals concerned. The link between earnings and benefits has been weakened. The 1912 Party Programme (written by Lenin) proposed a social insurance scheme in which benefits would be equal to lost earnings. This is no longer regarded as likely—or even desirable (Lantsev, 1976, p. 34):

The basic direction for the development of the fund [for the support] of the elderly and non-able-bodied as well as that of the fund for the temporarily incapacitated is to make the level of pensions approach more closely the level of wages. However, there can scarcely be any necessity, even in the distant future, of setting the target of attaining full equality between pensions and earnings. After all, the needs of working members of society are greater than those of the non-employed.

Pension Adjustment

The rigid interpretation of the principle (by the courts) that a pension cannot be higher than the wage from which it is calculated and the fact that Soviet pension law 'does not envisage the recalculation of pensions as earnings increase after citizens have become pensioners' (Livshits, 1972, p. 242) means that for individual pensioners the value of their pension is fixed for considerable periods of time. This feature of Soviet social security has come in for some criticism in the past fifteen years. And, indeed, it is puzzling in view of the supposed character of social insurance in a socialist state. When pensions are derived, on actuarial principles, from prior contributions, their fixity is understandable. But the Soviet scheme is non-contributory in a formal accounting sense and, in Marxist terms, is financed out of current income. So there need be no technical or formulaic relationship between benefits and previous earnings.

The fixity of pensions is seen to give rise to two sorts of problems. First (Lantsev, 1976, p. 112):

... the stability of pensions leads to a gradual deterioration in the living standards of the elderly. An increasing number of pensioners come to receive pensions of a value close to the minimum and the average value of the pension falls further and further below the value of the pension calculated from the average earnings of the current year.

And the Soviet practice of periodic increases in the minimum pension is thought to be inadequate, both because these adjustments occur infrequently and also because they only provide for the upgrading of pensions that would otherwise fall below the new minimum. Lantsev for one has called for the introduction of a more automatic and more flexible process of adjustment, although he has not suggested how this objective might be achieved (Lantsev, 1974, p. 135).

Secondly, it is pointed out that the stability of pensions over long periods of time can lead to a sort of horizontal inequity (Lantsev, 1976, pp. 111–112, 113):

... It can lead to the situation where workers, *rabotniki*, in the same occupation, with the same level of qualifications, may receive different pensions depending upon when they retire.

As a consequence of the stability of pensions, once awarded, the situation could arise when the labour of a more highly qualified worker or specialist appears to be equated, in the size of the pension, with that of a less skilled or unskilled worker if average earnings when the skilled man retires are much lower than when the unskilled man is awarded his pension...

These phenomena, in their social and economic consequences are undesirable.

(*See also* Khabibi, 1975, p. 285.) Lantsev does not elaborate further. The idea that such phenomena might be undesirable implies a more complicated concept of equity than has been apparent so far; it rather changes the usual interpretation placed upon the socialist principle of distribution. If an individual's pension should depend upon the value of his labour contribution, according to the socialist principle, and if the wage properly measures that value (again according to the socialist principle) then the pension should rightly depend upon previous earnings. But economic development and increases in labour productivity imply that the value of the labour supplied by an unskilled worker today, objectively measured, is greater than the value of that supplied, say, twenty years ago. And this is reflected in a rising level of earnings. Thus the phenomena regretted by Lantsev and Khabibi are a consequence of the assumed objective determination of wages. Their attitude implies, it seems to me, that an individual's pension should be determined by his merit (as measured by his qualifications) and not by the value of his past contribution. That is, their argument would seem to imply that the pension of an engineer, for example, whenever he retired, should always be higher than that of an unskilled labourer, that the distribution of benefits among pensioners should reflect the distribution of earnings among active occupational groups (although, possibly, with a lower degree of dispersion).

Recent Soviet discussions of pensions, then, display a general acceptance of the principles upon which the Soviet system is based. There is little criticism of the idea that entitlement should depend upon prior employment or that benefits should be related to earnings; also, most commentators appear to believe that the range of differentiation is appropriate. But this apparent satisfaction with the status quo is somewhat misleading. There are frequent criticisms of the consequences of particular regulations and the impression created by them is that both economists and lawyers would like to see a rationalization of the system, with greater attention being paid to horizontal equity. Second, it is felt that the distribution of pensioners by benefit is incorrect, that too many receive minimum or near-minimum pensions and are therefore in near-poverty (or are a burden on their families). Finally, many would claim that too large a proportion of available resources is wasted, either because pensions are paid to those in employment or because they are given to those still capable of supporting themselves. Among specialists at least, there is a widespread feeling that some reform of the retirement age is necessary. The more general question of equity, of the redistributive aims of the Soviet government, is taken up in the final section.

THE SOVIET CONCEPT OF EQUITY

Preceding sections of this paper have described recent Soviet attitudes towards the distribution of income under socialism, towards the scope for state intervention in the income-formation process and constraints upon its freedom of action. In this section I discuss the concept of equity or fairness that seems implicit in this material; I also produce some evidence to suggest that this is changing, or at least that there are differences of opinion about the future of the 'Soviet welfare state'. The paper concludes with a brief remark about the relevance of this material for the development of Soviet policy.

The socialization of the means of production, it is argued, by putting an end to exploitation 'raises socio-economic equality to a new and higher level' (Maier and Rakitskii, 1976, p. 191), and thus makes sure that all will be judged by the same yardstick—their labour. But the revolution does not usher in an era of formal equality, of equality in consumption; rather, the system of distribution adopted should (Maier and Rakitskii, 1976, pp. 190–191):

> ... actively facilitate increases in the effectiveness of social production, a more rational use of economic resources... [it should] strengthen and develop a socialist way of life. This can be achieved only by means of the integrated development of both distribution according to labour and distribution through social consumption funds.

Certainly there is a presumption that inequality will diminish in time, that, in the long run there should be a reduction in earnings differentials; but the importance of reconciling this with the maintenance of incentives is stressed (Sukharevskii, 1974, pp. 284–285). In practice, this is taken to imply the desirability of rewarding merit or achievement, of ensuring that those in responsible positions earn substantially more than ordinary state employees.

Second, it is accepted that the state should gradually both increase the amount of support it gives and extend its assistance to more groups in society. But, in the past, Soviet social welfare schemes have frequently restricted access to favoured categories of the population or have provided differentiated benefits for various groups of workers. And the impression is given in the writings of many academics that this is not only more efficient, not only in conformity with the demands of production, but is also fair (*see, for example*, Khabibi, 1975, p. 275 *or* Acharkan, 1967, p. 44). There is little emphasis upon universality, upon equal treatment for all; or rather, it is implicitly recognized that all are not equal. A disabled miner or steelworker is assumed to be different from (and more deserving of state support than) a disabled shopworker or peasant. When resources are scarce, it is just and proper that they should be concentrated on the former categories; in the last resort, the others may be left to fend for themselves.

Indeed, vestiges of this discrimination remain to this day. In spite of a constitutional guarantee that all who work, *vse trudyashchiesya*, had the right to a pension *kolkhozniki* were excluded from state schemes until 1965 and many are still treated less favourably than state employees. Certain categories of worker receive higher pensions, not only because their earnings while in employment are higher but also because more generous formulae are used to calculate the pension from their wage. For many temporary benefits, the war-disabled, trade-union members or those with an uninterrupted employment record are treated more favourably than other categories of state employee. However, over the past decade or so, many of these special provisions have been criticized. It has been suggested that they give rise to horizontal inequities, that they result in the unequal treatment of equals. That is, some have asked whether trade-union status, for example, or previous conditions of employment are relevant to the issue of determining the scale of support provided, whether particular transfers should be conceived of as rewards for previous activity (or as a stimulus to desirable behaviour in the future) or whether they should not more appropriately be related to current need.

The relative crudity of many Soviet welfare schemes also gives rise to horizontal inequities, but this has received far less attention from Soviet specialists. In any scheme there is a trade-off between equity and administrative simplicity. The more careful one is in taking account of differences in circumstances, the more complex one's regulations and the more difficult a scheme is to administer. But, in general, the more equitable it is. In the allowances they make for dependents and so on, most Soviet income-support schemes appear to have opted for administrative simplicity rather than equity. The same is true of the Soviet tax system.

Third, it has been forcibly and persuasively argued that the primary objective of the Soviet state is not the elimination of inequality through redistribution, but the reduction of those socio-economic barriers that give rise to unequal abilities, to differences in capacity for work. Equality of opportunity and not equality per se is the proper goal to pursue.

This last view has been attacked. Several authors have been critical of those (and this presumably includes Rakitskii) who argue (Mamontova, 1975, p. 295):

> ... that the basic function of social [consumption] funds can be reduced to ensuring the conditions necessary for effacing socio-economic differences in the development of work-skills, *sposobnosti k trudu*, and for the all-round development of all members of society.

Mamontova's criticism is part of a more general expression of discontent at the lack of progress that has been made towards reducing or eliminating poverty in the USSR.

This is ascribed by some to an excessive reliance upon the policy of raising the minimum wage. This, it is argued, does little to help those families whose income does not derive from work—the disabled, the elderly, widows and orphans. It is also relatively costly since it benefits many who are not among the most needy (Rzhanitsyna, 1971, pp. 15–16).

Mamontova herself is also critical of existing social welfare programmes. She claims that, as a result of tying a high proportion of cash transfers to earnings, the value of benefits increases with per capita incomes; she also claims that a similar pattern is observable for subsidized services (Mamontova, 1975, pp. 297–298). More generally (pp. 299, 301), she would like to see a change of emphasis in patterns of social expenditure and some reform in the way that it is administered:

> ... it must be admitted that social consumption funds could be used more to bring about reductions in family income differentiation. In our opinion social consumption funds are insufficiently exploited for this purpose at the present time. The principle of giving priority to poorer families in the allocation of particular transfers and subsidies is not always adhered to.... It is necessary now to adopt forms of material support which at the lowest possible cost ensure the maximum gain to the least well-off.

She would like to see the extension of means-tested benefits and a reduction in the support given to those in employment, those capable of supporting themselves.

In the arguments of those who have written about the shortcomings of Soviet anti-poverty policy, who have emphasized the necessity of doing more to raise the living-standards of the deprived, a new component can be discerned. There is less stress on mutual obligation, on the right to state help being dependent upon the prior fulfilment of duties. And there is a greater concern for need, for the responsibility of the state to all members of society.

CONCLUSIONS

In this paper I have been concerned with the writings of academic economists and lawyers, with specialists in the field of social security; one may legitimately ask how representative they are and whether they will have a significant influence on the future formulation of policy. Each of these questions is a separate topic that merits extensive discussion which the following remarks are not intended to preempt. First, I have no way of knowing what a majority of the Soviet population thinks about the extent of inequality in the USSR. Further, while I am sure that all of those whose work I have quoted know more than I do, I suspect that, given the shortcomings in Soviet data collection methods, they are relatively ignorant as well. However, the Soviet policy-making process means that public opinion is of less importance in the USSR than in a parliamentary democracy.

Second, it might be argued that the opinions I have quoted have appeared in relatively obscure specialist publications and that less importance should be attached to them than to the views expressed in the national press and in the writings and speeches of the Party leaders. There is something in this argument, but it also reflects a misunderstanding of policy-making in the USSR. The Soviet Union is a complex bureaucratic state and policy-formation is no longer the exclusive prerogative of a kitchen cabinet as it was in Stalin's later years. Many of those whose work I have quoted are employed in government research institutes and it is they who will proffer advice, suggest policies, draft the legislation. Their writing provides a valuable insight into an important strand of the Soviet policy-making process and thus merits serious consideration by those interested in the likely directions to be followed by Soviet social policy in the future.

REFERENCES

Acharkan V. A. (1967) *Gosudarstvennye pensii*, Moscow.

Archarkan V. A. (1971) Pensionnoye zakonodatelstvo i problema zanyatosti *Sotsialisticheskii Trud*, **1**, pp. 117–125.

Acharkan V. A. (1973) Aktualnye problemy pensionnogo obespecheniya In: Sarkisyan G. S. (1973), pp. 136–151.

Acharkan V. A. (1974) Sotsialisticheskii printsip raspredeleniya po trudu i sotsialnoye obespecheniye *Sotsialisticheskii Trud*, **11**, pp. 119–129.

Andreev V. S. (1974) *Pravo sotsialnogo obespecheniya v SSSR* Moscow.

Basov V. I. (1967) *Obshchestvennye fondy potrebleniya i byudzhet* Moscow.

Chapman J. (1963) *Real Wages in Soviet Russia since 1928* Cambridge, Mass.

Gordon L. A. et al. (1974) Razvitoi sotsializm: blagosostoyaniye rabochikh *Rabochii Klass i Sovremennyi Mir* **2–3**, pp. 53–72.

Kapustin E. I. (1974) Tarifnaya sistema i ee rol v organizatsii i regulirovanii zarabotnoi platy In: Volkov A. P. pp. 247–274.

Khabibi R. I. (1975) Sootnosheniye oplaty po trudu i obshchestvennykh fondov potrebleniya: sotsialno-ekonomicheskii aspekt In: Shvetsov A. P. pp. 272–287.

Kostin L. A. (1976) *Rost narodnogo blagosostoyaniya—glavnaya zabota partii* Moscow.

Kulikov V. S. (1972) *Rol finansov v povyshenii blagosostoyaniya sovetskogo naroda* Moscow.

Kunelskii L. E. (1971) Rost potrebleniya, uvelicheniye dokhodov i ikh tovarno-materialnoye obespecheniye *Sotsialisticheskii Trud* **12**, pp. 3–11.

Kuprienko L. P. (1976) *Vliyaniye urovnya zhizni na raspredeleniye trudovykh resursov* Moscow.

Lantsev M. S. (1974) Sovershenstvovaniye sistemy sotsialnogo obespecheniya v usloviyakh razvitogo sotsializma *Sotsialisticheskii Trud* **9**, pp. 129–137.

Lantsev M. S. (1976) *Sotsialnoye obespecheniye v SSSR* Moscow.

Lenin V. I. (1961) *Polnoye Sobraniye Sochineniy* (5 ed.) vol. 21, Moscow.

Livshits R. Z. (1972) *Zarabotnaya plata v SSSR: pravovye issledovaniya* Moscow.

McAuley A. (1967) Rationality and Central Planning *Soviet Studies* January, pp. 340–355.

McAuley A. (1977a) The Distribution of Earnings and Incomes in the Soviet Union *Soviet Studies.*

McAuley A. (1977b) *Soviet Anti-poverty Policy, 1955–1975* (Inst. Research on Poverty Discussion Paper No. 402–77) Madison, Wis.

McAuley A. (1978) *Economic Welfare in the Soviet Union: Poverty, Living Standards and Inequality* Madison, Wis.

Madison B. (1972) Social Services for Families and Children in the Soviet Union since 1967 *Slavic Review*, pp. 831–852.

Maier V. F. (1968) *Dokhody naseleniya i rost blagosostoyaniya naroda* Moscow.

Maier V. F. (1977) *Uroven zhizni naseleniya SSSR* Moscow.

Maier V. F. and Rakitskii B. V. (1976) Obshchestvennye fondy potrebleniya i rost blagosostoyaniya naroda In: *Oplata truda pri sotsializme: voprosy teorii i praktiki* Moscow and Warsaw, pp. 190–206.

Mamontova T. I. (1973) Povysheniye roli obshchestvennykh fondov potrebleniya v reshenii sotsialnykh problem In: Sarkisyan G. S., pp. 56–81.

Mamontova T. I. (1975) Vliyaniye obshchestvennykh fondov potrebleniya na differentsiatsiyu v urovne zhizni rabochikh i sluzhashchikh In: Shvetsov A. P., pp. 294–302.

Marx K. (1967) *Critique of the Gotha Program* New York.

Matthews M. (1978) *Privilege in the Soviet Union* London.

Medvedev R. (1975) *On Socialist Democracy* New York.

Musgrave R. (1959) *The Theory of Public Finance* New York.

Politicheskaya Ekonomiya (1959), uchebnik (3rd ed.) Moscow.

Rabkina N. E. and Rimashevskaya N. M. (1972) *Osnovy differentsiatsii zarabotnoi platy i dokhodov naseleniya* Moscow.

Rakitskii E. V. (1966) *Obshchestvennye fondy potrebleniya kak ekonomicheskaya kategoriya* Moscow.

Rzhanitsyna L. (1971) Obespecheniye vysokogo urovnya zhizni vsem trudyashchimsya *Sotsialisticheskii Trud* **8**, pp. 11–18.

Rzhanitsyna L. (1973) Obshchestvennye fondy potrebleniya—vazhnyi istochnik rosta blagosostoyaniya sovetskikh lyudei *Sotsialisticheskii Trud* **7**, pp. 78–85.

Sarkisyan G. S. (ed.) (1973) *Dokhody trudyashchikhsya i sotsialnye problemy urovnya zhizni naseleniya SSSR* Moscow.

Shvetsov A. P. (ed.) (1975) *Sotsialisticheskii obraz zhizni i narodnoye blagosostoyaniye* Saratov.

Sukharevskii B. M. (1974) Zarabotnaya plata v SSSR In: Volkov A. P. pp. 201–246.

Volkov A. P. (ed.) (1974) *Trud i zarabotnaya plata v SSSR* (2nd ed., revised) Moscow.

Zaitsev L. I. and Rashchikov I. D. (1972) *Sotsialnoye obespecheniye kolkhoznikov* Moscow.

DISCUSSION

by **R. Van Slooten,** *Director, Central Economics Service, Northern Ireland Department of Finance, Stormont, Belfast*

Like most of the participants at this Symposium I am no expert on the Soviet economy. But, to examine how Marxists tackle fundamental and familiar problems, such as equity *vs.* efficiency, from their very different ideological standpoint is always valuable. It is also difficult, for Russian economics must be translated not only out of the Russian but out of the, for most of us, unfamiliar Marxist terminology. McAuley's paper is both clear and stimulating.

He discusses three areas of state policy:

(i) Wage and salary determination;

(ii) Direct provision of social services;

(iii) Transfer payments.

I shall consider each in turn and then, as McAuley does, make some general remarks about the Soviet concept of equity and its application in practice.

Incentives, in the form of wage differentials, are apparently taken very seriously in Russia. In the socialist (as opposed to the communist) state each is rewarded 'according to his labour' and this involves the objective determination of earnings differentials, based on the widespread use of job-evaluation and centralized bureaucratic procedures. This meritocratic system is however moderated by a minimum wage provision. It was not made clear how this minimum (or the related subsistence level of income for non-workers) was determined; a comparison with UK experience in this area would also be interesting.

A second important avenue of redistribution is direct provision of social services, in particular health, education and housing. The criteria for selection are not altogether clear from McAuley's paper. He quotes Lantsev as emphasizing compensation for earnings loss (i.e. risk spreading) and compensation for special needs (e.g. arising from family size) but in both cases cash transfers would generally seem more appropriate. More convincingly, he quotes Rakitskii who suggests that equality of human capital and environmental conditions are important in achieving equality of income in the long-term. Here cash transfers might be inadequate, because individuals could not necessarily be relied upon to spend them in an appropriate manner. It is interesting to contrast the long-term approach to income distribution with the much heavier emphasis on redistributing current income which is characteristic in the West. It may be that Western emphasis is influenced by the more empirical nature of discussion and the greater ease of quantifying redistribution in the short term. While the above paternalistic principle is comprehensible, it does not automatically provide criteria for allocating social expenditure in practice, or for deciding which should be zero-priced, or which merely subsidized. Empirical information on the effects of such expenditure would be useful.

Further problems arise in the allocation of services which are in short supply. Apparently one criterion for access to social services is participation in the labour force. But how far is this criterion applied in practice? And how are those unable to work (e.g. the disabled) or alienated treated?

Turning now to transfer payments, McAuley's discussion concentrates on old age pensions. The Soviet view of pensions is markedly different from that pertaining in the West. Firstly, pensions are *conditional*—on the fulfilment of two constitutional obligations, i.e. to work and to defend one's country, and some people are altogether without pension entitlement. Secondly, there is no pretence at relating benefits to contributions; instead pensions are earnings-related subject to maxima and minima. There is no index-linking of pensions, only the minimum is periodically raised; hence, older pensioners tend to cluster towards the minimum. Thirdly, continued employment is no bar to receipt of a pension. McAuley suggests that while there is general acceptance of the principles upon which the Soviet pension system is based, several of the above features have come in for considerable criticism. Comparison with British controversies over pensions is interesting.

McAuley draws attention to the increased emphasis on welfare or equality as official objectives in the post-Stalin era. The emphasis is reflected both in Soviet research and in achievements in this area. An explanation of why and how these changes occurred would be of considerable interest.

As far as current attitudes are concerned, the Soviet concept of equity is, apparently, equality of opportunity, not equality per se. One pointer is the lack of emphasis on *universality*. It is implicitly recognized that *all are not* equal. Another pointer is the importance attached to social expenditure on goods and services which are seen as equalizing long-term income potential. Here it is possibly being unquestioningly assumed that equalization of opportunity combined with technical progress will lead inexorably to social equality. But the assumption is doubtful: both factors may reinforce rather than reduce elitism. This is perhaps a particularly interesting issue for discussion.

SUMMARY OF THE GENERAL DISCUSSION

Hare asked about the position of the private sector in the USSR. Obviously this was quantitatively small, but it might make a considerable difference to the distribution of income, since some private sector incomes might be quite high. Also, so far as attitudes were concerned, the source of income might be important as well as the quantity. McAuley felt that attitudes and theorizing about distribution largely ignored the private sector, which probably accounted for 10–15% of personal incomes. There were no private sector pension schemes—but one should remember that, except in the case of married women, one had to have a socialist job before being allowed to operate in the private sector at all.

Collard wondered whether there was any sort of market over time in Communist countries. For instance, could peasants lend intertemporally to one another? McAuley replied that moneylending probably did exist on an informal basis. It was not an approved activity. Peasants could borrow from the state for the purpose of house construction, and there were a limited number of financial assets that could be legally acquired. Szakolczai said that in Hungary there existed credit co-operatives, particularly for building purposes.

Le Grand commented that the Russian attitude to equity was similar to the American—there was an emphasis on access-type social policies, whereas West European countries tended to go in more for outcome-type policies. But equality of opportunity could still produce elitism, as for instance in civil services where entry is by competitive examination. Also he noted the quote by Mamontova (p. 256) which echoed his own view that subsidized services benefited the better off. McAuley agreed that the Soviet system was elitist—he felt that the official view was that elitism was necessary to foster development. Also there were simply not enough resources for effective outcome policies. The emphasis on subsidized services rather than cash benefits reflected the generally paternalistic attitudes of the Soviet state. Szakolczai commented that subsidies to cultural and intellectual services were felt necessary in order to maintain a large intellectual sector in the cause of economic progress; their aim was not really redistributive. He felt that there was no way in which one could avoid elitism completely; for example the sons of richer families would always be more likely to go to universities. Nicholson felt that the results of removing inequality of opportunity were very long-term, and not easily measured. McAuley agreed that this was true, but in his view the Soviet attitude to education as an important aid to mobility was too optimistic, conditioned by early successes. He thought that in the end the supply of skilled jobs would not match the demand for them, leading to social discontent.

Hammond suggested that there were some general lessons that could be drawn from the two papers about Eastern Europe. The most important was that the most effective redistribution policies were those aimed at improving the lot of the very poor. Then there was the question of choice of instruments. One instrument was price/tax policy, and the lesson from Hungary was that this had gone too far, and was causing efficiency problems. A second, and much better, instrument was social security policy. Winter disagreed with Hammond's interpretation of the Hungarian experience—he felt that Szakolczai's paper had argued that there had not been enough redistribution, given the pricing distortions. Collard also thought that this was not quite right—there had been redistribution, but of an undesirable nature. McAuley felt that the important point was that there was scope for improvement in both efficiency and equality at the same time—one was not actually on the efficiency–equality frontier at all.

McAuley was asked which he thought were the main inequality problems in the USSR. He mentioned three: discrimination between state employees and peasants, particularly marked in the Stalinist era, but less so now; discrimination between sexes, which still existed in practice, despite legislation on equal pay and opportunities dating back to 1936; and discrimination among ethnic groups, which showed itself in large regional disparities in per capita income, etc.

Champernowne asked about attitudes towards inequality at the upper end of the distribution, especially with reference to the privileges and perks of senior jobs. McAuley replied that there was very little information about high *incomes*, and even less about *perks*. From journalistic sources one could identify the standard forms of perk: extra cash handouts, access to restricted distribution networks for foreign or luxury goods, access to better town housing, country houses, chauffeur-driven cars, etc. Matthews had estimated that about 250 000 (0·25% of the employed population) had access to privileges of this sort. There was no academic debate about these practices; public response to them was rather mixed.

There was some discussion on direct *vs.* indirect taxes. Layard noted that East European countries seemed to rely heavily on indirect taxation, and hardly at all on income tax. Theoretically we teach that indirect taxes have the same disincentive effects as direct taxes, but was this really true? What exactly was the evidence? He could only think of a study by Ashenfelter and Abbott. Nicholson pointed to work being done for the Institute for Fiscal Studies by Reddaway and associates. McAuley felt that a lot depended on attitudes, and they in turn depended on the information available. Where the tax component of the price was unknown to the consumer there was less resistance. Szakolczai explained that one reason for the neglect of income tax in Eastern Europe was that the highest incomes were usually of doubtful legality, so that they would not be declared. Also, as the majority were employed by state enterprises anyway, it was administratively simpler to act directly on the primary distribution.

Nicholson offered a number of propositions for summing up the Symposium as a whole:

(i) The most redistributive policy instruments were social security benefits.

(ii) Benefits were more redistributive than taxes.

(iii) Therefore the progressivity of taxes was not important.

(iv) The best long-term way of reducing inequality was to engineer a reduction of pre-tax differentials.

(v) There should be more investment in opportunity-equalizing schemes.

McAuley stressed the need to be clear about the objectives of policy. Was the aim to raise the incomes of the poor, or to penalize the rich? Social security benefits would be very effective in the first case, but not in the second. He felt that the lesson from Eastern Europe was that price manipulation was not a good method of redistribution. Wages policy might be a better method than high levels of income tax, but to apply this in the West would require considerable institutional change and increase in bureaucracy.

Winter regretted that in the discussion no-one had touched on what had surely been a most important method of redistribution in Eastern Europe—that of revolution and expropriation.

INDEX